D1559692

Protecting the Presidential Candidates

Other books by Mel Ayton:

Plotting to Kill the President – Assassination Attempts from Washington to Hoover
Dark Soul of the South: The Life and Crimes of Racist Killer Joseph Paul Franklin
Justice Denied: Bermuda's Black Militants, The 'Third Man' and the Assassinations of a Police Chief and Governor
Beyond Reasonable Doubt – The Warren Report and Lee Harvey Oswald's Guilt and Motive 50 Years On, with David Von Pein
The JFK Assassination: Dispelling the Myths
Questions of Controversy: The Kennedy Brothers

Praise for Mel Ayton's *Hunting the President: Threats, Plots and Assassination Attempts – From FDR to Obama*:

'The only book of its kind and certainly the best book of its kind . . . A fascinating and very important book which I heartily recommend . . . it's easy to figure out why Mel Ayton's writing has drawn nearly universal praise in the past and for his present volume *Hunting the President* . . . Even for people who know American history; even for people who have a special expertise in the history of presidential assassinations; you're going to learn a great deal from [this] new book.' – Michael Medved, *The Michael Medved Show*

'*Hunting the President* by Mel Ayton shows that both threats and attempts are far more common than we know.' –Larry Getlen, *New York Post*

'Ayton . . . debunks conventional wisdom about presidential assassins' motivations. . . . Readers who pick up *Hunting the President* will take away much they didn't know before about many who've stalked presidents with murder in mind.' – Alan Wallace, *Pittsburgh Tribune*

'I picked up this book, boy, it's fascinating!' – *The Sean Hannity Show*

'I love the book . . . it's a great read.' – Peter Boyles, *The Peter Boyles Show*

Protecting the Presidential Candidates

From JFK to Biden

Mel Ayton

FRONTLINE
BOOKS

An imprint of
Pen & Sword Books Ltd
Yorkshire – Philadelphia

FRONTLINE
BOOKS

First published in Great Britain in 2021 by
Frontline Books
an imprint of Pen & Sword Books Ltd,
47 Church Street, Barnsley, S. Yorkshire, S70 2AS

Copyright © Mel Ayton 2021

ISBN 978 1 39901 408 3

The right of Mel Ayton to be identified as Author of this work has been asserted by him in accordance with the Copyright, Designs and Patents Act 1988.

A CIP catalogue record for this book is available from the British Library.

All rights reserved. No part of this book may be reproduced or transmitted in any form or by any means, electronic or mechanical including photocopying, recording or by any information storage and retrieval system, without permission from the Publisher in writing.

Typeset in Chennai, India
by Lapiz Digital Services.

Printed and bound by CPI Group (UK) Ltd, Croydon, CR0 4YY

Pen & Sword Books Ltd incorporates the imprints of Pen & Sword Archaeology, Atlas, Aviation, Battleground, Discovery, Family History, History, Maritime, Military, Naval, Politics, Social History, Transport, True Crime, Claymore Press, Frontline Books, Praetorian Press, Seaforth Publishing and White Owl

For a complete list of Pen & Sword titles please contact

PEN & SWORD BOOKS LTD
47 Church Street, Barnsley, South Yorkshire, S70 2AS, England
E-mail: enquiries@pen-and-sword.co.uk
Website: www.pen-and-sword.co.uk

Or

PEN AND SWORD BOOKS
1950 Lawrence Rd, Havertown, PA 19083, USA
E-mail: Uspen-and-sword@casematepublishers.com
Website: www.penandswordbooks.com

For my wife Sheila, my son Tim, my daughter Laura, my son-in-law Paul – and my grandchildren, Isabella, Sophia and Cameron, the joy of my life

Contents

Preface

Protecting the Presidential Candidates – from JFK to Biden is the third in a series of books I have written about presidential protection following the publication of *Hunting the President: Threats, Plots and Assassination Attempts – From FDR to Obama* (2014) and *Plotting to Kill the President – Assassination Attempts from Washington to Hoover* (2017).

According to the Secret Service it is during a presidential election year when a president or presidential candidate faces the highest risk of assassination. During this period the Secret Service is on its highest alert when candidates for the presidency, including sitting presidents, expose themselves to large and sometimes unruly crowds. It makes their protective mission a vital part of the election process.

Protecting the Presidential Candidates is the first book of its kind to chronicle the history of modern bodyguard protection for leading presidential candidates and presidents during election cycles. It is also the first book of its kind to tell the story of the role of state law-enforcement officers and private bodyguards in protecting presidential candidates.

The book also covers plots, threats and assassination attempts against leading candidates but omits a full examination of assassination plots and threats against presidents. Those incidents are chronicled in my books *Hunting the President – Threats, Plots and Assassination Attempts – From FDR to Obama* and *Plotting to Kill the President: Assassination Attempts from Washington to Hoover*.

It would be impossible to write about the protection all candidates have received from 1960 to 2020. There have, literally, been more than a hundred presidential candidates during this period. The majority of their presidential campaigns lasted only a few weeks or, at best, a few months. I have therefore chosen those politicians who the media characterised as 'front-runners' or 'future presidents' – the exception to the rule being the candidacies of Jesse Jackson and George Wallace. While historians never believed either candidate would eventually become president, they nevertheless described them as having ran important historical campaigns which placed the United States' defining issue of race at the centre.

There have been a number of assumptions held by the general public which *Protecting the Presidential Candidates* addresses. It has been assumed that protecting the lives of leading candidates has been wholly dependent on the Secret Service. Whenever reports appear in the media about a politician's 'bodyguards' it is generally assumed that presidents, vice presidents and presidential candidates are all guarded by the US Secret Service from the beginning of the presidential campaign season to its conclusion. *Protecting the Presidential Candidates* alters that assumption. Readers will probably be unaware, for example, that candidates like Jimmy Carter and Ronald Reagan campaigned for the presidency long before the official election cycle began, and they would also be unaware of the protection these candidates employed – which was very little. Jimmy Carter, for example, began his campaign with the protection of one Georgia State Police bodyguard, as did Ronald Reagan who was protected by a single California Highway Patrolman.

Readers will also learn that sitting state governors who ran for president, including Nelson Rockefeller, Bill Clinton, George W. Bush, Mitt Romney and George Wallace, began their campaigns with a small force of state police officers.

Many presidential candidates were either sitting or former vice presidents. *Protecting the Presidential Candidates* addresses the commonly held belief that vice presidents have never been the target of assassins. It has often been said that no one would attempt to kill a vice president because it would be pointless – nothing would change and the president would simply appoint another vice president closely allied to his policies. However, as this book demonstrates, there have been at least five assassination attempts directed against vice presidents; one of which has never before been revealed.

It is hoped that readers of *Protecting the Presidential Candidates* will learn much about the leading candidates for president over the past sixty years including how they coped with running for president in face of the prevailing dangers; how they interacted with their security details; how they managed the demands made upon them by their staff and security teams; how their private behaviour interfered with the protective mission; and how candidates responded to the numerous threats made against their lives.

Many stories revealed in *Protecting the Presidential Candidates* have remained largely hidden from the public; some buried in newspaper archives and others in oral histories, presidential libraries or official government documents. Additionally, most Secret Service agent memoirs do not chronicle the many assassination threats and assassination plots leading candidates have faced. Utilising FBI files and other government documents these stories can now be told.

Mel Ayton
Durham, England, 2021

Acknowledgements

I am grateful to many people who gave encouragement and wise advice during the production of this book, including authors Dan Moldea, Mark Olshaker and John Douglas, Frontline Books' John Grehan and Martin Mace, and my editor Alison Flowers. I am also grateful to Iowa Democratic Party activist Jim Williams who knew many of the presidential candidates I write about and who provided me with insightful information.

Chapter 1

The Torture Trail

'The candidate is a race horse and his staff are trying to enter them in every race around.'

Ronald Reagan

'The best time to listen to a politician is when he's on a stump on a street corner in the rain late at night when he's exhausted. Then he doesn't lie.'

Theodore H. White, author of *The Making of the President*

'I saw their strengths and weaknesses as each wrestled with life-and-death decisions.'

Former Secret Service agent Clint Hill

By 1960 the major political parties had discarded the old system of having party elders choose which candidate should be the nominee. Since that time the more democratic presidential primary process became the only viable route to the presidency – the exception being the nomination of 1968 Democrat Hubert H. Humphrey who eschewed the primary system relying on his influence with party bosses.

Presidential campaigns are a contest for control of power in the most powerful nation on earth. The contest of personalities and policies takes place in a war of ideas with sharp turning points along the way as candidates succumb to electoral approval or disapproval.

And campaigns have stretched out for a prohibitive length. The number of primaries has expanded exponentially since the early 1960s. Political journalist Robert Scheer called the primary process, '. . .[a] numbing effect of a modern mass media-observed campaign that requires such a high-wire act – balancing fundraising with integrity, superficial sloganeering with profound commitment, and homogenizing the entire unwieldy package into a marketable commodity – that in the end, the candidate is transformed into a caricature who has difficulty in remembering from whence he came'.[1]

Even those men and women who saw politics as an honourable way to serve their country ended up damaged by the pursuit. Words like 'exhausted', 'tortured' and 'crushing' were often used by the candidates to explain the gruelling process of fighting primary after primary to persuade the electorate they could appeal to a diverse nation and had what it takes to be president. It became a mind-numbing cross-country obstacle course. Accordingly, many politicians judged to be competent and popular have been deterred from trying.

The pressures can make or break a candidate. When 1972 front-runner Edmund Muskie was attacked by a New Hampshire newspaper he responded with a speech to an outdoor crowd and became emotional to the point of being on the verge of tears. Calm unravelled under stress. It made voters question the emotional stability required from a potential president. When George Romney ran for president in 1968 he made the mistake of telling voters he had been 'brainwashed' about Vietnam. The 1972 presidential candidate George McGovern was so exhausted by the time he arrived at the Democrats' Miami Beach convention he made the disastrous mistake of selecting as his running mate Thomas Eagleton, a man who had undergone electro-shock treatment for depression. The 77-year-old Joe Biden became so exhausted in running for president in 2020 it often left him sounding incoherent during television interviews and campaign speeches. In fact, so many candidates suffered from health problems brought on by campaigning they had to conceal these from the public.

The primary system has tempted literally hundreds of politicians to run for president because of federal subsidies. This type of politician runs not because he or she believes they could be successful but instead are offered an opportunity to raise their profile for other reasons like running for re-election as a governor, Senator or Congressman. Consequently, there have been many candidates who should not have received Secret Service protection including one notable Congressman, John G. Schmitz, a member of the extremist John Birch Society. According to one agent, 'He used to sit back there [in the limousine] smoking a stogie and just grooving on the idea that he had his own private police force . . . . I'd just shake my head and think, what a waste of taxpayer's money.'[2]

Other presidential candidates who never had a chance of winning the presidency were Georgia Governor Lester Maddox, a right-wing racist, and Shirley Chisholm, a black Congresswoman. In 1976, Maddox was the presidential candidate of the far-right American Independence Party. His candidacy disappeared almost without trace. Nonetheless, he received Secret Service protection for two weeks and glorified in the fact that he was protected by a federal agency. Chisholm entered the Democratic contest primarily to prove it was possible for a woman and an African American to run for president. She was under no illusions she could possibly win.

Not only is the primary system a marathon that punishes winners and losers alike, it also greatly increases the candidate's exposure to assassination from nationwide extremist groups and individuals who believe it is their God-given right to intervene in the electoral system and eliminate anyone they perceive as antagonistic to their cause. The effect campaigning had on the bodyguards was equally debilitating. Throughout the history of election campaigns agents frequently couldn't remember which town or city they were in and experienced the same exhaustion suffered by the candidates.

The bodyguards who formed the close protective detail around the presidential candidates included Secret Service agents (in the case of the president or vice president running for re-election it's the Presidential Protective Detail (PPD) and the Vice-Presidential Protective Detail (VPPD)), local police officers, state troopers and private citizens. They had unique access to the personal lives of the people they protected. Nobody except the candidate's wife was in such daily intimate proximity to the presidential aspirant and they often became privy to private and intimate conversations in limousines and hotel rooms and on golf courses and jogging trails.

Many bodyguards formed a close bond and friendship with their protectees. As one former bodyguard said, 'During these [private] moments [when no press was present] they weren't politicians, they were just regular people, who, after spending the vast majority of their waking hours in a fishbowl for all to observe and critique, were now off the clock. The human side could be refreshing to see.'[3]

Bodyguards have also witnessed embarrassing moments in a candidate's campaign with the realisation of how intrusive they have been at the most delicate of moments. The candidate may even forget a bodyguard is in the room, something that Dennis McCarthy recalled when he was guarding President Nixon. McCarthy once saw Nixon crying as the Watergate Scandal began to plague his presidency. State trooper bodyguards conspired with Arkansas Governor Clinton to hide amorous encounters from his wife when he campaigned for the presidency.

When Clinton became president his Secret Service bodyguards faced challenges to the discrete nature of their mission when an independent prosecutor ordered them to reveal confidential knowledge of the president's relationship with White House intern Monica Lewinsky. 'The president's day is your day,' former agent Marty Vencker said, 'nobody sees the president the way an agent does. The Secretary of State gets maybe half an hour with him. We were there all the time. And we saw the guy when his head was hanging the lowest.'[4] Bodyguards also witnessed affairs and marital discord and other behaviours because they became so part of their inner circle the protectee thought nothing about it.

Bodyguards also observed up close the rash behaviour of candidates when they campaigned. LBJ's recklessness in plunging into crowds during the 1964 presidential election was emulated in 1968 by presidential candidates Eugene McCarthy, Robert Kennedy and Richard Nixon. Robert Kennedy and Eugene McCarthy eschewed the offer of police bodyguard protection. Both candidates did not want to alienate anti-war youth and African American and Hispanic crowds who were believed to hold an animus towards local police departments and national law-enforcement agencies. The exception was candidate George Wallace who adhered to the security protocols laid down by his state troopers. However, when he ran for president in 1972, he let down his guard, left his bulletproof dais and was shot as he shook hands with his supporters.

Secret Service Chief U.E. Baughman said Richard Nixon was 'an assassin's delight' especially during election campaigns. Baughman said that Nixon came near to being killed on 'several occasions' for his wanton disregard for his safety, often climbing on the roof of his limousine to wave to the crowds of anti-war demonstrators. On one occasion his valet drove him out of his San Clemente, California, Western White House without informing his Secret Service detail. Nixon was in the back seat covered in a blanket; he had simply wanted to go a local restaurant without his bodyguards. However, reporters had spotted him and informed the Secret Service who soon caught up with him.

There were few occasions when Secret Service agents were caught off guard by the behaviour of Gerald Ford, Jimmy Carter, Ronald Reagan,

George H.W. Bush, George W. Bush and Barack Obama while they were campaigning. But they were seriously challenged by Bill Clinton and Donald Trump. Clinton's womanising caused problems with the state troopers who protected him during the initial phase of his 1992 candidacy. When Clinton was given Secret Service protection his agents faced the same problem. They were concerned at the way he was cavalier with regard to his safety and his reputation. When Donald Trump campaigned in 2016 and 2020 agents were faced with protecting a president who plunged into crowds and attracted vitriol not seen since the anti-war demonstrations during the Nixon years.

* * *

Whenever reports appear in the media about a politician's 'bodyguards', it is generally assumed that presidents, vice presidents and presidential candidates are all guarded by the US Secret Service. However, before presidential candidates qualify for Secret Service protection they are usually guarded by state troopers, state public safety officers or Capitol police officers, or they make private arrangements such as hiring private security guards. The Secret Service also has the ability to call in federal law-enforcement officers from other agencies to assist in protective duties, including airport baggage screeners from the Transportation Security Administration, DEA agents and immigration enforcement officers.

Presidential candidates are not given official protection until they have proved their worth in the primary election campaigns which run for the first six months of a presidential election year. Until then candidates must make their own security arrangements. Following the assassination of Senator Robert F. Kennedy in 1968, nearly all presidential candidates were given protection. An additional 150 agents were assigned for the job and borrowed from other Treasury Department agents – the Bureau of Alcohol, Firearms and Tobacco, the Customs Service and the formerly titled Bureau of Narcotics.

A criterion for protecting candidates has changed since 1968, however. The Secret Service protects only 'major' presidential candidates, or by executive order, and only those who request coverage. The Secretary of Homeland Security determines which presidential candidates are considered major after consultation with an advisory committee that includes the Speaker of the US House of Representatives; the House Minority Whip; the Senate Majority and Minority Leaders; and an additional member chosen by the committee itself. While protection for the president and vice president is mandatory, others can decline it if they choose. Once they are accepted, the Secretary of Homeland Security consults with the advisory committee and one additional member selected by the other members of the committee (usually from the Secret Service) and determines if a candidate is eligible for Secret Service protection.

If the candidate is eligible, they are notified of the committee's decision and asked if they would like protection. Specifically, presidential candidates become eligible for Secret Service protection, according to the Congressional Research Service, if they:

- Are publicly declared candidates.
- Are actively campaigning nationally and are contesting at least ten state primaries.
- Are pursuing the nomination of a qualified party, one whose presidential candidate received at least 10 per cent of the popular vote in the prior election.
- Are qualified for public matching funds of at least $100,000 and have raised at least $10 million in additional contributions.
- Have received by 1 April of the election year an average of 5 per cent in individual candidate preferences in the most recent national opinion polls by ABC, CBS, NBC and CNN, or have received at least 10 per cent of the votes cast for all candidates in two same-day or consecutive primaries or caucuses.
- Presidential and vice-presidential nominees and their spouses are to receive Secret Service protection within 120 days of a general presidential election. In modern history, however, major candidates receive Secret Service protection well before that time, usually early in the primary campaigns in the late winter and early spring.
- Major candidates are those that have considerable prominence among the public and have raised substantial money for their presidential campaigns.

Once the protection is authorised, it would be unusual for a candidate to then decline it.

Additionally, once a candidate has fulfilled the requirements to apply for Secret Service protection they may still retain their own private bodyguard detail. Most candidates for president begin their candidacy protected by local police agencies and private security firms before they are recognised as 'front-runners'. The 2016 presidential candidate Donald Trump, for example, had his own team of private bodyguards when he began his campaign. They continued to protect the candidate long after he was given Secret Service protection.

Unless a candidate is an incumbent and therefore already being protected, the Secret Service is not often present for early primary contests like Iowa and New Hampshire. By law, candidates are only required protection within 120 days of the general election. That means July of an election year is when the Secret Service usually begins guarding those candidates who have been successful in the primary election campaigns.

Presidential candidates can also get Secret Service protection if there appears to be a credible threat and protection can start earlier if warranted, such as Barack Obama who got his Secret Service detail in May 2007 after receiving numerous death threats. It was more than a year before he won the 2008 Democratic nomination. The 2016 candidate Ben Carson's political director G. Michael Brown said the candidate received threats that developed into serious safety concerns by the late summer of 2015. Secret Service protection for Carson began sometime around late October/early November 2015. Hillary Clinton already received protection before she ever entered the race due to her status as former First Lady. Other notable presidential candidates with early protection include Ted Kennedy in 1979, 411 days before Election Day, Jesse Jackson in 1987, 351 days before Election Day, John Kerry in 2004, 256 days before Election Day, and Mitt Romney in 2012, 278 days before Election Day.

A presidential candidate's detail is organised 'ad hoc' drawing from agents in the field. They are therefore relatively inexperienced compared with the details assigned to the president. However, each detail has a supervisor with presidential protective experience. The agency also takes into account the level of threat a candidate faces when he or she is assigned agents.

The Secret Service provides candidates with a bulletproof car, a lead car and a chase car. An advance party of agents go to the next city or town on the candidate's schedule. The advance-team agents are responsible for checking out the route the candidate will take to the venue. Ambush points are noted which is the reason why a candidate is always advised not to request a deviation from the route planned by the agents. The advance team also checks out recent purchases of weapons against a list of threateners who live in the vicinity of the candidate's scheduled event. They also seek advice about pertinent information held by local police departments, and 24-hour surveillance is kept on those individuals whom the Secret Service place on their 'watch list'. Often individuals who appear on the list will be told to stay clear of any of the candidate's scheduled appearances. The advance team is ready at the airport to meet the candidate when they arrive.

However, although most candidates appreciate the protection the Secret Service provides, some of them are not aware of what they are getting themselves into when they run for president. The 1992 presidential candidate Bob Kerrey said:

> If you were running for office, this is what I'd say to you. At some point, arriving in your life is an organization called the United States Secret Service. And when the Secret Service arrives, *you can't open your own car door.* They interfere with all your neighbours; anyone who wants to get in contact with you has to deal with them. So the best advice I could ever give to a candidate is, Think about this. You might *win.*[5]

The public are also generally unaware of the risks taken by the men and women who form the protective cloak around the president, vice president and presidential candidate. The agency lists thirty-eight agents on its 'Wall of Honour' who have died in the line of duty since 1902. They include White House police officer Leslie Coffelt who was at his security post at the front door of Blair House which was the temporary residence of President Truman who was upstairs taking a nap when two armed Puerto Rican nationalists attempted to storm the house to kill the president. In the shoot-out Officer Coffelt was killed.

Four agents died in an automobile accident while protecting Queen Elizabeth II on a visit to California in 1982. The car went off a mountain road. Six agents died in the Oklahoma terrorist bombing. During the Nixon administration an agent died in a helicopter accident. Seven agents were being taken by helicopter from Key Biscayne to join Nixon's detail in the Bahamas. The helicopter crashed. Six agents escaped but agent Cliff Dietrich was killed. The list also includes Julie Cross, a female agent murdered in 1981 in a robbery while part of a counterfeit surveillance operation at Los Angeles

International Airport.[6] Since 2000 two agents have died in the line of duty. Christopher Smith died of a heart attack in 2005. The most recent death is 42-year-old agent Nole Edward Remagen who died from a stroke when he accompanied President Trump on a trip to Scotland in 2018.

Many law-enforcement officers have been killed protecting the president or a presidential candidate, including Police Officer Victor Lozada of the Dallas Police Department who died in a motorcycle crash in 2008 while providing escort duty for presidential candidate Hillary Clinton. US Customs Service Criminal Investigator Manuel Zurita was killed while serving on President Clinton's protection detail in the Virgin Islands in 1998. He died when his boat hit a coral reef. In 2007 Police Officer Germaine F. Casey was killed while riding a motorcycle in George W. Bush's motorcade. In 2012 in Jupiter, Florida, a police officer died in a motorcycle accident while guarding President Obama.[7] In 1972 an Alabama state trooper was shot guarding presidential candidate George Wallace. Washington DC police officer Thomas Delahanty was wounded during the 1981 Reagan assassination attempt.

Like the Secret Service personnel surrounding the president, the basic duty of bodyguards protecting state governors who become presidential candidates (e.g. Wallace, Rockefeller, Reagan, Agnew, Dukakis, Clinton and Romney) is ensuring around the clock safety including campaign schedules organised before the candidate receives Secret Service protection. In the case of Congressmen and US Senators bodyguard protection is provided by Capitol police officers, private security and personal aides in association with local police forces – at least until they qualify for Secret Service protection.

There are historical reasons why state governors receive protection, whether they are running for president or not. Between 1790 and 1968 there were 8 assassination attempts on the approximately 1,330 people who served as governors in the United States. That translates into about six-tenths of 1 per cent of US governors being subjected to overt acts of violence during that period. Among recorded gubernatorial assassination attempts were attacks on Louisiana Governors William Pitt Kellogg in 1873 and Stephen B. Packard in 1877, New Jersey Governor John F. Fort in 1908 and Virginia Governor J. Lindsay Almond Jr in 1959.

However, the only recorded case of an assassination of a governor in office was that of Kentucky's William Goebel, who was shot and killed in his home state in 1900. The assassination apparently stemmed from disputed election results.

Studies have shown that a US president faces odds of 6 to 1 that an attempt will be made on his life. The odds are 143 to 1 for a Senator and 1,000 to 1 for a US Representative. The odds for a governor are 75 to 1.[8]

Like Secret Service agents, state troopers stand watch at governors' offices and mansions, typically armed with high-impact pistols and equipped with small walkie-talkies. They usually accompany the candidates to formal state functions as well as purely partisan political gatherings and campaign stops. Alabama Governor George Wallace, for example, had a security force of six full-time officers, four of whom normally accompanied him on trips outside the state. When he ran for president in presidential elections from 1964 to 1976, his guard was augmented by extra troopers who worked hand-in-hand with the Secret Service.

When a presidential candidate qualifies for Secret Service protection he or she is typically assigned about a half-dozen Secret Service agents who set aside their field-office jobs investigating counterfeiting and fraud for three-week shifts on protective detail. At public events and in motorcades, additional agents from the nearest field office and uniformed local police act as additional security. The other agents guarding a presidential candidate tend to be among the Secret Service's most junior.

The Secret Service security takes three forms. One is physical protection which includes guarding the home, coverage of the office and examination of vehicles and aeroplanes. Agents take control of the candidate's schedules, travel arrangements and checking out the venues where a candidate is due to speak. The venue is checked for bombs and possible evacuation routes are identified should an incident occur.

During a presidential election cycle the sitting president and vice president will already be protected by the Secret Service. Their immediate protection is provided by the Presidential Protective Detail (PPD), 'the brotherhood' or 'package' as some agents call it, and the Vice-Presidential Protective Detail (VPPD). Only a small percentage of agents will ever serve on the PPD and VPPD. Most agents are selected after years of having proven themselves as field agents or on other protective assignments. Additionally, a president or vice president may have a preference to be guarded by an individual agent. Former Secret Service Director James J. Rowley said, '. . . if the newly elected President expresses a preference for a certain man, you're generally willing to assign that man'.[9]

The Secret Service sends a team of agents to the places the president or presidential candidate will visit, whether it is a shopping mall, park or convention hall. They gather information about whether the area is safe and whether or not a hostile environment exists such as a political demonstration. They also liaise with local police forces to find out whether they have intelligence on a prospective threat. They will work closely with the candidate's staff and elicit information about any threatening behaviour or threatening letters and phone calls. The places of maximum danger are identified as those where the candidate's presence has been well-publicised. The least dangerous are the ones which are the least planned and least advertised.

Sometimes the security apparatus surrounding a president appears to be overwhelming. One agent who protected President Carter during a visit to Hannibal, Missouri said he counted '250' people who were carrying guns that day. 'There had to be a few wild cops who saw conspirators behind every bush', he said. 'I thought, God, nobody light a firecracker, we'll all get killed in the crossfire.'[10]

To protect the candidates, the Secret Service agents work in three different perimeters: an inner perimeter, a middle perimeter and an outer perimeter. The men working the inner perimeter are with the candidate to cover him and protect him in case there is an attempt on his life. When there is an incident that endangers the candidate an agent's training kicks in and he instinctively covers him or her to protect them from harm.

The middle-perimeter agents stand post at the entrances, exits and on the rooftops. They make sure the president, vice president or presidential candidate is entering a safe environment. Prior to entering a building the rooms must be cleared, emptied and secured chemically and biologically. Bomb dogs are used and all kinds of technical devices are employed to make sure there are no 'bugs' in his room and that it is environmentally safe.

Secret Service agents and police officers that are assigned the responsibility of controlling vehicular and pedestrian traffic within several blocks of where the president is going to be speaking or interacting with people cover the outer perimeter. As former agent Jim Cool said:

> You can never think about horizontal protection alone. There are helicopters patrolling the skies above the area where the president is engaged and there is also coverage below. When the president is travelling on an announced parade route, technicians will even go into the subterranean areas of a city and supervise the welding of manhole covers and sealing them so that no one with intent to

do malice can surface from below. . . . There are constant threats on the lives of the president and vice president. It is like Battlestar Galactica all the time, even worse since 9/11 . . .[11]

Agents are mindful of politics. 'The Secret Service realizes that isolation is not reality when you talk about a public official, and particularly during a campaign,' said former agent Eljay Bowron. 'If security prevents them from campaigning and accomplishing their mission, there's no point to them going out on the campaign trail.'[12]

Secret Service agent Joseph Petro said he worked with President Reagan's aides in promoting the president's public image while not endangering him. Negotiating, he said, was vital in order to avoid political disputes.

Normally, the Secret Service would prefer to perform its mission outside the public spotlight. But presidential candidates relish connecting with the public. It has given greater visibility to the bodyguards who are willing to place themselves between a presidential candidate and a would-be assassin. Accordingly, the Secret Service frequently comes into conflict with the candidate or the men and women who run their campaigns. For example, the Secret Service will usually request at least 20ft between the candidate and the campaign crowd but his aides will demand 4ft. The agents want him to enter the hotel through a rear door; the aides want him to stride past the cameras at the main entrance. 'There's definitely a conflict,' a staff member of Bill Clinton's 1992 campaign said. 'A campaign is, by definition, about meeting people and each person the candidate meets the Secret Service sees as a potential risk.'[13]

However, although bodyguards restrict the movements of candidates, a security detail can be politically advantageous. Agents give a 'presidential air' to their campaigns and can professionally facilitate a candidate's schedule. During the 1980 presidential campaign George H.W. Bush initially eschewed Secret Service protection until his advisers said he would look more 'presidential' with official bodyguards around him.

The Secret Service has sometimes taken loyalty to the point of lying for the protectee. One agent denied he was in a photograph taken of Kennedy with one of the president's mistresses even though it was clearly him. Agents lied to the press when Nixon managed to sneak out of his San Clemente summer home hidden under a blanket in the back seat of a car with his valet driving.[14]

Agents also have the difficult task of working around a protectee's impulsiveness. Former Secret Service agent Dan Emmett often saw presidents and presidential candidates act recklessly during election campaigning and even within the secure confines of the White House. President Jimmy Carter liked to walk to the South Lawn and talk to visitors on the other side of the fence. Bill Clinton liked to go jogging around the White House and Barack Obama would stroll from the White House to a local hamburger fast-food restaurant. George H.W. Bush wanted to see the aftermath of the 1992 Los Angeles riots. 'We thought he was just going to drive around,' Emmett said. However, '. . . he got out of the limo and was walking through south-central LA in a Brooks Brothers suit, with buildings still smouldering and store owners on the roofs with shotguns. You had people that close to the president with live weapons.'[15]

During the 2016 campaign Donald Trump's bodyguards were aware of the candidate's impulsiveness during campaigning. He would often stop his motorcade to greet supporters. On one occasion following his inauguration, agents had to scurry to surround him as he exited his limousine on Bingham Island near his home outside Palm Beach. They pushed back the crowds as they scrambled to make sure the door to the president's armoured SUV stayed open while he was out of the car. 'It's a Secret Service nightmare,' Dan Emmett said, 'but agents are trained for that . . . While the Secret Service would certainly prefer the president never, ever do that, they all do that.' Ultimately, it is the president who makes the decision. Former agent Danny Cecere said, 'You can give a suggestion. You can give advice. But ultimately it's up to the president.'[16]

Former Secret Service agent Dennis McCarthy concurs:

> That's what frightens us. When you can't see the hands, you don't know what's in the hands. I have walked up to people and said, 'Hey buddy, how ya doin'?' and reached down to grab his hand in his pocket to see if he's got a gun – and then just kept on walking. They don't realize what I've just done. Then all of a sudden they do – and they jerk their hands out of their pockets.

However, as the stops are 'random' they carry an element of surprise that works to agents' advantage. Potential assassins are unlikely to be in the vicinity – unless the would-be assassin is a 'stalker'. And, historically, presidential assassins of the past all knew where their targets would be when they aimed their weapons.

Bodyguards usually cannot remonstrate with the men and women they protect. If agents object to any travel arrangements or other security arrangements, there is nothing they can do except make objections, advise them, make suggestions, even object strenuously to what they think are bad ideas, but ultimately it is the protectee who makes the final decision. In 1972, for example, George Wallace had strayed away from a bulletproof lectern against his security detail's advice. 'They want maximum exposure', said Secret Service agent Frank O'Donnell, 'and we want minimum exposure. Everything's a compromise.'[17]

Accordingly, Secret Service and presidential candidate bodyguards always walk a fine line. On the one hand, the safety of the candidate is sacrosanct; on the other, the detail is extremely wary of being perceived as overbearing and over-protective.

Although the Secret Service has ten times as many agents as it did when JFK was assassinated in 1963, the agency still struggles to give adequate protection during presidential election years when their resources are stretched to the limit. Accordingly, agents worry they will be blamed if a successful assassination is carried out on a president or presidential candidate and that Congress, which controls financing for the agency, would not take the blame should that happen.

Just about every Secret Service agent receives an assignment to a presidential protection detail at some point in their career and it could be with the president, the vice president or a presidential candidate. Former agent Tim Wood described his experience as spending:

> Four to six years doing a protection assignment, and then you rotate back to the field for criminal investigations, I spent close to seven years on the president's detail. I did about six months with George H.W. Bush, then the first four years with President Clinton. Then I left and went to Seattle, as a criminal investigator working in the field. Then I went to Boise, Idaho, and got a promotion to be the resident agent in Boise, Idaho. From there I got a promotion to go back to the president's detail as a supervisor for the first two years of President George W. Bush.[18]

According to former Secret Service agent Frank O'Donnell, a veteran of twenty-four years with the agency who guarded candidates Edward M. Kennedy, Jesse Jackson and Michael Dukakis as well as Vice President George Bush and President Reagan, the younger agents loved being assigned to a candidate's detail. However, O'Donnell said, 'The older guys would rather be back at the field office.' Even so, he added, 'Everybody needs to do it at least once, because you'll be telling those stories for the rest of your career.'[19]

Because of the high burn-out rate of Secret Service agents protecting the president they usually work no more than five years on the presidential detail. This is because the agency recognises the heightened stress levels that result in protecting the chief executive. Dan Emmett said:

> Forgo sleep for 24 hours, skip lunch and dinner, stand outside of a house in the rain at 3 a.m. for several hours, take a cab to the airport and finally board a plane to a large city for a four-hour flight. Repeat this regimen for several days in a row. To make the simulation complete, you also need to fail to attend a child's birthday or graduation and miss the holidays or your wedding anniversary. . . . The routine is essentially shift work: Each agent assigned to the president works for a two-week period during the day, followed by two weeks on midnight shift and two weeks on the evening shift. At the end of this six-week cycle the agent goes into a two-week training phase, after which the cycle begins again. The continual changing of shifts, combined with constant travel to different time zones, is, of course, very hard on the body. Agents often burn out after four or five years.[20]

Bodyguards, whether they are state troopers, Secret Service agents or local security guards, typically work 8-hour shifts, though those shifts can come at any time of the day or night, and may take place anywhere in town, out of state, even out of country, sometimes with little notice. According to former Secret Service agent David See:

> We're in and out of a vehicle, in and out of a truck . . . walking around town. Whether or not you know where we are is a totally different story. But believe me we are there, believe me. . . . Most

people wouldn't notice this vehicle passing by. . . . You're looking for what doesn't look right, what's out of place here. . . . our primary responsibility is in the event of an attack to cover and evacuate that individual. My job's not to take cover and get behind something. We have drills that we do. They throw a lot of these sorts of things at you to get you that conditioning, that mental conditioning.[21]

Former Secret Service agent Marty Vencker said the campaigns he covered would be so stressful, 'I'd be running alongside the limo and I'd have to look down and read the sewer covers to see what city I was in. . . . on a given day we'd be travelling through four or five cities'.[22]

Commenting on the stress bodyguards have had to endure during the presidential election cycle, former Secret Service agent Tim Wood said that no other detail duty is quite as stressful as dealing with impromptu presidential greetings with private citizens standing behind a roped-off area. 'That's where agents earn their money,' he said. 'You have no idea what an uncontrolled crowd might do. To minimise threats, agents are constantly scanning for hands stuffed in pockets or other signs of suspicious activity. Their omnipresent sunglasses? Those are for crowd-scanning without tipping off potential suspects, and to ward off any liquids or other projectiles thrown in their direction.'[23]

Agents also have to come to terms with the post-traumatic stress many of them may suffer following incidents of violence. Agents Jerry Blaine and Clint Hill spoke of how the memories of the assassination of JFK remained with them long after the tragedy. Agents Jimmy Taylor and Larry Dominguez said they never got over feelings of guilt following the attempted assassination of George Wallace. In Dominguez's case, those feelings were exacerbated as he protected President Reagan during John Hinckley's 1981 assassination attempt.[24]

When an election cycle ends the candidate's bodyguards often feel a sense of relief. In 1976 when then Director of the Secret Service H. Stuart Knight was asked how he felt when a candidate dropped out of the race he said:

Good. But that's a purely selfish, non-political comment. In 1968, following the assassination of Robert Kennedy, we were suddenly given all the candidates to cover. The Secret Service agents really got put through the wringer. There is a tremendous emotional and psychological strain apart from the obvious physical strain. There is long hours, no sleep. The agents get keyed up and it takes a lot out of them. Military doctors have compared it to battle fatigue. One thing that generates this response is that there is very little margin for error in our business. Therefore, we demand perfection.[25]

There are other personal problems agents have dealt with. Bodyguards have frequently become so much a part of the families they have protected they have ended up acting like servants – carrying out duties that have often been characterised as 'menial', including babysitting, carrying luggage and collecting shopping packages. Often bodyguards have balked when asked by the president or the president's family members to carry out such tasks.

Agents can also expect the unexpected and not just from the intentions of would-be assassins lurking amid large crowds. When he was president, Ronald Reagan carried a .38 revolver in his briefcase 'just in case'. When Reagan was on his ranch, he used to carry the pistol and once scared an agent by firing it without warning.[26]

* * *

Threats to a presidential candidate come from many quarters. As former Secret Service agent Gerald Blaine observed, '. . . the tools of the assassin are far more sophisticated. Sniper rifles can strike a person's head from over a mile away with accuracy. Missiles, radioactive materials, biological weapons, chemicals, explosive devices and the dreaded nuclear weapon are available.'[27]

The Internet and advanced technology has also drastically changed how Secret Service officials prepare for presidential candidate events. Former Secret Service agent Todd Madison believes that, 'Evolution in technology has created a new physical risk – not only does the ground need to be secured, but we now must consider what is coming from above in the form of drones.' According to Madison, 'Threat levels can also vary by location. Risks and threats will shift as a candidate travels around the country and attends different events, so each location needs its own security plan and those plans need to adjust as the environment changes. Consider the local rhetoric and political outlook and whether it is negative, positive or neutral toward a candidate.'[28]

Accordingly, the danger to presidential candidates is real. 'In every campaign', said Eljay Bowron, 'they have determined that there have been people – for lack of a better word – stalking candidates with ill intent.'[29] Former

Secret Service Director H. Stuart Knight said, '. . . the Presidency is certainly a dangerous job, and so is campaigning for the Presidency. Candidates say that's the price you have to pay if you're going to be in public life.'[30]

The Secret Service has investigated literally thousands of assassination threats. However, there is no way of knowing how many plots or planned attacks have been made against presidents or presidential candidates. One agent likened the agency to a lighthouse. 'You do not know how many ships a lighthouse has saved,' he said.[31] And, given the number of threats and the grave possibility some might be serious, the Secret Service has had no choice but to investigate. As Marty Vencker observed:

> It might be just another [false] story but it couldn't be ignored. The intelligence guys would read poison-pen letters around the clock and tape phone calls passed along by the White House operators. . . . the wacko communiqués could range from a trite crayon drawing of Richard Nixon with a knife through his eye to an incoherent phone conversation that ended with the ear-splitting sound of the caller blowing his brains out.[32]

Former Secret Service agent Joseph Petro considered the 'many times' an attacker has waited to strike but had been stopped because of the heavy bodyguard protection around a president or presidential candidate. 'We don't know', Petro said, '. . . [but likely] . . . more than we will ever know'.[33] Personal security specialist Gavin de Becker said, 'How you look – literally how you look at people – can enhance deterrence . . . There are many cases where attacks were deterred by the conspicuous currency of protectors – by the appearances that matter.'[34]

The Secret Service has always refused to say how many open threats they investigate against political leaders and their families and no one will ever know for sure how many plots or planned attacks have been thwarted by the agency. Their records are closed to public scrutiny. However, there have likely been many more assassination threats and assassination attempts than previously suspected.

Accordingly, it is problematic in quantifying the number of 'known' assassination attempts presidential candidates have faced since 1960 during election campaigns. However, a general guide is possible. An 'attempted assassination' can be defined as an armed individual who has approached a presidential candidate with ill intent or had an opportunity to knife or shoot a candidate even if they have been foiled at the last minute by stringent security or other circumstances. The category includes armed individuals who stalked a candidate. They are identified in the forthcoming chapters and include would-be assassins of President Lyndon Johnson, Senator Barry Goldwater, Senator Robert Kennedy, Alabama Governor George Wallace, Senator Ted Kennedy, President Richard Nixon, Senator Eugene McCarthy, New York Mayor John Lyndsay, Senator Gary Hart, President George H.W. Bush and President Donald Trump while they campaigned. Other categories of would-be assassins of presidential candidates include plotters who planned to kill a candidate but did not have the opportunity to approach them. Their stories are replete throughout the book.

Although some researchers conclude there is no such thing as a 'profile of the assassin', the majority of threateners can, arguably, fit a group portrait – that of an unemployed young white male, a failure and a drifter, unloved and unable to love with little or no contact with women; if they developed a relationship with a woman, they frequently experienced emotional difficulties; they were loveless, obsessional, lonely, hating, frustrated and psychically and socially alienated; almost all had some form of personality disorder. Most of them were deceptively calm, well-behaved, often shy individuals who grew up controlling themselves until an incident in their lives acted as a catalyst for action. This description can also apply to those lone wolf would-be Islamist assassins who became a serious problem for the Secret Service since the 1990s.

Most would-be assassins also shared a pattern of behaviour – a chain of thinking that led them into seeing assassination as acceptable. For almost all of them, attacks or near-lethal approaches occurred after a period of downward spiral in their lives. Many had been hospitalised at least once for psychiatric reasons, ranging from long-term treatment to brief admissions for suicidal threats. The most frequent motive that assassins offered for attacking a public figure was to achieve notoriety or fame. As University of New Hampshire professor Stuart Palmer observed, 'You can become a TV star or an assassin. [For some people] becoming an assassin, known to everyone by the media is certainly pretty good second best.'[35]

Other assassins wanted to avenge a perceived wrong, to end their pain by being imprisoned or hospitalised or killed, to save the country or the world, to achieve a special relationship with the target. Many would-be assassins suffered from delusional thinking. Others had a mixture of motives including psychological and political.

During election cycles from 1960 to 2020 the front-runner candidates who faced the most danger were the politicians who inspired the greatest emotional response. Among the many presidential candidates who have received numerous threats since 1960 other than the president the list includes Robert F. Kennedy, Ted Kennedy, George Wallace, Jesse Jackson, Ronald Reagan and Donald Trump; candidates who attracted love and hatred in equal measure. As *Chicago Tribune* journalist Mike Royko observed, '[Jesse Jackson] . . . inspires strong and deep emotions, stronger and deeper than any politician in my adult life. While that gift can be a ticket to success in politics, it can also be a ticket to the emergency room. Those who have attracted assassins – the Kennedys, Reagan, King, Wallace – have one thing in common: they weren't bland. They generated electricity.'[36]

* * *

The assassination of President Kennedy persuaded many in government that the time when presidents and presidential candidates could wade into crowds to shake hands and greet the public should come to an end. However, this idea was never put into practice by presidential candidates in the decades that followed and led to numerous attempts by attackers to breach their security cordons – sometimes ending in tragedy.

Chapter 2

Camelot's Sentinels

'If I had reacted about five tenths of a second faster, or maybe a second faster . . . I wouldn't be here today . . . I could have taken the third shot.'

'I still have nightmares about it. I wish I had taken that third bullet for him. I wonder: maybe if I had moved a little faster, he might still be alive today?'

Secret Service agent Clint Hill

In 1960, when Senator John F. Kennedy campaigned around the country for president he did not have Secret Service protection until he won the November general election as the Democratic Party nominee. The candidate relied on local police law-enforcement agencies, Senate aides and family members to escort him when he gave campaign speeches. Two aides in particular, Dave Powers and Kenny O'Donnell, helped organise his schedule and travel arrangements and liaised with local police.

Often JFK's campaign became chaotic. In fact, the campaign was so disorganised the candidate once got lost. The press had been saying that Kennedy and his running mate, Lyndon Johnson, had not been 'getting along' so campaign organisers arranged for the candidates to meet up in New York for a television programme. After a parade down Broadway, the group intended ending up at Columbus Circle. However, the Kennedy retinue 'got lost' even though they had the Police Commissioner with them in the same car. Kennedy had to stop the car himself to ask directions at a gas station.[1]

JFK's womanising was well known to his aides when he was campaigning around the country. His affairs were also known to the Washington press corps, but the journalistic tradition of the time dictated that the private affairs of politicians could not be printed. A Georgetown housewife, obsessed with exposing the womanising candidate for president, became a public nuisance in the 1960 Kennedy presidential campaign but the general public did not care to hear or believe her story.

Recently uncovered notes Kennedy wrote during the 1960 election campaign trail – scrawled notes to his aides while he was suffering from a bout of laryngitis – show the candidate was worried that his womanising might damage his chances of winning the presidential election. 'I got into a blonde', Kennedy wrote in one missive. Concerned his behaviour might be exposed, he wrote, 'I suppose they are going to hit me with something before we are finished.'[2]

Kennedy's notorious philandering did not begin with his accession to the presidency. He was unfaithful throughout his marriage to Jacqueline Bouvier Kennedy. During the 1960 presidential primary campaign elections he told one of his lovers that he would divorce his wife. He was soon disabused of that idea when his father, Joseph P. Kennedy, objected, telling him it would ruin his chances of becoming president.

During a stop-over in Las Vegas during his 1960 primary election campaign he was introduced to Judith Campbell by Frank Sinatra, who supported Kennedy's candidacy. Campbell, later known as Judith Exner, was a 25-year-old beautiful Elizabeth Taylor lookalike. A month after the meeting they become lovers. He even slept with Campbell in the Georgetown home he shared with his wife and two children the night before his inauguration and as president-elect his Secret Service agents were privy to the affair.

At one point during the campaign JFK asked Campbell to carry a satchel containing at least $250,000 to Chicago mobster Sam Giancana who had also recently been introduced to Campbell by Sinatra. It was Kennedy Sr who arranged the mobster's assistance in helping JFK win votes in the corrupt precincts of Chicago. Throughout her years with JFK, Campbell was under intense FBI surveillance due to her association with the mobster. FBI Director J. Edgar Hoover chose not to make this information public at least in part because revealing it would indicate the extent of his illegal bugging and would damage his and the FBI's reputations.

By the autumn of 1962, JFK had been warned by Hoover that the liaison threatened his presidency. Campbell was dropped, although Kennedy continued to have affairs with other women. Many years later Campbell claimed to have got pregnant by JFK during their last sexual encounter. According to Campbell, JFK told her not to keep the baby and to seek help from Giancana in terminating the pregnancy.[3]

Following his election in November 1960 the Secret Service appointed a detail to guard the president-elect. The bodyguards were composed of thirty-eight special agents. In addition, there were six special agent-drivers, eight special agents assigned to the Kennedy family and five special agents detailed to the Kennedy home in Hyannis Port.

Many Kennedy agents expressed an admiration for the newly elected president. Clint Hill, who was responsible for Jacqueline Kennedy's security, said Kennedy was, 'Very charismatic and friendly. He treated us like family, forming a close personal relationship. President Kennedy always called us by our first name, while Mrs. Kennedy always referred to (me) as "Mr. Hill", and had the children do so as well.'[4]

Kennedy's agents noted how different he was from President Eisenhower. 'He made a point of knowing our names,' former Secret Service agent Ken Giannoules said. President Eisenhower's agents were simply addressed as 'agent'.[5] However, Kennedy's personal style of campaigning posed a problem for the Secret Service. He was known to cause deep concern because he relished contact with the crowds.

Many of JFK's agents believed his private transgressions put his presidency at risk. Secret Service men who stood by as the president met women in hotels around the country were appalled, as a steady stream of high-priced prostitutes were brought in to have sex with him. However, there was one affair his bodyguards were unaware of. Mimi Beardsley was a 19-year-old intern who worked in the White House and travelled with the president around the country on presidential trips. A seat on Air Force One was always reserved for her. She was told by Kennedy's aides to wait in hotel rooms until Kennedy wanted to see her.[6]

Agent Larry Newman said Kennedy's detail 'loved Kennedy' and 'loved the fact he made an effort to learn the names of the agents and some personal details about them'. However, he called his appointment to the president's detail a 'baptism by fire'. On one occasion he was guarding the president at the Olympic Hotel in Seattle in November 1961 when a local sheriff came out of the elevator with two 'high-class call girls' and proclaimed that he was taking them to the presidential suite. Newman tried to stop them, but presidential aide Dave Powers intervened and ushered the women into the hotel room. The local sheriff who was assigned to assist the Secret Service informed the prostitutes that if they ever revealed their assignations with the president they would be sent to a psychiatric hospital.

Newman said the Kennedy detail was not concerned about the immorality of his personal lifestyle, but this did cause morale problems with the agents. 'This was the President of the United States', Newman said, 'and you felt impotent and you couldn't do your job. It was frustrating.' The agents were concerned that the president was putting himself at high risk. 'We didn't know if these women were carrying listening devices,' Newman said, 'if they had syringes that carried some type of poison or if they had Pentax cameras that would photograph the president for blackmail. Your security is only [as good] as its weakest link and the weak link was [Dave] Powers bringing these girls in.' Newman continued, '. . . we grieve that he would conduct himself in such a way as to make us so vulnerable and make the country so vulnerable'.[7]

Kennedy agent Tim McIntyre also told investigative reporter Seymour Hersh that his shift supervisor, Emory Roberts, took him aside and warned him, 'You're going to see . . . stuff with the President. Just forget about it. Keep it to yourself. Don't even talk to your wife.' In McIntyre's view, a public scandal about Kennedy's incessant womanising was inevitable. 'It would have had to come out in the next year or so. In the [1964] campaign, maybe,' he said. McIntyre said he and some of his colleagues felt 'abused' by their service on behalf of President Kennedy. He said he eventually realised that he had compromised his law-enforcement beliefs to the point where he wondered whether it was 'time to get out of there. I was disappointed by what I saw.'[8]

At the time of the Seattle Hotel incident Kennedy's bodyguards were briefed that there was a high risk of assassination. They were told an assassin had attempted to kill Cuban leader Fidel Castro as the Cuban leader launched a ship. The bullet meant for the Cuban leader hit the ship's propeller instead. The agents were warned that Castro might be organising a 'retaliatory strike'.[9]

Kennedy's agents were also concerned about the type of 'medication' he was receiving. When Kennedy was running for president in the 1960 primary elections his brother-in-law Stanislaus Radziwell (married to Jacqueline Kennedy's sister, Lee) recommended Dr Max Jacobson for treatment of his back pains. 'He was the batwing and chicken blood doctor,' Newman said. The medication turned out to be a cocktail of amphetamines. Kate Thom Kelley, the wife of one of JFK's friends, said:

I don't know how much he knew about it, I don't know how much his doctors knew about the drugs. Some of it was experimental. But, you know, the only thing that we can say is that so far there is no evidence that it interfered with his judgment. He certainly lived through and was president during some of the most frightening moments in recent history.[10]

One of the senior agents, Newman said, knew what Jacobson was prescribing for Kennedy, 'and tried to keep him away from the president . . .'.[11]

After Kennedy took office he continued having assignations with numerous women who were brought to the White House. Occasionally he would meet them at New York's Carlyle Hotel where the Kennedy family had an apartment. Kennedy's women included not only Judith Campbell but socialite Mary Pinchot Meyer, an artist who lived in Georgetown in Washington DC, East German suspected spy Ellen Rometsch and two other call girls from communist countries, Maria Novotny and Suzy Chang. The latter two women were also involved with British defence minister John Profumo and a Soviet naval attaché stationed in London.

The FBI learned of the Rometsch-Kennedy connection and began to investigate her. Attorney General Bobby Kennedy arranged to have her deported and she was flown back to Germany on a US Air Force transport plane.

According to investigative journalist Seymour Hersh, the Secret Service stood guard outside the White House swimming pool when the president swam naked with two of his favourite female assistants, Priscilla Wear and Jill Cowen, nicknamed Fiddle and Faddle. Wear already had the nickname Fiddle when she joined the White House staff, so Kennedy aides applied the name Faddle to Cowen. The president was often joined by his brothers, Bobby and Teddy.[12]

Kennedy's agents also revealed the president had sex with Marilyn Monroe at New York hotels and in a loft above the Justice Department office of Robert Kennedy, the president's brother. The loft had a double bed that RFK used when he needed to stay over at the Justice Department. The unnamed agent told journalist Ronald Kessler, '[Kennedy] had liaisons with Marilyn Monroe there. The Secret Service knew about it.'[13]

Don Hewitt, the host of the 1960 presidential television debates, knew Kennedy well. Hewitt described Kennedy as 'indiscreet' and that he:

... didn't know that a young kid was going to brag about having it off with the president. Jack Kennedy didn't realize. . . . Well, most of the women who had things with Jack Kennedy were very secret about it. Judith Exner wasn't. It's almost irresistible to say you're having an affair with the president. So it was reckless. . . . So, you know, he was very human, but it wasn't very smart. And it's hubris.[14]

Samuel Beer, a Massachusetts Democrat colleague of Kennedy's, said Kennedy liked 'really lower-class, vulgar women . . . with the exception being Washington socialite Mary Pinchot Meyer'. Beer said Kennedy had, '. . . a terrible relationship with this Mafia woman [Judith Campbell Exner]. . . . Who then wrote about it; it was true. It was an awful chance that he took.'[15]

There is little doubt that Kennedy was aware that if any stories about his private life were made public it would put an end to his 1964 re-election bid.

* * *

There were a number of 'scares' during the Kennedy campaign that turned out to be innocuous including an incident on 4 November 1960 when Kennedy was campaigning in Chicago. Police arrested two men, 23-year-old Puerto Rican Jaime Cruz Alejandro and 61-year-old African American minister Israel Dabney, who separately approached the Democratic presidential candidate armed with pistols. Both men were arrested and charged with a misdemeanour for carrying a concealed weapon and both denied having any intent to harm Kennedy.[16]

Although there were no serious plots to kill Kennedy during the 1960 campaign, he was targeted after he became president-elect and it occurred within weeks of his election. Kennedy had retired to his father's estate in Palm Beach for deserved rest from the rigours of the campaign trail. On Sunday morning, 11 December 1960 a car slowed down and came to a halt across the street from the Kennedy residence. Inside the house were members of the Kennedy family including John and Jackie Kennedy and their children. Inside the car sat 73-year-old Richard Pavlick, a postal clerk from Belmont, New Hampshire. The car contained seven sticks of dynamite that could be detonated by the simple closing of a switch. His intention was to wait until Kennedy entered his car then drive his own forward into Kennedy's, blowing himself and the president-elect up.

Pavlick watched the house and knew Kennedy would be going to Sunday Mass at 10.00 am. As Kennedy opened the door of his house, surrounded by agents and accompanied by his wife and children, Pavlick's conscience was pricked. He didn't wish to harm Jackie or the children. He followed the president to Mass and stood yards away from him inside the church when agents were alerted by his demeanour. Pavlick walked away, got in his car but did not throw the bomb switch a second time because Kennedy was surrounded by children outside the church. He drove off in the opposite direction.

Police were soon tipped off by acquaintances in his home town and alerted local police about his purported assassination plans. On Thursday, 15 December, after a nationwide manhunt, he was arrested for reckless driving and admitted the dynamite found in the car was to assassinate Kennedy. He was eventually handed over to Secret Service agents who charged him with attempted murder and unlawful possession of explosives. He subsequently spent six years in various federal prisons and mental institutions.

Pavlick was not alone in his desire to kill Kennedy. The threats and Secret Service investigations would grow to incredible proportions over the following three years. In 1961 alone the Secret Service investigated 870 threatening letters addressed to the president. White House police officers turned back 643 persons who tried to argue or force their way into the White House. The figures were 50 per cent higher than those for the final year of the Eisenhower administration.[17]

During his presidency threats to assassinate Kennedy included:

- In early April 1961 agents received reports that a pro-Castro group in the United States planned either to kill JFK and his wife and children or kidnap his daughter Caroline Kennedy. The group was put under surveillance and agents believed the plot was foiled for this reason.
- A threat to shoot JFK by a Nashville man on 18 May 1963. As Kennedy was giving a speech at a local high school the would-be assassin approached the president armed with a pistol hidden in a sack. Alerted by the man's suspicious demeanour, agents arrested him. JFK was seconds from death.
- A few weeks before JFK's November 1963 Dallas trip Thomas Valle, a Marine Corps veteran and expert marksman who hated JFK, taped a collage of photos and stories about the president to the walls of his Chicago apartment room. The collage was accompanied by threatening remarks. After a tip-off from his landlady Valle was arrested. Agents discovered he had an M1

rifle and hundreds of rounds of ammunition. The incident occurred shortly before the president's trip to Chicago.

- In October 1963 Wayne Gainey, who said the Ku Klux Klan had authorised him to kill the president, was arrested after he said he was going to assassinate Kennedy during the president's visit to Tampa, Florida.
- John William Warrington had written five letters threatening JFK for his association with Martin Luther King postmarked 15, 16 and 17 October in Tampa. In October 1963 Warrington wrote he would be 'lying in ambush' armed with a rifle when the president visited Florida.
- A group of Irishmen who threatened to kill Kennedy on his June 1963 visit to Ireland.
- Joseph A. Milteer, a right-wing racist, told an acquaintance he knew about 'a mobile, unidentified rifleman shooting from a window in a tall building with a high-powered rifle fitted with a scope'. The assassin would be waiting to kill Kennedy on the president's November 1963 trip to Miami.
- In November 1963 two anti-Castro Cubans, Thomas Mosley and Homer Echevarria, threatened to 'take care of Kennedy'.
- On 21 November 1963 a Dallas college student, Russell McLarry, said he planned to be 'waiting with a gun to shoot JFK' when the president visited Dallas the following day. McLarry was arrested and when he appeared in court he said he was 'not sorry the president was killed. . . . I don't remember exactly what I said. The statement I made was a joke. If I can be tried for a joke and found guilty – well, that's the extent of it.' The following 10 January a federal grand jury apparently believed him and jurors refused to indict McLarry on a charge of threatening the president.
- George J. King Jr, an extreme right-winger who hated Jews and African Americans, was heard in August 1963 discussing the possibility of killing the president. He was arrested before his plans came to fruition for the illegal sale of machine guns.[18]

At the time of JFK's visit to Dallas the Secret Service's 'watch list' included numerous people who had threatened to kill the president. However,

Kennedy agent Gerald Blaine said, 'There weren't ANY active threats in Texas.'[19]

* * *

In late November 1963 President Kennedy was in Texas primarily for political reasons – to heal a rift in the Democratic Party and to raise funds for his 1964 re-election campaign. He told his friend Senator George Smathers that he wished he could escape the trip which he called 'a pain in the neck'.

There were warnings that the President's reception might be hostile. Lately, Texas had been in an unfriendly mood toward the Kennedy administration. Partly, this arose from the Civil Rights Movement which Kennedy had supported; partly it was aroused by right-wing militant groups like the John Birch Society. Vice President Lyndon Johnson, himself a Texan, was frequently vilified. Ambassador to the United Nations Adlai Stevenson had recently been spat upon and hit with a picket sign in Dallas. Placards were being distributed bearing the president's image and the legend 'Wanted for Treason'. Even Governor John Connally was worried and some of JFK's aides were uneasy about the trip.

There were twenty-eight special agents in the presidential entourage. Agent Winston Lawson, along with Jesse Curry, the Dallas police chief, sat in the lead car, directly in front of Kennedy's. Behind them Secret Service agents William Greer and Roy Kellerman were in the driver and passenger seats of the president's limousine, a 1961 midnight-blue four-door Lincoln. This second car carried the Kennedys and Texas Governor John Connally and his wife. Four retractable side steps and two steps with handles on the rear of the car had been added to allow Secret Service agents to jump on or off during the motorcade. The vehicle was heavy, unwieldy and difficult to manoeuvre, especially when turning corners as the limousine driver discovered when he turned onto Elm Street right next to a sniper's perch at the Texas School Book Depository.

The third car was a 1955 black Cadillac convertible driven by Secret Service agent Sam Kinney. It was Kinney's job to stay a few feet behind the presidential limousine at all times to prevent another vehicle from intervening. Paul Landis, Jack Ready and Clint Hill rode the running boards along the sides of the car. Agents George Hickey, Emory Roberts and Glen Bennett sat inside the vehicle.

Agent Mike Howard was one of the Secret Service bodyguards who protected President Kennedy in Dallas. He said, 'The crowds were tremendous. . . .

People were lining the streets even though a soft rain was falling. President Kennedy made them roll down the windows in the motorcade even though everyone inside was getting wet. He wanted to see the people he was waving to. And people were bending over for a glimpse inside as the car passed by.'[20]

The actual route in Dallas was selected by Secret Service agents Forrest V. Sorrels and Winston G. Lawson to traverse the distance between the Dallas airport and the site of the luncheon where the President was to speak to business and political leaders.

To the rear of Kennedy's limousine was a car carrying the Johnsons and Texas Senator Ralph Yarborough. Secret Service agent Rufus Youngblood, who was also in the car, heard an 'explosive noise'. In the second car behind Johnson Dallas Mayor Earl Cabell's wife saw a 'projection' sticking out of a window of the book depository building. From a press car at the rear of the motorcade, Robert Jackson, a *Dallas Times Herald* photographer, saw a rifle being slowly drawn back through an open window. Directly across from the building, Amos Euins, a 15-year-old schoolboy, saw a man shoot twice from a window.

Jackie Kennedy, who was sat next to her husband in the limousine, heard a sound similar to a motorcycle noise and a cry from Governor Connally which caused her to look to her right. On turning she saw a 'quizzical look' on her husband's face. Jacqueline Kennedy said:

> They were gunning the motorcycles. There were these little back-fires. There was one noise like that. I thought it was a backfire. Then next I saw Connally grabbing his arms and saying no, no, no, no with his fist beating. . . . He was holding out his hand . . . I could see a piece of his skull coming off. It was flesh-coloured, not white – he was holding out his hand . . . I can see this perfectly clean piece detaching itself from his head. Then he slumped in my lap, his blood and his brains were in my lap . . .[21]

Dallas was imprinted in agent Clint Hill's mind. Two seconds after the first shot was fired Hill ran for Kennedy's limousine. Kennedy had torn a groin muscle when he swam in the White House pool in September 1963. Forced to wear a full-body brace, he was held erect, unable to bend forward when Lee Harvey Oswald's bullets struck him in the back of his neck and tore into the rear right side of his head. In 2009 Hill could still '. . . see it . . . can hear that third shot, see the president slump sideways into Mrs Kennedy's lap and see her scramble across the back of the car trying to pick up pieces of his brain and skull'.[22]

After Kennedy was taken to Parkland Hospital Secret Service agents Richard Johnsen and Andy Berger stood guard outside the operating room. Their instructions were to bar anyone who did not have permission from the doctors to enter. At one point, an FBI investigator tried to get in. The agents refused and the FBI agent had to be subdued before they instructed him to leave the area.

Agent Mike Howard said he was convinced that Lee Harvey Oswald fired the lethal shots from a window at the Texas School Book Depository where Oswald worked. He also said he saw Oswald and his wife Marina together after his arrest and it led him to believe Oswald was guilty. He saw Marina Oswald's facial expressions as Oswald talked to her in Russian. Howard believed Marina recoiled because her husband had just admitted to her that he had assassinated the president.[23]

* * *

When John F. Kennedy prepared to run for a second term in office he had just faced down the Soviet Union over the Cuban Missile Crisis and the country was in the middle of the Cold War. When Vice President Lyndon Johnson was hurriedly sworn in as commander-in-chief he knew that an attack on the president could possibly be the start of a pre-emptive nuclear strike against the United States. The CIA was aware of Soviet plans to eliminate US leaders if a war broke out. The new president was fearful 40 million Americans might die in a nuclear exchange.

In the months following the assassination President Johnson wanted to end the intense speculation engendered by the assassination. Was the Soviet Union to blame? Could the finger of guilt be pointed at Cuba's dictator Fidel Castro? The US public was also desperate to know what exactly had happened and if the assassination could have been prevented.

President Johnson's response was to appoint the Warren Commission. It was charged with investigating the circumstances surrounding the assassination and was headed by the Chief Justice of the Supreme Court, Earl Warren. The Commission's final report, which was released during the 1964 presidential election campaign, was impressive – twenty-seven volumes of witness testimony, exhibits and reports. The Warren Commission heard 552 witnesses and received more than 3,000 reports from law-enforcement agencies which had conducted 26,000 interviews.

One of the ways the Warren Report made an immediate and long-term impact was on US Secret Service procedures. The Warren Commission determined that the Secret Service and other federal agencies, including the FBI, needed 'sweeping revision' going forward in order to better protect the president and anticipate threats. However, the report reserved its most stinging criticism for the Secret Service.

In some respects, the report stated, the Secret Service was not equipped to deal with the president's style of leadership, in particular Kennedy's love of large crowds and his need to be close to the public. '(Kennedy's) very position as representative of the people', the report stated, 'prevents him from effectively shielding himself from the people. He cannot and will not take the precautions of a dictator or a sovereign. Under our system, measures must be sought to afford security without impeding the President's performance of his many functions.'[24]

During the visit to Dallas, the report continued, President Kennedy insisted on riding in an open car without any Secret Service agents in the vehicle; the route took them through the centre of Dallas, where crowds lined the streets and cheering supporters occupied every window.

The report included concerns about the agency's advance intelligence work on potential threats to the president. It found that the Secret Service should have taken a 'broader view' of information that was considered a threat to the president.

The Secret Service's lack of written guidelines on advance preparations and coordinating with local law enforcement was also criticised. While the motorcade route and the stops along it were well-coordinated, the report concluded, the buildings lining the route were not searched and no counter-measures were put in place to prevent a shooting. 'Examination of these procedures shows that in most respects they were well conceived and ably executed by the personnel of the Service. Against the background of the critical events of November 22, however, certain shortcomings and lapses from the high standards which the Commission believes should prevail in the field of Presidential protection are evident.'[25]

The report found no issue with the conduct of the Secret Service agents present at the assassination, 'Their actions demonstrate that the President and the Nation can expect courage and devotion to duty from the agents of the Secret Service.'[26] However, the Commission noted that the agency was under-staffed and under-funded and thus unable to complete its mission of security to the best possible standard. It recommended an increase in personnel and budget to ensure the agency was able fully to prepare for presidential trips.

More than a decade after publication of the Warren Report a new investigation into the circumstances surrounding the JFK assassination was carried out. The House Select Committee on Assassinations (HSCA) concurred with the findings of the Warren Commission with regard to the Secret Service's responsibilities on the day of the assassination. The Committee criticised agencies and departments of government in the fulfilment of their duties, especially the Secret Service which, the committee concluded, did not give President Kennedy adequate protection. The agencies 'performed with varying degrees of competency in the fulfilment of their duties', the HSCA concluded. Secret Service agents in the motorcade were inadequately prepared to protect the president and the agency was 'deficient in the performance of its duties'.[27]

Both reports cited the fact that nine of the Secret Service men who were in Dallas with the president the day he died had been out until the early hours of the morning visiting a nightclub. A few of them were sleep deprived and had been drinking while travelling with the president, an activity that was clearly prohibited by Secret Service protocols. Following the Warren Report's publication and in response to suggestions the agents were less than dedicated and professional, Secret Service Chief James Rowley would later testify that none of his men were impaired when they reported for work that morning.

Although the agents denied they did not have more than one or two alcoholic drinks, the truth finally came out decades later when the nightclub's owner admitted to the *Fort Worth Star-Telegraph* that he '. . . got a call from the White House asking us not to say anything about the agents' drinking because their image had suffered enough as it was. We didn't say anything but those guys were bombed. They were drinking pure Everclear [a strong alcoholic drink].'[28]

Both government reports agreed that the first shot fired by Lee Harvey Oswald from the Texas School Book Depository missed. During the critical time between the second shot which entered Kennedy's back and exited his throat and the third shot to Kennedy's head the Secret Service agents failed to take evasive action. Roy Kellerman, the leader of the security detail, looked puzzled. He thought a firecracker had gone off. Arlen Specter, one of the lead lawyers for the Warren Commission, said Kellerman 'was the wrong man for the job – he was 48 years old, big, and his reflexes were not quick'.[29]

William Greer, at the wheel of the president's car, did not immediately speed up or swerve away from the shots. Had Greer swerved or accelerated the presidential limousine Oswald's third and fatal shot may have missed. Paul Landis and Jack Ready in the vehicle behind Kennedy's did not jump forward to protect the president with their bodies. Agent William Greer was clearly '. . . tormented by his actions in the motorcade, including his failure to hit the accelerator immediately after hearing the first shot'. Greer later apologised to Jacqueline Kennedy after the limousine arrived at Parkland Hospital saying, 'Oh, Mrs. Kennedy, oh my God, oh my God. I didn't mean to do it. I didn't hear, I should have swerved the car, I couldn't help it. Oh Mrs. Kennedy . . . if only I had seen in time.'[30]

However, the two government reports did not go into any great detail about the president's actions that day which may have contributed to his assassination. As the decades passed agents began to speak out about why Kennedy's immediate bodyguards had not been in a position to take the bullets meant for the president. According to author Ronald Kessler, who interviewed a number of agents who had been on Kennedy's detail, this desire to be seen by voters eventually contributed to his death. Kennedy wanted to be physically close to the voters, so he was impatient with agents who wanted to surround him. When Kennedy became president agents would stand on the running boards at the side of the presidential limousine. But agents invariably blocked crowds from seeing the president. 'Despite warnings of violence in Dallas', Kessler wrote, 'he refused to let Secret Service agents ride on the rear running board of his limousine in the motorcade on November 22, 1963. Since the "kill shot" to the president's head came 4.9 seconds after the first shot that hit him, Secret Service agents would have had a chance to protect him.'

Kennedy Agent Chuck Taylor told Kessler that, 'If agents had been allowed on the rear running boards, they would have pushed the president down and jumped on him to protect him before the fatal shot.' Secret Service Director Lewis Merletti concurred, 'An analysis of the ensuing assassination,' Merletti said, 'including the trajectory of the bullets which struck the president, indicates that it might have been thwarted had agents been stationed on the car's running boards.'[31]

However, Kessler's criticisms have been challenged by other agents. Agent Gerald Behn, the head of the White House detail, who was not in Dallas that day, told one writer, 'I don't remember Kennedy ever saying that he didn't want anybody on the back of his car.'[32]

Further criticism of the Secret Service was provided by agent John Norris, 'Except for George Hickey and Clint Hill, [many of the others] just basically sat there with their thumbs up their butts while the president was gunned down in front of them.'[33]

Former Agent Gerald Blaine also provided new information about the actions of the Secret Service agents that day in his book *The Kennedy Detail*. Blaine wrote of how sleep deprivation meant many agents often struggled to stay awake. 'Working double shifts had become so common since Kennedy became president', Blaine wrote, 'that it was now almost routine. . . . The three eight-hour shift rotation operated normally when the president was in the White House, but when he was travelling . . . there simply weren't enough bodies.' Blaine also commented about how motorcades '. . . were the Secret Service's nemeses . . . There were an endless number of variables . . . and you could never predict how a crowd would react'.[34]

Five decades after the assassination Clint Hill would place the blame on the Secret Service's bureaucracy. 'The only time you ever really got anything accomplished was after an incident occurred,' Clint Hill said. When the Secret Service asked Congress to appropriate money for overtime or extra men, he said, they often got their support too late. 'After the incident they would come back and give us what we had asked for in the first place.'[35]

* * *

The Secret Service acted immediately on the commission's criticisms and implemented major changes. A larger budget and the creation of hundreds more staff positions allowed the agency to expand and improve upon its protection details and advance preparation. By the time the Warren Report was published, the agency had already completely revamped its presidential motorcade requirements to address the vulnerabilities that were exploited in Dallas.

The presidential limousine was redesigned to permit two Secret Service men to sit facing the President in jump seats. In the car following the President's limousine, an agent with an automatic rifle was required to sit facing toward the rear – clearly a response to the circumstances of JFK's assassination when agents were unaware Lee Harvey Oswald was shooting from above and behind. Better coordination with other federal agencies and local law enforcement were also put into place to ensure that the Secret

Service would be capable of providing the president with the best possible protection.

Before Kennedy was killed, Secret Service files with names of persons potentially dangerous to the president contained no more than 400 names. Secret Service procedures broadened criteria increasing the numbers to 8,000 people, although that number was later criticised by a former agent who said the agency was simply adding to the list just about anyone who was under the slightest of suspicions. When President Johnson visited El Paso in September 1964, the new security measures were in effect. Before his arrival, agents inspected every hotel and high building along his 20-mile route from the airport into the city. The agents compared the names of 'transient people' with those on the growing list of potential presidential assassins.

As the pace of the 1964 presidential election increased the Warren Commission issued its report. However, the Commission's suggested protective measures appeared to have had little effect on the way the new president behaved as he travelled around the nation seeking votes.

Chapter 3

Lyndon Johnson's Secret Servants

'. . . in one respect [Johnson] was little different from any other president we had to deal with. He had that same peculiar fatalistic attitude about his own safety.'

Secret Service agent Rufus Youngblood

'Of all the presidents, he was probably the most professional politician. Politics was his hobby. He was also the most down-to-earth human being who was in the White House during my time there. Little things bothered the hell out of him. He said to me once that the big decisions didn't bother him, but some of the little bitty things. . . . He would tell you how to turn a screw clockwise or counter clockwise.'

Secret Service agent Rufus Youngblood

Following JFK's election, the laws at the time did not provide for official Secret Service protection for the vice president on a full-time basis. However, a Secret Service detail could be assigned 'at his request'. When Johnson was asked by Kennedy to make visits abroad a Secret Service detail was assigned consisting of detail head, H. Stuart Knight, and his assistant head, Rufus Youngblood. Other agents were assigned if necessary.

The Secret Service believed the 1951 law was too weak and said a vice president was not in a position to evaluate whether or not he needed protection. The law giving the vice president mandatory protection did not pass until October 1962, a fact that went unnoticed because of the Cuban Missile Crisis.[1] Accordingly, the official Vice-Presidential Protective Detail was expanded to twenty-six agents with H. Stuart Knight as head of the detail, Youngblood as his deputy. The detail included agents Lem Johns, Glenn Weaver, Paul Rindle, Jim Goodenough, Woody Taylor and Jerry Bechtle. Johnson wanted Congress to repeal the new law, but he was unsuccessful.

According to White House Air Force steward Jack Woodward, Vice President Johnson did not like the Secret Service and would try and sneak away from his agents.[2] So the agents asked him to be, Woodward said, 'a kind of . . . interim spy, to keep the Secret Service aware when Mr Johnson would sneak off somewhere . . . He was a difficult man. . . .'.[3]

Vice President Johnson's agents concurred with Woodward and knew he was a difficult person to guard. He once attempted to have an agent fired because a helicopter didn't appear at the precise time to whisk him away from Eleanor Roosevelt's funeral. 'President Kennedy called Johnson and told him to lay off the Secret Service agent', one agent said, '[and] that it had not been an intentional error . . . Kennedy always told us, "you guys don't want anything to ever happen to me, because then you'd have to work for Johnson".'[4]

* * *

The presidential journey to Dallas in late November 1963 brought both President John F. Kennedy and Vice President Johnson together to raise funds for their 1964 re-election campaign. On arrival the president and vice president rode in separate open limousines through the streets of downtown Dallas on their way to a luncheon at the Dallas Trade Mart. When Kennedy was shot, Johnson was two cars back and heard the shots. Rufus Youngblood threw himself on Johnson covering the vice president's body to protect him from further shots. To Johnson it was unclear if the president was the only intended target or if this was a grand conspiracy. Until Johnson left Dallas to return to Washington DC a few hours later he believed he might be in grave danger.

Johnson no doubt saw Kennedy's assassination as a tragic event but it did rescue him from the vice presidency, which he saw as a powerless position. He had gone from being influential Senate Majority Leader to a position which was, in the words of a previous vice president, 'worthless'. It left him deeply depressed. Johnson also worried about whether JFK was going to retain him as his vice president in the coming election year. Although he hated his job, he didn't want to be embarrassed by rejection.

Following Johnson's accession to the presidency, the vice president's detail was integrated with the president's. Johnson always felt more comfortable with the agents who had protected him when he was vice president and it led to tensions within the newly formed detail. The JFK detail had come under intense scrutiny because of the tragedy that had just occurred and the criticism aimed at the agency overall.

The new president was forever grateful to agent Rufus Youngblood for protecting him. He told an audience in Georgia before the 1964 election, 'My life is in the hands of Georgia, and it is 24 hours a day under the direction of Rufus Youngblood and no greater or nobler son has this state ever produced and no braver or more courageous man.'[5] In 1969 Johnson privately recalled to an aide how, when the shots in Dallas were fired, the 'tougher and better and more intelligent [agent] than them all' had bravely 'put his body on me' on the floor of the vice-presidential car.

However, Johnson was always distrustful of the Secret Service which led him to worry about it. He asked Assistant Director of the FBI Cartha Deloach to place an FBI agent on Air Force One to provide him with extra security. Deloach was worried he was encroaching on the work of the Secret Service but went ahead and appointed FBI Special Agent Orin Bartlett to accompany the president. Deloach later informed Secret Service Director James Rowley of the assignment. Rowley did not object. '[Johnson] was not a coward,' Deloach said, 'he was a very strong man but he . . . felt to have the FBI and the FBI's strength and the FBI's knowledge' would be advantageous.[6]

Johnson also frequently complained about his agents. When he travelled he said, the Secret Service would, 'notify everybody in town what time you're coming, how you're coming, where you're coming and how to kill you, if you want to. They do everything except kill you.' Johnson wanted his agents to:

> Let us go and get in the car and keep their damn mouth shut, we'll go down a back road and nobody ever knows we're there. But they get their si-rines [*sic*] going, forty cops leading you, and all that kind of stuff. So I don't care about haulin' any more of them than necessary because the most that I've ever been in danger is with a bunch of Secret Service men. They don't know how to operate their guns. Hell, I had 10 of 'em out there one day trying to kill a snake, and they couldn't kill it. They just emptied the gun . . .[7]

Johnson was also dismissive of some of his other bodyguards. He had a low opinion of Roy Kellerman, the agent who rode in the front passenger seat of Kennedy's car. Johnson said Kellerman was 'about as loyal a man as you could find . . . but dumb as an ox'.[8] 'Not all the Secret Service are sharp,' he said. 'It has always worried me that they weren't. They are the most dedicated and among the most courageous men we've got. But they don't always match that in brains. But the problem is you pay a man four or five hundred dollars a month and you get just what you pay for.'[9]

By all rights, Johnson should have had plenty of motivation to play it safe and defer to the Secret Service about his personal security. But he regularly overrode the advice of his bodyguards and waded into crowds, despite repeated warnings by his agents. 'Some of the scariest moments in Secret Service history happened while the organization protected Lyndon B. Johnson,' Clint Hill said. Johnson was both unpredictable and uncooperative, which, in the eyes of the bodyguards, was a bad combination. 'You'd think Johnson would be plenty happy to have Secret Service agents around him after JFK's assassination, but apparently, he wasn't exactly grateful,' Hill added.[10]

Johnson's agents were well aware of the new president's sexual escapades. As a Senator, one of his affairs was with the wife of a Texas newspaper publisher, another with a Washington reporter for the Hearst newspapers. One agent alleged Johnson had sex with one of his secretaries in the Oval Office. Johnson criticised the agent for not warning him that his wife was on her way. Lady Bird ended up walking in on the pair, so an alarm system was installed to prevent it from happening again.[11] 'He was a competitive womanizer,' historian Robert Dallek said. 'When people mentioned Kennedy's many affairs, Johnson would bang the table and declare that he had more women by accident than Kennedy ever had on purpose.'[12]

Clint Hill, who was assigned to Johnson's detail after the Kennedy assassination, said Johnson could be crude, 'and if he was driving across the countryside and needed to use the bathroom, he would stop and use the natural terrain to relieve himself even with women in the car'.[13] On one occasion when Johnson was driving his own car on his ranch he told an agent in the follow-up car that if he didn't keep his distance he would shoot his car's tyres out.[14]

Other agents also portrayed Johnson as a bully, terrorising aides and associates. He lashed out when agents didn't immediately respond to his orders. When Johnson was running late for an event, he ordered an agent to jump the curb to avoid traffic. The agent refused. The next day he was fired. But Johnson's secretary intervened and he kept his job.[15] In fact, Johnson was forever 'firing' his agents. However, he usually forgot about it and they kept their jobs.

Some of Johnson's staff concurred with this characterisation of the president. Air Force One steward Jack Woodward said:

> I can't say there was really one person I ever disliked. But I didn't cotton to Johnson because of his 'bull-in-the-china-cabinet' type of carrying on. He wanted everyone to know who he was, and what he was. . . . He would be getting into conferences with his staff [on board the plane] . . . and if someone is disagreeing with him, the first thing to come off was his shoe and he would pound the table with his heel.[16]

However, Secret Service agents Clint Hill and Rufus Youngblood, who both developed a close relationship with Johnson, believed he was a mixture of both good and bad. Clint Hill said he was:

> . . . a professional politician and always active, sometimes a little uncouth and unpredictable. Over the years with him I would see 'the Johnson treatment,' where he would berate someone because things did not go exactly as he wanted. Yet, even though he rarely apologized, before he left office, he did apologize to the agents. I thought it was very considerate of him.[17]

It was Clint Hill who Johnson turned to after Robert Kennedy was assassinated. Johnson feared he would meet the same fate. Before he attended a memorial service for Martin Luther King Jr he phoned the agent and told him he had had a premonition he would be murdered. Hill said Johnson asked him to '. . . stay as close as possible during the service'.[18]

Rufus Youngblood said Johnson's mood swings were like a 'pendulum', but he was also '. . . the most sentimental of men sometimes almost to the point of becoming maudlin'.[19] Youngblood said Johnson was appreciative of the dedication of his agents. After the vice president's 1962 world tour Johnson said that although it had been a 'rough trip', he wanted the agents to know he hadn't seen the 'slightest sign' that any agent had 'wavered' and he appreciated all they had done.[20]

Hill also observed the compassionate side of the president, especially the times when the president had to grapple with the Vietnam War. The president, Hill said, was caught between his anti-communist views and the pain of sending young men into combat. Johnson made frequent visits to a local Catholic church, seeking guidance and solace. Hill's observations about Johnson were confirmed by White-House aide Bill Moyers. Moyers said Johnson would '. . . just go within himself, just disappear – morose, self-pitying, angry. . . . He was a tormented man.'[21]

* * *

As the 1964 election approached it appeared the lessons of the Warren Commission, which made numerous suggestions about how to improve presidential security, had been forgotten and Johnson's dislike of bodyguard protection would place him in danger on numerous occasions. As former agent Dennis McCarthy said, LBJ had a 'he-man image of himself [and] resented having agents around him all the time. He didn't like the idea of needing protection from anyone.'[22]

Johnson risked his life, in part, because he wanted to exceed the popular vote of his hero, Franklin D. Roosevelt, who won in 1936 with 60 per cent of the vote. Johnson also wanted to shed the image of an accidental president and poor substitute for JFK. A 'landslide' vote in the 1964 election would provide that kind of acceptance by the US public.

In October 1964 LBJ was the victim of a planned assassination attempt but it was foiled by a tip-off and an investigation by the Secret Service. Johnson was visiting Buffalo, New York, for a campaign speech when agents received information about a man who had made 'assassination plans'. When agents arrived at his workplace to interview him, they observed a rifle lying on the ledge of a window overlooking the street below. When agents searched him they found a single cartridge in his pocket. The building where the man worked was on the presidential motorcade route. When questioned, he said he was a brigadier general in the Minutemen and that he needed only 'one bullet to do the job'. He was arrested and committed to a mental hospital.[23]

During the 1964 presidential election campaign, one of the difficulties the Secret Service faced protecting LBJ was the fact that he would constantly jump out of his car to shake hands with people. A close friend, Margaret Chase Smith, said she saw Johnson during the campaign and was shocked at what he did and was not approving of it. 'I saw him over in Lewiston, for instance,' Smith said. 'He kept putting his hand out, and he'd get out of the car. His hands were bleeding from scratches. People are rough at times like that.'[24]

During his New England campaign tour Johnson would terrify his agents by ordering his car to stop then stand up in his limousine and exhort crowds to vote for him using a bull-horn. He was perfectly silhouetted against the sky which made his agents fear he would be in the telescopic sights of a would-be assassin. On one occasion during the campaign Johnson's body-guards believed that a car in the motorcade, which had erupted in flames due to a faulty engine, had been bombed. The president's car was quickly evacuated. On another occasion Johnson was travelling in his limousine in Florida when a loud explosion was heard. Johnson looked startled but his head of detail quickly deduced it was a blowout of a car tyre.[25]

Only a week after he received the Warren Report LBJ complained to his vice-presidential running mate, Hubert Humphrey, about criticism from the Senate Majority Leader Mike Mansfield and others that he was risking his life by wading into crowds. Johnson said:

> Just tell them that the Secret Service has never had the slightest concern. . . . What they need to cover is the route that a candidate follows – the buildings and the cowards that lurk in the dark. There is not any problem with getting out and shaking hands. Kennedy shook hands with three or four groups. That wasn't what killed Kennedy.[26]

Revealing his ignorance of the assassinations of Presidents Garfield and McKinley, Johnson said, 'No president has ever been assassinated by shaking hands with somebody or being in a crowd. They are assassinated when they go to a theatre, or when they drive down the street and somebody can hide.' Two weeks later, Johnson once again risked his life by insisting that Robert Kennedy, who was running for a New York Senate seat, stand with him in an open limousine during a motorcade ride through Brooklyn.[27]

Director of the Secret Service, James Rowley, appeared not to have any concerns about Johnson's style of electioneering. Rowley said, 'There was a lot of concern . . . but on the other hand what worked to our advantage . . . is the element of surprise . . . So we're flexible enough to meet a given situation.'[28]

During his five years as president, Johnson would become the most threat-ened president in modern times. By 1968 anti-war demonstrators had finally forced him to accept safer venues for public statements or speeches. Many of them were made at heavily guarded military bases around the country and he rarely left the confines of the White House after his 'resignation speech' on 31 March 1968.

After Johnson left office he became much more appreciative of the work of his bodyguards. He told a group of agents:

> I have abused you. I have criticised you. I have been inconsiderate of you . . . I have spent more of my time telling you what you did wrong than what you did right. But . . . I remember in Australia when I just couldn't keep back the tears when I looked in the faces of Jerry Kivett, Dick Johnson, Jerry McKinney, Lem Johns, and Bob Heyn, and the dearest of all, Rufus Youngblood, with that paint streaming down their faces, splattered all over them, but their chins up and their president safe . . . I remember Bob Taylor standing there and letting the Cadillac run over his foot in order to protect his president from harm.[29]

* * *

Senator Barry Goldwater was the Republican nominee for president in 1964. Johnson defeated him in a landslide election. The Republican standard bearer carried only six states – Alabama, Arizona, Georgia, Louisiana, Mississippi and South Carolina – and won less than 39 per cent of the popular vote.

Goldwater had never lusted after the presidency and was never entirely sure he wanted it. 'I have no plans for it. I have no staff for it, no program for it, no ambition for it,' he told *Time* magazine in early 1963.[30]

However, a group of conservative businessmen and industrialists joined forces to persuade Goldwater to run. Although they were friends of the Senator, they had little political experience to run his campaign. In 1963, before the JFK assassination, Goldwater had assumed that he'd run against Kennedy, whom he had always regarded as a friend. In fact, Goldwater hoped that if he did decide to run for president and secured the Republican Party nomination, both men could travel around the country together engaging in a series of Lincoln-Douglas-style debates. However, he did not really believe he stood a chance against the increasingly popular Kennedy. Goldwater wanted to use the opportunity the election afforded him to spread the message of conservatism.

For his part, Kennedy hoped that Goldwater would run against him – but not out of friendship. Kennedy believed he would self-destruct once the general campaign began. 'People will start asking him questions', he told his friend, *The Washington Post* reporter Ben Bradlee, 'and he's so damn quick on the trigger, he'll answer them. And when he does, it will be all over.'[31]

Following JFK's assassination Goldwater remained one of the Republican Party's favourites to run against Johnson in the coming election. However, he was not so keen to run against the new president. Goldwater now had to contend with a man who would 'slap you on the back today and stab you in the back tomorrow'.[32]

Like Donald Trump today, Goldwater was regarded as a divisive figure even within his own party. Ideologically, Goldwater was a strict constructionist who believed in the supremacy of state rights – a particularly controversial position to take at the peak of the Civil Rights era. He preached that since the New Deal the federal government had become so big, so powerful and so authoritative that government itself posed a threat to the principles of US liberty.

Kennedy's prescient assessment of Goldwater was accurate. Following his nomination Goldwater gave a stirring acceptance speech in which he said, 'I would remind you that extremism in the defence of liberty is no vice and let me remind you also that moderation in the pursuit of justice is no virtue', and he once talked of lobbing a nuclear bomb into the 'men's room of the Kremlin'. Many voters believed he would be 'trigger-happy' with the nuclear button. He also appeared to advocate the use of tactical nuclear weapons in North Vietnam. LBJ portrayed him as too reckless to trust and told voters the Republican candidate would put the nation at risk of nuclear war.

In fact, allegations of Goldwater's instability surfaced during the campaign and he sued two magazines for reporting them. His wife testified in court that her husband had never suffered any mental illness or shown any sign of one or of any mental disturbance whatever and that he had never consulted a psychiatrist or received psychiatric treatment. Dr Leslie Kober of Phoenix, Arizona, Senator Goldwater's friend and personal physician for many years, and Harry Rosenzweig, another lifelong friend of the Senator, all denied that Goldwater had ever had 'a nervous breakdown' in the 'medical sense of the phrase'.

One of the magazines also alleged that Goldwater was so unhinged and paranoid that during the Republican Party convention in San Francisco, 'for the first time in American history' armed guards were posted around a non-incumbent presidential candidate, 'even before he was nominated' and 'his aides began to realize how paranoid he was'. Replying to allegations about his armed guards, Goldwater said if the writer had bothered to 'only casually check . . . he would have discovered that there were armed guards posted about his [Republican Party opponent], Governor William Scranton . . . at the same Mark Hopkins Hotel'.[33]

In 1964 the Secret Service only extended protection to the president, the vice president, the president-elect and vice president-elect. And, unlike Goldwater, Johnson had the advantage of a Secret Service detail – the motorcades were planned, the routes checked in advance. Testifying to a Senate Committee in 1975, Goldwater made light of the fact that he did not have the advantage of being protected by the Secret Service. 'I didn't have any Secret Service protection,' Goldwater said, 'from the time I was first suspected of being a candidate until the day after that cliff-hanger.'[34] Secret Service agent Rufus Youngblood said Goldwater's campaign '. . . had to provide whatever protective forces they felt they might need' from private funds.[35] However, despite having limited protection Goldwater insisted he, '. . . never felt in danger. I feel that when the Lord wants you He's going to take you. . . . If a fellow wants to assassinate somebody, he can do it. I get one or two threats a week. I think they're mostly crackpots.'[36]

When President Johnson was asked if he considered Goldwater's safety an issue, he said:

> I haven't explored that subject. If the Senator felt that he was in danger in any way and felt the necessity of protection and felt that we ought to carefully consider adopting a policy of protecting candidates, I would be glad to review it carefully and try to work out some kind of an agreement that would be satisfactory to him. He has not told me of his views on the matter.[37]

During the 1964 Republican Party primary election campaigns Goldwater had a single 'security man' and driver, Charlie Justice, an automobile dealer who volunteered as a helper at the start of the campaign. He also enlisted the assistance of local police departments when he campaigned around the country.

Los Angeles County Sheriff Peter Pitchess, who was on leave for the campaign, was 'more or less in charge of [my] safety', Goldwater said. During his twenty-three years as sheriff, Pitchess eliminated the county's violent extremist group, the Posse Comitatus, introduced the use of helicopters for car chases and crowd control, and set up one of the first SWAT teams in the United States. He linked the geographically separated offices and jails with teletype machines for faster communication, and computerised the offices' records in the 1960s.[38]

In a memo to his deputy Clyde Tolson, FBI Director J. Edgar Hoover heaped praise on Pitchess and wrote:

> . . . the Senator had hired a rather substantial squad or security detail to protect him. I stated the Senator had procured the services of a Deputy Sheriff from Los Angeles Sheriff's Office. I stated this man is a good man and is a graduate of the FBI National Academy and he has, in turn, built up a substantial squad that furnishes the senator protection on his travels.[39]

Goldwater's campaign spent between $300,000 and $400,000 for the protection of the Pinkerton National Detective Agency. The Pinkertons were used 'mostly in hotels where we stayed,' Goldwater said.

During the 1964 Republican Party convention Goldwater and his chief opponent for the nomination, William Scranton, were staying at the same hotel, the Mark Hopkins. The hotel was situated on Knob Hill which was owned by film star Gene Autry. The Scranton campaign team was on the twelfth floor. Directly above them was the Goldwater campaign team on the fourteenth and fifteenth floors, with the Senator occupying Suite 1502. Scranton himself occupied the Royal Suite on the sixteenth floor. Goldwater stayed in the Presidential Suite on the seventeenth floor.[40]

The Pinkerton Agency guarded the Goldwater floors at the hotel from both the press and possible 'Scranton spies'. Electronic experts were hired by Goldwater's aides to check the interweaving floors for listening devices. The guards, who wore grey suits, were stationed at every exit – six per 8-hour shift around the clock but reporters and photographers still managed to acquire special badges giving them access to the floors. Whenever Goldwater left the hotel, he exited through an underground passage that emerged more than a block away. Sometimes the Senator, a licensed National Guard pilot, left the hotel to go flying and one day he 'buzzed' the Republican Party Convention centre.

Goldwater sometimes took a service lift up to his suite to avoid having to mingle with other guests at the hotel in any of the three public lifts. He often emerged from the lift in the company of kitchen staff. The Republican Party nominee was assigned two private bodyguards at the convention, one of whom, Vern Stephens, received a slight injury to his groin when he tried to prevent access to Goldwater by a zealous guest.[41]

Following his nomination, Goldwater travelled around the country in a Boeing 727, a three-engine jet, flying at very nearly the speed of sound. The plane was named the Yai Bi Ken, which is Navajo for 'House in the Sky'. The candidate was usually accompanied by his wife, five or six campaign advisers and more than fifty journalists.[42]

Goldwater's vice-presidential nominee, New York Congressman William E. Miller, was concerned about Goldwater's security at a time when '. . . emotions [were] running high . . . [due to] . . . the nature of the times and the intensity of feelings'.

Miller also told the press that the Republican campaign headquarters was giving 'serious consideration' to the 'question of security' for the Republican nominee and that there was a serious possibility that violence might surround the nominee's campaign. He believed the law should be changed to extend Secret Service protection to presidential nominees as well as to the president and said he would ask for the introduction of legislation to provide Secret Service protection for a candidate from the time of his nomination until the election.[43]

However, Miller's proposed law was not put into effect. As Secret Service agent Rufus Youngblood recognised, 'The bill had failed to pass. It was going to take another assassination to get it through.'[44]

Goldwater agreed with Miller and spoke about the possibility that one of his campaign appearances might touch off racial violence because of his stand against the Civil Rights bill and the resulting opposition of African Americans to his candidacy. It could cause some people to consider him a racial bigot, he said. Since he was reported to regard the racial situation in the country as tense and dangerous, Goldwater feared that those who took this view might collide with some of his own more ardent supporters. He was also accused by some media of making it possible for 'great numbers of unapologetic white supremacists' to hold 'great carnivals of white supremacy'.[45]

Efforts to provide improved Secret Service protection for Goldwater were underlined by threats against his life. FBI Director J. Edgar Hoover acknowledged the FBI knew about the threats Goldwater had received, '. . . threats of bombs, none of which has materialized, and in those instances we immediately notify the security man in charge of the Senator's detail so the information is promptly passed on just as we do for the Secret Service if there is a threat against the president'.[46]

Goldwater said he never had any contact with the FBI during his campaign. The FBI reports, however, indicate that Goldwater's aides received information about the threats whenever they arose. The only time he made contact, Goldwater said, was when agents told him how to safeguard his home in Phoenix 'electronically'. Goldwater said he paid for the cost which he estimated at $8,600. Goldwater added, 'I think the only time a Secret Service man saw me was on Election Day. . . . when I never campaigned and I was out trimming the cactus in my garden. . . . I didn't see [the FBI agent] . . .'.[47] According to Rufus Youngblood, Secret Service agents were despatched to 'the unprotected nominees to be at their sides on November 3rd when the vote count would begin. . . . On November 4th, the Secret Service quietly slipped out of [Goldwater's home in] Phoenix . . .'.[48]

Goldwater also said he never felt in any real danger during the campaign, although he had been pelted by 'three eggs and two stones' and he lost the sleeve of his coat three times when he waded into crowds. On some days, Goldwater said, he shook 5,000 hands. The Senator was also fatalistic with regard to his safety. 'I am convinced', he said, 'that if any man or woman wants to kill a candidate, if they are willing to risk their lives, they can do it regardless of the Secret Service, private service, FBI or the Sheriffs. There is just no way.'[49]

There were numerous threats to Goldwater's life even before he became the Republican Party nominee. In 1958 Goldwater's 'pilot and guard' reported he had received information about a man in Sunflower, Arizona, who said the Senator 'owed him $500 and that the next time he saw Goldwater he was going to kill him'.[50]

On 6 October 1960 the FBI reported a phone call in which the caller said, 'Listen and listen carefully. When Goldwater comes to town he will never leave alive.' Following the assassination of JFK, threatening telephone calls 'flooded' Goldwater's senate office.[51]

Threats to Goldwater during the 1964 campaign caused some disruption. For example, a threatening telephone call was received by police in Springfield, Illinois, in August 1964, shortly before Goldwater was to return to Washington after a speech. It resulted in his chartered airliner being diverted to another airport. Goldwater's plane had originally been scheduled to land at National Airport, just across the Potomac from Washington. But the plane came in at less crowded Dulles International Airport, some 30 miles from the capital, after hurried consultations with Federal Aviation Agency (FAA) officials and the FBI.

The long-distance telephone call was made by a man who identified himself as 'Lt. Bruce Allen'. He told Springfield police Sergeant John Nolan, 'they are going to hit [underworld slang for kill] and shoot Goldwater between 3:30 and 4 this afternoon'. Nolan asked who was going to try to kill Goldwater and the answer came back, 'Puerto Ricans'. The caller hung up when Nolan asked where he was calling from.[52]

Other threats to Goldwater during the 1964 campaign included:

- In July 1964 Samuel Weiner, who had spent time in a mental hospital and was described as a 'psychopath', appeared at one of Goldwater's campaign events in Scottsdale, Arizona. He was described as an 'extremist' who 'might possibly be capable of inflicting bodily harm on the candidate'. The FBI said Weiner intended to cause a disturbance by alleging he had been wrongly incarcerated and was suing Goldwater and other authorities for $250,000 for illegal arrest. When he was removed from the venue he continued to be 'obnoxious'. He was arrested and charged with disturbing the peace.[53]
- In July 1964 a Los Angeles businessman stated that a pro-Castro acquaintance threatened that if Goldwater was elected president he would 'personally assassinate him'. The FBI contacted the Secret Service and Goldwater's staff to report the threat but no arrests were made.[54]
- The FBI reported letters which included threats and reported they were 'making a number of investigations as appropriate'. A typical letter that required investigation was from a Forest Service officer in charge of campgrounds in California. The worker said his agency had just hired a young man to 'work in the back country' and that the new employee was a member of a '. . . group or club that are sworn to kill . . . Barry Goldwater if he gets elected'. FBI files do not indicate whether or not any arrests were made.[55]

In 1975 Goldwater revealed how he had been stalked by a would-be assassin who carried a rifle. He was told about it by one of his bodyguards. 'I had one threat', Goldwater said, 'from a man with a rifle someplace in Ohio but they [bodyguards] talked him into waiting until my plane took off.'[56]

Chapter 4

The Hubert H. Humphrey Assassination Plots

'I never admired Humphrey more than . . . at one of his presidential rallies. . . . He came into an auditorium packed with a couple of thousands of baying, chanting students and he walked with his wife to the podium through a downpour of awful insults and shouted obscenities and when he got up to speak, he couldn't make it.'

Journalist Alistair Cooke

'He knew what our intelligence had warned us of on that trip [Vietnam] and he was aware that he was one of the prime targets . . .'

Secret Service agent Rufus Youngblood

A general assumption exists that no one has attempted to assassinate a US vice president; the reasoning being the holder of the office has no real political power and has a low profile. An assassin would go after the man with the real political power, it was reasoned, and that would be the president.

While it is true that no vice president has been assassinated, it is generally accepted by historians and biographers that two attempts to assassinate a vice president have been made; the attempt to assassinate Abraham Lincoln's vice president, Andrew Johnson, and the attempted assassination of Woodrow Wilson's vice president, Thomas Marshall.

The alleged attempt to assassinate Vice President Andrew Johnson was not really an assassination attempt at all. John Wilkes Booth's co-conspirator, George Atzerodt, was given the task of killing Johnson but he never attempted to carry it out. He got drunk in a hotel bar instead. (Another plotter attacked Secretary of State William Seward. The Secretary of State then was second in line in terms of presidential succession. President pro tempore of the Senate, Lafayette Foster, a Republican Senator from

Connecticut, would have become president had the plot resulted in the actual assassination of Vice President Johnson in addition to President Lincoln. Booth's plan was to decapitate the head of government and his successors.)

The second incident involving an attempt to assassinate a vice president occurred on the evening of 2 July 1915 when Eric Muenter, an anarchist who opposed US support of the Allied war effort, broke into the Senate chamber, laid dynamite around Vice President Thomas R. Marshall's office door, and set it with a timer. Muenter was later apprehended and confessed to the attempted assassination of the vice president.[1]

However, there is compelling evidence that two more vice presidents should now be added to that list – Theodore Roosevelt's vice president, Charles W. Fairbanks, and Lyndon Johnson's vice president, Hubert Humphrey. The attempt to assassinate Fairbanks is revealed here for the first time.

Following President McKinley's assassination in 1901 Senator Charles Fairbanks became an outspoken advocate for banning anarchists from entering the country. In a speech he gave after the death of McKinley he said, 'The anarchist stands as the personification of the destroyer. . . . it certainly is consistent with the spirit of our constitution to protect ourselves against anarchism by Federal action of a drastic character'.[2]

The attempted assassination against Fairbanks occurred in Flint, Michigan, in June 1905, the year he became Theodore Roosevelt's vice president. He travelled to Flint to lay the cornerstone of the new federal building. The ceremony was attended by a 2,000-strong crowd.

Fairbanks had been speaking for 20 minutes when 32-year-old James McConnell, later described as a 'blacksmith' and 'anarchist', forced his way through the crowd to Fairbanks' side holding a revolver concealed in his hip pocket. Four 'police detectives' caught the would-be assassin and 'choked him into submission'. After McConnell was placed in a police wagon to be taken to the Saginaw Street Police Station, he told police officers that '. . . his time would come soon; that he would yet be able to carry out his purpose and assassinate the vice president'. The crowd reacted angrily. Soldiers from the nearby army base in Fort Wayne who took part in the ceremony and parade shouted 'Lynch him!' and followed the wagon. During the confrontation between the crowd and the police the anarchist reportedly pleaded with the arresting officers to protect him. After the incident Fairbanks continued with his speech, apparently unfazed.[3]

As federal laws protecting vice presidents had not yet been enacted the unnamed anarchist was charged with disorderly conduct. Flint police said the anarchist had stalked Fairbanks from Chicago and had intended to shoot him there. Fairbanks had stayed in Chicago en route east from the Lewis and Clark Exposition in Portland, Oregon.[4]

Responding to the attempted assassination, Fairbanks said he had been unaware that an attempt had been made on his life and 'treated the matter lightly'.[5]

* * *

When John F. Kennedy was assassinated in 1963 Speaker John McCormack was next in line to assume the presidency on the death of the president and vice president. When he heard the (false) news the president and vice president had been assassinated McCormack believed he was no longer Speaker of the House but President of the United States. As he became aware of this possibility, he experienced a severe attack of vertigo as he stood up. Returning to his seat and allowing the momentous news to sink in, he was shortly afterwards informed that the vice president was unharmed. McCormack's face showed intense relief.

The abrupt transition of 1963 persuaded many in government that the issue of succession should be addressed by Congress because the next two offices in the line of succession were occupied by the ill 72-year-old McCormack and 86-year-old President Pro Tempore of the Senate Carl Hayden. Between 1789 and 1963 sixteen vacancies had occurred in the vice presidency. Neither the Constitution nor the succession acts addressed the issue of their replacement and there were lengthy lapses when the nation was without a vice president.

The problem was eventually solved in 1967 with the passing of the Twenty-Fifth Amendment which simultaneously empowered a president to nominate a vice president when that office became vacant. The provision was used twice, first in 1973 when President Richard Nixon appointed Gerald Ford to replace Spiro Agnew, who had resigned, and again in 1974, with the appointment of Nelson Rockefeller after Nixon himself resigned and Ford became president. (The Amendment also addressed the issue of presidential disability allowing for the disabled president to be succeeded by an 'Acting President'.)

President Johnson would go without a vice president for nearly fourteen months until his January 1965 inauguration when Hubert Humphrey was sworn in as the new vice president. No sooner had Humphrey taken the oath of office he was faced with the prospect of succeeding to the presidency. Two days after the inauguration Humphrey was informed in the middle of the night, by a 'hotline' connected to the White House, that President Johnson had been taken to hospital with an undefined illness. Within the hour a call from one of Johnson's aides informed that the president was not seriously ill. For an hour Humphrey had to contemplate the possibility he was the new president.[6]

When Humphrey was selected to be Lyndon Johnson's vice-presidential running mate in the 1964 election he was one of the premier political figures of his time and was seen as a future president for the next two decades. However, he never achieved the presidential office he so coveted. He pursued the presidency on four occasions, 1960, 1968, 1972 and 1976.

When President Johnson said in March 1968 that he would not pursue the Democratic Party nomination Humphrey decided run in his place. Competing against Senators Robert Kennedy and Eugene McCarthy for the party nomination, he was considered to be the 'establishment' candidate and was known as the 'happy warrior' because of his cheery personality and optimistic approach to politics. In August of that year he won the nomination.

Humphrey's general election campaign against Richard Nixon got off to a disastrous start. In August 1968, at the Democratic Party convention held in Chicago his attempts at unity failed. His references to the 'Politics of Joy' appeared out of touch with the anti-war riots and protests going on around the city. Furthermore, Humphrey had difficulty distancing himself from President Johnson's unpopular war policy since he had been an advocate of it. He lost a close election to Nixon.

Humphrey's confidant W. Averell Harriman, head of the peace talks in Paris to end the Vietnam War, said, 'I know that, as president, Hubert would have stopped the Vietnam War in 1969. . . . His election would have avoided the extended tragedy of the Vietnam War as well as Watergate. In addition, I believe that period would have been a time of economic and social progress under an irresistibly optimistic, wise, and determined president.'[7]

Humphrey returned to politics in 1970, when he was once again elected to the Senate. In 1972, he ran for the Democratic nomination and announced his candidacy on 10 January 1972 in Philadelphia. Humphrey won some primaries, including those in Ohio, Indiana and Pennsylvania, but was defeated by George McGovern in several others, including the crucial California primary. McGovern went on to win the 1972 Democratic Party nomination.

On 22 April 1974, Humphrey said that he would not enter the upcoming Democratic presidential primaries for the 1976 presidential election but thought he might have a chance at the nomination if the convention became deadlocked. He said at the time that he was urging fellow Senator and Minnesotan Walter Mondale to run, despite believing Ted Kennedy would enter the race as well and likely succeed. Leading up to the election cycle, Humphrey said, 'Here's a time in my life when I appear to have more support than at any other time in my life. But it's too financially, politically, and physically debilitating – and I'm just not going to do it.' In December 1975, a Gallup poll was released showing Humphrey and Ronald Reagan as the leading Democratic and Republican candidates for the following year's presidential election.[8] But Humphrey prevaricated too long and was unable to garner support after Jimmy Carter took the lead in the Democratic primaries.

In August 1976, Humphrey was diagnosed with cancer but was nonetheless re-elected to the Senate. He remained active there until his death in January 1978.

* * *

Humphrey did not have any Secret Service protection during the 1964 campaign. His detail arrived to guard him on the evening of the election. Humphrey was in the ballroom at the Sheraton Ritz Hotel in Minneapolis when his agents arrived to guard him. As the new vice president remembered, '. . . sometime around midnight, there was a thrilling moment when the Secret Service agents appeared suddenly at the doors and around my table. I was Vice-President-Elect.'[9]

Humphrey developed a strong and trusting relationship with his Secret Service detail from the beginning. He was protected by an eighteen-man force headed by agent Glenn Weaver and his deputy Walt Coughlin. The detail included agents Jerry Parr, Dennis McCarthy, Roger Warner, Jimmy Taylor, Elmer Moore, Roger Counts, Jack Giuffre, Bob Burke and Rick Barbuto. There were five agents in each shift plus three supervisors. Their shifts lasted for 12 to 16 hours. From 1965 to 1968 it was common for the detail to work more than 1,000 hours overtime each year.[10]

Agents who protected the US vice president were aware of a 'pecking order' within the agency. The Presidential Protective Division looked down on agents who protected the vice president. According to former agent Joseph Petro, who had first served in the vice president's detail and was later promoted to the president's detail, the PPD agents acted as an 'elite force' and were sometimes disdainful towards the vice president's agents.[11]

Humphrey's agents were under the overall supervision of Secret Service Assistant Director Rufus Youngblood who would often travel with the vice president. During the 1968 election year, 'the year from hell' as Humphrey called it, the vice president's detail increased to only 27 men while the president's detail numbered over 100 agents. They not only had the responsibility of guarding Humphrey but also carried the burdens of travel and security.[12]

The bodyguards, Humphrey said, 'worked under very severe constraints' and there were 'limits as to what they can do'. Humphrey said he had '. . . an intimate working relationship with the Secret Service' and considered 'many of its members to be personal friends'.[13]

According to Secret Service agent Clint Hill, Humphrey's agents were 'burnt out'.[14] One agent who guarded the vice president, Jim Connally, shot himself in 1973 after succumbing to alcoholism which was thought to have been brought on by the stressful life he led as an agent. According to agent Marty Vencker, Connally also lived with the fear he was going to be fired because of his addiction.[15]

Humphrey travelled incessantly and stood in for the beleaguered President Johnson on diplomatic trips abroad. It was Humphrey's courage when he visited Vietnam and confronted anti-war hecklers in speeches around the nation that gained him respect from his agents. They admired how a calm Humphrey acted during crowd disruptions. During one speech at a university a demonstrator stood near Humphrey's platform and began screaming insults at the vice president. One of Humphrey's agents reacted by putting his '. . . fist down the [demonstrator's] throat. . . . I think I broke my hand', he said. The vice president did not condone the agent's behaviour but he fully understood why he acted as he did and did not report the assault.[16]

In 1966 Humphrey visited the US Marine Base at Da Nang, South Vietnam. Dennis McCarthy advanced the trip and two days before Humphrey's visit the agent's plane was hit by small arms fire. During the same two days McCarthy had been present when the Vietcong began shelling the base. When Humphrey arrived, '. . . he walked through the [hospital] wards pinning medals on pyjama-clad Marines,' McCarthy wrote. 'He was his usual cheerful self seemingly unconcerned with the danger and living up to his political nickname, the Happy Warrior. But the rest of us kept listening for the tell-tale whistle of incoming rounds.'[17] Former agent Rufus Youngblood said Humphrey was '. . . a real trooper in Vietnam, going out to visit the troops in the combat area and not restricting his activities to the comparative safety of Saigon'.[18]

Humphrey's agents once more admired the vice president's courage when he visited South Vietnam for a second time, in October 1967, for the inauguration of South Vietnam's President Thieu and Vice President Ky. During the outdoor ceremonies the agents expected mortar fire to erupt at any time. At a palace reception Humphrey was standing near an open door leading into the palace gardens when flashes and loud explosions erupted. The building shook as guests ran for cover. The firing site was later found to be 3 miles from the palace. Youngblood admired how there was a 'sparkle in his eyes that had come to be something of a trademark with him. . . . I really admired the guy'.[19]

Secret Service agents also witnessed the compassion of the vice president during his visits to Vietnam. When Jerry Parr accompanied Humphrey to a soldiers' hospital, he saw '. . . a dramatic change' in the vice president's face. Humphrey 'turned pale' as he saw the terrible wounds the soldiers had suffered. Humphrey had talked about the war in Vietnam 'intellectually', Parr said, 'But that hospital tour got the war out of his head and into his gut.' Humphrey's agents also observed the vice president when he despaired about the war, 'I detest this war! I detest it! But I have to support my president,' Humphrey said.[20]

There were, however, occasions when the vice president clashed with his detail. Chuck Vance took a different approach to Johnson's agents when he was faced with demands he walk the vice president's dog. Vance replied, 'I'm sorry, Mr. Vice President, we're not allowed to do that. But we'll be glad to walk you, sir.'[21]

* * *

The vice presidency of Hubert Humphrey was arguably the most difficult and dangerous of all the vice presidents. He was beset by anti-war demonstrations around the country and from 1965 to 1968 he was heckled and threatened by anti-war student demonstrators, especially during the presidential election year of 1968. Agents had to be constantly on their guard for missiles thrown at the candidate and had to think of new ways of taking Humphrey from the safe confines of a limousine to the relative safety of an auditorium of hotel.

The difference between the 1964 and 1968 elections, Humphrey said, was ' . . . the difference between a balmy breeze and a hurricane. There is no comparison . . . during the 1968 period . . . there were constant threats of violence and physical disruption'. Humphrey believed it was a time in US history that no one could understand '. . . unless [they] had gone through it'. The 1968 Democratic presidential nominee felt that, 'There wasn't a time that you didn't feel that there was something terrible that could happen, that could be terribly bad to you and your family . . . it isn't just the candidate'. Humphrey said that members of his family were also threatened.[22]

The worst heckling of Humphrey's 1968 campaign was in Seattle. The Civic Arena was filled with 4,000 supporters. There were 200 protesters gathered in a balcony corner of the arena to the right of the platform where Humphrey delivered his speech. Shouts of 'Stop the war' drowned Humphrey out before his agents waded into the crowd of protestors and escorted the ring leaders out.

Humphrey's agents also regarded 1968 as the 'year from hell', according to Marilyn Parr, wife of agent Jerry Parr. 'War protests were so strong that President Johnson seldom left the White House,' Parr said. 'Instead, he sent Hubert Humphrey, his vice president and Democratic presidential candidate, to face the turmoil in the streets, riots in urban neighbourhoods and endless demonstrations on college campuses.'[23]

Humphrey's son, Hubert Humphrey III, said, 'It's amazing the country didn't come apart at the seams. Dad had a bit of a fatalistic point of view. He said, "If someone wants to get me and give up their life in the process, they'll do it".' D.J. Leary, who served on Humphrey's staff in 1968, said, 'There was a very real sense of violence in the air. Humphrey was aware of it. He said he got up every morning and it was like a dull ache in the back of the head – after a while you didn't notice it anymore.'[24]

During his campaign the vice president visited seventy-six colleges. Carolyn Parr said:

> Only two speeches were free of heckling. The vice president's detail had to do what the president's detail should have been doing, with only 18 agents. . . . No one got a day off. More often than not, they worked double shifts, sometimes travelling or doing seat-of-the-pants advances one step ahead of the VP. Then as now, most of the overtime was uncompensated. But most of the agents would have chosen normal hours instead of overtime pay.[25]

Wherever Humphrey went he was met with abuse. At Stanford in March 1967, for example, demonstrators mobbed his car screaming 'War criminal!', 'Murderer!' and 'Burn, Baby, Burn!' Several tried to break through the police cordon, and a can of urine was thrown over one of the agents.

On one occasion Secret Service agent Chuck Vance saw Humphrey react violently when he was confronted by a protestor. When the vice president returned to his hotel late at night during the 1968 Democratic National Convention he passed through a line of demonstrators shouting 'Dump the Hump'. Humphrey thought one of the group was being friendly when he was asked to shake hands. As Humphrey approached him the man turned his hand over and shouted 'Dump the Hump'. According to Vance, 'Humphrey formed a fist and punched him in the chest. We weren't sure what would happen, so we whisked him away and into the elevator. There was total silence until about the 16th floor. Then, all of a sudden, we heard a voice from the back of the elevator say, "Boy that felt good".'[26]

* * *

Hubert Humphrey lived under the threat of assassination all his political life, especially during the time he was Lyndon Johnson's vice president. He was also threatened numerous times when he ran for president in 1968. In fact, as a presidential candidate that year there were 'hundreds of threats', including threats to bomb, shoot and hire Hell's Angels to kill him. Some of the threats were made under the influence of alcohol or were judged by the FBI and Secret Service to be the result of an ill-considered comment in a public place. Most of the threats came in the form of letters and telephone calls.

Hubert Humphrey's first brush with assassination occurred shortly after he became mayor of Minneapolis in 1947. Humphrey had begun to clean up the crime-ridden city, telling voters, 'The gangsters of Chicago are out to take over the city and are on their way to doing so unless they are stopped. We are starting to see business move out of the city – and people are going, too, to the suburbs. This must be halted if Minneapolis is to go on as a city.'

Not long after Humphrey began his anti-crime campaign his office received a number of anonymous telephone threats which lasted for months. They originated with the anti-Semitic, anti-black and anti-communist 'Democratic Nationalist Party', a right-wing hate group.

On the night of 6 February 1947, Mayor Humphrey was returning to his home in southeast Minneapolis. He was late from a dinner with a legislative delegation. Usually, he was accompanied to the door by driver and bodyguard Vern Bartholomew, a police officer armed with a .38 pistol. However, Humphrey waved off Bartholomew so friends could ride home in his car. Three shots rang out as Humphrey walked to his front door. His wife, Muriel, said she'd heard the shots, but had thought that they were backfires from a car. For the next few weeks, when Officer Bartholomew drove Humphrey home, he made sure to look out for any suspicious activity before walking the mayor to his door. No one was ever arrested for the assassination attempt.[27]

No sooner had Humphrey been appointed as Johnson's vice-presidential running mate in August 1964 the FBI began to receive numerous 'tip-offs' that his life was in danger. The threats included a bizarre tale of a man who contacted the agency to report that the vice president was 'going to be shot'. When he was asked to explain his statement the anonymous caller said he had a TV built into his brain which showed moving pictures of incidents about to happen.[28]

In October 1964 a gunsmith, Daniel D. Farell, attended a campaign speech given by Humphrey outside a railroad terminal in Upper Derby, Pennsylvania. He was arrested after saying he would kill the vice-presidential candidate. In a later court appearance Farell was fined $10.[29] The same month 46-year-old freelance writer Sidney Warner was seized by police as he stood in a Chicago crowd listening to the Democrat nominee speak. He was arrested for saying Senator Hubert H. Humphrey should be killed, and held under a $10,000 bond for a psychiatric examination.[30] The following month 22-year-old Puerto Rican musician Israel Nunez Feliciano was arrested by Secret Service agents after threatening to kill Humphrey in the Virgin Islands.[31]

Following Humphrey's election as vice president the threats increased. 'During the period I received protection,' Humphrey said, 'there were possibly more dissident elements at work in American society than at any other time in my lifetime. The period 1965 through 1968 insofar as I was concerned was a period of tremendous tension and danger and the possibilities of physical harm always were there.'[32]

An incident that was characterised by the FBI as an 'alleged attempt on the life of Vice President Humphrey at Hollywood Palladium, Los Angeles' occurred on 12 July 1965. The FBI considered the matter a 'Secret Service responsibility'. Following an investigation, the Secret Service advised the Bureau that the threatener was ' . . . intoxicated at the time . . . was denied access to Vice President Humphrey and . . . was kept under surveillance'.[33]

A more serious alert involved a caller who told FBI agents that a ' . . . states righter had paid a man $10,000 to shoot Vice President Humphrey with a high-powered rifle at the Forest Hills Cemetery'. However, the FBI was unable to trace the call.[34]

In July 1967, 19-year-old Ronald Eugene Read, a soldier from Fort Richardson, Anchorage, brandished a .44 calibre Magnum revolver in the vicinity of Humphrey when he made a stop-over in the Alaskan city after visiting South Korea. Humphrey was staying at a hotel downtown when bus passengers spotted Read displaying a pistol at the side entrance to Humphrey's hotel. The bus driver contacted the police. Read was arrested, jailed and was held in lieu of a $100,000 bail. With little to go on except a suspicion he had been stalking the vice president, the judge accepted a firearms charge guilty plea.[35]

Many Humphrey threateners were clearly deranged. In 1967 the Secret Service received reports about a 'young man' in San Francisco who had been overheard saying Humphrey should be kidnapped and held 'under water' until a headline appeared in the *New York Times* stating, 'The US is withdrawing all troops out of Vietnam'. Humphrey had been staying at San Francisco's Hilton Hotel when the threat was made. The same threatener suggested that after the kidnapping Humphrey's head should be shaved, he should be given a false beard and be forced to take LSD to keep him under control. The FBI and Secret Service investigated the threat but was unsuccessful in tracking down the culprit.[36]

Humphrey's Secret Service agents were especially concerned about the possibility of violence when Humphrey made trips abroad. In 1967 during a trip to Italy for meetings with the Italian prime minister and Pope Paul VI, Humphrey had been instructed by his agents to be sure that when he exited his limousine he should walk at an appropriate pace to the entrance of a building. However, when Humphrey attended an opera concert he waited outside the opera house providing the opportunity for the secretary of the Milan Young Communist League, Gianni Buzzan, to throw a plastic bag filled with yellow paint at him. Buzzan missed the vice president but hit the director of the opera house 'chest on'.[37]

When Humphrey travelled abroad, numerous FBI reports warned him of impending anti-war demonstrations organised by left-wing political groups. Anti-war demonstrators were armed with paint, urine and nail-studded balls which posed a very real physical risk. While Humphrey was in Florence,

Italy, on 1 April 1967, 23-year-old Giulio Stocchi threw eggs at the vice president and missed. He was seized by Humphrey's agents who turned him over to Italian officers.[38] In Brussels, Belgium, on 9 April 1967, demonstrators led by communists threw rotten eggs and fruit at Humphrey's car, also hitting several of his bodyguards.[39]

However, there were also false alarms during Humphrey's time as vice president, including a visit to West Germany's capital, Bonn, that year. Humphrey met with government leaders there before going on to West Berlin. The day before Humphrey arrived police rounded up eleven German left-wing extremists who they alleged had been plotting to kill the vice president when he arrived in the city. The group was accused of threatening Humphrey's life by using 'bombs, plastic bags filled with chemicals and other dangerous objects such as stones'.[40] However, the 'bombs' were nothing more than smoke candles and paint. The alleged assassination attempt became known as the 'Pudding Bomb Assassination Attempt'.[41]

In October 1968 an assassination plot was revealed by the *Santa Monica Evening Outlook* newspaper carrying the headline, 'Plot to Kill HHH in Venice Bared'. The headline was a reference to Humphrey's planned visit to the coastal town near Los Angeles on 24 October 1968, when he was due to give a campaign speech. The article stated the visit had been cancelled because the FBI and Secret Service had uncovered an assassination plot. However, the FBI LA office said it had not received any information about the alleged 'assassination plot'.[42]

In August 1968, the FBI learned of a plot to assassinate 'several prominent political leaders' including Humphrey. The information came from an unidentified source that leaders of dissident groups and youth gangs were plotting the assassinations. The FBI monitored movements of several groups and individuals during the Chicago Democratic convention and brought in suspects for questioning including community leader Reverend John Fry and members of the Blackstone Rangers, a Chicago street gang.

The gang members were questioned by a federal grand jury which considered evidence that the Rangers were planning to 'riot in the Chicago Loop, disrupt the Convention, and assassinate Eugene McCarthy and Hubert Humphrey'.[43] However, there was insufficient evidence to prosecute. Humphrey acknowledged the alleged plot when he told reports, 'I was targeted by an assassination team and supposedly to be taken care of.'[44] He also remarked that, 'If someone wants to get me and give up their life in the process they'll do it.'[45]

When the vice president lost the 1968 election his wife Muriel told agent Hal Thomas, 'Well, at least now he'll live.'[46]

* * *

There were three serious assassination attempts on the life of Hubert Humphrey when he was vice president. The first, attempt, and arguably the most dangerous, occurred in 1965.

Humphrey was invited to speak in Baton Rouge by a friend, Victor Bussie, head of the Louisiana AFL/CIO Unions. The date set for the speech was 9 April 1965, at the Jack Tar Capitol House Hotel in Baton Rouge.

Louisiana State Policeman Joe Cooper worked undercover for the FBI from 1963 to 1965, infiltrating a Ku Klux Klan organisation, the 'Feliciana Klan'. Cooper served in the Klan's KBI (Klan Bureau of Investigation). He was approached by a Ku Klux Klan member and asked if he could provide security information about the impending visit of Humphrey to Louisiana. The Klan, Cooper reported to his FBI contacts, was plotting to assassinate the vice president when he visited Baton Rouge. The Klan wanted Humphrey killed because he was 'an integrationist'.

When he made contact with FBI agents, Cooper supplied the names of two of the plotters. FBI agents followed the alleged conspirators and took photographs but they were not arrested. The FBI in turn advised Cooper he should tell his Klan contacts Humphrey's security would be heavy '. . . along the route of the Vice President's motorcade . . .', but he was also told to suggest, 'it might not be as tight at the Capitol House'. The Secret Service feared that if their surveillance was discovered others would take the place of the two men who had been tracked.

When the information about the plot was relayed to the Secret Service, Humphrey's agents advised the vice president he should call off his visit. However, Humphrey insisted he was safely protected and refused to cancel the event.

When Humphrey arrived in Baton Rouge he rode with the governor in a limousine to the governor's mansion. Later the two men rode together to the hotel. Security forces were everywhere along the route, covering the motorcade with high-powered rifles stationed on rooftops. Humphrey, escorted by Governor McKeithen, entered the hotel's ballroom and walked to the speaker's platform. FBI and Secret Service agents were present observing all visitors coming and going. The man given the task of shooting Humphrey, a union member who had a ticket to get into the ballroom, was spotted immediately.

He had taken a seat at the rear. Two FBI agents sat down in front of him. Secret Service men sat on both sides. A further two members of the team sat behind. The gunman stood up and reached for his pistol which he had concealed under his coat. The federal agents subdued him and led him out through a kitchen door. The second would-be assassin was also arrested and removed from the ballroom. When agents searched his car they found a gun. There was a third man on the assassination team but he left before Humphrey arrived.

The plotters were questioned but were never charged. Cooper said FBI agents told him they did not have sufficient evidence. 'I know this guy would have killed Humphrey,' Cooper said. 'He was a crack shot. He could part your hair without touching your scalp.'

Word about the attempt on Humphrey's life was not allowed to leak out until two years later, when the *New Orleans States-Item* printed part of the story. They described an attempt on Humphrey's life by a 'right-wing organization' but did not mention the Klan by name.[47]

Within a few years, all three of the men who were arrested for the assassination attempt were dead. One was shot to death by his wife. Another was killed when a metal door fell on him. The third, a young man, died of a heart attack. Emile W. Weber, Joe Cooper's attorney, said, 'There is absolutely no question in my mind that Joe saved Hubert Humphrey's life.'[48]

Possible corroboration for the attempt on Humphrey's life is chronicled in the FBI files. In a memo dated 8 February 1965 an FBI agent wrote:

> Information set forth re: possible picketing by the Klan in connection with the visit of Vice President Hubert H. Humphrey in Baton Rouge, Louisiana and New Orleans on April 9 1965, being furnished to Department of Justice, Secret Service, military intelligence and appropriate local authorities including officials of Louisiana State University where the Vice President is scheduled to speak. Matter being closely followed.[49]

However, a follow-up memo dated 3 March 1965 titled 'Visit of Vice President Hubert H. Humphrey to Baton Rouge, Louisiana April 9 1965' is completely redacted – which may or may not suggest that an informant or undercover agent's name, and background information about the agent, had been withheld. A further memo dated 1 April 1965 'From Cartha DeLoach to Mr Mohr' was heavily redacted except for one comment, 'Was Humphrey notified? I discussed the matter with [redacted] approximately two weeks ago. Not only was [redacted] advised but additionally I left him with a blind memorandum containing all facts in the matter. He was very grateful and stated that the Vice President would be definitely alerted.'[50]

The second assassination attempt against Vice President Humphrey occurred during a vice-presidential trip to Australia, 18–20 February 1966. Humphrey's visit was to discuss the war in Vietnam in which Australia had committed troops.

An Australian youth, 19-year-old Peter Kocan, became enamoured with Lee Harvey Oswald and was an admirer of Hitler. During Humphrey's visit Kocan attempted to position himself near the vice president in order to shoot him. As Humphrey's Secret Service protection was too tight Kocan decided it was too risky and left. The fact the would-be assassin went on to shoot a leading Australian politician led the Secret Service to believe it was an extremely serious threat. If Humphrey's detail had been lax in their duties, the Secret Service believed, it was very likely Kocan would have gone ahead with his assassination attempt.

Kocan turned his attentions to an Australian politician. On the evening of 21 June 1966, while Labour Party leader Arthur Calwell was campaigning, Kocan tried to assassinate him. After Calwell left the meeting and just as his car was about to drive off, Kocan approached the passenger side of the vehicle, aimed a sawn-off rifle at Calwell's head and fired at point-blank range. The closed window deflected the bullet, which lodged harmlessly in Calwell's coat lapel. He sustained only minor facial injuries from broken glass.

When asked about his motive, Kocan told police, 'I had to do something to set me aside from all the other nobodies.' He also admitted to police his plan to assassinate Humphrey but he was never charged. Kocan was tried and found guilty of attempted murder in late December 1966 and was sentenced to life imprisonment. He was later transferred to a hospital for the mentally ill and was released in 1976.[51]

The third incident identified as an 'assassination attempt' by the Secret Service occurred in October 1967 during the inauguration ceremonies for South Vietnam's President Thieu. The vice president's motorcade lined up in the Presidential Palace's circular drive when Glenn Weaver intuitively thought they had been waiting there too long for safety. He ordered Rick Barbuto, the limousine driver, to move. A minute after Barbuto drove the car away two cars in front of the limousine were hit by a mortar and a driver was killed. Rufus Youngblood said Humphrey was aware he was one of the primary targets and that '. . . the Viet Cong would have scored a real coup if the vice president of the US had been killed'. According to agent Jerry Parr, 'It was clearly intended for the vice president.'[52]

Chapter 5

The Stalking of Robert Kennedy

'I play Russian roulette every time I get up in the morning but I just don't care. There's nothing I could do about it anyway.'

Robert F. Kennedy

'You have to be hyper vigilant. You had one president murdered, one shot and wounded, a governor shot and wounded and paralyzed, two attempts on Ford, and you had Martin Luther King killed. You know it's out there. You just don't know where.'

Former agent Jerry Parr

'What if I had come up behind Sirhan a few seconds sooner and caused him to miss? This is exactly what would probably have happened had RFK had Secret Service protection. How different the world would be.'

Warren Rogers, RFK assassination witness

On 31 March 1968, President Lyndon Johnson unexpectedly withdrew from the nomination process for the presidency, leaving the contest open to Robert Kennedy and Eugene McCarthy. Kennedy, the brother of assassinated President John F. Kennedy, soon became the front-runner in the race for the Democratic nomination.

Kennedy had a reputation as a 'fatalist', always prepared for tragedy. Relaxing in the rear of a plane during the primary campaigns, he was asked by a reporter if he thought someone would seek to harm him. Kennedy said, 'Well, let's not talk about that.' On another occasion while campaigning he said, 'I play Russian roulette every time I get up in the morning but I just don't care. There's nothing I could do about it anyway.' Kennedy added, 'Of course, I worry about what would happen to my family, to the children. But they would be taken care of . . .'.[1]

When Kennedy was asked about the dangers of unruly crowds and riding in open-top cars while he campaigned, he said he did not worry about it. 'There's no sense in worrying about those things. If they want you, they can get you.' he said. A reporter asked Kennedy if he had thought about his assassination as bringing on a national crisis. 'Perhaps it would, I suppose so,' he said. 'But what can I do about that? I'll tell you one thing, if I'm elected president you won't see me riding around in any of those awful cars [closed-top cars brought in after the JFK assassination]'. Kennedy said he would ride in open-top limousines if elected president, 'So I really don't care about anything happening to me . . . This isn't really such a happy existence, is it?' he said.[2]

There were numerous threats against Kennedy's life during his quixotic run for the presidency, including an incident in New York's JFK airport when a man with a concealed gun followed Kennedy to the departure gate before he was stopped by airport security and searched. In Washington DC, the FBI arrested a man who had been impersonating the Senator by staying at hotels and signing his vouchers 'Robert F. Kennedy'. There was also an atmosphere of danger surrounding his campaign.[3]

But there were also threats involving his private life that he would have to face during his run for the presidency. If they were revealed at the time, they would have derailed his campaign.

There have been many allegations over the past five decades that Robert Kennedy had engaged in adulterous affairs, including relationships with Hollywood stars Marilyn Monroe, Kim Novak and Lee Remick. Kennedy supporters have dismissed the allegations, claiming writers and authors had used unreliable sources. It has long been a contentious issue among writers and historians. In 2020, for example, author J. Randy Taraborrelli wrote, 'Where Bobby was concerned, maybe he cheated on Ethel, but we don't know for sure and, based on what we do know of his character, it's doubtful.'[4] Also in 2020, Ted Kennedy biographer Neal Gabler said, 'Save for Bobby, infidelity had been a family inheritance . . . all except Bobby, who, by most accounts if not by most rumors, was faithful to Ethel . . .'.[5] Additionally, there was scepticism about a previously secret Russian intelligence report, released in 1997, which appeared to prove the Kennedy had engaged in affairs with women from the start of his married life. The report stated that during his visit to Russia in 1955 Kennedy asked his Intourist Guide to send 'a woman of loose morals' up to his room.[6]

However, it is the statements made by five people who were close to the Senator that finally renders the naysayers wrong. The statements made about Kennedy's adulterous affairs come from political aides Arthur Schlesinger Jr and Richard Goodwin; two Hollywood friends of the Senator, Richard Burton and Dame Joan Collins; and his brother-in-law George Terrien.

In the 1980s Arthur Schlesinger spoke to author Anthony Summers for his book *Goddess*. Schlesinger said Kennedy had liaisons with women especially when he was 'travelling'.[7]

Richard Goodwin, a political aide to Presidents Kennedy and Johnson and close friend of Robert Kennedy, said there was no question that 'Bobby' had extramarital affairs. 'Of course he did,' Goodwin said. 'That's a Kennedy family tradition . . . He wasn't sort of randomly random like his brother (Jack) or Teddy, for that matter. Not at all. He was much more selective and limited . . . Everyone was doing it, including the press. That's why they never reported it.'[8]

Richard Burton's diaries were not written for publication which adds verisimilitude to his story about Kennedy's affairs. The diaries were only published after Burton's death. Additionally, the British actor, unlike some sources for anti-Kennedy books, had no axe to grind which further adds to his veracity. Burton wrote of RFK:

> The Kennedy family are notorious satyrs. I was amazed when Bobby K took Margot Fonteyn off into a back bedroom at Pierre Salinger's house in (Beverly Hills) and my asking Salinger, when they came back, 'where the hell have they been?' and Salinger's fat-faced reply which was a finger over the lips . . . Maybe . . . the Kennedys do believe that they can get away with anything. Gawd [*sic*] Help him . . . I know, too, that when Jack Kennedy was running for President and stayed with Frank Sinatra at Palm Springs, that the place was like a whore-house, with Jack as chief customer . . . Christ, the chances those fellers took.[9]

In January 2021 Joan Collins revealed how she once turned down Kennedy's advances, reminding him he was a married man. She refused to expand on her revelations saying, 'Ethel, his widow is still alive so I really don't want to go into it too much because I wouldn't want to hurt her.'[10]

Kennedy's brother-in law George Terrien is one of the most important witnesses, and perhaps *the* most important witness to allege RFK had a sexual relationship with Marilyn Monroe. Terrien had been Bobby Kennedy's college roommate and later married Ethel Kennedy's sister, Georgeann. Terrien said that during a telephone conversation with the then Attorney General, Kennedy admitted he had sex with her. Kennedy also believed Monroe had fallen in love with him, according to Terrien.[11]

* * *

When Kennedy returned to his home in Hyannis Port during the primary campaigns the Kennedy family chauffer, Frank Saunders, was given the task of protecting the 'exhausted' Senator.

The day after Martin Luther King was assassinated Saunders had been approached by the Secret Service and handed a loaded .38 pistol. The agents told Saunders to carry it as they were afraid that someone might try to kill Kennedy. Saunders said he didn't want the pistol but the agents insisted. They wanted him to have it, 'just in case'. Saunders began to carry the pistol, hiding it in a holster under his sports jacket. However, by the time of the Indiana primary in May he decided he would stop wearing it. 'The compound was a private preserve,' Saunders said, 'a safe haven. It was crazy to even think that somebody might try and kill Robert Kennedy.'[12]

Throughout Robert Kennedy's eighty-five-day presidential campaign his only 'official' bodyguard had been former FBI agent Bill Barry. As the Senator travelled around the country, walking through surging crowds and greeting supporters from his open-top car, Barry was often his only shield. Later, during his campaigning for the California primary, Kennedy enlisted two friends, former Olympic decathlon champion Rafer Johnson and professional football player Roosevelt Grier to assist Barry.

Kennedy met Barry when he was Attorney General in the JFK administration. Along with this cabinet position came protection in the form of an FBI bodyguard and driver. Barry met Kennedy when he acted as an FBI agent detailed to meet and protect the Attorney General during his visits to New York and later when he became a Senator travelling around the state. Historian Arthur Schlesinger Jr said the two men had a '. . . kindred spirit in many ways, including scepticism about [FBI Director] J. Edgar Hoover'.[13]

Hoover loathed the Kennedys. When he learned that Barry had taken holidays to be Robert Kennedy's driver during the former Attorney General's 1964 New York senatorial campaign, he had Barry transferred to Mobile, Alabama. In turn, Barry's response was to resign from the FBI and begin work as a bank vice president, remaining close to the Kennedy family. When Robert Kennedy announced his candidacy for the presidency in March 1968 Barry was given the responsibility for Kennedy's security. By the end of the California campaign Bill Barry had become 'exhausted'.[14]

Kennedy received additional close bodyguard protection from Grier and Johnson during the final phase of the primary campaign which ended with the California election.

Rafer Johnson was a two-time Olympic decathlon medallist (silver in 1956 and gold in 1960) and former starter for the UCLA basketball team. At Rome, he was the first black person to carry the US flag in an Olympic opening ceremony. Following his successful athletic career, Johnson found employment in Hollywood appearing in films alongside stars like Frank Sinatra, Bob Hope and Elvis Presley. Before the Rome Olympics, he had to choose between a top role in the film *Spartacus* and a spot in the Olympics. He chose the Olympics.

Johnson had met Robert Kennedy in 1960, when he was honoured by the 'People to People' programme as athlete of the year at a ceremony in New York. Kennedy was the presenter, and Johnson told him he would like to participate in the new Peace Corps programme which was instituted by the JFK administration. Kennedy, determining that Johnson was serious, flew him back to the White House with him and a friendship began. In 1968 Johnson was asked to campaign for Kennedy when the Senator made visits to California in preparation for the June primary election. He was soon enlisted to become one of the Senator's protectors during campaign stops.[15]

Rosey Grier, the 6ft 5in Rams football player, first met Robert Kennedy when Ethel Kennedy invited him to a celebrity event in Washington DC in 1967. At their first meeting Kennedy humorously punched him in the stomach then suggested a game of touch football with relatives and friends joining in. 'It broke the ice . . .,' Grier said.[16]

Shortly after that initial meeting, Grier received a call from Kennedy aide Joan Braden who was working on the Senator's presidential campaign. She invited Grier to join the campaign which had started on 16 March 1968. Grier accepted because he knew he was helping a candidate who stood for 'racial and economic justice'. Following the assassination of Martin Luther King, Grier thought it vital Kennedy be elected, '. . . the final thing', Grier said, 'was that we were [going to] make a difference in our world'.[17]

Grier's role in the campaign was never defined but it was accepted he would assist in bodyguard protection as well as being a friend of the family. His celebrity would also help in the campaign because Grier was African American, a voting group that favoured the Senator. Grier was especially helpful when he assisted Kennedy's campaign visits to Watts, an African American suburb of Los Angeles, which had achieved notoriety when riots erupted there in 1964.

Once the 1968 campaign got underway Barry found himself receiving little cooperation from the candidate when it came to protective measures he wanted to implement. Kennedy allowed Barry to help him navigate the sometimes unruly crowds that enveloped him but refused his bodyguard's suggestions for improved security. Kennedy insisted on close contact with his supporters to show he was strong enough and brave enough to inherit his brother's legacy.[18]

In April 1968, during one campaign stopover in Lansing, Michigan, police informed Barry that a man with a rifle had been spotted entering an office building across the street from Kennedy's hotel. Taking precautions, Barry arranged for the Senator to leave the hotel via an underground garage instead of leaving by the front entrance. When Kennedy heard of Barry's arrangements he became angry and told his bodyguard, 'Don't ever do anything like that again. . . . Don't make any decisions or changes without my permission. I make the decisions around here. If somebody's going to shoot me, they'll shoot me. But I'm not sneaking around like a thief in the night.'[19]

The possibility of violence and danger was very much in the minds of the people who were around the Senator. It was generally accepted the memory of his assassinated brother had 'something to do with it', according to *LIFE* reporter Louden Wainwright. In April in Logansport, Indiana, armed police stood on rooftops overlooking the outdoor venue where Kennedy spoke to his supporters. In May, Kennedy's motorcade suddenly pulled off the road as the Senator and his wife hunched down in the back seat of their open top car. Ethel Kennedy had only asked for the car to pull in as she was feeling the cold and wanted to put on a coat, but it left reporters believing it may have been an assassination attempt. In San Francisco's Chinatown on the last day of the California primary election campaign every member of the Kennedy group flinched at the sound of firecrackers and bursting balloons.[20]

In his moment of victory, having won the California primary election on 4 June, Kennedy said, 'To my old friend, if I may, Rafer Johnson, is here. And to Rosey Grier, who said that he'd take care of anybody who didn't vote for me.'[21] Within minutes Kennedy lay on the floor of the Ambassador Hotel pantry having received a mortal gunshot wound to the head.

* * *

Sirhan Sirhan, a 24-year-old Palestinian immigrant who lived in Pasadena, California, sought meaning to his increasingly hopeless life in the United States by embracing anti-Semitism, anti-Americanism and Palestinian nationalism. His parents taught him the Jews were 'evil' and 'stole their home'. They also taught him to hate, despise and fear Jews. As a part-time gardener Sirhan came to hate the Jews whose gardens he tended. He referred to them as 'f****** Jews', 'the goddamn Zionists' and the 'f****** Zionists'.[22]

Those close to Sirhan, and who knew him well, included his brothers Munir, Sharif and Adel and friends Walter Crowe, Lou Shelby, John and Patricia Strathmann and Elsie Boyko, as well as his former boss John Weidner. They all agreed that Sirhan had hated Jews and been intense and emotional whenever he discussed the relationship between Arabs and Israelis.

Although some acquaintances of Sirhan said he was pleasant and well-mannered, that it is not the lasting impressions of those who knew him best. His brother Munir, the youngest of the Sirhan brothers, said Sirhan was 'stubborn' and had 'tantrums'.[23] William A. Spaniard, a 24-year-old Pasadena friend of Sirhan's, said the young Palestinian was 'a taciturn individual'.[24]

After Sirhan's short spell at Pasadena College he worked at the Grande Vista Del Rio Ranch in Corona, California. He revealed the violent side of his character when he was employed there as an exercise boy/trainee jockey. According to two exercise girls who worked at the ranch, Sirhan treated the horses 'cruelly'. Additionally, a horse trainer saw Sirhan mistreat a horse, 'kicking and hitting it with his fists'. Sirhan, he said, '. . . was in a rage of temper'. By way of explanation Sirhan told him the horse 'provoked him'.[25]

Sirhan's brother Adel said his brother became angry in the year before the presidential election about television reports on the Middle East and would 'walk across the room with a sour face very fast and get away'.[26] Another brother, Sharif, told Egyptian journalist Mahmoud Abel-Hadi that following the broadcast of a pro-Israeli television speech Kennedy gave while campaigning in California, Sirhan 'left the room putting his hands on his ears and almost weeping'.[27]

Walter Crowe, who had known Sirhan from the time they were young adults, unsuccessfully tried to organise Students for a Democratic Society events on the Pasadena College Campus, which Sirhan briefly attended. Crowe said Sirhan was virulently anti-Semitic and professed hatred for the Jews and the state of Israel and believed Sirhan's mother, Mary Sirhan, propagated these views to her son.[28]

Crowe believed Al Fattah's terrorist acts were justified and that Palestinian terrorists had gained the respect of the Arab world. He said Sirhan spoke of 'total commitment' to the Palestinian cause and took a left-wing position on issues such as racism and the Vietnam War. However, Crowe said, Sirhan was a 'reactionary' when it came to the Arab-Israeli conflict. Crowe believed that Sirhan saw himself as a 'committed revolutionary' willing to undertake 'revolutionary action'. Sirhan was for 'violence whenever, as long as it's needed'. Later, Crowe came to feel guilt about the part he may have played in putting ideas of terrorist acts into Sirhan's head and reinforcing Sirhan's resolve to commit a violent political act.[29]

Lou Shelby knew the Sirhan family intimately. He described Sirhan as 'intensely nationalistic with regard to his Arab identity'. According to Shelby:

> We had a really big argument on Middle East politics . . . we switched back and forth between Arabic and English. Sirhan's outlook was completely Arab nationalist – the Arabs were in the right and had made no mistakes. I tried to reason with him and to point out that one could be in the right but still make mistakes. But he was adamant. According to him, America was to blame for the Arabs' misfortunes – because of the power of Zionism [in the United States]. The only Arab leader he really admired was Nasser and he thought Nasser's policies were right. The Arabs had to build themselves up and fight Israel – that was the only way.[30]

John and Patricia Strathmann had been 'good friends' with Sirhan since High School. According to John, Sirhan was an admirer of Hitler, especially his treatment of the Jews, and was impressed with Hitler's *Mein Kampf.* John also said Sirhan became 'intense' and 'mad' about the Arab-Israeli Six Day War. Patricia said Sirhan became 'burning mad . . . furious' about the war. Sirhan's friend Elsie Boyko said Sirhan had always been intense and emotional whenever he discussed the Arab-Israeli conflict and was critical of US foreign policy regarding Israel.[31]

At first, Sirhan became enamoured with Robert Kennedy as he believed the Senator was for the 'underdog' in society and would naturally support Palestinians. However, when Kennedy announced his support for sending bomber jets to Israel Sirhan became furious at what he thought was a 'betrayal'. He thought he would be 'like his brother', the president, and help the Arabs but:

> Hell, he f***** up. That's all he did. . . . He asked for it. He should have been smarter than that. You know, the Arabs had emotions. He knew how they felt about it. But, hell, he didn't have to come out right at the f****** time when the Arab–Israeli war erupted. Oh! I couldn't take it! I couldn't take it![32]

Sirhan began using mind-control techniques in promoting his goal of killing Senator Kennedy. He concentrated in front of a mirror and thought about his intended victim. He wrote in his notebooks, '. . . Senator Kennedy must be sacrificed for the cause of the poor exploited people . . . the glorious United States of America will eventually be felled by a blow of an assassin's bullet . . .'. When Kennedy brought his campaign to California in May 1968 Sirhan wrote, 'My determination to eliminate RFK is becoming more the more of an unshakable obsession. . . . RFK must die – RFK must be killed Robert F Kennedy must be assassinated RFK must be assassinated RFK must be assassinated. . . . RFK must be assassinated before 5 June 68. . .'.[33]

Sirhan started to put his plan of killing Robert Kennedy into action. He bought a .22 calibre pistol with his brother Munir and began to stalk the candidate.

According to Joseph and Margaret Sheehan, Sirhan had attended the Los Angeles Sports Arena Kennedy rally on Friday, 24 May 1968. Following Kennedy's speech, the Sheehans waited outside the arena to catch a glimpse of the presidential candidate. In the crowd was Sirhan who looked 'completely out of character with that crowd. . . . very quiet, intent and purposeful in a frightening way'. Margaret Sheehan thought Sirhan was 'intense and sinister'.[34]

On Sunday night, 2 June, Sirhan was seen at the Ambassador Hotel on Wilshire Boulevard, Los Angeles, at approximately 7.30 pm. Sirhan had discovered that Kennedy was due to give a speech in the hotel's Palm Terrace Room. William Blume, who had been a fellow employee at a health-food store owned by John Weidner when Sirhan worked there, said he recognized him. He observed Sirhan in the lobby area adjacent to the Palm Terrace Room.

Sirhan elbowed his way to the front of the crowd waiting for RFK to give his speech. Sirhan had been close to an aisle RFK was due to walk down. However, Sirhan grew impatient and left the area before Kennedy arrived. The Senator was late because he had taken his children to Disneyland.[35]

Completing his speech, Kennedy walked through the kitchen area. Miriam Davis, a hostess for the event that evening, walked around the hotel for 20 minutes after the Senator had finished. She saw Sirhan sitting in the pantry area. Either Sirhan had missed Kennedy's journey through the pantry or he had lain in wait but was unable to get near him.[36]

There is also compelling evidence Sirhan stalked Kennedy in San Diego on 3 June during the Senator's last day of campaigning. Sirhan said he drove 'someplace in that direction' on that day. He told Michael McCowan, a Sirhan defence investigator, he had put 350 miles on the car's odometer. The 260-mile round trip from Pasadena to San Diego might explain the extra miles Sirhan clocked up.[37]

On Tuesday morning, 4 June, at 8.00 am, Sirhan bought a newspaper at Washington Boulevard and Lake Avenue in Pasadena. At 11.00 am he drove to the San Gabriel Valley Gun Club in Fish Canyon in Duarte, an LA suburb, and was one of the first to arrive at 11.30 am. He registered using his real name and correct address. Sirhan rapid-fired his gun, expending between 300 and 400 bullets.[38]

* * *

The security arrangements were sparse at the Ambassador Hotel. Los Angeles Police Chief Thomas Reddin said after Kennedy's assassination the Senator's staff had twice turned down offers of police protection for the candidate. Reddin said the response was not unusual as presidential candidates did not normally want policemen around them because they wanted 'no barrier against the voter'.[39]

According to police officer Daryl Gates, who would later become Los Angeles Police Chief:

> Had we been [at the Ambassador that night] I have no doubt
> we would have pre-planned Kennedy's route from the Embassy
> Ballroom . . . to the Colonial Room . . . and we would have had
> enough officers on hand to protect him . . . but Kennedy's people
> were adamant, if not abusive, in their demands that the police not
> even come close to the senator while he was in Los Angeles . . . he
> wanted no uniforms around at all, none that could be captured in
> a photograph or on a piece of film. Kennedy desired to be seen as a
> man of the people, charging into crowds alone.[40]

Gates said that, in retrospect, the Los Angeles Police Department should
have insisted on security for RFK. However, Gates was worried that, had the
LAPD assigned plain-clothes officers inside the Ambassador without RFK's
knowledge, Kennedy's aides would have accused the police of spying.[41]

Los Angeles Police officer Gene Scherrer who was assigned to liase with
Kennedy's campaign staff said, 'He didn't want his followers – the poor, the
blacks, the ethnic groups, the liberals – to see him surrounded by police
types. I argued with him about it the last day, but he told me not to come to
the Ambassador that night.'[42] Nevertheless, there were three or four squads,
which included eight to ten men each, strategically located around the hotel.[43]

William Gardner, the head of the Ambassador Hotel's security force, said
he received no request to provide personal security for Robert Kennedy, but
he had anticipated security problems and hired eight 'Ace Security' guards
in addition to the ten plain-clothes hotel security staff.

Gardner said that Kennedy had been a guest at the hotel on previous
occasions during the 1968 campaign and that it was made clear to him that
'the Senator did not want any uniformed security guards in his presence nor
did he want any armed individuals as guards'. In addition to the security
force of eighteen guards. six uniformed fire inspectors were assigned to the
hotel for the evening to enforce fire and occupancy regulations.[44]

Nine guards were deployed in the Embassy Ballroom itself where Kennedy
was scheduled to deliver his victory speech. Two security guards were at the
foot of the stairs where Kennedy was expected to descend for his appearance;
two uniformed guards were outside the ballroom doors and two more in
plain clothes, in the hallway leading to the main lobby. Two guards, Stanley
Kawalee and Thane Cesar, were assigned to accompany him through the
pantry after he had delivered his speech.[45]

Over 1,800 Kennedy people were in the Ambassador Hotel Embassy Ballroom on the night of Kennedy's primary election victory. Three other political events were being held in the hotel. The hotel's security contingent, therefore, faced a tremendous challenge in trying to deal with the huge crowds. Security was stretched to the limit controlling access at the main doors and hallways.[46]

* * *

Despite a request by Robert Kennedy for Gene Scherrer to stay away from the Ambassador Hotel on the night of the California primary election, the LAPD officer nevertheless decided to go. 'I don't know why, I just did,' Scherrer said; he also had a 'premonition' that something bad was going to happen.[47]

Kennedy arrived at the hotel at approximately 8.15 pm and went immediately to his suite of rooms, 511 and 512. When CBS declared victory for Kennedy at 11.00 pm, Kennedy prepared himself for his victory speech. The crowd in the Embassy Ballroom reacted enthusiastically to the news.

Kennedy volunteer Susan Harris had befriended reporters Jon Akass and John Pilger. She delivered drinks to them and, to avoid the crowd in the ballroom, found a shortcut through the pantry which was situated behind the Embassy Ballroom. Returning to talk to the reporters, she told them, 'There's a little guy in there [the pantry] who keeps looking at me kind of funny, just staring as if he's waiting around for something.' She later identified 'the little guy' as Sirhan Sirhan.

Robert Kennedy and his three bodyguards, accompanied by Kennedy aides, left the Senator's fifth floor suite at 11.45 pm. to take a service lift to the kitchen area. Kennedy told an aide he didn't want to go through the crowd to get to the stage and so a hotel worker showed them to the freight lift. Reporter Constance Lawn ran down the stairs and through the kitchen. As she passed through the pantry, which was lit by three blue fluorescent tubes slotted in the ceiling, someone called out asking if Kennedy was coming that way. Lawn answered in the affirmative and also remembered catching a glimpse of a swarthy looking young man who she later identified as Sirhan.

The Kennedy supporters in the Embassy Ballroom were now convinced that their candidate could arrive at the Democratic convention in Chicago in August with enough momentum to secure the party nomination for president. By winning both the California and South Dakota primaries, Kennedy had moved into a position to seriously challenge Vice President Hubert H. Humphrey for the nomination.

John Frankenheimer, at whose Malibu home Kennedy had been staying the night before voting day, was standing behind the Embassy Ballroom stage as Kennedy delivered his speech. Frankenheimer said:

> I was standing there in the archway feeling like someone in '*The Manchurian Candidate*' [The film Frankenheimer directed]. I can see Bobby's face on a big television monitor . . . and I can see his back for real. As I stood there a figure went by me and it was as if there was electricity coming out of his body. I've never felt anything like it before or since. Of course, it was Sirhan Sirhan.[48]

Following his speech, Kennedy heard a voice say, 'This way, Senator.' It was now approximately 12.13 am on 5 June, the first anniversary of the Arab-Israeli Six Day War.

Kennedy had asked Bill Barry to look after his wife and so he did not accompany the Senator through the pantry. A surge of people surrounded Kennedy as kitchen workers lined up behind a steam table to greet him. As Juan Perez shook his hand, he said, 'Señor Kennedy, mucho gusto!' Kennedy moved on to shake hands with some cooks and busboy Juan Romero. At the moment he turned to his left to shake Romero's hand Sirhan began firing his pistol.

The closest bodyguard to Kennedy was Thane Cesar who was standing directly behind the Senator. He was inches away from him as Kennedy shook hands with the kitchen staff. Cesar saw 'flashes' and was blinded by the 'bright floodlights'. He saw 'an extended arm, a gun, and the flash from the barrel of the weapon'. As soon as Cesar saw the flash and heard the gunshots he ducked but stumbled and fell forward. When he rose from the floor he pulled out his .38 pistol and held it in his hand with the gun at a 45 degree angle but uncocked.[49]

Kennedy was hit in the head and collapsed as he reached out and grabbed Cesar's clip-on tie. He fell on his back as the seventy-seven-strong pantry crowd began to scream and panic, pushing and shoving one another.

Bullets were sprayed around the room as Grier and Johnson and a host of others jumped on the assailant as Sirhan held on tightly to his Iver Johnson .22 pistol, expending all eight bullets. Kennedy was mortally wounded in the head. Five others in the crowd were also shot but survived their wounds. Eventually, Sirhan was subdued. Shortly afterwards police officers arrived at the hotel and Sirhan was taken to a nearby police station.

Warren Rogers, who participated in the melee that ensued after shots were fired had often thought, 'What if I had come up behind Sirhan a few seconds sooner and caused him to miss? This is exactly what would probably have happened had RFK had Secret Service protection. How different the world would be.'[50]

* * *

Years later, Sirhan gave a political motivation for his crime. It related to Kennedy's support of Israel in the Arab-Israeli conflict. In 1989, in an interview with David Frost, he said, 'My only connection with Robert Kennedy was his sole support of Israel and his deliberate attempt to send those 50 bombers to Israel to obviously do harm to the Palestinians.'[51]

The motive was clear – Robert Kennedy was killed by an avowed Palestinian nationalist, a man whose loyalty to his homeland outweighed his allegiance to the country that gave him refuge after his family fled the Middle East.

Sirhan later claimed to have suffered amnesia following the shooting. However, it was one of his defence investigators during Sirhan's 1969 trial who debunked that idea. Michael McCowan said his client remembered everything that happened that night including looking Kennedy in the eyes before he shot him. Sirhan's claim was clearly a ruse and held out some promise his conviction might someday be overturned but it was also a way of admitting his crime which guaranteed him praise from fellow Arabs and Palestinians.[52]

* * *

As the years passed one of Kennedy's bodyguards, Ace Security Guard Thane Eugene Cesar, who had been standing behind the Senator when he was shot, was frequently accused by conspiracy theorists of having colluded with the assassin. Cesar was fingered as the co-assassin who fired the fatal shot to Kennedy's head.

Cesar worked on the assembly line at Lockheed Aircraft. Early in 1968 he had applied for the position of security guard at Ace Guard Service because he was desperate to earn extra money and the additional $3 an hour wage was enticing. He worked part time for Ace on occasion, and in the late afternoon on 4 June he received a call to report to the Ambassador Hotel for duty. Cesar said that he was called late because another guard had telephoned at the last minute to say he could not show up for work and that he was not there as a 'bodyguard' but for 'crowd control'.

At 11.15 pm he was assigned to check credentials at the Colonial Room doorway and clear the way for the Kennedy entourage en route. As the crowd entered through the kitchen pantry food service area, he took up his duty and followed Senator Kennedy closely behind and to the right. Seconds later, when the shooting began, Cesar hit the floor and drew his weapon only as he began to get up. He insisted he did not fire it.

Cesar was interviewed during a reinvestigation of the assassination by the Los Angeles Special Counsel Thomas Kranz in the mid-1970s. He told investigators that he could have left the Ambassador without talking to anyone about the incident as no one seemed to be interested in taking his statement. Instead, he told LAPD officers that he had been inside the pantry at the time of the shooting, and they took him to Ramparts Police Station, where he was questioned. However, officers failed to examine his .38 pistol. Cesar also told the Kranz team that Ted Charach, who had filmed him for a documentary, *The Second Gun*, had taken his statements out of context and exaggerated them.

For more than fifty years Cesar had to live with the accusation that he was Robert Kennedy's real killer. Every anniversary of the assassination produced more allegations and 'proof' he had lied about his involvement in the purported conspiracy despite overwhelming evidence that not one witness saw Cesar shoot Kennedy.

As witness Vincent DiPierro told *The Washington Post*'s Ronald Kessler in 1974, as Sirhan began firing, he lunged forward, bringing the muzzle of his Iver Johnson revolver to within inches of Kennedy's head. 'It would be impossible for there to be a second gun,' DiPierro told Kessler. 'I saw the first shot. Kennedy fell at my feet. His blood splattered on me. I had a clear view of Kennedy and Sirhan.'[53]

In a 2018 radio interview, DiPierro's memory of the events in the pantry that night had not diminished with the passage of time:

I saw the gun come from the right side of my eye and [Sirhan's arm] was outstretched. . . . we always talk about the upward trajectory . . . well, Sirhan was shorter than Robert and he was also stretched out so that his arm was an extended version going in an upward trajectory . . . no one ever really brought it up. . . . there was nobody between Robert, Sirhan and me . . . I heard popping of balloons . . . the first shot was directly to his head . . . I got sprayed with the bullet to his head . . . there was a pause because Robert's hands went up to his head. . . . the third bullet hit the top of his jacket . . . the fourth shot went through my shirt . . . I didn't get hit . . . A lot of people said there were more than 8 shots. Well, there was a lot of popping, a lot of banging. I only saw 7 shots come out of the gun. There were 8.[54]

Acclaimed investigative journalist Dan Moldea, who wrote the definitive book on the shooting, found no evidence that Cesar had worked for the Mafia, the CIA or billionaire Howard Hughes, and the Ace security guard had not been a member of a right-wing political organisation or worked as a freelance hit-man, as conspiracy advocates alleged. Moldea also discovered that Cesar had never been a wealthy man, and there was no evidence that he had received any funds from conspirators. Moldea said, 'At the time of my first interview with him, Cesar had only $2,500 in his bank account and still owed the bulk of the $88,000 mortgage on his house. He owed $8,000 on a truck and $5,000 for another personal loan.' Cesar told Moldea, 'No matter what anybody says or any report they come up with, you know, I know, I didn't do it. The police department knows I didn't do it. There're just a few people out there who want to make something out of something that isn't there – even though I know that some of the evidence makes me look bad.'[55]

The falsehoods promoted by conspiracy theorists over the past five decades – the 'girl in a polka dot dress' who purportedly hypnotically controlled Sirhan; the multiple teams of CIA-controlled assassins skulking around the Los Angeles Ambassador Hotel; the allegations that Sirhan was never close enough to RFK to fire the fatal shot; the allegations of Sirhan firing 'blanks'; and the accusations against Cesar and Ambassador Hotel witness Michael Wayne – have all been addressed and debunked over the years.[56]

* * *

Reflecting on the tragic events that took place in the Ambassador Hotel former agent Marty Vencker said the tragedy need not have occurred. Professional bodyguards were important, he said, because they knew they had to stay above politics and not be taken in by the glitz and glamour of a political event. Kennedy's bodyguards were caught off-guard because they were Kennedy supporters. '[They] were caught up in the happiness of him winning the California primary,' Vencker said. 'You have to stay detached.'[57] Former agent Joseph Petro posed the question 'Would Bobby Kennedy have been murdered . . . if he'd had Secret Service protection?' Petro concluded with a '. . . qualified no. Had Secret Service agents been around, had [they] been around, Sirhan Sirhan would have had to change his tactic. Without the Secret Service, Bobby Kennedy was much more vulnerable.'[58]

Not long after Kennedy died, when campaigning was suspended temporarily, the violent atmosphere which took Kennedy's life appeared to return. One of the candidates who opposed Kennedy for the Democratic nomination, Eugene McCarthy, visited St John's University in Minnesota, where he once taught, for rest and recuperation. McCarthy, Secret Service codename 'Snowstorm', had been physically affected by the tragedy according to some of his friends. One of them said the Senator had felt 'guilt' at taunting RFK during the campaign. He recalled a remark McCarthy had made about Kennedy – 'Demagoguing to the last,' McCarthy said. Another aide heard him say that Kennedy 'brought it on himself', a reference to RFK's support for Israel.[59]

One night at dinner, eating with the faculty, McCarthy engaged in an argument with one of the teachers, an unnamed monk. The monk was carrying a concealed revolver and tried to attack Senator McCarthy with it after a disagreement. However, the monk was restrained by McCarthy's Secret Service detail.[60]

Chapter 6

Guarding Governor Reagan

'It's ironic that the two presidents [Kennedy and Reagan] who most tolerated and believed in protection while I was in the Secret Service are the only two who were shot.'

Former Secret Service agent Lynn Meredith

Former film star and former president of the Screen Actors Guild, Republican Party stalwart Ronald Reagan announced his candidacy for Governor of California on 4 January 1966 before a nationwide television audience. He '... had never ... campaigned for an elected position' before and no one 'ever did more ... to launch a national political career', historian H.W. Brands wrote. Reagan had only been a Republican for two years, having identified with liberal causes for much of his life as a registered Democrat. 'And with one speech (given during his cross country speaking tours for General Electric) he became the most attractive Republican in America'.[1] In 1964 Reagan's support in Barry Goldwater's presidential run further enhanced his appeal to prospective voters.

Reagan was easily elected to the governorship by a margin of nearly 1 million votes over the incumbent Democrat, Pat Brown, and was instantly characterised as a leading Republican candidate for president appearing on the cover of *Newsweek* the week following his win.

Stu Spencer, who worked on Reagan's campaign for governor, was not surprised by the ex-Hollywood star's victory over his Democratic opponent Pat Brown. 'He was the best candidate I've ever dealt with,' Spencer said. 'I've dealt with a lot of good candidates, but he was exceptional. Why? Number one, he had a core, he had a sense, he had a belief system. His ego never got in his way.'[2]

During the 1966 campaign Reagan's security team included former LAPD police officer Bill Friedman, the first to be hired, and retired LAPD Lieutenant Niel Nielson. The team also included an armed California

Highway Patrol officer, Dale Rowlee, who became Reagan's driver. He would later be appointed to Governor Reagan's security detail during the period when Reagan was governor-elect and then governor.

The Reagan team were given the use of a DC-3 plane by the owner of American Turkey Farms. Not only did the owners provide the plane but also the services of a pilot and stewardess and flew the candidate all over California.

Los Angeles Police Department motorcycle/traffic police officer Chuck Ward volunteered as personal security for candidate Reagan and stayed on when Reagan was governor-elect. When Reagan took office in January 1966 Ward was called on for bodyguard work in-state and out-of-state when required. Ward said his work for Reagan was a 'labour of love . . . he treated me fine . . . Just like I was a friend . . . he never issued any orders'.[3]

When Reagan first arrived in Sacramento the security for the state's thirty-third governor was practically non-existent but a contingent of California State Police bodyguards was soon organised. The new unit all attended gun qualifying courses both in southern California and at the California Highway Patrol Academy in Sacramento. Art Van Court became the governor's security chief. Soon after Reagan's inauguration bulletproof glass and electronic locks on the doors were installed in his office. Reagan's press secretary, Paul Beck, explained the increased security measures as necessary because the governor's office 'is wide open to the whole [Sacramento] capitol park'. Peck added that Reagan received '. . . an average of five death threats a week . . .'.[4]

Reagan's governorship occurred during a time of growing unrest on university campuses. Van Court, a former Los Angeles police officer who always carried a gun, was characterised as 'Reagan's bodyguard'. He walked by Reagan's side when the governor attended a board of regents meeting on one of the campuses. Reagan's limousine had been surrounded by screaming protestors who rocked the car. As Reagan exited the vehicle Van Court protected the governor as they made their way to the entrance of the building. 'You took your life in your hands when you were going with Reagan to a lot of places in those days,' Governor Reagan's chief of staff, William P. Clark Jr, said, 'particularly to a college campus because of the radical element.'[5]

Two highway patrol officers on the security team had the 'complete trust' of Reagan – Dale Rowlee and Willard 'Barney' Barnett. Dale Rowlee, a devout Christian who spent more time at the ranch with Reagan than anyone apart from Reagan's wife Nancy, was responsible for protecting Reagan during the governor's visits to Northern California. Barney, who had previous experience acting as a bodyguard for visiting dignitaries to Los Angeles, was responsible for Reagan's trips to Southern California. He came from the same California Highway Patrol unit as his 'back-up', Wayne Waddell, and also Rowlee. 'Reagan had no friends as most of us use that word,' his chief of staff said. 'There was no one with whom he would just hang out [with]. . . . with the exception of Willard "Barney" Barnett, California Highway Patrol officer and confidant-at the ranch.' In 1970 his security chief was Ed Rickey, who had served on Reagan's Secret Service detail in 1968.[6]

Barnett arrived on the scene as soon as Reagan became governor in November 1966 and stayed with the ex-governor after Reagan left office in January 1975. In Barney the Reagans had a dedicated and trusted security person with a law-enforcement background and a driver having defensive driving skills. As Reagan's political career progressed the couple also knew Barney could work with the Secret Service, given his law-enforcement experience.

Reagan's first introduction as a governor to personal security was shortly after he took office. Reagan had hit a 'panic button' that alerted State Capitol Police to 'immediate and present danger'. Bill Clark Jr, the Ventura County Chairman of the Reagan for Governor Committee, remembered how, '. . . doors swung open . . . we were being confronted by two or more men with drawn pistols levelled at our heads. The previous Pat Brown administration had the alarm installed but had forgotten to inform new administration members and Reagan.'[7]

In June 1968, following the assassination of Robert Kennedy, when President Johnson declared that all candidates from both parties should receive Secret Service protection, the Secret Service '. . . found itself in a hectic scramble putting together multiple security details and coordinating plans for the national conventions of both the Democratic and Republican Parties', agent Michael Endicott said.[8]

Reagan was considered 'technically' to be a candidate even though he never said he was running for the presidency. Reagan had agreed to run as a 'favourite son' candidate for the presidency because the Republican Party had been split between conservatives and liberals ever since the 1964 California primary election when the conservative Barry Goldwater defeated the liberal Nelson Rockefeller for the Republican Party nomination. In 1966 Reagan saw the need to bring the party back together. One of the ways he did it was to invoke his '11th Commandment' – speak no ill or evil of another Republican.

Reagan said the detail had been offered because after the assassination of Robert Kennedy the authorities believed '. . . foreign agents were plotting to kill other American officials'.[9] A newly appointed Secret Service detail arrived at the governor's 'Executive Residence' on 45th Street, Sacramento. It was led by agent John Simpson. On meeting the governor Simpson asked him if he would accept the detail being assigned to him and Reagan agreed after a short discussion with his staff. Ed Meese who had been appointed Reagan's legal advisor in late 1966 said, 'For the first time [Reagan] had a real substantial body of security agents protecting him.'[10]

Shortly after the detail arrived Reagan said he joined them at a shooting range near Lake Malibu, where he used to own a ranch. Reagan told his agents he believed the correct position when firing was to 'crouch'. Agent Simpson corrected him, explaining that '. . . if we are ever shooting at someone, we're between him and his target and we don't crouch'. Reagan said he looked '. . . at these guys, perfect strangers, who had taken a job where, if anyone was shooting at me, they were going to stand up straight between him and me and make themselves a target. I was amazed and grateful.'[11]

Reagan was the victim of numerous threats during his time as governor and his security detail was well aware of the climate of the times during his run for the presidency in 1968. Many threats came from radical groups in California including left-wing anti-war dissenters and Black Power militants. He was a special target among radical groups because he took a hard-line approach to campus disorder and violet anti-war protests. He responded to one campus demonstration by saying, 'If it's to be a bloodbath, let it be now.'[12]

Reagan's closest brush with danger during his 1968 run for the presidency occurred during the two months he was protected by the Secret Service. It came, Reagan said, '. . . at the peak of the rioting on our university campuses'.[13]

On 22 June Michael Endicott was assigned to Reagan's Secret Service detail and was asked to meet the Secret Service head of detail, John Simpson, and other agents including Doug Duncan, Ed Hickey and John O'Toole at Washington DC's Marriott Hotel where Reagan had given a speech. Reagan, Van Court and the detail flew on a private plane to Los Angeles with a brief campaign stop in Kentucky. The remainder of the detail took separate flights to Sacramento to guard Reagan's home, 341 45th Street, and his Capitol office which was 5 minutes away. Agents from the Los Angeles office provided extra security for Reagan when the party landed at Los Angeles then drove to his Pacific Palisades home.

Endicott said Governor Reagan '. . . wasn't living in the governor's mansion, because it had fallen into disrepair and was being renovated, so he was living in Sacramento in a nice home. One night we got an anonymous tip that there might be some type of terrorist activity about to go down, courtesy of the Black Panther Party.'[14]

On 9 July 1968 agents Doug Duncan, Bob Horan, Bob Barker and Michael Endicott were on duty working the 4 to midnight shift at the mansion, which was situated near the Oak Cliff area of the city. Oak Cliff was known to police as an African American 'flashpoint' section of the city in the event of civil disruption. Sacramento police had informed Reagan's detail that police intelligence indicated that 'racial unrest was likely' that night but after small disturbances broke out the police had apparently 'stabilised the situation'.

At about 10.30 pm Endicott was stationed at one of the 'guard positions' in his car outside the house armed with a six-shot Colt revolver and an Uzi machine gun. He was talking to another agent Bob Horan when they received a radio message from Duncan telling them that two men were approaching the house armed with Molotov cocktails. Endicott passed his Uzi to Horan who ran to the front door. Endicott exited his car and yelled at the two men ordering them to halt. Before the men had a chance to light the petrol bombs they discarded them and ran away.[15]

Duncan gave chase and managed to get off a shot but the attackers had already jumped in their car and disappeared. Endicott gave chase to the second attacker but stopped when he realised the governor's mansion may have been under attack from a second group.

When Sacramento police arrived at the scene Endicott spoke to them then noticed Reagan was standing on the front lawn wearing a bathrobe and listening in. When Endicott spoke to the governor, Reagan told Endicott, 'Well, this is certainly much more exciting than watching "The Invaders" [a popular TV show at the time]'. Reagan had watched the show before retiring to bed. 'I was asleep one night', Reagan said, 'when I heard a loud noise outside our window that could only have been a gunshot fired very close to the governor's mansion.' Reagan got out of bed and walked into the hall and was met by an agent who told him not to go near the windows.[16] Before he left the house Reagan had asked an agent if it was 'ok' to take his pistol with him.[17]

The Sacramento police and Secret Service investigated the incident but were unable to bring any charges as their informants refused to testify. They did learn, however, that the group that organised the attack planned to enter the mansion via the back door of the property but when they saw 'the agent with the shotgun' they changed their minds.[18]

Reagan said that his wife Nancy was '. . . very upset by the near miss but I calmed her down assuring her the two men had gone'. When Reagan told reporters who arrived at the mansion after the alarm was raised that an agent had fired a warning shot, the agent interjected and said, 'Governor, we don't fire warning shots. I just missed the bastard.'[19]

In August 1968, when the Republican Party convention concluded with the nomination of Richard Nixon, Meese said, 'All of a sudden, the day after the convention was over, Secret Service security vanished . . . so then I was left with the responsibility of "What do we do now?"' Meese decided to ask agent Simpson to assist him in recruiting someone from the Secret Service to set up a security force for the governor which became known as the 'Executive Protection Service'.[20]

In 1970 during his re-election campaign Reagan revealed that eighty California National Guard military policemen, armed with .45 calibre pistols, had been on active duty '. . . to be bodyguards for key state officials'. The governor said he made the decision based on intelligence concerning 'the general atmosphere of threats from radical groups to try to disrupt the election process'. The guardsmen, Reagan said, had been assigned to a 'great many people' and had been offered to opposing candidates for election as well as state officers including the governor, lieutenant governor, Secretary of State, Controller, Attorney General and Treasurer.[21]

In 1971 Dennis LeBlanc, a California State Police officer, was assigned to the governor's security. When Reagan left the governorship he retained LeBlanc as one of his personal bodyguards. LeBlanc took a leave of absence from the California Highway Patrol between 1972 and 1974 and became responsible for Reagan's security when the former governor travelled around the country for three years giving speeches in preparation for his run for the White House in 1976. It was a time LeBlanc described as 'pretty hectic'.[22] In fact, LeBlanc was Reagan's sole bodyguard and driver during those trips. LeBlanc would later work for Reagan in the White House as deputy director of special support services.

During this period LeBlanc said Reagan was:

> . . . constantly writing a lot of the time. It was on a legal pad where he'd write things out longhand. . . . he would always fly first class

> . . . he'd sit by the window and I'd sit in the aisle seat next to him.
> It didn't matter whether or not there was a movie being shown and
> all the lights were out – he'd turn on his reading light and would
> constantly be writing. Beginning in 1975, LeBlanc said, '[Reagan]
> drove up to the ranch from Los Angeles and back down the same
> way many, many times for the next two years. Either Barney or I
> would drive and Reagan would sit in the back seat with his legal
> pad writing.'[23]

LeBlanc, who described himself as a 'jack of all trades', also had the job
of supervising Reagan's 688-acre Santa Barbara ranch, Rancho del Cielo
('Ranch in the Sky'). Reagan was about to finish his second term as governor
and he was looking for a refuge from the pressures of the outside world.
Reagan, who many friends considered a 'frustrated cowboy', was instantly
taken with the property. In November 1974, the Reagans bought it for about
$527,000. They renamed it Rancho del Cielo and set about refurbishing the
rundown property. It provided the couple with the joy and serenity that no
other place had given them.

The house on the ranch was little more than a shack with a corrugated
aluminium roof. With the help of LeBlanc and Barney Barnett, both of whom
stayed in the small bunkhouse behind the main house, Reagan knocked out
the walls, laid a vinyl floor in the veranda and installed a tile roof. The ranch,
situated almost 30 miles northwest of Santa Barbara, was a 2½-hour journey
and situated in a remote area.[24]

Working with Reagan on the ranch, LeBlanc came to see him as:

> . . . a guy's guy, a great person to work with. He didn't ask me to do
> anything he wouldn't do. . . . the natural tendency is to go ahead
> and do those harder things so he didn't have to do them. He didn't
> like that. He wanted to be involved in everything . . . he always
> gave you that relaxed feeling.

LeBlanc also observed how Reagan enjoyed 'a simple life' working with the
ranch hands. 'He's not a simple man,' LeBlanc said, 'but he's not a complicated man. He was just a great guy to be around.'

Former agent Louis Mason recalled how the president interacted with
others no matter what station in life they held. He recalled the time when

Reagan was having trouble sleeping one night. Not wanting to wake his wife at 2.00 am, Reagan knocked on the door where Secret Service agents were billeted and asked if they would play a game of cards with him. 'He was very respectful,' Mason said. 'He asked us for permission to come into a room in his own house. . . . He was an everyday man. He was not like, "I'm Mr. President, and that's how you will address me." When you were with him, you felt like you were with a friend.'[25]

Secret Service agent John R. Barletta spent many hours on horseback at the ranch with the president and wife Nancy, and observed first-hand their strong, loving relationship. During one ride Barletta saved Reagan's life when the president was thrown by a bolting horse. Barletta said he was ready to give CPR as the unconscious Reagan wasn't breathing. When he heard him cough, he put an oxygen mask on him, '. . . his tongue was curled and his eyes were back in his head,' Barletta said. A helicopter was called and soon the president recovered.[26]

However, it was Dennis LeBlanc who witnessed the downside of the Reagan presidency during the president's visits to his ranch. LeBlanc said Reagan always treasured his time there especially after he became president, but he also brought the burdens of his office with him. When a Korean airliner was shot down early in his presidency and later when the Space Shuttle *Challenger* exploded, LeBlanc saw Reagan phoning the relatives of the victims from his ranch house. He was 'visibly affected', LeBlanc said. 'It really hurt him.'[27]

Many journalists on the campaign trail liked Reagan and concurred with his agents' characterisation of the candidate. Few of them who spent time with him disliked him. They also liked the fact he was never 'mean-spirited' and had a sense of humour.

Secret Service agents knew that guarding candidates they disliked should not interfere with their protective mission. This was not a problem for Reagan's details who always looked forward to guarding him during his presidential campaign runs in 1968, 1976 and 1980. In fact, in their zeal to look after a candidate they admired they were sometimes accused of being too protective, keeping supporters away, which provoked criticisms that Reagan looked 'too imperial'.

Although Reagan was '. . . always personable with the [Secret Service] agents he did not get personal,' former agent Joseph Petro said, 'he knew faces' but did not think it was necessary to memorise their names. Reagan referred to his guards as 'the fellas' and it was rare to find one agent who did not like him. Reagan's bodyguards during the 1980 presidential campaign described him as moral, honest, respectful and dignified.[28]

The 1976 election was the first presidential campaign where candidates received Secret Service protection when they qualified for matching funds from the Federal Election Committee. During the campaign Secret Service bodyguards were assigned to 'any candidate who raised at least $5000 out of at least twenty states'.[29]

Reagan was assigned a team of twenty-one agents led by agent Joe Parris. The candidate respected the professionalism of his protective detail and did not challenge the advice his agents gave him about what was best for his protection. Although later, when Reagan became president, he did not like wearing the protective but uncomfortable 4lb Kevlar bulletproof vest, there were times his agents insisted upon it and he complied.[30]

Marty Vencker joined Reagan's Secret Service detail in late 1975 when the candidate was living in Pacific Palisades. Vencker witnessed how Reagan's neighbours became angry and frustrated as his detail blocked streets to ensure the candidate's safety. 'But Reagan had great support with us,' Vencker said. 'Maybe it was because he'd made four Warner Brothers movies based on the life of [Secret Service agent] William Henry Moran.'[31]

Vencker was with Reagan on a campaign plane flight when the candidate nearly died. As the plane took off the agent saw Reagan quickly rise from his seat and gasp. A peanut had stuck in his throat. A Reagan aide quickly grabbed him and performed the Heimlich manoeuvre, saving his life.[32]

Former Secret Service agent Thomas Blecha remembers that during the campaign Reagan came out of his home in Bel Air to drive to Rancho del Cielo. Another agent noticed that he was wearing a pistol and asked what that was for. 'Well, just in case you guys can't do the job, I can help out,' Reagan replied.[33]

A number of biographers have stated Reagan never carried a gun. Biographer Lou Cannon, said, 'It's so off the wall that I don't know what to say. I think it's a fantasy, at best.'[34]

However, Jim Kuhn, Reagan's former executive assistant and right-hand man, saw a .38 pistol in Reagan's briefcase. Reagan's Secret Service body-guard John Barletta also saw Reagan with a pistol during a flight to Japan after he left the presidency. Barletta reports that Reagan told his agent-in-charge Garrick Newman, 'If you ever need another weapon, I've got one here', showing Newman his snub-nosed revolver he kept in his briefcase. 'They don't search me, you know,' Reagan said.[35] Barletta also said that Reagan was in the habit of carrying a gun long before he became president. When Reagan was working for the General Electric Company, giving speeches to the company's workers around the country, he once opened his hotel window after hearing screams and saw a woman being accosted by a man. Reagan pointed his pistol at the attacker to warn him off.[36]

Craig Shirley also reports that Reagan had begun the practice of carrying a gun after John Hinckley's 1981 assassination attempt. Shirley said that Reagan defied his wife and the Secret Service and 'routinely' brought the gun aboard flights on Air Force One and Marine One. The 78-year-old president thought he just might click open his briefcase in order to 'help out'. When suffering with Alzheimer's, the Secret Service took the gun from him in 1994.[37]

During the primary election campaign Robert Powis became one of Reagan's favourite agents. Powis worked out of the Secret Service's Los Angeles office. During campaign rallies he would help Reagan by guiding him to spectators wanting to shake the candidate's hand. He would engage him in long conversations especially when Reagan visited his newly purchased ranch. Agents accompanied the former governor on his daily horse rides and helped him to clear brush and chop wood. Each day his agents would notice something they thought was quite odd, given the fact they knew he was an unassuming man without any signs of vanity. Reagan would lie down beside his pool with a sun reflector. 'Getting a coat of tan', he would tell his bodyguards.[38]

The most disturbing threat to Reagan during the campaign came from a fan of 'Squeaky' Fromme, one of Charles Manson's girlfriends who had tried to shoot President Ford months earlier. His name was Michael Lance Carvin.

In November 1975 the Secret Service investigated Carvin. He was the son of a wealthy real-estate broker and a drop-out from the University of Denver and the University Tampa. He worked in the Denver area before returning to Florida in September 1975. Carvin had recently been acting 'strangely' according to his parents. He had been watching newscasts about Squeaky Fromme and said, 'She is right. She must go free.' On a trip to Las Vegas he tried to buy a gun but did not satisfy state laws.

On 10 November 1975 Carvin phoned the Secret Service's office in Denver from the Light House Point public telephone and threatened to harm Reagan as well as President Ford and Vice President Nelson Rockefeller unless Squeaky Fromme was freed.

Shortly after announcing his intention to challenge President Ford for the Republican Party presidential nomination Reagan went to Miami to give a 15-minute outdoor speech to about 400 supporters gathered in front of a Ramada Inn near Miami's International Airport. At the conclusion of his speech, he stepped off the podium and moved along a security rope set up to keep crowds 15yd away.

As Reagan shook hands agents dived into the crowd and grabbed Carvin as he pointed a fake .45 calibre toy gun at the candidate. Three Secret Service agents reacted swiftly and subdued Carvin before handing him over to local police officers. Reagan later said he had '. . . gone over to that side of the audience to see an old friend. I just thought someone had fallen down and I was persuaded by the Secret Service to leave.'[39] Reagan appeared to be unfazed by the purported attempt on his life and never stopped smiling. Alluding to the fact that being attacked seemed like a rite of passage, an aide later told the press that, '[If Reagan] didn't feel like a candidate before he does now.'[40] It was an eerie forerunner to the attack made by John Hinckley in March 1981.

Two court-appointed psychiatrists found Carvin sane and competent to stand trial. In April 1976 a Florida jury convicted Carvin of numerous violations including making oral telephone threats against the lives of President Ford, Vice-President Rockefeller and Reagan. He was also convicted of attempting to intimidate and interfere with Reagan during campaigning by aiming 'an authentic-looking toy gun' at the candidate.

The judge sentenced Carvin to four-and-a-half years in prison for the telephone threats (three terms, to be served concurrently), one year for impeding Reagan's campaigning, served consecutively to the four-and-a-half year term, and three four-and-a-half year terms for the letter threats, to be served concurrently with each other and consecutively with the one-year term.[41]

However, because he was free before sentencing, he was able to jump bail. He left his parent's Pompano Beach home on 3 June 1976 taking his father's car and $60 in cash and several of his father's credit cards. After a tip-off from a store clerk he was caught the next day at a central Florida convenience store.[42] Carvin was paroled in 1982.

In 1998 Carvin became a 'repeat threatener' when he sent four letters to radio talk-show host Howard Stern from his home in Las Vegas. In one letter the 44-year-old Carvin threatened Stern and his family calling him 'Dead Man Walking'. In another threat Carvin wrote, 'I will absolutely without a doubt, kill you and this is 100% guaranteed.' For this offence Carvin was given a two-and-a-half year prison sentence.[43]

Following the attack on Reagan a Secret Service local field office spokes-man said that because of the enormous field of candidates that year 'it could only get worse'.[44] Responding to Carvin's assault, Reagan said, 'I don't think there's anything you can do except place your confidence in these guys, and they're awfully good.' According to author Craig Shirley, the attack on Reagan was 'the beginning of Reagan's lifelong love affair with the Secret Service'.[45]

* * *

By late 1979 the list of Republican presidential candidates had grown to include Senators Howard Baker, Bob Dole, Lowell Weicker, John Anderson, Philip Crane, John Connally and George H.W. Bush. However, it was Reagan who dominated the primaries, driving from the field all the candidates except George Bush, who posed the strongest challenge. Bush had won primaries in Pennsylvania and Michigan, but it was not enough to turn the tide.

On 20 May 1980, after Reagan won the Michigan and Oregon primary elections he had secured enough delegates to guarantee victory as the Republican Party nominee and chose George H.W. Bush to be his running mate.

During the campaign Reagan received numerous threats including a threatener from the 'American Indian Party' who asked Senator Hayakawa to help him, 'even to the point of killing Reagan'. Another threat warned Reagan not to go to Oregon, 'If Reagan comes here he may get his head blown off.'[46]

However, the most serious threat to Reagan came after his election. At the time of Reagan's inauguration in January 1981 Jerry Parr was the head of Reagan's Secret Service detail and it was Parr who saved Reagan's life when the president was shot outside the Washington Hilton Hotel on 30 March 1981.

As Reagan exited the hotel and strolled to his car shots rang out, striking White House Press Secretary James Brady in the head and Washington DC police officer Thomas Delahanty in the neck. Secret Service agent Timothy McCarthy attempted to shield Reagan with his own body and was shot in the abdomen. One bullet hit the window of the limousine, while the sixth and final struck the president under his left arm, and soon lodged in his lung.

Parr landed on top of Reagan, who hit the car's transmission hump hard. Reagan didn't know a flattened Devastator slug had bounced off a rib and lodged an inch from his heart. After telling the driver to go back to the White House, Parr ran his hands over Reagan's body, but found no injury. Then he noticed bright red blood on Reagan's lips, which his Secret Service medical training told him must have come from the president's lungs. He told the driver to head for George Washington University Hospital. The president had already lost 3 pints of blood when he staggered into the emergency room.[47] Parr saved Reagan's life by recognising he had to ignore White House protocol which stipulated the president should be taken to the secure White House after any attack. Instead, Parr directed the driver to the hospital. Parr said:

> He was pale, though lucid. His lips were turning a little bit blue. I didn't have to be a doctor to sense someone really in trouble. There was no choice. He was bleeding so badly from his mouth. It was frothy, red blood. I've had other agents who were in my position before me say 'Jerry, I'd have taken him to the White House first.' I tell them, if you'd seen him, like I saw him, you'd have known that was the wrong place to go.[48]

If Parr had gone first to the White House Reagan might possibly have died by the time he arrived at the hospital. 'The real hero – and I give him every credit – is Tim McCarthy, who spread his big Irish body out there and takes one of those shots that certainly would have hit me or the president,' said Parr. 'It happened on my watch. I feel responsible that [Hinckley] got that close in the first place.'[49]

Parr's daughter Kim said Nancy Reagan credited her father for saving her husband's life. 'Nancy Reagan never blamed my father or the Secret Service for the assassination attempt on her husband,' Kim said. 'She was a very classy lady. Ever since the 1981 assassination attempt, she and my dad had been very close and they continued to be good friends throughout their lives,' Kim said. 'Looking back, it's obvious she just had class and undying support for her husband and for the office of the Presidency. She really was a great lady.'

'Jerry Parr was one of my true heroes,' Nancy Reagan said. 'Without Jerry looking out for Ronnie on March 30, 1981, I would have certainly lost my best friend and roommate to an assassin's bullet.'[50] However, Reagan's agents were criticised for their poor protection measures. According to journalist Ron Kessler, the Secret Service wanted Reagan to emerge from a speech at the Washington Hilton without any spectators present. The Reagan White House staff overruled the Secret Service, though, insisting for public-relations purposes that crowds have access to the president. The Secret Service improperly backed down, Kessler alleges, and let unscreened bystanders within 15ft of Reagan. As a result, John W. Hinckley Jr had a clear shot and almost killed the president.[51]

Following the assassination attempt the Secret Service became plagued with 'copycat threats'. The agency said they were 'worried publicity over the . . . threat to President Reagan's life could prompt a string of "copycat" assassination attempts'. In the six-month period following the attempt on Reagan's life the average number of threats increased by over 150 per cent compared with a similar period the previous year.[52] The Secret Service were on high alert investigating threats to 'finish the job' by unconnected individuals all across the United States resulting in numerous investigations. One investigation centered around a Nebraska farmer who became a taxi driver. He had become obsessed with film actress Jessica Savitch. Copying Hinckley, he wrote a series of letters to her implying he might kill Reagan in order to win her love.[53]

Throughout his presidency Reagan was targeted by numerous would-be assassins who were as dangerous as Hinckley, including:

- A would-be armed assassin nicknamed 'Catman' stalked President Reagan to Gracie Mansion in New York, but his shot was apparently blocked by agents. Catman was so named by agents because he had sent threatening letters to the president along with numerous photos of cats.[54]
- Mary Frances Carrier stalked President Reagan to Dumfries, Virginia, a location where the president rode horses. On 1 April

1981, two days after Reagan was shot, Carrier was stopped by local police on harassment charges. In her car they found an envelope that bore several phrases threatening the president, including the phrase 'Murder the President' and an 'an arsenal of weapons'. When questioned by Secret Service agent Kevin Mitchell, Carrier said, 'It is too bad Hinckley wasn't successful in killing that son-of-a-bitch. . . . if need be I would shoot him . . .' She was found guilty of threatening the president.[55]

• After Reagan left office Gregory Stuart Gordon climbed the fence of his Bel Air home and attempted to 'strangle' the former president before he was subdued by agents.[56]

* * *

John Hinckley, the man who attempted to assassinate President Reagan on 30 March 1981, was found not guilty by reason of insanity and was ordered to live at St Elizabeth's Hospital in Washington DC, for treatment. Over the years, the court loosened restrictions on him. In the last decade the amount of time Hinckley has been allowed out increased as doctors said he was no longer a danger to the public or himself. While at St Elizabeth's he began a romantic friendship with a former patient, Cynthia Bruce.

In 2009 a judge allowed John Hinckley multiple ten-day visits to his mother's home in Williamsburg. Federal judge Paul Freidman freed Hinckley after thirty-five years of confinement at St Elizabeth's Hospital on 5 August 2016. The Hollywood actress Jodie Foster, with whom he became obsessed when he shot Reagan and wanted to 'win her love', was horrified at the news.

Hinckley's release was permitted on the condition he live with his mother, who was widowed in 2008. She agreed to allow her son to stay at her home as part of his eventual return to society. Another condition of the release was for Hinckley to see a psychiatrist once a week in Williamsburg.

Hinckley's release came with many other restrictions including a prohibition on using alcohol, possessing any firearms, possessing memorabilia of Jodie Foster and he was prohibited from contacting many people associated with the assassination including the Reagan family. He was also prohibited from watching violent films, speaking to the press and visiting past homes of US presidents.[57]

Chapter 7

Searchlight and Pathfinder

'If somebody is going to make an attack, he will be able to do so even though [Secret Service agents] are surrounding me.'

Richard Nixon

'They'll never impeach me as long as I have him [Agnew] here.'

Richard Nixon

'If a discussion to eliminate me – through an automobile accident, a fake suicide or whatever, the order would not have been traced back to the White House . . . [It was] an indiscrete threat from the White House that made me fear for my life.'

Spiro Agnew

On Election Day, 8 November 1960, following a hard-fought campaign for the presidency against his Democrat opponent, John F. Kennedy, Richard Nixon decided to go to Mexico. He had been scheduled to head to the Ambassador Hotel in Los Angeles to wait for the election results but on the way there, riding in a black Cadillac limousine and accompanied by one Secret Service agent and a military aide, he changed his mind and headed for Mexico. The group changed vehicles and walked to a follow-up car driven by a Los Angeles police officer. Nixon took over driving and they managed to evade the waiting press at the Ambassador.

The Nixon group drove to La Habra, California, where Nixon visited his mother before driving south along the Pacific Highway, stopping off at a gas station where he told a startled gas-station attendant he was simply going for a 'little ride', something he often did as it was one of the few sources of relaxation for him.

After crossing the border and having lunch in Tijuana, Nixon handed over driving duties to the LAPD officer and sat in the convertible's rear seat and headed back north. During the return journey Nixon wanted to stop off at the Mission of San Juan Capistrano. It was 'one of my favourite Catholic places,' Nixon said. When they arrived the vice president proceeded to give the group a tour of the Mission. 'For a few minutes, we sat in the empty pews for an interlude of complete escape,' Nixon later recalled. Nixon and his three road-trip companions arrived back in Los Angeles to await the results of the 1960 presidential election. Nixon was either going to be the thirty-fifth president or a retired politician.[1]

Nixon lost the 1960 election to Kennedy. However, he was never to experience the freedom he enjoyed on his Mexican trip when, four years later, he once again won the Republican nomination for president.

* * *

Nixon was not unfamiliar with presidential security arrangements. When he became vice president in 1953 he met with Secret Service Chief U.E. Baughman and told him he did not want Secret Service protection while he was in Washington but agreed to minimal protection elsewhere. Later, he said he would accept two bodyguards in Washington and more when he was out of town.[2]

During the eight years as vice president Nixon had a harmonious relationship with his detail. He was, 'Always scrupulously polite and very appreciative of everything we did,' Baughman said. However, Baughman added, he had, '. . . utter disregard for his own personal safety during his eight years as vice president'. Baughman had come to think of Nixon as 'an assassin's delight, a murderer's dreamboat'.[3] Another Nixon bodyguard said the vice president had, '. . . delusions of safety' and was 'far too brave for his own good'.[4]

However, Nixon's agents admired the vice president's courage. During a visit to Burma they accompanied him to a village where communist agitators were addressing villagers in English. It was an anti-American 'frenzy', according to agent Rufus Youngblood. Nixon told his detail to stay behind as he walked towards the speaker and engaged him in a conversation. Youngblood said Nixon's actions calmed the crowd. 'The mood of the crowd changed', he said, 'to a much friendlier tone.'[5]

Former agent Ken Giannoules protected Nixon during the 1960 campaign. 'There was nothing "buddy-buddy" about the job,' Giannoules said. 'Our job was to protect the president, the Office of the President. We did not have personal relationships with the presidents or their families.' However, he did take note of the differences in style of the people he protected. 'Nixon was all business,' Giannoules says. 'And so was his staff. You could set your watch based on his itinerary. He followed it to the minute.'[6]

The candidate gave specific instructions that the Secret Service should provide him with only a small detail for the 1960 campaign. In August at a Greensboro, North Carolina, election rally he gave the Secret Service specific instructions about his protection in the midst of the crowd telling them not to interfere with the crowd's attempts to reach out to him. It resulted in an agency report spelling out how their job was rendered impossible. The agents were prevented from dealing with the 'manhandling' Nixon experienced from the 'mad, mauling melee' the report stated.[7]

Nixon continued to ignore the advice of his agents and waded into what they described as 'uncontrollable crowds'. During an election campaign stop in Chicago the Secret Service was unable to prevent Nixon from sustaining a knee injury when he was giving an outdoor speech on the city streets and was jostled by the crowd. Strict instructions were given to the police who were told to back off when Nixon campaigned. As a result, his two daughters were nearly trampled to death outside the Blackstone Hotel. The Secret Service concluded all three members of the family were 'extremely close to personal injury for several minutes'.[8]

Nixon had the advantage over Democrat hopeful John F. Kennedy in the election. He had eight years' experience as Eisenhower's vice president and acquitted himself well on two occasions when Eisenhower was taken ill and he had stepped in to become *ipso facto* head of the government. Nevertheless, he lost the election to Kennedy but only by a narrow vote margin.

When Nixon became president-elect in November 1968 he acted oblivious to the changes in security that had been instituted in the years following the 1960 election. He felt he could act independently of his bodyguards leaving the constraints of his security behind. Former agent Lynn Meredith said that on his last full-time protective assignment with Nixon, '[He] would walk between his office and apartment in New York City every day at lunchtime – something that would never be allowed now.'[9]

Former Secret Service agent Clint Hill believed President Nixon, now codenamed 'Searchlight', was suspicious of the Secret Service and was frequently unwilling to heed their impartial advice. He thought Nixon's aides John Ehrlichman and Bob Haldeman were 'unscrupulous' and a bad influence on the president.[10]

Hill also believed Nixon had '. . . an ego that needed to be stroked so badly that the man was willing to take calculated risks – risks that might cost him his life'.[11] Hill said Nixon was 'much more distrustful of the agents and clearly he was taking risks that flew in the face of Secret Service recommendations'.[12]

Nixon's bodyguard would rarely interact personally with him, according to former agent Michael Endicott. The role they held was 'distant and impersonal'.

According to Larry Buendorf this was altogether quite natural. 'Nixon was very shy,' Buendorf said. 'He would greet you, he'd acknowledge that you were there, but you could see that he was pretty much focused on a lot of other things as a president probably should be. Some presidents acknowledge their agents all the time; others are tied up with other things.'[13] Nixon told his Director of the White House Military Office he would never become 'familiar' with his agents. 'They've got a job. I've got a job,' Nixon said. 'The minute you start getting familiar with people, they start taking advantage. I always hold those guys at arm's length. I think they're great guys and do a fine job but I don't believe in letting your staff move into the quarters.'[14]

However, the image of a 'remote' Nixon was not always a description some of his agents agreed with. Agent Dennis McCarthy recalled the December 1972 night he was stationed on the back porch of the house Nixon was staying in during a presidential trip to the Azores for a meeting with the French president. McCarthy heard a radio broadcast of a football match coming from Nixon's room. After the game had ended Nixon exited his room and began to discuss the game with McCarthy. 'For half an hour', McCarthy said, 'we discussed the playoffs, the season, and the [Redskins'] chances in the Super Bowl, just like two guys getting together over a couple of beers to discuss the game . . .'.[15]

There were times, however, when Nixon would reveal his dark side. His aide, John Ehrlichman, said Nixon approved of 'strong-arm tactics' when it came to handling unruly protestors. He instructed Ehrlichman to 'have the Secret Service rough up hecklers' during the 1968 campaign. The agents balked at Ehrlichman's instructions and refused. When Nixon was told they would not commit any violent acts he asked his aide to organise 'some kind of flying goon squad of our own to rough up the hecklers, take down their signs and silence them'. Nixon's team began to hire off-duty police officers and firemen to act as 'ushers'. They willingly removed demonstrators who blocked the candidate's way, sometimes using violence.[16] But agents did appreciate the way Nixon organised his campaign. Learning from experience he did not work his staff to the point of exhaustion and agents were appreciative of the way he had periodic breaks in his schedule, promoting efficiency and durability in his staff and his agents.[17]

In 1972 Nixon's re-election campaign was equally less stressful on agents. His strategy was not the campaign his Democrat opponent George McGovern wanted – which was to engage Nixon on the issues. Instead, Nixon adopted a 'Rose Garden' campaign highlighting his successes like withdrawal from Vietnam, the economic and diplomatic opening to China and a nuclear arms deal with Russia.

However, Nixon did not stick to his plans. During summer and autumn 1972 he campaigned across the country, frequently responding to anti-Vietnam demonstrators with bravado. During one campaign event he deliberately taunted Vietnam War protestors, raising his hands in his V for victory sign and the crowd threw rocks, eggs and bottles. Many people were injured. 'To this day I don't understand the ego that must drive someone to risk his life and those of others for a few moments of adoration,' former agent Clint Hill said.[18] Former agent Marty Vencker said it was a challenge guarding the 'grandstanding' Nixon when he was campaigning. During his campaign rallies supporting Republican candidates in the 1970 mid-term elections, Vencker said that anti-Vietnam demonstrators threw rocks and left ten dents in the president's limousine.[19]

The Secret Service also soon became a subject of controversy during Nixon's presidency. The agency faced allegations it was losing its independence and pandering to political favouritism. Agent Rufus Youngblood accused Nixon's aides of trying to 'bend the service to their will'. The evidence to support Youngblood increased after the election when it was revealed Nixon had enlisted Secret Service agents to spy on his political opponents, Edward Kennedy and George McGovern.[20]

Secret Service agents told author Ronald Kessler they considered Nixon to be one of the 'strangest of presidents'. One agent spoke of how Nixon would take walks on the beach at his Key Biscayne 'Florida White House', wearing a sports jacket and tie. He thought it looked 'strange'. According to Kessler, Nixon was extremely depressed a lot of the time, and more so during the Watergate Scandal. As his depression and paranoia accelerated, he drank excessively and reacted to events around him to the point of paranoia. Kessler also reported that Nixon had a poor relationship with his family, and was, in many ways, a recluse. Pat Nixon was quiet most of the time. One agent who spoke to Kessler said, '[Nixon] seemed to have no relationship with his wife, Pat.' When the Nixons were in their San Clemente, California, 'Western White House' Nixon would play a nine-hole golf game with his family. During the entire hour-and-a-half game, one agent said, the President did not say one word to his wife and daughters.

Nixon's wife Pat was suffering the strains of the Watergate crisis that was quickly enveloping her husband and she soon took to drinking excessively. She often couldn't remember things, one agent said, including where her own house was. Agents, who were on alert for illegal immigrants coming ashore at the beach near the San Clemente house, on one occasion found the First Lady in the bushes on her hands and knees trying to find her way back.[21]

There were certainly some stresses throughout their marriage according to an old friend and adviser to Nixon, Father John Cronin. Cronin said that when Nixon was vice president he asked him to go to his home in the Washington suburbs to get some papers. 'When I knocked', Cronin said, 'Pat opened the door and said . . . "He can't get back in by sending a priest!"' Cronin returned to Washington and Nixon told him he and his wife were '. . . just having a little problem now'. Cronin realised that Nixon was not going home at night. 'He kept a hotel room in the District for nights when he had to stay late at the Senate, or for other reasons. And he was just living there,' he said.[22]

Additionally, there is some evidence that Nixon had battered his wife on three occasions; once when he lost the lost the race for California Governor in 1962; the second incident occurred during Nixon's time in the White House; and the third incident happened shortly after his resignation at his San Clemente beach home. During that incident Pat Nixon was taken to hospital. She told doctors her husband had hit her.[23]

Veteran Secret Service agent Rufus Youngblood concurs with the descriptions of Nixon's character provided by some of Nixon's former agents. Youngblood liked Nixon when he was vice president but believed he had changed. 'Time had done something to him,' Youngblood said.[24]

George McGovern, Nixon's opponent in the 1972 presidential election, said that although Nixon was not a 'bad president in many senses of the word' – opening the door to China, establishing a policy of detente with the Soviet Union and removing troops from Vietnam – he had 'one big flaw, and that was his personal paranoia that somebody was going to take what was rightly his away from him'.[25]

However, there were some agents on Nixon's detail who offer a different characterisation of Nixon. Their stories reveal more about Nixon's personality than anything Kessler's sources might offer. Many of them spoke of the president as a 'moral man' who was always respectful to his agents and the White-House staff. Former agent Louis Mason said he did not condone what Nixon did with regard to Watergate, but he believed Nixon's presidency actually taught some 'valuable lessons about leadership'. Though Nixon was not the only person involved in the scandal he was loyal to his people and didn't 'throw people under the bus . . . I'm not saying he didn't do something wrong,' Mason said, '. . . all of them were wrong, but he took responsibility. What you have to learn in business and what you have to learn in your dealings with others is, don't do anything you are not willing to stand up and take responsibility for.'[26]

Agent Michael Endicott also saw a different Nixon. Endicott would join Nixon for swims in the ocean. 'When we were in up to our waists [in the sea],' Endicott said, 'he said, "Let's go" and we both dove into the water at the same time. . . . when he rolled over and began treading water I was nearby. He talked about the stimulating plunge into the water and how much he enjoyed Red Beach.'[27] Former Secret Service agent Marty Vencker said Nixon '. . . treated you like a human being. He always asked about your mother, and when somebody in your family was sick, Nixon was the first to send a card or flowers.'[28] White-House staff concurred. Kate Andersen Bower said, 'The Nixons were formal with the staff but they were kind – and his kindness made watching the president's slow unravelling so painful.'[29]

Additionally, Nixon had a sense of humour; a description of the president which is missing in Kessler's account. Nixon was watching television one afternoon at his San Clemente home while feeding biscuits to one of his dogs. 'Nixon took a dog biscuit', former agent Richard Rapasky said, 'and was looking at it and then takes a bite out of it.'[30] Air Force One pilot Colonel Ralph Albertazzie flew Nixon to California after the president's resignation. Greeting Nixon, he told him he was going to be his pilot. Graciously Nixon replied, 'Well, Ralph, sorry I never made you a general.' Albertazzie replied, 'Sir, there's still time.'[31]

Agent Mike Endicott also saw Nixon in a different light. Endicott said that some agents do indeed have a '. . . close relationship with the person they protect. It is a private matter and generally not made public. Richard Nixon did not necessarily have a public persona as being warm and friendly but we know differently.'[32]

A number of agents also witnessed how Nixon was far from being the aloof and arrogant president as some of his detractors have portrayed him. One evening, Nixon built a fire and forgot to open the flue damper. In the chaos that erupted agents came running. 'Can you find him?' one of the agents asked the other. 'No, I can't find the son of a bitch,' the other agent said. From the bedroom, Nixon responded, 'Son of a bitch is here trying to find a matching pair of socks.'[33]

Additionally, the agents who spoke to Kessler related many stories that occurred during the most stressful part of Nixon's presidency. Nixon was drinking, he was exhausted and he was physically and mentally unwell. He also had to bear the burden of being the first president in United States history to resign his office.

The descriptions of Nixon provided by many agents are supported by reporter Seymour Hersh, who said the president was 'invariably kind and courteous' to secretaries and valets. More than once, Hersh said, 'he would wait silently and without complaint the few times he was put on hold by an officious secretary or an unaware operator'.[34]

Towards the end of his presidency Secret Service agents saw how disturbed the president was becoming due to the stress of the Watergate investigations. During a five-nation trip to the Middle East, including Egypt, Nixon was suffering from a resurgence of phlebitis, a condition that could result in a blood clot. Ignoring medical advice, in Cairo he shocked his bodyguards by wading into crowds shaking hands. The agents barely managed to extricate him and take him to his limousine. He rode in open-top cars once in Saudi Arabia without his bodyguards. When Nixon's doctor Major General Walter Tkach told agent Dick Kaiser of his concerns, Kaiser responded, 'You can't protect a president who wants to kill himself.'[35] Marty Vencker said, 'Sometimes [it] seemed that he went out of his way to take his place as a martyr beside Jack Kennedy.' Vencker recalled that during Nixon's first term his favourite limousine was the SS 100X – the restored midnight-blue Lincoln Continental in which Kennedy was shot.[36]

Nixon's ill-health resulted in his 'dying' on the operating table. Stephen Bull said that in September 1974 Nixon underwent a surgical procedure to prevent the phlebitis clot from breaking free and going to his heart. He went into cardiac arrest and 'flat-lined'. 'He was dead for whatever that period of time was, two, three, five seconds', Bull said, '. . . it was quite more severe than I think anyone ever realized'.[37]

Nixon's values were traditional – God, country, family. He believed he was right to defend those values during his presidency in the face of free love, drugs, denial of God, selfishness and indulgence. However, it is easy to see why he was hated. His presidency ended in ignominy following the exposure of his abuse of power. Despite his immense political skills, intelligence, ability and achievements, he allowed his uncontrollable paranoia to destroy him. Nixon didn't need to use political dirty tricks to win re-election in 1972, but he did exactly that against the Democratic National Committee and the Democrat nominee, George McGovern. Nixon and his top aides covered up the break-in at the Democratic National Committee headquarters at the Watergate Hotel in Washington DC, and by summer 1974, it was revealed that a secret White-House taping system held evidence of the cover-up. When the recordings of Nixon's conversations were eventually released it was all over for the thirty-seventh president. The recordings revealed Nixon had lied about covering up the Watergate break-in and he resigned before his impending impeachment.

* * *

President Nixon received numerous death threats as vice president and president including an attempt by a mentally ill Samuel Byke who was shot and killed by police officers as he tried to hijack a plane to crash it into the White House.

However, during his 1972 campaign he was the victim of two serious attempts on his life. The first attempt came from Arthur Bremer who stalked Nixon during a presidential trip to Canada. He wrote in his diary that he did not expect to survive the assassination attempt. 'I was supposed to be Dead a week & a day ago,' he wrote. 'Or at least infamous.' He added that he believed his diary would be examined as closely as the Dead Sea Scrolls once he took his victim down.[38]

Bremer often wrote flatteringly about the Secret Service agents he observed protecting the president. Bremer noted one 'smart [Secret Service] agent' who impressed him, two vigilant 'SS with binoculars' and a fourth 'squared-away agent', whom he nicknamed 'Mr. Moustache' for his 'neatly run operation'. Bremer wrote in his diary, 'What a dope! Those noisemakers were all on news film! He should of photographed the quiet ones.'[39]

Unfortunately for Bremer Nixon's security was too stringent and, frustrated by his failure to assassinate the president, he turned to his diary once again. In it the would-be assassin recorded that he despaired of ever getting near the president. Bremer then turned his attentions to George Wallace (see Chapter 9).

The second serious threat came from a 27-year-old 'well-off' investment banker and right-wing radical, Andrew B. Topping. Topping's wife had committed suicide on 6 July 1972, shortly after the birth of their son. He blamed 'pro rightist forces beyond his control' for his wife's death. When police came to his apartment to investigate they noticed Topping had 'several guns'. One of the weapons found in a closet was a .45 Webley, the same kind of weapon Topping's wife used to kill herself. Topping was arrested and charged with firearms violations but released on his own recognisance pending his trial.

A week before his arrest on the gun charges Topping had made a request for an appointment to see President Nixon. His request prompted Secret Service agents to interview him and carry out a background check. A short while later one of Topping's acquaintances arrived at Secret Service offices in New York and told agents that Topping had asked him for assistance in finding an assassin who would kill the president. The Secret Service responded by arranging for one of their undercover agents, Stewart J. Henry, to pose as an assassin for hire as a ruse to trap the would-be assassin.

On Thursday, 10 August 1972, Henry and the unnamed acquaintance met with Topping at the Central Park Boat Basin in New York City. After negotiations, Topping handed over $1,000 and made it clear the money was 'to kill Nixon'. The 'assassination' was planned for the following week. Topping was immediately arrested and taken to a local police station. He was charged with 'threatening and attempting to kill the president of the United States'.[40]

* * *

John Simpson was appointed head of Spiro Agnew's detail when the former Maryland Governor was chosen as Nixon's vice-presidential candidate at the Republican National Convention in Miami in August 1968. Michael Endicott was also assigned to the detail and after the convention was over he escorted Agnew, now Secret Service codenamed 'Pathfinder', to San Diego aboard Agnew's new campaign plane and then on to Hawaii for a campaign stop. It was the start of one of the most difficult assignments for the Secret Service as anti-war demonstrators flooded campaign rallies and heckled the man who acted as Nixon's 'hatchet man'.

Agnew's combative style during the campaign won over many supporters on the right by his attacks on liberals. After the election Agnew continued to berate the left and became well known for his speeches attacking liberals as, 'an effete corps of impudent snobs who characterize themselves as intellectuals' and his denunciation of the media as 'nattering nabobs of negativism'. During his time in office he became the hero of the 'silent majority' of Americans who supported the Nixon administration.

When Spiro Agnew was inaugurated in January 1969 he became the most closely guarded of any vice president in US history. Although his detail was made up of only ten agents or so watching him during visits to small towns, he had up to twenty-five agents acting as a moving wall on college campuses where emotions ran high.

The Special Agent in Charge of the Vice Presidential Protective Division was Samuel E. Sulliman, a Bucknell University graduate who had worked in the White House as well as the Boston, Chicago and Washington field offices. He succeeded John Simpson following the vice president's inauguration. Many of the agents on Agnew's detail were hold-overs from Vice President Humphrey's detail.

Agnew's agents had a 'good relationship' with the vice president according to one of them, agent Clint Hill. In fact, Hill developed a 'friendship' with Agnew. Whenever the vice president was travelling by plane Agnew would ask Hill and the vice president's doctor to join him in a game of pinochle.[41] 'He was extremely respectful of our team of agents', Hill said, 'and he trusted us to the point that if we made a recommendation or told him not to do something, he complied without question.' During a vice-presidential visit to a Vietnam military base, which was experiencing incoming sniper fire, Agnew asked Hill if it was safe. 'That was typical of my relationship with Agnew,' Hill said. 'He trusted my judgement and never questioned my decisions.'[42]

Before vice presidents lived in the vice-presidential mansion, holders of the office lived in their own homes. Agnew's apartment was on the fourth floor in the east wing of the Sheraton-Park Hotel in Washington DC. Inside the seven-room layout – occupied by his wife Judy and their teenage daughter Kim, one of their four children – was a battery of four surveillance cameras. The Secret Service also installed a hidden buzzer under the rug of the front door that signalled any pressure. These electronic and electric watchdogs connected with a next-door Secret Service apartment. Under the law at the time, there was no specific provision for protection of a vice president's wife, but Judy Agnew was always accompanied by at least one agent when she went out.

When Agnew travelled around the country or abroad, the Secret Service accorded him the same advance planning it gave President Nixon, involving inspection of hotels and other public places to be used and consultations with local police on such matters as parade routes.[43]

During his time as vice president Agnew had many close calls when anti-war demonstrators attended his speaking venues. During a visit to Manila anti-American protestors hurled a 4in bottle of explosive powder at his limousine and as his motorcade entered the US Embassy compound three Molotov cocktail bombs were thrown. The bomb thrown at Agnew landed 15ft away emitting smoke but failed to explode.[44]

Unaware of events that were to follow, the press speculated in 1973 that Nixon would have to resign because of his involvement in the Watergate Scandal and be replaced by his vice president. The press also characterised Agnew as the leading contender for the Republican presidential nomination in 1976.

The idea that Agnew was a future president was not an opinion shared by President Nixon or some of Nixon's supporters. Nixon was disappointed in the way Agnew conducted his trips abroad and spent too much time playing golf. Nixon, Ehrlichman and Haldeman believed Agnew did not perform well on a 1971 trip to Africa. In an Oval Office conversation, in which they discussed how to dump Agnew from the 1972 ticket, the Africa trip was brought up. Nixon was also irritated that the vice president seemed to be 'too buddy-buddy with the Secret Service [and] too undisciplined with his staff,' he said.[45] The person Nixon wanted as his vice-presidential candidate in 1972 was John Connally, the former Texas Governor who was Treasury Secretary, and he was still trying to persuade Connally to replace Agnew on the ticket just three days before the 1972 Republican Party convention. However, the conservative wing of the Republican Party was favourably inclined towards the man who took on the liberal press and liberal establishment and Agnew remained on the ticket.

As the president's troubles over Watergate mounted, some Nixon loyalists saw Agnew as insurance against impeachment, certain that Congress, if they brought impeachment proceedings against Nixon, would not want to turn over the White House to a relatively untested, highly controversial vice president. 'They'll never impeach me as long as I have him here,' Nixon said.[46]

* * *

Agnew was the opposite of Nixon as far as personal morality was concerned. Throughout his term as vice president he was involved in extramarital affairs, including one affair with a staffer, while promoting family values. In fact, he purchased an expensive watch and other quality jewellery for her. Unknown to the public and press, his Secret Service agents drove Agnew to meetings with girlfriends in Washington hotels and arranged for women to stay in adjoining hotel rooms when Agnew was travelling. Agents on his detail once clandestinely took Agnew to a room on the fourth floor of Washington's Regis Hotel and left him there unguarded for 3 hours, at his request. A former agent on Agnew's detail said, 'Leaving him in an unsecured location was a breach of security. As agents, it was embarrassing because we were facilitating his adultery. We felt like pimps.'[47]

However, a large number of Agnew's agents respected him and found the vice president and his wife to be very friendly and accommodating. 'Agnew was kind of a cop buff,' recalled former Secret Service agent Chuck Vance. 'He enjoyed being with the agents and their wives. He would throw parties for them, and they would throw parties for him.'[48]

Agents said the reduction in stress after Agnew took over from Hubert Humphrey was 'dramatic' mainly because of the increase in vice-presidential protection and the assignment of forty-eight agents compared with the twenty-seven agents under Humphrey.[49] Jerry Parr said the new vice president and his wife Judy '. . . to a unique degree . . . recognised our humanity and appreciated our service. They asked about our families and looked at photos of our kids.'[50] When the Agnews flew to Hawaii in October 1970 they asked the agents' wives to accompany them seeing no reason why an empty Air Force plane would incur any extra cost to the government if they could utilise the empty seats. Parr called it an 'incredibly generous gesture'.[51] When Parr arranged a house party for the detail the Agnews attended they worried that agents on that particular shift would miss the party. Parr said the agents had 'unconsciously moved from professional detached concern' for the Agnews to 'affection'.[52]

On his numerous trips to Greece in his capacity as a Secret Service agent, Ken Giannoules accompanied Agnew who was the only Greek-American to hold the office of vice president. The 1971 trip took Agnew to Athens and Thessaloniki, and then he delivered an address at the square in Kalamata – the Peloponnese region from where Giannoules' family originated.

'He didn't know any Greek, so I taught him a few Greek words on the helicopter ride – a few things to include in his speech,' Giannoules said.

The agent had hopes that the Greek-American would one day become president. Though Giannoules didn't have occasion to spend much time with Agnew – he was not on Agnew's permanent detail – he heard a lot of positive stories about the vice president from his colleagues. 'Not everyone follows directions well,' Giannoules elaborated, 'but Agnew always did. His wife [Judy] was especially nice.'[53]

The agents on Agnew's detail were, however, not immune from criticism. Some media outlets accused them of '. . . riding roughshod over all who get in their way, that they can exercise rudeness when it suits their mood . . . the suspicious nature of the Secret Service has been extreme'.[54]

Agnew's presumed accession to the presidency appeared to be just as improbable as his fall when reports began to appear in the press that he had accepted bribes. During his time as Governor of Maryland Agnew had received large amounts of cash from Maryland contractors and when he became vice president the practice continued. Agnew, like governors before him, saw the payments as a 'facilitating fee' but they were actually bribes in order to award contracts to those who paid up.

In summer 1973 the Justice Department began to investigate Agnew after they received information he accepted $100,000 in cash brides when he served as Baltimore County executive in Maryland prior to the vice presidency as well as taking bribes as vice president.

Agnew did not deny receiving the payments and that any payments he received from Maryland government contractors did not influence his actions as governor. He also insisted that no contracts had been awarded to 'incompetent engineering contractors'.

Agnew's defenders argued that had the vice president admitted his crimes he might well have made a case that he was the victim of overzealous prosecutors who denied him his civil rights leading to his inability to receive a fair trial. Instead, in October 1973, Agnew decided to plead *nolo contendere* (no contest) to the charges and agreed to resign. Historians have speculated that had Agnew known how weak Nixon was with respect to the Watergate Scandal he would have fought the charges.

Agnew's agents witnessed the terrible strain the vice president was under. During rides in the vice president's limousine they often heard Judy Agnew weeping and observed how Agnew had lost weight during the crisis.[55]

However, Agnew tried to keep his humour intact. During his trip to the courthouse Agnew humorously surmised he might end up in jail. The agents accompanying him offered to go with him. When Agnew resigned, Secret Service agent Giannoules '. . . felt utter disappointment'.[56]

The bond between Agnew and his agents was so strong that when he resigned from office a number of them volunteered when off duty to move his effects out of his office in the Old Executive Office Building across the street from the White House into his temporary offices on Lafayette Square.[57] Agnew's disgrace was taken personally by Jerry Parr who saw the vice president as a 'father-figure'.[58]

Following Agnew's resignation it was revealed the former vice president feared for his life during the summer months when the bribery scandal erupted. Agnew was worried that if he did not resign he would be killed and he elaborated on this in his memoirs. Shortly before his resignation, he wrote, he received 'an indiscrete threat from the White House that made me fear for my life'. Quoting from a memorandum sent by his White House military aide General Mike Dunn, Agnew said Dunn had met with Nixon's Chief of Staff Alexander Haig and been told that there was an 'ironclad' case against his boss for corruption and also evidence to show Agnew had evaded income tax. Haig told Dunn, 'The clock is running . . . anything may be in the offing . . . It can and will get nasty and dirty . . . the president has a lot of power – don't forget that'. Agnew said the warning 'sent a chill through my body . . . I might have a convenient "accident"'. Agnew said he knew that there were 'men in the White House' who professed to speak for the president and could order the CIA to carry out 'missions that were very unhealthy for people who were considered enemies . . . I might have been in grave danger'. Agnew became 'frightened' and 'feared' for his life. 'If a discussion to eliminate me – through an automobile accident, a fake suicide or whatever,' Agnew wrote, 'the order would not have been traced back to the White House.'[59]

However, the most credible context for Agnew's 'worries' was that Alexander Haig had meant Agnew could be sent to jail for his malfeasance in office.

In 1980 Agnew also blamed 'Zionists' for his ousting. He wrote to Fahd bin Abdulaziz Al Saud, then crown prince of Saudi Arabia, saying:

I need desperately your financial support. Your highness is already familiar with the unrelenting Zionist efforts to destroy me . . . the Zionists in the United States knew that I would never agree to the continuance of the unfair and disastrous favouring of Israel and they had to get me out of office there so that I would not succeed Nixon.

Since 1974, Agnew said, 'The Zionists have orchestrated a well-organized attack on me [through lawsuits], to bleed me of my resources to continue my effort to inform the American people of their control of the media and other influential sectors of American society.'[60]

The Secret Service acceded to President Nixon's wishes that the former vice president retain his detail following his resignation. He was protected for four months by twenty-one agents assigned to guard him. The agents were with Agnew at Frank Sinatra's house in Palm Springs when the General Accounting Office announced that the protection was a 'violation of the law'.

The Secret Service looked to Nixon to decide what they should do. Nixon had been caught up in his own battle to save his presidency during the Watergate crisis and he quickly abandoned his support for his former vice president saying that '. . . it is revolting that a penny of public funds should be spent on this impenitent felon as he lives the high life'.[61]

Accordingly, the head of the detail received a message from Washington to cease guarding the former vice president. Agnew said the agents were withdrawn:

> . . . while I was visiting Frank Sinatra to attend the late Jack Benny's 80th birthday party in mid-February 1974 . . . suddenly one evening the Secret Service with me [twelve agents who Agnew jokingly referred to as the 'Dirty Dozen'] received orders to cease my protection at midnight. The White House communications people came in that same evening and pulled out the White House phones, and the agents left at midnight. I had not been notified by anyone until the head of my detail informed me. It was an eerie occasion and a sad one . . . It was like losing part of my family when they left.[62]

* * *

Agnew received numerous threats against his life during his vice presidency including:

- During a visit to Auckland New Zealand Agnew met with Prime Minister Keith Holyoake as a dozen anti-war demonstrators stood vigil outside his hotel. The group were the remains of a 500-strong protest march. During the early hours a 32-year-old unemployed man, Sydney James Arthur, phoned the hotel on two occasions stating that Agnew's assassination was being planned by the 'Progressive Youth Movement', the organisers of the protest. The caller described the would-be assassin's modus operandi – he would go to the hotel suite armed with a Colt .45 revolver while wearing a government messenger's uniform. Arthur was arrested in the hotel lobby and sent to a psychiatric hospital for observation.[63]
- In 1970 the FBI received information from an Air Force Intelligence officer that a radical New York City group, the 'East Side Crazies', were planning to assassinate Agnew. Despite an intensive investigation no member of the organisation was charged.[64]
- During a visit to Frank Sinatra's home in Palm Springs California to play golf two Secret Service agents heard what sounded like gunshots. They also heard what to them sounded like an 'incoming round whine through the trees about 20 feet up, causing birds in the trees to fly'. The Secret Service agents and Sheriff's deputies checked out the area but found nothing. The FBI reported that agents '. . . believed it to be a shot but could not be sure'. No arrests were made.[65]
- In May 1972 Agnew's limousine approached the Lausche Building Fairgrounds in Columbus, Ohio, for a fundraising dinner. There were 300 anti-war protestors present and as 50 surged towards Agnew's car, a 1970 Cadillac Fleetwood, a missile, later believed to be a rock, struck the rear window breaking the glass. After an intensive investigation the FBI and the Secret Service were unable to identify the protestor who threw the rock.[66]

- In September 1973 the FBI received a phone call providing information that a man threatened to 'put a bullet in the vice president's head'. The caller had just had dinner with the threatener who said he would be travelling to the airport the next morning armed with his Winchester Magnum rifle which was fitted with a telescopic sight. When he was interviewed by the FBI, he said he had decided not to go to the airport. No charges were made.[67]
- In 1974 the Bristol, Tennessee, Chief of Police informed the FBI that an African American man he had arrested threatened to kill the former vice president. He was described as a mental patient who had been arrested for assault with a deadly weapon, carrying a concealed weapon and resisting arrest. The threatener had stated that when he was released from hospital he was going to 'get a gun and kill Spiro Agnew'. No charges were made against the mentally ill man.[68]
- In 1974 the Symbionese Liberation Army, which kidnapped Patricia Hearst, threatened to kill a number of government leaders including the former vice president. The group members were either arrested on terrorism and kidnapping charges later or died in a shoot-out with police in Los Angeles.[69]

In 1996 77-year-old Agnew died of undiagnosed acute leukaemia at Atlantic General Hospital in Berlin, Maryland, near his summer home in Ocean City. (His year-round home was in Rancho Mirage, California.) Following his death, former Senator and 1996 Republican Party presidential candidate Bob Dole eulogised him as a hero – a man who '. . . earned the support of millions of his countrymen because he was never afraid to speak out and stand up for America'.[70] A number of agents asked Judy Agnew to allow for a larger funeral to accommodate them.

Chapter 8

Beating Nixon

'. . . the Presidency is certainly a dangerous job, and so is campaigning for the Presidency. Candidates say that's the price you have to pay if you're going to be in public life.'

Former Secret Service Director H. Stuart Knight

'The members of McGovern's Secret Service detail took some of the sting out of the final result – 49 states lost, only Massachusetts and the District of Columbia won – with a surprise for him the next morning. Overnight, they'd had one of the presidential limousines flown in, and it was idling curbside, when he came down for the motorcade that would take him to the airport and the flight back to Washington.'

Democratic Party consultant Bob Shrum

Following the 1968 assassination of Robert Kennedy President Johnson had made it clear he wanted *all* the candidates protected for the continuing presidential election campaign. The many assignments took a toll on the Secret Service. In 1968, agents put in more than 270,000 hours of overtime. Accordingly, the mission of protecting candidates in a violent and volatile time in US politics became a near impossible task.[1]

The new security procedures had an effect on individual candidates. They ranged from very little for men like Vice President Humphrey and George C. Wallace, who were already heavily protected, to considerable for Senator Eugene McCarthy. Rockefeller had been used to having bodyguards around him and did not see his life, as other candidates did, as disrupted. McCarthy, who never had a bodyguard, could now avail himself of improvements in his campaign including having a hotel room awaiting him on his campaign trips. His improved security also included having his hotel rooms searched in advance for bombs. However, McCarthy was not originally receptive to his twenty-seven-man security detail. On a visit to Phoenix after the assassination, he said the protection was something of a nuisance but at least had the virtue of 'interfering with television cameramen'.

Twenty-one Secret Service agents were assigned to each presidential candidate, to work in three 8-hour shifts of seven men each. At any one time, however, there were only two or three agents with the candidate while the others checked out the campaign rally sites or leapfrogged ahead to advance security arrangements in the next city on the schedule. The Secret Service agents were assisted in their protective mission by locally based Secret Service agents, state troopers, local police, plain-clothes detectives and treasury agents not attached to the Secret Service.

New York Governor Nelson Rockefeller was Richard Nixon's primary opponent for the 1968 Republican Party nomination. He had spent millions of dollars of his own money in unsuccessful attempts to win the Republican nomination in 1960 and 1964. On a visit to Washington in the early 1960s, as Rockefeller's private plane flew over the city, he saw the White House visible below. A passenger asked him how long had it had been since he first wanted to live there. Rockefeller replied, 'Ever since I was a kid. After all, when you think of what I had, what else was there to aspire to?'[2]

In 1967 Rockefeller routinely employed only one state trooper as his bodyguard and occasional chauffeur even though he was continually referred to by the press as a '1968 presidential candidate'. Rockefeller had reason to deploy extra guards because he had recently received a 'death plot' against him by 'gambling interests' who had been the 'objects of a state-wide crackdown'.[3]

In 1968 the Secret Service detail assigned to Governor Rockefeller worked harmoniously with his state trooper bodyguards. Agents protecting him were naturally apprehensive following the assassination of Robert Kennedy. When Rockefeller resumed his campaign for president he delivered a speech at the Baltimore Hotel in Los Angeles. He was protected by ten agents, New York State Police and Los Angeles police officers. Following the speech, the bodyguards escorted the governor during a tour of Watts, the Los Angeles riot-torn neighbourhood. When Rockefeller gave a televised statement eulogising Kennedy the security detail was so nervous they demanded that all the doors in the studio be locked.[4]

Rockefeller enjoyed a good relationship with his assigned agents. For their part, they recognised that his down-to earth personality belied the fact he was born into US aristocracy. However, some of his detail could not understand why the governor was a Republican when his policy positions were clearly liberal. When Rockefeller addressed the National Press Club his detail spoke openly to a reporter about their protectee. One of his agents was amazed Rockefeller acted like a Democrat. 'I thought that guy was supposed to be a Republican', the agent said, 'but he made a 20-minute speech, and for 15 minutes of it he eulogized the political philosophy of a Democrat, the late Senator Bob Kennedy. He even got in a plug for another Democrat, Senator Eugene McCarthy, whom he praised for doing so well in the New Hampshire primary.'

Another agent observed, 'I thought we were to keep tabs on a guy who was trying to pick up support in the GOP Convention, but that's not how his presidential speech came through to me. Bob Kennedy left almost 400 delegates behind him, and Rocky sounded as if he were trying to snatch them for use at the Democratic Convention.'

A third agent agreed:

> It sure is a crazy mixed-up assignment that the chief sent us on this time. We're supposed to guard a Republican governor, but he was muffled to the ears in the martyr hood of a late Democratic senator. He kept quoting the late senator's lines. He took a swipe at GOP National Chairman Ray Bliss as well as mussing up Dick Nixon. If I were Hubert Humphrey or Gene McCarthy, I'd be worried about Rockefeller's switching parties and slashing his way to nomination in Chicago.

The agent in charge of the detail reminded the group that protection of the candidate was the main priority despite the political views of their protectee. 'You fellows are just setting up a lot of excuses,' he said. 'It doesn't make any difference . . . we're still responsible for keeping him alive.'⁵

Rockefeller lost the 1968 party nomination to Nixon who went on to win the general presidential election against his Democratic Party opponent Hubert Humphrey. The apex of Rockefeller's career came in 1973 when Vice President Spiro Agnew resigned and the former New York Governor and presidential aspirant was chosen by President Ford to be his vice president.

Throughout his political career Rockefeller had been the victim of numerous threats against his life from political extremist groups including the American Indian Movement, the Black Panthers, the Black Liberation Army, the Ku Klux Klan, the Attica Brigade, Christian Identity and the Posse Comitatus.

Serious threats to Rockefeller's life included:

- In February 1967 the FBI considered an incident involving a potential stalker as serious enough to carry out a full investigation. In a heavily redacted FBI memo agents refer to a woman who '. . . discussed the wealth of the Rockefeller family and that she could draw a map of the Rockefeller estate [Pocantico] and knew the guards and when their shifts changed, [She] claimed to represent the American Nazi party and wanted . . . to supply 8 Colorado Minutemen to work with . . . 8 members of the American Nazi party to kill Nelson Rockefeller'. The information came from an informant who 'wanted to clear [redacted] from any action that was undertaken against the Rockefeller family'. The subsequent FBI investigation did not result in any arrests.[6]

- When an inmate from the Bronx State Mental Hospital escaped the FBI initiated a manhunt because the patient had threatened to kill Rockefeller. When he was on the run he had written to his wife stating he was going to kill not only Rockefeller but also President Nixon. His wife took the letters to New York Police's 45th Precinct where she was interviewed. The matter was handed over to the Secret Service. The FBI files do not disclose whether or not the patient was apprehended or charged with threatening a public official.[7]

However, the most dangerous threat to Rockefeller's life came from the Posse Comitatus ('power of the county') in 1975 after he became vice president. The organisation was a loosely based coalition of anti-government white supremacist groups with a membership of around 15,000. The FBI estimated that perhaps 150,000 others supported them during the 1970s. A single group was usually made up of two or three dozen members. Posse organisations were unanimous in their belief in local self-rule; most groups claimed independence from federal (and in many cases state) authority, recognising only the local level of governmental authority.

The central core of their beliefs was 'Christian Identity', an extremist ideology that alleged Jews were 'gradually taking over the U.S. banking and financial systems'. Jews were purportedly the offspring of Satan and they had 'seized the land and the power of white Christians'. Christian Identity groups advocated the extermination of 'the blacks, browns and other minorities' who were the 'henchmen' of Jews.

The Posse first began to attract media attention in 1974, when Thomas Stockheimer, the leader of the Posse in Wisconsin, was tried and convicted for assaulting an Internal Revenue Service agent.

But it was a 1975 threat to federal government leaders that first brought national attention to the extremist group. Nelson Rockefeller became a top target for the Posse because the vice president was considered to be one of the major 'money czars' involved in an alleged global conspiracy. The Trilateral Commission, of which Rockefeller was a member, was the '. . . ultimate evil – Jewish bankers who are conspiring to take over the world and ruin their lives'. The Posse alleged the commission was trying to force farmers off the land through the banks and the Federal Deposit Insurance Corporation so it could control food production and the economy.

In 1975 a group of Posse members based in Little Rock, Arkansas, plotted to assassinate Rockefeller. An informant reported the plot to the FBI which conducted an 'extremist matter/white hate' investigation and 'foiled the plot'. However, there is no indication that anyone was ever tried for the offence of threatening the vice president.[8]

During their investigation of the Rockefeller plot the FBI uncovered seventy-five Posse chapters in twenty-three states. They also discovered that the organisation appealed to people living in the rural Midwest as the farm crisis of the 1970s worsened. The Posse saw the crisis as an opportunity to spread their message and create a white, Christian republic. Subsequently, the profile of the extremist organisation rose leading to further investigations by the Bureau from 1980 to 1986 on possible domestic security/terrorism activities.

The group eventually lost momentum after a number of violent confrontations with law enforcement and was eventually supplanted by better organised anti-government and racist groups.

* * *

By 1972 the ranks of anti-war demonstrators had swollen making the campaign season as dangerous as 1968. Secret Service intelligence had informed agents of new ways college student leaders had thought up in order to disrupt a candidate's speech or prevent a candidate's limousine from arriving at a speaking venue.

In fact, the 1972 presidential campaign began to take on the image of battlefield conditions. The candidate's car would be followed by a Secret Service follow-up car. Behind that would be the 'war wagon', an ordinary saloon car that would be stocked with heavier weapons, ammunition taped to the ceiling and Uzi machine guns which were easily spotted by the crowds.

The work of the agents was demanding. One day an agent would be in snowy New Hampshire and the next in sunny Florida, sweating profusely due to the clothing protocols in place. Many agents became anxious and nervous as the candidate arrived at a venue like a college campus. They knew they would often be met with hostility. They would breathe a sigh of relief when the candidate reached the relative safety of a hotel lobby.

Undermanned due to the new primary election protocols giving security coverage to an increased number of candidates, the stress of the job took its toll. There were no criteria in effect at the time for choosing which candidates would receive protection. 'We didn't have any criteria for choosing who'd get protection,' former Secret Service agent Jerry Parr said. '. . . Yes, even Benjamin Spock, the baby expert, got Secret Service protection when he ran for president in 1972.'

One former agent told of how three agents suffered nervous breakdowns due to overwork. One agent was found in a New Jersey forest walking around aimlessly with a gun in his hand. Another agent walked away from the candidate's plane as the party boarded. The plane left without him. A third agent became so disturbed he began to talk of dreams he had in which he encountered 'faceless assassins'.[9]

During the Miami Republican and Democratic party conventions in the summer of 1972 the Secret Service were assisted by the Bureau of Alcohol, Tobacco and Firearms (ATF). Bureau Director Rex Davis said it was 'an honour to receive the request [for assistance] since in our eyes it meant the Secret Service placed special confidence in our Special Agents to perform this vital service to the nation'.

In 1972 the ATF had over 100 agents assigned to the conventions and they worked under the direction of the Secret Service. The Bureau was later instrumental in foiling assassination plots against President Nixon, Davis said, including a September 1973 plot in which an ATF agent working undercover was offered $25,000 to kill the president. The Secret Service was immediately contacted and the would-be assassin was arrested the day after he made the offer. In the second instance quoted by David an ATF agent met with an informant who gave information that a member of a 'militant organisation' had met with the informant. The would-be assassin was 'a twice convicted felon, armed with three high-powered rifles and a possible automatic weapon,' Davis said, and he was 'en route to a city where a meeting with a militant organisation was to take place to discuss the president's visit to that city'.[10]

The new law stipulating which candidates were provided with protection in 1972 provided for a special advisory committee made up of the Democrat Senate Majority Leader Mike Mansfield; the Senate Minority Leader, Hugh Scott; the House Speaker, Carl Albert; the House Minority Leader, Gerald R. Ford of Michigan; and a public member, former Senator Thomas Kuchel of California, to decide which candidates should receive protection.

The committee worked with John B. Connally, Secretary of the Treasury, who was in overall charge of the Secret Service. It decided that protection, which cost up to $200,000 a month for each candidate, would be extended to those having at least 5 per cent of the vote in the Harris or Gallup opinion polls. If unannounced candidates drew 20 per cent in the polls they too would receive protection. This excluded Shirley Chisholm and Wilbur Mills. The criteria for protection of candidates were gradually refined over the coming decades.[11]

At the outset of the campaign New York Mayor John Lindsay was considered a front-runner for the Democratic Party nomination. He felt his personal guard, New York City Police Officer Pat Vecchio, was sufficient protection and decided to forego any Secret Service protection offered if he went on to be successful in the primaries. He said it would spoil his 'New York City style of campaigning'.

Lindsay had a poor showing in the Wisconsin primary and withdrew from the race in April 1972. However, he still faced threats of assassination. In June 1968, in the week after the assassination of Senator Robert F. Kennedy, Carlos Alberto Valle stalked him. When the mayor appeared on the steps of city hall for an outdoor ceremony, a police officer noticed Valle had a knife protruding from his belt. The officer pulled the knife out and arrested the would-be assassin. Valle was sent to a mental institution, and no charges were made against him. Nine months later he called the local offices of the FBI and Secret Service and threatened to kill President Nixon. In 1981 he threatened to assassinate President Reagan.[12]

The majority of the candidates fell by the wayside during the primary campaign leaving Humphrey, Muskie, McGovern and Wallace as the leading contenders. Nixon was challenged by Republican anti-war candidate and Congressman 'Pete' McCloskey, but it was a quixotic effort.

Even though he had announced he would not be a candidate, Ted Kennedy was still considered to be the candidate to beat in the event he changed his mind and threw his hat into the ring.

Nixon clearly identified which opponents had the best chance of ending up securing the Democratic nomination and running against him in the November general election. On 28 May 1971, thirteen months before the June 1972 Watergate break-in, he directed his top aide to use wiretapping and permanent tails and coverage on the leading Democrats, Edward M. Kennedy, Edmund S. Muskie and Hubert H. Humphrey.

At the time, George McGovern was showing little support in the polls and therefore was not a threat to the president. 'Keep after 'em,' Nixon told White House Chief of Staff H.R. (Bob) Haldeman in an Oval Office conversation on 28 May 1971. Nixon wanted to dig up information on their families and finances. 'Maybe we can get a scandal on any of the leading Democrats,' Nixon added, 'I don't know. Maybe it's the wrong thing to do . . . but I have a feeling if you're gonna start, you got to start now.'[13]

Despite a widespread appreciation of the risks of traditional campaigning – open motorcades, speeches from unprotected podiums and shaking hands with spectators at rallies – candidates continued to campaign in this way.[14]

Edmund Muskie was considered to be the leading candidate at the start of the Democratic primary season mainly due to his outstanding performance as Hubert Humphrey's vice-presidential running mate in 1968. During the 1968 campaign Muskie shot to prominence when he engaged a heckler at a campaign appearance in Pennsylvania. Muskie didn't insult or talk over him, or insist that he be silenced or evicted. Instead, he invited him to come up and share the microphone to state his case, provided he would then quietly let Muskie make his response. The audience and the national media were impressed.

Nixon's re-election team hired Elmer Wyatt to spy on Muskie. The retired cab driver was accepted by campaign staff as a volunteer, and he became the candidate's chauffeur. He was paid a thousand dollars a month by Nixon's men. One of his jobs as a volunteer was to ferry documents from Muskie's Senate office to campaign headquarters. There were so many documents to Xerox that Wyatt rented an apartment and a Xerox machine. He would make copies of everything and send them to the Nixon campaign.

That was just one of the many 'dirty tricks' the Nixon team engaged in while working to undermine Muskie. Some of the others were nothing more than juvenile pranks. On more than one occasion, members of Nixon's team sneaked into a hotel where the Muskie people were staying, stole all their shoes from the hallway and threw them in a trash can.

Muskie's candidacy appeared to be crumbling. He began to '. . . get crotchety at night about going places the staff had set up for him . . . he started muttering about how the bastards were pushing him too far and fast, trying to kill him'. The campaign was clearly having an effect on his emotional state.[15]

The attacks and dirty tricks played on Muskie came to a breaking point in February 1972, when a New Hampshire newspaper published a fake letter to the editor that had been planted by the Nixon campaign. In the letter, Muskie was accused of laughing when a member of his staff referred to French-Canadians by the insulting term 'Canucks'. The newspaper also ran an unflattering piece about Muskie's wife, which portrayed her as a crude joke-teller.

On the morning of 26 February 1972, shortly before the 7 March New Hampshire primary, Muskie stood in front of the offices of the *Union Leader*, calling its publisher William Loeb a liar and criticising him for impugning the character of his wife. Newspapers reported that Muskie cried openly, allegedly breaking down three times. Muskie maintained that if his voice cracked, it cracked from anger; Muskie's nemesis was the same editor who referred to him in the 1968 election as 'Moscow Muskie'. The tears, Muskie claimed, were actually snowflakes melting on his face.[16]

The attack nevertheless had a devastating effect on Muskie's presidential hopes. Despite winning both Iowa and New Hampshire, his campaign lost momentum and he withdrew from the race leaving only two viable candidates during spring and summer 1972 – Hubert Humphrey and George McGovern (Wallace, though he won the support of millions of voters, was never realistically believed to have any chance at the Democrat nomination).

At first Muskie failed to gain the respect of some of his bodyguards during his short presidential campaign. When he was campaigning, Muskie demanded that the Secret Service carry his golf bags. An agent on his detail refused and later told author Ronald Kessler, 'He took vacations in Kennebunkport. He would play 18 holes of golf every day. He would cheat and kick the ball in the hole with his foot and pick it up and put it in.'[17]

Despite running a short campaign, Muskie was still subject to threats against his life. Many were classed as 'serious' by his Secret Service detail. The head of the detail told him that '. . . at the outside there might have been 35 . . . possible threats which were deemed serious enough to investigate . . . of those 35, perhaps two or three were regarded as of sufficient seriousness for the agents actually to interview the persons involved'.[18] Muskie believed that of the thirty-five cases the majority of them were '. . . people who had backgrounds of mental disorder of one kind or another'.[19] One individual who threatened Muskie was so mentally ill prosecutors decided not to charge him.

Muskie's support for the Clean Air Act and the Clean Water Act passed by Congress in 1972 also got him into trouble. It provoked an unknown letter writer in Bryantown, Maryland, to include the Senator in a 'death list' of Democrat candidates who were going to be 'blown to bits' in their Capitol offices on 4 May 1972, according to the letter writer. Both the FBI and Secret Service were especially concerned about the threats as a year previously a major bomb blast had caused serious damage to the Capitol building, though no injuries were sustained.

Muskie also received hand written letters with similar letters going to George McGovern and Ted Kennedy. The Muskie letter stated he was going to be assassinated. 'The bomb is supposed to be dynamite with a contact fuse. It is pre-planned', the threatener stated, '[and] the bomb is to be placed under chairs.' The FBI took fingerprints from the letter but was unable to find any matches.[20]

In January 1972 Muskie received a threatening letter signed by 'G.C. Carlton' who lived in Bryn Mawr, Pennsylvania. The letter stated that Senator Ted Kennedy and Senator Edward Brooks 'should be shot'. Additionally, the letter stated that Muskie should be 'deported back to Poland or Rome', and 'somebody should fill you and the bastard harp Kennedy full of lead'. The letter concluded with the wish that Kennedy and Muskie should 'rot in hell'.

In February 1972 the FBI discovered the letter writer had a few aliases but the agency could not find enough evidence to determine the threatener's real identity. The investigation was closed down after an assistant US Attorney in Philadelphia decided the threat did not come under the relevant federal statute for 'threats'.

The same month a caller phoned a number of media outlets claiming that Muskie and Wallace were the targets of the 'Black Military Underground For Revolutionary Justice'. FBI agents interviewed the caller, a Boston man, who they described as 'rambling' and 'emotionally disturbed'. The suspect had attended a meeting the purpose of which was to discuss the assassinations of Edmund Muskie and George Wallace. The plotters were purportedly going to use a new type of bomb that would 'burn rather than explode'. The suspect said he did not want to see Muskie killed as the Senator was a 'good man'. Agents concluded he was mentally ill and the revolutionary organisation he cited was 'dreamed up'. Prosecutors declined to prosecute on the basis of his 'mental instability'.[21]

* * *

Although Edmund Muskie was ahead in the polls, it was George McGovern who Nixon wanted to run against because he was a liberal who adopted left-wing policies. In fact, McGovern became known as the candidate for 'Acid, Amnesty, and Abortion'. Nixon believed he could easily defeat him. Accordingly, Nixon's re-election team worked hard during 1971 and 1972 to undermine Muskie and to deliver the nomination to McGovern – essentially, to pick their opponent.

In the months following Muskie's downfall George McGovern's primary election successes put him in the lead. Although McGovern was initially considered a losing candidate, he came second in the Iowa and New Hampshire primaries and eventually won primaries in many states across the nation. In June 1972 his win over Hubert Humphrey in California secured his nomination.

McGovern had arrived at the position of front-runner for a number of reasons. At first McGovern believed that Ted Kennedy would become the main contender to take on Nixon after his first term in office. However, in 1969 he '. . . heard what happened [at Chappaquiddick; see p. 169 below]. I woke up the next morning with the sun shining in my face, and while I don't believe too much in hunches, I woke up and thought, you know, I'm going to be the Democratic nominee for President because Ted won't run now for sure.'[22]

After the assassination attempt on Wallace in May 1972, McGovern requested – and received – additional security. McGovern also cancelled all campaign activities in the days after Wallace was shot.

McGovern flew 51,465 air miles travelling between 64 cities within less than 3 months of general election campaigning. He campaigned seven days a week, 16 hours a day, for almost two years. 'Fatigue is a treacherous thing. You are haunted by it, yet not fully aware of it. It keeps you from doing your best at anything, whether it's chasing a pretty girl, or making a good speech, or choosing a running mate.' He asked 1964 Republican presidential candidate Barry Goldwater what lessons he'd learned from his defeat to Lyndon Johnson. 'Don't get exhausted,' Goldwater replied. 'It's lying out there ready to trap you and make you do all sorts of half-arsed things.'[23]

McGovern said he was 'very high' on the Secret Service. 'I think they are a highly competent, dedicated and capable group of public servants . . . I can . . . tell you that it is my own judgement that some of us are alive today because we had Secret Service protection,' he said.[24]

McGovern was also aware of the dangers he faced when campaigning, particularly as he approached the closing weeks of the campaign. He understood why campaigners like him risked danger when greeting crowds of supporters. It was a 'kind of symbolic demonstration' which showed that candidates were 'close to the people' he said. McGovern also said candidates felt obliged to 'plunge into crowds' when their spirits were low after having been attacked by the press or by their opponents. 'It lifts their spirits', McGovern said and 'demonstrated that the candidate was "brave"'.[25]

As McGovern emerged as Nixon's leading opponent the president urged aide Charles Colson to have the Secret Service spy on him. Confidential information that McGovern had met with an alleged 'left-wing subversive' was picked up by agent James C. Bolton and promptly passed on to the White House. Bolton had promised to keep his father, an administrative assistant to Republican Representative Glenn R. Davis, informed about the McGovern campaign. The father passed on his son's reports. However, the story of McGovern meeting with the alleged 'left-wing subversive' was untrue.

In 1974 the House Judiciary Committee stated that Nixon had 'repeatedly engaged in conduct violating the constitutional rights of citizens . . . misused . . . the Secret Service . . . to conduct or continue electronic surveillance or other investigations for purposes unrelated to national security . . .'. It was one of the reasons why Nixon's presidency eventually ended in his resignation. Bolton was forced to resign from the agency.[26]

McGovern was also the victim of a plot by White House aides to connect him to the George Wallace assassination attempt. The Senator said he learned about the plot:

> . . . very quickly afterwards, and then it came out in the hearings of Senator [Samuel] Ervin's committee. That's when we had the proof. . . . So when Wallace was shot, I'm sure that Nixon had a joyous evening of celebrating that he was home free. And he ordered his staff to get out there to Wisconsin and fill that apartment of this fellow who shot Wallace with McGovern literature.[27]

Nixon was also probably aware of information the FBI held involving allegations McGovern had fathered an illegitimate child. If revealed at the time it would have destroyed the Senator's candidacy. Aides to McGovern had been tipped off by supporters in Terre Haute, Indiana, that someone, presumably a Nixon loyalist, had been seeking to get hold of a copy of a birth certificate that listed McGovern as the father of a daughter born to a woman who moved to Indiana to give birth to the child in secret. There was also a threat that it would soon become public. McGovern's aides swiftly informed him about the story so he would be prepared when it became public. However, he decided to keep silent in the hope that Nixon would choose not to leak the information. The reason Nixon declined remains a mystery. It is possible the president's enormous lead in the polls was influential, making any revelation unnecessary.

In 1975 McGovern wrote a letter to FBI Director Clarence Kelley asking for the release of his FBI file. On 16 April, two FBI inspectors met with McGovern in Washington. There was a chance, he told the agents, that he might enter the presidential primaries in 1976 then related how he did not want to make the same mistake he made in selecting Thomas Eagleton without a proper vetting procedure. If he succeeded in winning the 1976 Democrat nomination, he said, he wanted to be able to tell any potential running mate if the FBI possessed derogatory information about him. Specifically, he asked if the FBI had information about a child he fathered as a young man.[28]

A month later, on 14 May, the agents met again with McGovern. They were authorised to give McGovern an oral account of what was in his records. They shared with McGovern that in 1960, during a thorough background search after he had been nominated to serve in John F. Kennedy's administration, FBI investigators verified an allegation that McGovern had fathered a child. McGovern did not make any comment as to the veracity of the allegations, probably because he knew it to be true.[29]

One agent in McGovern's 1972 detail was not impressed with the way the candidate 'flip-flopped' in support of his chosen vice-presidential running mate, Senator Thomas Eagleton, after Eagleton admitted he had received electro-shock treatment for depression. In fact, some agents joked about what should have been considered a serious issue. They kept asking each other if the 'jumper cables' had been packed in the vice-presidential candidate's car – '. . . so we can get Eagleton started if he stalls'.[30]

Despite the problems McGovern had with some of his agents, his detail liked the candidate and thought he was a 'decent guy'. McGovern, for his part, felt loyalty to the men who were prepared to put themselves between him and an assassin's bullet. During a press conference he made a point of responding to a news story which characterised his agents as 'thugs'. McGovern publicly thanked his detail for 'risking their lives'.[31]

A wide range of candidates – from Shirley Chisholm and Julian Bond to Dr Benjamin Spock – were all formally proposed as McGovern's running mate. The Democratic Party nominee bypassed Jimmy Carter, who had simultaneously campaigned against the South Dakota Senator while lobbying to join his ticket, and chose Senator Thomas Eagleton of Missouri. Days later, when news broke of Eagleton's history of shock therapy and hospitalisation for depression, McGovern replaced Eagleton with Sargent Shriver, founder of the Peace Corps, former US Ambassador to France and brother-in-law of Ted Kennedy.[32]

Shriver was also liked by his detail which was headed by agent Barney Boyette, an agent who had experience of campaigns having worked on Edmund Muskie's 1968 detail. Other agents included Marty Vencker, Michael Endicott and Larry Buendorf. 'You couldn't help but like the guy,' Vencker said. Of all the details Vencker worked on in his time as a Secret Service agent it was Shriver's detail he liked the most. Vencker was also aware that Shriver knew that George McGovern would never win the election. Nevertheless, he said, Shriver did not despair and relished the opportunity to campaign for liberal causes he believed in.[33]

Marty Vencker was responsible for guarding the vice-presidential candidate's Maryland home. He enjoyed watching the 'Kennedys' play touch football on the estate's lawn and how the family revelled in the fact that another member of the family was running for high office. In turn the Kennedys, including the Shrivers, embraced the Secret Service agents as 'part of the family'. Vencker and Buendorf were often solicited to join in their football games. Endicott thought Shriver was 'bright and hard-working, sociable, fun-loving . . . a happy-go-lucky person'. When Endicott was told to accompany the candidate to a sauna Shriver told him not to forget his gun. Joking with his wife, Shriver then chastised the agent for 'bringing his gun into a sauna'.[34]

Shriver gave it his all during the 1972 general election campaign. During one week on the hustings he flew more than 11,000 miles. The plane was specially equipped with a travelling campaign headquarters in the forward cabin and an office and communications centre at the rear. The press and the Secret Service were seated in-between.

During the campaign there were threats against Shriver's life which were investigated by the FBI including a threat reported by a woman who said her son might be stalking the candidate. Her son had attempted to purchase a pistol when he was in Milwaukee. The mere fact he wanted to buy a handgun alarmed her after she had observed her son appearing in a photograph of a crowd surrounding Shriver in San Francisco. The report concluded, 'Milwaukee advised by subsequent teletype 11/6/72, at request of Secret Service six Milwaukee Agents surveilled| [suspect] in Madison . . . until Shriver completed his visit there'. The campaign rally was conducted without incident.[35]

* * *

McGovern had plenty of enemies and was the recipient of numerous threats to assassinate him. Many threats were the result of the Senator's anti-war policies and his liberal/left agenda if he became president. Most threateners denounced him as a radical, or communist and, in some cases, a traitor. The FBI's McGovern file contains about sixty-five cases involving extortion and assassination threats, along with a record of all correspondence between McGovern and the Bureau.

Many threats were quite bizarre. One informant sent candidates Muskie, McGovern, Kennedy and the 'Speaker of the House' a letter telling of how he learned about an assassination plot by using a Ouija board.

Another 'informant' wrote to McGovern's campaign headquarters in June 1972. It was delivered to the FBI for investigation. The letter warned that McGovern was going to be assassinated. The letter writer blamed the CIA for JFK's assassination and the writer came to that conclusion after 'reading 15 books on the subject'. The letter writer warned, 'I firmly believe the CIA will also kill you . . . if you persist in your bid for the Presidency. It is vitally imperative that you be made aware of your own personal danger.' In another missive investigated by the Bureau an informant said a leader of the American Indian Movement, Russell Means, was going to 'get that son-of-a-bitch' McGovern when he arrived at Pierre, South Dakota, for a campaign rally.[36]

There were numerous threats made by mentally unstable individuals who contacted the FBI, McGovern's local headquarters and local police departments including:

- In October 1972 a New York City police officer received a phone call stating, 'Senator McGovern will be at the Americana Hotel and he will be shot tonight'. The Secret Service opened an investigation but the suspect was tracked down and arrested by officers in the 17th Precinct and sent to Bellevue Hospital for psychiatric examination.[37]
- On 8 November 1972 a mentally unstable man entered the McGovern campaign headquarters in Atlanta and said he had been trying to kill McGovern for five months. He said he had been hired by the American Communist Party and that all US government officials should be 'done away with'. When he was interviewed by the Secret Service he denied making the threats. There was insufficient evidence to prosecute.[38]

Other reports of assassination threats were taken seriously, including:

- On 16 May 1972 the FBI received a report from a CB radio operator that he overheard a CB operator in the 'West Indies . . . call number [redacted] talking to a CB operator in Miami, Florida, call number unknown, in which statement made that McGovern would be assassinated prior to reaching convention . . . he determined . . . that two men, one West Indies extract,

currently following McGovern with intent to assassinate
. . .'.[39] However, agents were unable to track down a suspect or
suspects.
* When McGovern was staying at the Doral Beach Hotel during
the Democrat convention police arrested two men who were
members of the Republic of New Africa, a black separatist
group, for carrying concealed weapons. The two men who lived
in Jackson, Mississippi, were identified as 32-year-old Malek
Sonebeyatta and 33-year-old Ahmed Obatemi. One of them
had been arrested in the lobby of McGovern's hotel and the
other as he sat in his car parked on the ramp of the hotel. Two
guns were found under the car's front seat. The police also discovered the men were carrying multiple identifications. Their
lawyer John Brittain Jr said the two men denied knowing that
the weapons were in the car. He also said that the authorities
were trying to frame the radical organisation. McGovern cancelled a campaign meeting at the Deauville Hotel after his aides
received reports of the arrests. The Secret Service was unable
to determine whether or not the two men at McGovern's hotel
were stalking the candidate.[40]
* In October 1972 a caller phoned McGovern's Philadelphia campaign headquarters and said, 'If he is for the Blacks, there will
be a revolution here. If McGovern speaks today at Cheney State
[College] he will be bombed.'[41]
* In June 1972 the FBI investigated a telephone threat in which
a bomb had been allegedly planted on McGovern's chartered
plane.[42]

McGovern continued to receive threats long after his unsuccessful 1972
presidential campaign including:

* In January 1973 a North Dakota Highway Patrol officer arrested
a man in Fargo for drunk driving. He resisted arrest and when
the officer searched his car he found a .22 Beretta automatic
pistol. There was no record of the gun on the national database.
During his arrest he threatened to shoot McGovern. Later it was
discovered he had a history of mental illness. He was sentenced

to ten days in jail and fined $100. He was also to undergo a psychiatric examination. However, charges of threatening the candidate were dropped by US Attorney Harold G. Bullis who said the threat did not 'violate Title 18, Section 1751, of the US Code or the Congressional Assassination Statute'.[43]

- In 1975 McGovern, who was tipped as a candidate for the 1976 Democratic Party presidential nomination, was informed by the FBI of a threat received by Greensboro, North Carolina, police. They had received information that McGovern would be assassinated while he was speaking at Charlotte's University of North Carolina. No arrests were made.[44]

* * *

George McGovern was so unpopular during the 1972 election campaign that anything he or the Democrats had to say was either dismissed or ignored. To make matters worse, Richard Nixon was so far ahead in the polls the average voter could not believe the likelihood that the Republican Party would commit so many acts of election sabotage when the Democratic Party was such a weak opponent. McGovern talked about Watergate; he made grand claims about the administration's complicity. However, the general public began to see him as some kind of conspiracy theorist. Had the public been given evidence of the role Nixon played in the Watergate Scandal it is reasonable to assume McGovern's chances of winning the election would have increased dramatically.

For his part George McGovern was sanguine about his presidential run, 'After the shooting of Wallace', he said, '[and] when I realized it was just going to be a two-way race – with Wallace's support, probably 90% of it at least, going to Nixon – I had serious doubts whether any Democrat could have defeated him at that point.' McGovern's realisation that he could not win came when the '. . . Eagleton thing erupted'.[45]

Chapter 9

The Populist

'Somebody's going to get me one of these days. I can just see a little guy out there that nobody's paying any attention to. He reaches into his pocket and out comes the little gun, like that Sirhan guy that got [Robert] Kennedy.'

George Wallace

'[The prosecutor would] like society to be protected from someone like me. Looking back on my life, I would have liked it if society had protected me from myself. That's all I've got to say.'

Wallace's would-be assassin, Arthur Bremer

'I think the Service did everything it could have done [to protect George Wallace]. It's interesting that Governor Wallace feels that we saved his life. He doesn't say we failed to protect him. He thinks we kept him from being killed.'

H. Stuart Knight, Former Director of the Secret Service

Campaigning as a champion of segregation, George Corley Wallace won the 1962 governor's race in Alabama and was soon catapulted on to the national political stage when he clashed with the Kennedy administration over Civil Rights. In 1963, facing off with federal marshals, he memorably stood in the doorway of the University of Alabama vowing to prevent black students from enrolling. His governorship saw some of the worst violence of the Civil Rrights era, including the Birmingham church bombing, which killed four young girls.

During his unsuccessful bid for the presidency in 1964 he was accompanied by his state troopers when he campaigned across the nation in the Democratic primary elections. Wallace defended his stance on Civil Rights (civil wrongs, as he put it), stating that northerners and southerners alike believed in the separation of the races. While his stump speeches were peppered with such rhetoric, many of his supporters merely tolerated his views on race, drawn more to his campaign for limited-government and 'states' rights'.

Wallace believed he did not stand any chance of winning, especially against President Johnson, but he believed his prospective strong showing could influence the coming general election. His successes shocked the establishment. In Wisconsin, a state far removed from the South, Wallace won a striking 34 per cent of the Democratic vote.

Wallace ran again for president in 1968 as an independent candidate. Although he was still a controversial political figure due to his continuing support for racial segregation and states' rights, his political rallies were met with enthusiastic and impassioned crowds. However, across the nation he was seen as a 'hate' figure by moderates. His opponents yelled 'Sieg Heil' or 'What about Selma?' (the latter referring to the brutal attack by police on Civil Rights marchers in that city) at the candidate, who would yell back, sometimes losing his place in his speech. The demonstrators brought signs that said, 'God Bless George Hitler, The Smiling Bigot', 'Why don't you die?' and 'Not even Jesus could forgive what you did'. His rallies encouraged violence against critics and sometimes ended in fist fights between Wallace supporters and a mixed bag of black protestors and anti-war students. According to journalist Jack Nelson, the crowds at Wallace's political rallies were 'scary' and 'chilling'.[1]

Wallace had every reason to be concerned about his security. In 1968 racially motivated inner city riots, assassinations and civil discord caused by virulent opposition to the Vietnam War were rife. He retained his state trooper bodyguard protection even though he was assigned a Secret Service detail in June following the assassination of Robert Kennedy.

Wallace's campaigns adhered to a set format. Typically, he campaigned in white working class neighbourhoods and fairgrounds accompanied by a retinue which included the actor Chill Wills. State Trooper Lieutenant Jemison would frequently stand behind Wills as the often inebriated film actor would lose his balance. Wills would then announce a concert by the Oak Ridge Boys, the Four Sunshine Sisters and Knoxville gospel singer Wally Fowler followed by Wallace's entrance, surrounded by state troopers.[2] Fights often erupted, the candidate becoming the target of a variety of objects including bottles and rocks. Wallace's daughter, Peggy Wallace Kennedy, travelled with her father in the summer of 1968. At one rally she said state troopers '. . . pretty much carried us to the car. Just took us from the crowd to get us to the cars' when projectiles started flying.[3]

During his campaign bomb scares at Wallace events and threats on his life became common. He was forced to sneak in and out of events on campuses, surrounded by armed guards at all times. His security staff even took to placing small strips of tape on the cracks around the hood of his car, so they could tell if it had been opened and possibly tampered with. Many protestors were publicly vocal about their hatred for Wallace and some issued clear threats against his life. Wallace often cited remarks made by Black Power militant H. Rap Brown at a Montgomery protest rally in which Brown said, 'If anybody gives you a gun, use it on Lurleen and George, because they are your enemies.'[4]

Accordingly, Wallace's security arrangements in 1968 were strict. Before the RFK assassination, when all candidates were offered Secret Service protection, Wallace had a protective wall of seventeen state troopers, including Alabama state troopers Lieutenant Floyd Jemison, Captain E.C. Dothard and Corporal Meady L. Hillyer. The troopers were nicknamed the 'Maginot Line' and were armed with .38 and .357 calibre Magnum revolvers. During 'meet and greet' sessions with his supporters at campaign rallies the troopers formed a line facing the candidate. A trooper was stationed each side of him. The arrangement formed a narrow corridor and supporters would walk through it to shake his hand. Wallace had also been fitted for a bulletproof vest, but he would never wear it. He felt uncomfortable and the vest was too confining.

Wallace's troopers 'revered' him. One trooper said, '. . . there ain't but three people can walk on water – Jesus Christ, [Alabama football coach] Bear Bryant and George Wallace'.[5] A Secret Service agent said Wallace was 'most considerate' and gave the Secret Service 'more than enough advance notice of his movements'.[6]

Wallace would deliver his speeches from behind an 800lb armour plated podium. During the campaign it had become both emblematic and also a logistical burden. The massive bulletproof podium, which disguised the fact the candidate was short in stature, was cumbersome and created transport problems for his security staff. The small Wallace campaign aircraft was of inadequate payload capacity to carry it, even if it were dismantled in sections. The podium had to be moved from city to city by automobile.

State Trooper E.C. Dothard was described as being closer to Governor Wallace than any other member of the campaign entourage. Reporters who travelled with the Wallace party described the police captain as 'the most popular cop' who had a 'laconic, droll wit'. Jemison had been a Wallace body-guard since the early 1960s. 'We always tried to keep the security on the tight side . . .', Jemison said, 'the Governor, he's on the friendly side, you know. He'd spend 50 minutes talking behind the bullet-proof podium and then an hour out in front of it shaking hands.'[7]

Like Wallace, the troopers were suspicious of the press. Once, when a reporter wrote a less-than-flattering story about the governor, E.C. Dothard approached him and said, 'The governor's real mad at you. He's getting god-damn sick and tired of you always using them 'postrophes when you quote him.' Dothard had been referring to Wallace's southern drawl. When the journalist was attacked by Wallace in a speech the crowd began to verbally attack him. However, Jemison told him, 'The governor said not to worry. I'm to look out for you if the crowd gets too worked up.' The reporter did not find Jamison's remarks 'reassuring'.[8]

However, notwithstanding the chaos of Wallace's campaign he carried 5 states, finished with 10 million votes, about 13.5 per cent of the vote, won 46 electoral votes and drew votes from both main candidates, Richard Nixon and Hubert Humphrey, in the general election.[9]

Although Wallace was considered to be a leading challenger for the 1972 Democratic Party presidential nomination, he was, in reality, an interloper who did not stand a chance even though he gained the support of millions of voters in the primary elections. However, Wallace said he wanted to enter the race, 'To keep the others honest.'[10]

By 1972 Wallace's security screen was regarded as one of the tightest and most thoroughly kept in political history. His Secret Service detail consisted of twenty agents and at least three of his Alabama state troopers. James Kelly was appointed head of his Secret Service detail and Nick Zorvas, who was based in Atlanta, was second in command. Both men were responsible for administering all security arrangements for the Wallace campaign and accompanied the candidate personally at all times.[11]

However, the agents became anxious that Wallace showed an almost physical need to immerse himself in the throngs that he allowed to press in on him. His bodyguards were frequently defeated by the exuberance and the hand-clasping adoration that greeted the candidate. 'It's the democratic way,' Zarvos said. 'The candidates have to go to the people and shake hands.'[12]

Wallace had often remarked privately that he was 'the most threatened candidate in the country'. However, State Trooper Jemison said that by May 1972 he had received 'no threats at all lately – you know, not anything you could pin down'.[13]

Wallace complained to his staff that the stop-and-fly airport rallies that had become a tradition in his campaign placed a burden on people who wanted to see him. Airports were far removed from cities, often at the end of narrow access roads that resulted in traffic jams. It was for this reason Wallace decided he would hold rallies at shopping malls. The first of his shopping centre rallies was staged in Marquette, Michigan, and the turnout seemed to confirm the Wallace's judgment that these rallies would bring him closer to the people.

Wallace was philosophical about the vitriol and animosity directed towards him by protestors. He said during a campaign rally in Michigan:

> Hell, I don't mind the kids [heckling]. They're just young and full of spit and vinegar. They ain't the ones I fear. The ones that scare me are the ones you don't notice . . . I can see a little guy out there that nobody's paying attention to. He reaches into his jacket and out comes the little gun, like that Sirhan guy that got Kennedy.

He told a *TIME* reporter, 'Somebody's going to get killed before this primary is over.'[14]

Wallace was especially worried about his Maryland primary campaign and wanted to cancel it but his aides persuaded him it was important to attend the scheduled shopping mall rallies in the Maryland towns of Wheaton and Laurel. His concerns were not without foundation. In early May 200 African Americans in Hagerstown, shouting obscenities, forced Wallace to cancel the scheduled rally. On 11 May in Frederick he was hit in the shoulder by a rock thrown by a demonstrator. On 15 May at Wheaton a crowd of 3,000 included hecklers who threw rocks and coins, striking his bulletproof lectern.[15] Later that day Wallace arrived in Laurel. Around fifty county and state policemen ringed the platforms from which Wallace spoke. In addition, an unknown number of plain-clothes policemen and Secret Service agents mingled with the crowd.

* * *

Marty Vencker, who had guarded Wallace periodically during the 1972 campaign, said, 'You learn to look for the face that doesn't belong. The guy who's nervous and perspiring when most people around him are having a good time.' Agents were trained to look for men and women whose eyes betrayed them, glittering with hatred.

Vencker had spotted a 'strange-looking guy . . . he had that red, white and blue outfit on, silver sunglasses, that simpering grin' a few weeks before Wallace's Maryland campaign visit. Vencker later learned he had spotted 'a killer in the crowd' who turned out to be Arthur Bremer.[16]

Bremer was 21, 5ft 6in and from Milwaukee. He was born into a quarrelsome household, the son of a truck driver and a mother who stayed at home raising her children. Bremer grew up socially awkward and lonely and was known to children in his neighbourhood as 'Crazy Man' because 'he garbled like Donald Duck'.

After leaving school Bremer worked as a busboy at the Milwaukee Athletic Club. However, his habit of talking to himself disturbed the customers, some of whom believed he was suffering a mental illness. In October 1971 it was decided to give him a new job working in the kitchen. Bremer was unhappy with this demotion and the following month obtained a job as a school janitor.

While working at the school he met 15-year-old Joan Pemrich. However, Bremer's quirky, intense behaviour became too much for her. She said she was embarrassed by the way he yelled and stamped his feet at a rock concert. After three dates Joan refused to see him anymore as she considered him to be 'goofy' and 'weird'. On 13 January 1972, Joan's mother told Bremer to leave her daughter alone.

Bremer was devastated. He repeatedly phoned her, begging her to see him again but the girl flatly refused. Pained at the rejection, he shaved his head, 'to show her that inside I felt as empty as my shaved head'. On one occasion he followed her and pulled off his knit cap, showing her his bald pate. She walked away from him without speaking.

Soon afterwards Bremer purchased two handguns, a .38 calibre pistol and a 9mm Browning automatic. After an incident where he fired bullets into a ceiling he was arrested by the Milwaukee police. He was charged with disorderly conduct, fined and ordered to undergo a psychiatric evaluation.

Bremer began keeping a diary. In it he expressed a desire for fame and notoriety. For inspiration he checked out two books from the public library in Milwaukee, both of them about Robert Kennedy's assassin Sirhan Sirhan.

'Now I start my diary of my personal plot to kill by pistol either Richard Nixon or George Wallace,' he wrote. 'How will the news associations describe me? An unemployed painter? An unemployed part-time busboy? A colledge (still can't spell it) drop-out? . . . I have it. "An unemployed malcontent who fancys himself a writer".'[17]

Bremer spent most of the next few months travelling around the country armed with his handguns which he kept in his 1967 Rebel Rambler. He began to formulate plans to kill President Nixon or George Wallace. He kept track of Nixon's movements during the 1972 primary campaigns and began stalking him. Following Nixon to Ottawa, he hoped to kill the president in order to achieve 'fame'. Writing in his diary at the time he stated, 'It is my personal plan to assassinate by pistol either Richard Nixon or George Wallace.' He wanted to 'do something bold and dramatic, forceful and dynamic, a statement of my manhood for the world to see'. Bremer believed his assassination attempt would '. . . be among the best read pages since the scrolls in those caves'.

By 4 May 1972 Bremer realised it would be almost impossible to assassinate the president. Nixon was too heavily guarded and the would-be assassin became frustrated that 'demonstrators' were always coming between him and his target. 'Can't kill Nixie boy if you can't get close to him,' he wrote in his diary.

Like many would-be assassins, Bremer switched to an easier target. He chose Wallace because he believed the candidate's security was visibly more relaxed. 'These SS men are a different crew than was in Dearborn,' Bremer wrote. 'No suspicions. Another security breakdown.'[18]

What the candidates stood for politically seemed of little importance to Bremer. He considered assassinating Democratic Party candidate George McGovern but decided he was too marginal a figure. He fretted that Wallace, his second-choice victim, would not bestow on him the infamy he craved. He mused that the assassination he planned would lack the greatest impact if Wallace's most liberal rival for the Democrat presidential nomination gained popularity. 'The whole country's going liberal,' a distressed Bremer wrote in his diary. 'I can see it in McGovern. You know my biggest failure may be when I kill Wallace.'

However, he eventually settled on Wallace. The candidate would 'have the honour' of being his victim. Bremer began stalking him and decided on a 'cute' declaration to shout when he gunned him down. It was, 'A penny for your thoughts'.[19]

Early on the morning of 9 May 1972, Bremer took a car ferry to Ludington, Michigan, and visited the Wallace campaign headquarters in the town of Silver Spring, offering to be a volunteer. The next evening he attended a Wallace rally in Lansing. Two nights later, he was present at a Wallace rally in Cadillac and stayed overnight at the Reid Hotel in Kalamazoo.[20]

On 13 May 1972, two days before the shooting, Bremer visited the Dearborn Youth Centre. There were windows on the sides of the hall and 'people at the 2 windowpanes closest to the door could, however, see all unobstructed. . . . I thought of the [Secret Service]. The thin glass was weakly reinforced with wire mesh. But no trouble for a bullet at all. That was my plan.'

On the afternoon of 13 May, Kalamazoo Police received an anonymous phone call saying a 'suspicious looking person had been sitting in a car near the National Guard Armory'. When police caught up with him Bremer said he was waiting for the Wallace rally to begin and wanted to secure a good seat. He was photographed at the rally that evening and his proximity to Wallace showed he had an opportunity to shoot him. However, Bremer failed to seize the opportunity because two 15-year-old girls were in front of him. 'I let Wallace go only to spare these 2 stupid innocent delighted kids,' he wrote. Bremer made his final diary entry on 14 May 1972 and drove to Maryland.

Wallace returned to Maryland after a short stay in Montgomery then flew to Washington DC. His entourage consisted of E.C. Dothard and other state troopers and around twenty Secret Service agents. His security also consisted of Maryland and Prince George's County uniformed and plain-clothes police.

On 15 May 1972 Bremer turned up for a Wallace rally at Wheaton Plaza, a shopping centre. He was dressed in dark glasses, patriotic red, white and blue and was wearing a campaign button which said 'Wallace in '72'. He strongly applauded the candidate as others in the crowd heckled. Two tomatoes were thrown at Wallace during the rally but missed. Based on this reception, Wallace refused to shake hands with anyone present, denying Bremer the opportunity to shoot him.

Wallace moved on to the sprawling, U-shaped Laurel Shopping Centre, 16 miles away. About 1,000 people were present; they were mostly quiet and it was generally a friendly crowd. Between fifty and sixty Prince George's County and Maryland state policemen had ringed his speaking platform.

In addition, an unknown number of plain-clothes police officers and Secret Service agents mingled in the crowd. There was minor heckling, but it did not last. After he had finished speaking, Wallace shook hands with some of those present, against the advice of his agents.

Secret Service agent William Breen said:

> The crowd was cheering and everyone was responding well to him. He certainly could electrify a crowd. And when he concluded his speech, he was supposed to leave the podium and go directly to the car. There were not to be any intermediate stops. And as he started – I was the point agent – he was to follow me. And I was going to go right over to the automobile. He was to get in and that was it, we were off to wherever we were going.[21]

Prince George's County Police Corporal Mike Landrum remembered pointing out Bremer to a Secret Service agent before the rally.[22]

At approximately 4.00 pm after delivering his speech, and on the spur of the moment, Wallace stepped off the platform to shake hands. He autographed photos and spoke to a number of officials when a cry rang out, 'Over here, George, over here.' It was Bremer. Wallace responded by walking over to the crowd accompanied by Dothard and agents Nick Zarvos and Jimmy Taylor. As Wallace shook hands with his supporters an outstretched arm appeared between campaign workers Ross and Mabel Speigel.

Bremer aimed his .38 revolver at Wallace's abdomen and fired five shots. Madeline Saunders and Ross Speigel grabbed Bremer's arm. Speigel '. . . just climbed up on this man . . . [and] down we went. The gun was still firing when we took him down.'[23] Bremer's plan to yell his carefully chosen catchphrase, 'A penny for your thoughts!', was forgotten as he fired his gun.

Nick Zarvos clutched his throat then bent down vomiting blood. Wallace's wife Cornelia lunged towards her husband using her body to protect him from a potential second shooter. Dothard grabbed his stomach and fell in front of *TIME* Correspondent Joseph Kane. A bullet from Bremer's gun had grazed Dothard's stomach and, though injured, he yelled, 'Take care of the Governor first!'[24]

Dora Thompson, a campaign volunteer, slumped to the ground with a bullet in her right leg. Music by Billy Grammer suddenly stopped. As a blanket of police smothered Bremer, there were shrieks and isolated cries of 'Kill him! Kill him!'[25]

Bremer hit Wallace four times. Wallace fell back and lost a pint of blood, going into a mild state of shock. One bullet lodged in his spinal cord. The other bullets hit Wallace in the abdomen and chest. He lay there, conscious but stunned. Blood streamed from his right arm and through his shirt at the lower right ribs.

Three other people present were wounded unintentionally by bullets that had gone through Wallace – Dothard was shot in the stomach, Dora Thompson was shot in the leg and Nick Zarvos was shot in the neck. Dr Richard Longoria, the doctor who treated Dothard, said the state trooper had '. . . a superficial wound of the abdominal wall with some irritation surrounding it, that was about three or four, two inches in diameter'. He said the abdominal wall was located on the lower ribs. Zarvos' speech was severely impaired following the shooting. He later testified at Bremer's trial, 'I had a 38 bullet enter the lower throat area, here, went across paralyzing my right vocal cord and entering lodged in the jawbone, fractured the jawbone and I have nerve damage to the lower lip area. There is no feeling and I lost four or five teeth.'[26]

Bremer was also tacked to the ground by Mike Landrum and put in a headlock. Landrum pushed him through an angry crowd for about 60yd to a police cruiser as some in the crowd tried to grab the officer's handgun so they could shoot Bremer. 'It happened so quickly,' Landrum said. 'My strongest impression was how quickly events can change.' Landrum remembered pointing out Bremer to a Secret Service agent before the rally.[27]

Though ashen from shock and loss of blood after having been shot four times, Wallace never lost consciousness. An ambulance arrived 10 minutes after the shooting and it took 25 more minutes from Laurel to Holy Cross Hospital in Silver Spring, Maryland. Wallace spent much of the time consoling his terrified wife Cornelia.

Following his arrest, Bremer asked police officers if he had killed Wallace. The officers humoured Bremer and told him he had. 'Yeah, yeah, you killed him. He's dead,' Landrum said. Meanwhile, doctors treated Bremer for a head injury sustained when spectators pounced on him. When Bremer learned he also had wounded a Secret Service agent, an Alabama state trooper and a Wallace campaign worker, he blamed spectators who 'deflected his arm'.

Just after midnight, Bremer was arraigned and taken to the Baltimore County Jail, where he would be held for the next two months. When police searched Bremer's car they described it as a 'hotel on wheels'. In it they found blankets, pillows, a blue steel 9mm fourteen-shot Browning semi-automatic pistol, binoculars, a woman's umbrella, a tape recorder, a portable radio with police band, an electric shaver, photographic equipment, a garment bag with several changes of clothes, a toilet kit, a 1972 copy of a *Writers' Yearbook* and the two books he had borrowed from the Milwaukee public library ten days earlier. Bremer was charged with four counts of assault with intent to murder and was arraigned in Baltimore on two federal charges. One of the federal charges was interfering with the civil rights of a candidate for federal office, a provision of the 1968 Civil Rights Act. The second charge was for assaulting a federal officer, Secret Service agent Nick Zarvos.

President Richard Nixon ordered the FBI to take jurisdiction of the investigation away from the Secret Service. 'Get the FBI. Order, at my direction, the FBI!' he said. Nixon wanted to avoid any accusations of a cover-up or incompetent handling of the criminal case so he ordered John Ehrlichman to take control of the investigation. Nixon said, 'I want a report, and I don't want any cover up. You know, this could be like the Kennedy thing. This son of a bitch [Secret Service Director] Rowley is a dumb bastard, you know. He is dumb as hell. We've got to get somebody over there right away. . . . Secret Service will f*** this up! They do everything!'[28]

Bremer's trial lasted only five days, beginning on 31 July 1972. It was only two-and-a-half months after he shot Wallace. His attorney, Benjamin Lipsitz, argued that Bremer was a 'schizophrenic' who could not be held responsible for his actions. Eight psychiatrists and two psychologists testified but they were divided on the issue of his sanity. The defence argued that Bremer was schizophrenic and legally insane at the time of the shooting, and that he had 'no emotional capacity to understand anything'. The prosecution argued that Bremer, while disturbed and in need of psychiatric treatment, was sane. Bremer knew what he was doing, had been seeking glory and was still sorry that Wallace had not died. Jonas Rappeport, the chief psychiatrist for the circuit court in Baltimore, who spent 9 hours with Bremer in June 1972 on four separate occasions, said Bremer's state of mind did not 'substantially impair his capacity to understand the criminality of his actions'.

On 4 August 1972, the jury of six men and six women took 95 minutes to reach their verdict. Bremer was sentenced to sixty-three years in prison for shooting Wallace and three other people. When asked if he had anything to say, Bremer replied, 'Well, Mr. Marshall mentioned that he would like society to be protected from someone like me. Looking back on my life I would have liked it if society had protected me from myself. That's all I have to say at this time.' The sentence was reduced to fifty-three years on 28 September 1972 after an appeal. On 6 July 1973 Bremer's second appeal to have the sentence reduced further was rejected.[29]

Bremer served his sentence at the Maryland Correctional Institution (MCI-H) in Hagerstown, Maryland. He was placed in solitary confinement for thirty days after a fight on 6 October 1972 and was reprimanded after another fight in December 1972. After a third fight in February 1973 he was placed in solitary again for thirty days. He declined to receive mental health treatment or evaluation. During his time in prison he was visited multiple times by his parents before they died.

Bremer worked in the prison library and was described by the chairman of the Maryland Parole Commission, David Blumberg, as 'compliant and unobtrusive'. However, parole boards over the years concluded that releasing him would be risky. He argued in his June 1996 hearing that, 'Shooting segregationist dinosaurs wasn't as bad as harming mainstream politicians.' The unrepentant attitude disturbed the Wallace family. 'I just don't know if justice has been served when I consider how much my father suffered,' his son George Wallace III said. Wallace's son reached out to Bremer in the early 1990s and suggested a meeting. Bremer's response, according to two FBI agents, was to jump on the bars of his cell and make sounds like a monkey.[30] Bremer was emulating the behaviour of RFK assassin Sirhan Sirhan, who exhibited the same behaviour when he attempted to prove he had been a hypnotised assassin.

Despite his lack of contrition, Bremer was released from prison on 9 November 2007, at the age of 57, having served thirty-five years of his original sentence. His probation ends in 2025. Conditions of his release include electronic monitoring and staying away from elected officials and candidates. He must undergo a mental health evaluation and receive treatment if the state deems it necessary, and he may not leave the state without written permission from the state agency that will supervise him until the end of his probation.

On his release Bremer said that one of the things he wanted most was the ability to make toast. He wouldn't talk about the past. Bremer was offered a job at a cleaning and home restoration business. 'He's been a blessing to us,' his employer said. 'I think what has made it work . . . it has to do with his willingness to hit the reset button and really work on that'.[31]

* * *

Wallace had ignored his agents' advice to avoid plunging into the crowd after he finished giving his speech. His eagerness to shake hands with his supporters was a tragic mistake.

Eugene T. Rossides, former Assistant Secretary of the Treasury Department, said the attack on Wallace could not have been prevented even if more bodyguards had been assigned to the candidate. 'Exposing himself so openly', Rossides said, 'he was a prime target.'[32] If Wallace had adhered to the security protocol of the 'Maginot Line' he used in his 1968 campaign, it is unlikely he would have been shot.

Wallace's near-death experience had a profound impact on him, '. . . transforming his views on race . . . the fiery rhetoric disappeared. He began to reach out to blacks and apologise for his positions on race.' In 1974 during his re-election campaign for Governor of Alabama he received large support from the state's black population. The black community also helped him win his final term as governor in 1982.[33]

Forty years after the assassination Stan Orenstein, the FBI agent who reported to the hospital immediately after the assassination to take charge of the investigation, said, 'I think in the ensuing years until his death, he always fell back on his experience in Maryland. It changed his life.' A few days later he interviewed a recovering Wallace in the Holy Cross Hospital room. 'When Bremer shot him, I firmly believe it made a sea change in his attitude,' Orenstein said. 'I think it was strictly politics with him. He didn't get any particular joy out of being brutal to black people and he wasn't involved in that. But the shooting changed his attitude toward black people.'[34]

By the time Wallace participated in his last campaign for president in 1976 much had changed. No other presidential candidate, with the possible exception of President Ford, was so isolated from the voters. The campaign was like an armed camp. Wallace's 1976 speaking lectern became a bulletproof enclosure; open only at the back with foot-high sheets of inch-thick protective glass. When Wallace was asked if he feared for his life, the candidate replied, 'If you want to be in politics you have to be willing to pay the price. I can tell you that price can be pretty high.'[35]

Because the bullet damaged one of his vocal cords, Zarvos was instructed not to speak for two months. When Zarvos visited Wallace in the hospital later that year, he used a drawing slate to communicate. Zarvos retired in the 1980s. By 1997, he was living in Sarasota, Florida, working occasionally as a consultant. A local newspaper story from that year described how Zarvos still spoke with a rasp because of the shooting twenty-five years before. In 2002, Zarvos, along with three other Secret Service agents who were guarding Wallace on 15 May 1972, received the Director's Award of Valour, the agency's highest honour.

Seven months after the assassination attempt, Wallace named E.C. Dothard the director of the Alabama Department of Public Safety. In 1974, the Colonel E.C. Dothard Safety Education Museum was opened in Montgomery. It included a monument to law-enforcement officers killed in the line of duty. Dothard died in December 1989, of a self-inflicted gunshot wound in a hospital where he was being treated for terminal cancer. He was 58 years old.[36]

Hearing of his death, George Wallace said Dothard was a very close personal friend and a fine citizen 'who gave his entire life to law enforcement, . . . he travelled all over the world with me . . .'.[37]

Wallace was forgiving of the man who tried to assassinate him. 'I am a born-again Christian. I love you,' Wallace wrote to Arthur Bremer in 1995. 'I hope that we can get to know each other better. We have heard of each other a long time.'[38]

The assassination attempt left Wallace suffering a lifetime of pain and medical complications brought on by his paralysis and he also suffered with Parkinson's disease later in life. Wallace died in 1998. He was 79. Following his death Civil Rights leader Congressman John Lewis said, 'With all his failings Mr Wallace deserves recognition for seeking redemption for his mistakes, for his willingness to change and to set things straight with those he harmed and with his God.'[39]

Chapter 10

Jimmy Who?

'A President has to [mix with crowds]. If he didn't, that would indicate he was intimidated. I don't think this country can stand the idea of its President cowering in the White House.'
Director of the Secret Service H. Stuart Knight, 1976

Following Nixon's resignation in August 1974 Gerald Ford, who succeeded Spiro Agnew as vice president in October 1973, took the presidential oath of office. In the build-up to the presidential election of 1976 Ford remained acutely aware that he was the only person in US history to become the chief executive without being elected. Additionally, his pardon of Richard Nixon became intensely controversial during the campaign.[1]

One of Ford's first acts as president was to arrange a reception for his Vice Presidential Protective Detail (VPPD) and their wives. 'To say the [Nixon detail] guys were seriously annoyed', Ford agent Joseph Petro said, 'is an understatement. They worked while we sipped cocktails with the president.'[2]

Ford was characterised by his agents as a 'true gentleman who treated the Secret Service with respect and dignity' and as having a great sense of humour. Agent Clint Hill thought Ford was '. . . a great guy: humble, respectful and kind. . . . [he] had a reputation as a bumbler but he was incredibly athletic. He swam every day, was a good skier and played tennis. He was an ordinary man intent on doing the right thing.'[3]

In fact, Ford was so adept and skilful on the slopes he often taunted agents to keep up with him. After failing, the Secret Service appointed an agent to Ford's detail who would ski backwards in front of the President and 'wave as the President tried to catch up with him'.

Agent Larry Buendorf, who was in charge of Ford's ski team, said, 'Deep down, Ford wanted people to understand what an athlete he really was.'

However, even after Ford left the presidency, he couldn't shirk the image the media presented of him as an accident-prone president. In 1977 Ford

149

Director of the United States Secret Service James J. Rowley (centre) with thirteen of JFK's White House Secret Service agents, 20 December 1961. (Photo: JFK Library)

President Lyndon Johnson campaigning with Robert Kennedy and surrounded by Johnson's Secret Service agents, 1964. Robert Kennedy while campaigning said, 'I play Russian roulette every time I get up in the morning but I just don't care. There's nothing I could do about it anyway.' In June 1968 he was assassinated by a Palestinian lone-wolf terrorist while campaigning. (Photo: Library of Congress)

 Governor of California Ronald Reagan's closest brush with death during his 1968 run for the presidency occurred during the two months he was protected by the US Secret Service. On 9 July 1968 agents Doug Duncan, Bob Horan, Bob Barker and Michael Endicott were on duty when two men attacked Reagan's residence armed with Molotov cocktails. (Photo: Library of Congress)

George Wallace's security arrangements in 1968 were strict. Before the RFK assassination, when all candidates were offered Secret Service protection, Wallace had a protective wall of seventeen state troopers nicknamed the 'Maginot Line'. During 'meet and greet' sessions with his supporters at campaign rallies the troopers formed a line facing the candidate. A trooper was stationed each side of him. The arrangement formed a narrow corridor and supporters would walk through it to shake his hand. If Wallace had adhered to this strict security protocol, it is unlikely he would have been shot during his campaign for the presidency in 1972. (Photo: Newsweek, Public Domain)

New York Mayor John Lindsay was considered a front-runner for the 1972 Democratic Party nomination. When the mayor appeared on the steps of New York's City Hall for an outdoor ceremony, a police officer noticed a would-be assassin, Carlos Valle, had a knife protruding from his belt. He was arrested by police and sent to a mental facility. Nine months later he called the local offices of the FBI and Secret Service and threatened to kill President Nixon. In 1981 he threatened to assassinate President Reagan. (Photo: Library of Congress)

Following the 1976 election Ford's detail transferred to President-Elect Jimmy Carter. The detail was initially headed by Richard Keiser. As a hold-over from President Ford's detail, Keiser was the agent who had often been mistaken for Ford when he appeared at the door of Air Force One before the president disembarked the plane. When Keiser was asked if he thought an assassin might mistake him for Ford, Keiser replied, 'I hope so.' (Photo: copyright Mel Ayton)

Kennedy chauffeur Frank Saunders who acted as a part-time bodyguard for Robert and Edward Kennedy revealed how Edward Kennedy had crashed his car in Palm Beach, Florida, six months before the tragic accident at Chappaquiddick. Kennedy, who Saunders described as inebriated, concluded that the Senator's car 'had to be speeding to miss the turn'. (Photo: copyright Mel Ayton)

The relationship between agents and Jesse Jackson's campaign staff soon deteriorated. Agents recognised that the staff had no experience when it came to running a national campaign. Impulsive changes to the candidate's schedule also created tension. 'No security detail can be effective under such circumstances', Secret Service agent Dennis McCarthy said, 'and a constant battle between agents and Jackson's staff members developed'. Jackson was told by the US Secret Service he had received the greatest number of threats of any candidate who had run for the presidency before. (Public Domain)

Gary Hart lost the 1984 Democratic Party nomination to former Vice President Walter Mondale but became the front-runner for the 1988 nomination. However, he withdrew from the race following a scandal he was involved in. During the 1984 campaign a would-be assassin was arrested at his San Francisco hotel armed with a .38 pistol. (Photo: Library of Congress)

Michael Dukakis, the 1988 Democratic Party presidential candidate, campaigning in Detroit, Michigan, guarded by Secret Service agents. Dukakis said he had 'no security . . . in Massachusetts and would not have it' when he was governor of the state. Dukakis found that being guarded around was 'very unpleasant'. He thought he had lost a lot of 'what I had as governor', meeting constituents in an 'easy and informal way'. However, he admired the work of the Secret Service even though he found it 'rather difficult', he said. (Photo: copyright Mel Ayton)

Nearly a year after Clinton was inaugurated as the 42nd president five state troopers who were part of his security detail when he was Governor of Arkansas were interviewed by journalist David Brock. The result was a shocking portrayal of a man who would arguably not have been elected president if their stories had been published during the 1992 presidential election campaign. (Photo: The White House)

Senator Robert Dole, 1996 presidential candidate, said that once he had won nomination he found being protected by the Secret Service was 'frustrating'. 'Anytime I wanted to talk to constituents, buy a suit, buy groceries', Dole said, 'I was walled off by the Secret Service'. He said the experience '. . . drove me up a wall'. When asked his views of what he was getting himself into he quoted his opponent, Bill Clinton, who said the White House was 'the crown jewel of the federal corrections system'. (Photo: copyright Mel Ayton)

Barack Obama during his 2009 inauguration and surrounded by his Secret Service bodyguards. During the 2008 presidential election he had received numerous threats including one in which six people, linked to a militia group in rural Pennsylvania, were arrested with stockpiles of assault rifles and homemade bombs. (Photo: The White House)

In Arkansas Hillary Clinton would send her state-trooper bodyguards to run errands and carry her bags. When she arrived in Washington she discovered that such behaviour did not go down well with the Secret Service. Protocol dictated agents were required to keep their hands free in case their protectees were attacked. When some agents refused to carry her bags they were quickly reassigned to other duties. (Photo: The White House)

During the 2016 and 2020 presidential campaigns Donald Trump was vilified as arrogant, obnoxious, racist and a megalomaniac. However, a number of agents went on the record to challenge these views. They revealed Trump's personality was in direct contradiction to the negative image portrayed in the media. He was very respectful and grateful to them, the agents said. (Photo: The White House)

Protecting the Presidential Candidates includes a previously unknown assassination attempt against the life of Theodore Roosevelt's vice president. Charles Fairbanks had been giving a speech to a crowd for 20 minutes when 32-year-old James McConnell, later described as an 'anarchist', forced his way through to Fairbanks' side holding a revolver concealed in his hip pocket. Four 'police detectives' caught the would-be assassin and 'choked him into submission'. McConnell later admitted he had been attempting to kill Fairbanks. (Photo: Library of Congress, Harris and Ewing, 1905–45)

visited New York's Shubert Theatre to see *A Chorus Line*. At the conclusion of the show, he stepped on to the stage but misplaced his foot and nearly fell into the orchestra pit 7ft below. The agent grabbed him and was later commended for saving Ford from 'certain very serious injuries from the resulting fall'. Later, Ford invited the agent to his hotel suite to thank him for saving his life.[4]

Ford had a temper, according to Buendorf. 'You could see it coming', he said, 'and that's when you'd beat a retreat. Give him a little room.' There were a few things that Ford did not like, Buendorf said:

> Not being on time was a big factor for him. I've heard him dress down campaigners that he'd gone out to campaign for and had them in the back seat of that limo and lectured them about timeliness, because he was a man that went by the clock. And that's where you get to it all the time because he'd get in the limo in Vail and go, 'Okay, go on to Denver. That's an hour and ten minutes. Let's see if we can break the record.' And I'd be going, 'Who's going to pay the ticket?' 'Well, I know you can go 67 in a 60. [That's] seven miles over.' And I'd go, 'Who's giving you this advice?' There'd be one of those exchanges in the car. 'Ah, you always go by the book', Ford would say. Then it'd be 'Buendorf', it wouldn't be 'Larry'.[5]

Buendorf said Ford and his wife Betty also had a well-developed sense of humour:

> [Betty] was the one who could really pull his chain every now and then [and] would often give him the business. I'd get up in the front and kind of see him and he'd always go, 'Buendorf, what're you laughing at?' 'Just talking to the driver,' I would say. He knew. . . . And he'd snort a little bit, but he knew he'd been had . . . they had a lot of fun together.[6]

Ronald Kessler who interviewed many Secret Service agents concluded, 'Unlike many other presidents Ford never engaged in any dalliances.' However, Kessler was clearly writing about Ford as president and not as a Congressman. According to LBJ aide and friend Bobby Baker, Ford had a sexual relationship with one of the women Baker arranged for politicians to meet in the 1950s and 1960s. Baker said Ford had sexual relations with Ellen Rometsch, a woman from West Germany who was married to a United States serviceman. In late 1963 Rometsch was sent back to Germany after Bobby Kennedy discovered she was having a relationship with his brother, the president. The allegation was confirmed, in part, by acclaimed historian and journalist Theodore H. White, who wrote in his 1978 memoirs that only three presidential candidates he had ever met '. . . had denied themselves the pleasures invited by that aphrodisiac (power)'. He named the candidates as Harry Truman, Jimmy Carter and George Romney (father of 2012 Republican presidential candidate Mitt Romney).[7]

During the 1976 presidential election year the Director of the Secret Service, H. Stuart Knight, was asked if he feared for Ford's life. 'I think if it comes to the point where the President has to be concerned with it', he said, 'then we in the Secret Service are not doing our job. I remember when Dwight Eisenhower was President; we were at a small country club just outside Gettysburg, and someone asked him, "Aren't you ever worried about being attacked?" He said, "No, I don't worry about that. I have people who worry about that for me." That is the only healthy attitude to have.'[8]

As the 1976 campaign season began two assassination attempts against Ford that occurred the previous year were uppermost in the minds of his protective detail. Within a span of seventeen days two women, Lunette 'Squeaky' Fromme and Sara Jane Moore, tried to shoot Ford in California.

Following the attempts on his life Ford took Buendorf aside and thanked him. 'He brought it up many times in his speech when he'd talk and he'd mention me by name. So, I mean, I got my thanks out of that. For me, it was about being confronted with something and doing the right thing. If I had missed, then I'd be the buffoon,' he said.

After Fromme's attempt on Ford's life Buendorf 'got very close' to the Ford family. However, he said:

> You have a professional responsibility to maintain that fine line. . . .
> But, at the same time, there's a respect that he has for you and a
> respect that you have for him. There are times when you need to
> be close. You know, on a golf course, he had a bad set of knees . . . I
> would ease up to him to 'talk', but really basically letting him lean
> on me as we're going up the hill and never create any attention to

the fact that he might have needed somebody to put a hand on. . . . because he did not like someone to reach out and assist noticeably.[9]

The second assassination attempt against Gerald Ford by Sara Jane Moore occurred in San Francisco outside the St Francis Hotel, a short distance from Union Square. Of the two assassination attempts, Larry Buendorf considered this attempt to be the most serious. 'Well, when you get rounds off, that obviously changes the whole scenario,' Buendorf said.[10]

A Secret Service agent assigned to check on the would-be assassin after Moore's release from prison became friendly with her and was subject to disciplinary measures by the agency.

There were a number of myths surrounding Moore's assassination attempt. Ronald Kessler, for example, wrote that Oliver Sipple, a disabled former US Marine and Vietnam veteran, pushed Sara Jane Moore's arm as she aimed her gun and shot at President Ford. He also wrote that the bullet flew several feet over the president's head and Secret Service agents Ron Pontius and Jack Merchant pushed Moore to the sidewalk and arrested her.[11]

The facts of the case are more nuanced. Sipple did grab Moore's arm, but not until after she got off her first shot, which missed Ford's head by only 6in. After her first shot, people realised something had happened and Sipple lunged at Moore and fouled a second, potentially deadly, shot.

Kessler's account also states that Secret Service agents Ron Pontius, Ford's Secret Service head of detail together with agent Jack Merchant tackled Moore to the sidewalk and arrested her. However, Pontius and Merchant were assigned to guard President Ford and were standing with Ford across the street from Moore. They did not leave Ford's side. In fact, they grabbed the president and pushed him into the limousine and sped away.

San Francisco police officer Tim Hettrich subdued Moore. Hettrich was assigned to crowd detail and was stationed on the sidewalk near Moore. Hettrich pulled the gun from her and handed it over to Secret Service agent Dotson Reeves, who grappled with Moore on the sidewalk.[12]

One of the reasons Moore attempted to shoot Ford was because '[Nelson Rockefeller] would be elevated to the presidency and the people would see who the actual leaders of the country are'. Moore said the assassination would force people to 'see, what we have now is a phoney government. Nobody ever elected Rocky to the vice presidency; he was governor of a state. Nobody elected Ford president; he was a representative for a congressional district.

We've never had a true democracy here or anything even approaching it; now we don't even have representative government.'[13]

Ford's attitude to the possibility of assassination was altogether one of resignation accompanied by an acceptance of the risks. After the two incidents Ford said he would continue with his style of campaigning and that no president should 'capitulate to the wrong forces in this country' and that the 'ever-present threat' was part of the job of being president. He continued, '. . . there's no way you can get 100% security unless you sit in the White House immunized. But you can't isolate yourself. The job entails certain responsibilities. One of those responsibilities is moving around seeing people and appearing in public. If you're in the job, you have to accept that gamble.'[14]

* * *

On 12 January 1971 Jimmy Carter was inaugurated Governor of Georgia. One of his first acts in office was to make it possible for African Americans to join the state patrol. He also chose a black officer to serve in his personal security force. On one occasion, when he was invited to speak at a country club, the members asked he not bring his black bodyguard with him. Carter ignored them and when he turned up to give his speech the black officer was by his side.

Governor Carter's contingent of personal bodyguards was named the 'Executive Security Team'. It reported directly to the Deputy Commissioner for Public Safety. Carter's bodyguards dressed in plain clothes while state troopers on duty protecting the governor's mansion were in uniform.

Shuttled from one part of Georgia to another by the state patrol or by the planes at his disposal, he was accompanied by his Georgia State Patrol personal bodyguard, Richard Cicero Coleman, better known by his nickname, 'Stock'. Coleman acquired the nickname when he was in 5th grade. 'He was real fat', his brother Henry Randolph Coleman said, 'and people called him Stock'. Coleman joined the Marines 'weighing 265 pounds and came out weighing 190, 195'. But the nickname stuck.[15]

Coleman was also the head of Carter's security detail. He was born in Eastman, Georgia, and in 1968, after graduating from Dodge County High School, he joined the Marines. Following his discharge, he began his career with the Georgia State Patrol. Coleman was an above-average state trooper eventually earning an Associate's Degree in Criminal Justice from Reinhardt University and also graduating from the FBI Academy in Quantico, Virginia. Rare for that time, he was also dubbed 'intellectual'.

Coleman travelled with Carter throughout the state, acting not only as the governor's sole bodyguard but also his driver. He reportedly had a submachine gun 'just like that used by the Secret Service', he once said.[16] Long after he left his duties as Jimmy Carter's personal bodyguard Coleman worked on security for the 1996 Olympics held in Atlanta. In fact, the security team had only two members – Coleman and an Atlanta police lieutenant, both working on part-time loan from their employers.

It was widely believed that once Carter ended his term as Governor of Georgia he would return to his hometown of Plains to run the family's peanut business. However, when his mother Lillian Carter asked her son what he was going to do after he left office Carter replied, 'I'll run for president.' 'It shocked me,' Lillian Carter said, 'but after five minutes I realised he was in earnest.'[17]

Within a year after Carter was elected governor his two aides, Jody Powell and Hamilton Jordan, were planning to advance their boss' ambitions. They strategised with the newest members of Carter's team, Gerald Rafshoon and Peter G. Bourne, a British-born psychiatrist who had worked on mental-health issues with Carter's wife, Rosalynn.

In 1972 the aides schemed to persuade the Democrat presidential nominee George McGovern to accept the governor as his vice-presidential running mate. Jordan and Rafshoon travelled to the Democratic National Convention in Miami Beach and solicited the help of Gary Hart, then campaign manager for McGovern. After the Democrat nominee bypassed Carter his aides set their sights on the 1976 presidential election. 'Jimmy saw that Ted Kennedy drank too much; Ed Muskie had a temper; Hubert Humphrey was nice, but his time was over,' Jerry Rafshoon said.[18]

George McGovern was a liberal who opposed the war in Vietnam. Carter watched McGovern run a campaign in which he was portrayed by his opponents as a radical extremist, and that ended with McGovern's overwhelming defeat at the hands of Republican incumbent Richard Nixon. Carter reasoned that the next election would require a different type of Democrat.

In December 1974, more than a year before the first Democratic primary and the final month of Carter's term as governor, he travelled to Washington and announced his candidacy before the National Press Club. When Carter began his campaign for president he was '. . . just driving around first of all with Jody [Powell] and me all by ourselves', he said.[19]

Carter spent months in Iowa preparing for its first-in-the-nation caucus. For much of the time his only companion during these trips was Jody
Powell. The two men shared motel rooms and stayed at supporters' homes
which provided the candidate with an image as a 'man of the people'. Carter
appeared at three factory shifts per day to shake hands. He campaigned at
football games, rodeos and livestock and tobacco sale barns. He sought the
votes of farmers, police officers, firefighters, refuse-collection workers and
cleaning crews.

Carter was assigned a Secret Service detail in October 1975, a full year
before the 1976 presidential election and given the code name 'Dasher'. The
practice of staying at supporters' homes caused anxious moments for his
agents. Unlike hotels, private homes required increased security. Additionally,
it caused disruption in the neighbourhood as roads and intersections had to
be closed off to accommodate the candidate's travels.

Because of the proliferation of presidential primaries along with the public
exposure of the candidates, the Secret Service's job was greater than ever
before. And, as a reaction to the 1975 attempts to assassinate President Ford,
Congress quickly provided Secret Service protection for not only Carter
but also Milton Shapp, Fred Harris, George Wallace, Morris Udall, Lloyd
Bentsen, Sargent Shriver, Henry Jackson, Birch Bayh, Terry Sandford and
Ronald Reagan. In 1976 primaries were held in thirty states and the District
of Columbia. Security for the candidates appeared almost impossible.

Friends and family members assisted Carter and formed the 'Peanut
Brigade'. They travelled across the country promoting Plains' favourite son.
The group included Carter's mother, who was known as 'Miz Lillian'. She
was described as very 'motherly and affectionate' by her bodyguard, Georgia
State Patrol officer Ray Hathcock. Miz Lillian accepted Hathcock, who she
described as a 'burly man with a boyish face' reluctantly. 'We travelled in
about a dozen foreign countries and in all the states except Alaska, North
Dakota and Hawaii', Hathcock said, 'and travelling with Miss Lillian was
great.'[20]

Carter had entered the 1976 presidential race with extremely low name
recognition and seemingly little chance against nationally better known politicians. When agent Marty Vencker was appointed to the Carter detail his
reaction was similar to most Americans. 'Jimmy Who?' he asked.[21] However,
Carter gained national recognition early in the primary season by winning
the Iowa caucuses and the New Hampshire primary.

By the summer of 1976 Carter was the presumptive Democratic Party nominee and went on to win the nomination later in July. However, along-side his increasing popularity came ever larger crowds, some hostile to the candidate's positions on social issues. During one campaign stop-over in Scranton, Pennsylvania, his protective detail became alarmed as they struggled to control a 1,000-strong crowd made up of Carter supporters and angry, anti-abortion demonstrators. Carter's detail formed a ring around him as he arrived at his downtown hotel. Agents protected Carter from bodily harm by preventing some in the crowd from pushing the candidate. The chanting reached a screaming pitch as the candidate was pushed and pulled. Carter kept his composure, tried to greet individuals in the crowd and reached out to shake hands. With difficulty the agents bundled the candidate to the safe confines of the hotel lobby. Unfazed, Carter turned and waved at the crowd as the demonstrators shouted 'Life, Life, Life'.[22]

Carter encountered a number of problems with his detail when he was out campaigning. Agents who protected him were often chided by press secretary Jody Powell for not allowing the media to get quality pictures of the candidate.

During one campaign stop when Carter joined a parade in Manhattan's Garment District, agents refused to allow a camera truck travelling in front of the candidate's car to slow down enough to get photographs. The agents needed an unblocked route so they could get Carter out of the area if something happened but press secretary Jody Powell became frustrated as he needed good coverage of his candidate. 'I'm hanging over the side of the truck screaming and shouting at the agent, who is ignoring me,' Powell said. 'So finally, I jumped off the truck, ran around it, and stood in front of it, just to make it stop.'

The agents argued with Powell as the Carter aide shouted, 'This is the big event of the day, and you guys are really screwing it up.' Powell 'just wanted to keep them arguing, because by this time [the photographers] were beginning to get shots'. Carter's agents decided to over-rule Powell by asking a New York police officer to intervene. 'In a few seconds,' Powell said, 'one of New York's finest – the biggest policeman I've ever seen – picks me up under my arm pits, sets me down to one side and says very softly, "Don't you ever do that again".'[23]

During the early hours of 3 November 1976, the day after voters cast their ballot, the state of Mississippi put Carter over the top. Networks declared that the country had just chosen Jimmy Carter as president of the United States – the first Southerner elected to the White House since Zachary Taylor in 1848.

During the primary campaign Carter had been assigned agents composed mainly of men and women from Secret Service field offices. Following the election Ford's detail transferred to President-Elect Carter and the new president's Secret Service code name was changed to 'Deacon'. The detail was initially headed by Richard Keiser, but he was eventually replaced by Jerry Parr. Parr worked alongside other detail members Larry Cunningham, Jack Smith, Jim Cool, Doug Laird and Marty Vencker.

Keiser was a hold-over from President Ford's detail. He was the agent who had often been mistaken for Ford when he appeared at the door of Air Force One before the president disembarked the plane. When Keiser was asked if he thought an assassin might mistake him for Ford, Keiser replied, 'I hope so.'[24]

Carter told Keiser that he wanted to avoid the trappings of an imperial presidency by avoiding police sirens whenever the presidential motorcade tried to avoid traffic jams. It would later result in press criticism for false cost-cutting.

The president often took chances with his own personal safety and there were occasions when his detail faced anxious moments. No sooner had Carter been inaugurated he exited his limousine and began walking down Pennsylvania Avenue accompanied by his wife. However, contrary to reports in the media, it had been well planned in advance according to Carter's son Chip:

> We planned that [at] Thanksgiving . . . and the Secret Service and I sat down with mom and dad and it was a suggestion that we had for them from the people at the inauguration, and the Secret Service and everybody agreed that it would be great to do, but not if anybody knew it was going to happen. So we never told a soul after that. . . . we knew it was going to happen.[25]

President Carter was viewed by his agents as distant and 'cool' and there were often times when agents thought he took too many risks. On one occasion, during a trip on the Mississippi River, Carter was impatient for the riverboat's gangplank to be laid down and jumped from the boat to the dock. If he had missed, he would have fallen 30ft and possibly been crushed by the boat. When he shone a spotlight on himself during the trip agents became anxious as they realised he had become a highly visible target for a sniper.[26]

There were also incidents that led them to believe the president's life was in danger. On one occasion agent Jim Cool was on duty watching Carter pitch in a softball game in Plains when he heard a 'thunderous blast'. Looking in the direction of the sound he realised that the service station owned and operated by Carter's brother Billy was engulfed in flames. Cool said:

> President Carter started running toward the station and we started running after him. Everyone expected the worst, but no one was seriously injured. A tanker truck had just pulled into the station and simultaneously someone had put a quarter in the Coke machine. Somehow the friction from the coin created an arc that resulted in a fiery explosion. About half the station was destroyed in the blast.[27]

On another occasion during a visit to New York, Carter's agents sprinted to an apartment building when a rifle with a telescopic sight emerged from a window. They discovered it belonged to a young boy who wanted to watch the president using the telescopic sight.[28]

There were also occasions when agents believed Carter was about to be physically assaulted. During a press briefing about the SALT talks in the White House a man began protesting against nuclear warheads. White House Press Officer Susan Ehrhardt said, 'He was from Iowa and he was with . . . the anti-nuclear group and he had been in jail many times before and I don't know how he slipped through Secret Service. I was really kind of shocked.' Within seconds the protestor was removed.[29]

Carter, the first president to take up jogging, caused some security problems for agents when, tiring of having his runs restricted to the White House grounds, he took to the streets. Agent Doyle Miller and the rest of the detail ran alongside, in front and behind the president and his physician during his routes. But agents, although used to running 3 to 4 miles daily to keep in shape, found it tough keeping up when weighted down with radio equipment and weapons. Soon bicycles were used during long jaunts to allow agents to keep up with the president and provide security.[30]

Often agent Jack Smith would be included in the group of agents who were assigned to jog with the president. Smith was a long-distance runner who often outran Carter. When the president competed in a public marathon run Smith attempted to persuade him to slow down, concerned about his health. Carter ignored him and eventually collapsed. He was placed in the rear of a car and agents called for the president's doctor, who gave him oxygen. Carter soon recovered.[31]

During Carter's presidency an incident at Camp David nearly resulted in the president being shot by a Marine guard. The guard, who was new to his posting, had been told that at night a particular footpath was never used so when Carter and his wife took an evening stroll along the path the Marine clicked his M-16 rifle and pointed it at the couple who he believed to be intruders. One of Carter's agents immediately stepped in front of the president and calmly spoke to the nervous soldier.[32]

After four years of grappling with inflation, a poor economy and oil price rises Carter entered his 1980 race for re-election with low poll ratings. Not long before the campaign began he went fishing with one of his agents at his Plains home. Soon they heard a rustling in nearby trees. It was a large rabbit escaping from a fox. The rabbit jumped in the water and swam towards Carter's boat. When Carter saw the rabbit swimming towards him he allegedly picked up a paddle and tried to hit it. When the press got wind of the incident Carter was ridiculed and led to editorial cartoons that gave some voters the perception that Carter was ineffectual as a president.

However, the story was exaggerated. Agent Doyle Miller said, 'It was just one of those times when everybody was sitting around Plains and nobody had anything to do and somebody mentioned the rabbit and it got so blown out of proportion it was ridiculous.' Miller was with Carter when the rabbit jumped into a pond and headed for the president's fishing boat. He said Carter did not hit the animal with a paddle.[33]

In Ronald Kessler's books about the Secret Service some agents who protected Carter spoke about him in such a negative way it seriously damaged his reputation. Kessler wrote, 'If the Secret Service considered Richard Nixon the strangest president Jimmy Carter was known as the least likable.'[34]

The Carters never really understood the Secret Service's role, according to Kessler. A former agent told the journalist that Carter '. . . tried to project the image of himself as a man of the people by carrying his own luggage when travelling' – but only when the press was in sight. In private, Kessler wrote, he would ask the Secret Service to carry his luggage. Another agent told Kessler that when the Carters were staying at their home in Plains, Georgia, the nuclear football, the device that the president uses to launch antiballistic missiles, was not permitted on the grounds of the Carter home. It was kept with an agent in Americus, about 15 miles away. The decision allegedly negated the possibility that Carter would be unable to respond quickly to a nuclear attack.

Kessler also wrote that Carter 'would regularly make a show of going to the Oval Office at 5 a.m. or 6 a.m. to call attention to how hard he was working for the American people'. The truth of the matter, agent Robert B. Sulliman Jr said, was that Carter '. . . would work for half an hour, then close the curtains and take a nap . . . His staff would tell the press he was working.'

Kessler also wrote of how Carter treated his agents and others who served him with utter disdain. Carter allegedly told agents not to look at him or speak to him, even to say hello, when he went to the Oval Office. 'For three and a half years, agent John Piasecky was on Carter's detail – including seven months of driving him in the presidential limousine – and Carter never spoke to him,' Kessler wrote. Carter was also allegedly 'moody and mistrustful'.[35]

Ronald Kessler was not the first writer to relate stories of how agents on Carter's White House Detail considered the thirty-ninth president to be 'aloof'. Agents Marty Vencker and Dennis McCarthy provided similar descriptions of Carter decades ago. In 1988 Marty Vencker, for example, described Carter as 'chilly' and 'remote . . . and so unlike Ford who agents described as friendly'.[36]

However, Carter was not alone in disengaging from his security detail when he wanted quiet moments. One of Ford's agents said there were times when:

> [He] went from Palm Springs to New York City in the limo, to L.A., from L.A. to New York City, board meetings, back to the airport, fly back to L.A. and drive back to Palm Springs and never say a word and I sat right next to him all the time. It was just the matter of giving him the space. If he wanted to talk to me, I would talk, but I wasn't going to sit there and hold a discussion about world events, because, first of all, I just wouldn't do that.[37]

Although the agents interviewed by Kessler were being truthful many agents' stories lacked context. Kessler interviewed a handful of agents who worked on Carter's detail out of a total White House presidential detail of 120 agents. It is not altogether clear or conclusive from Kessler's accounts that all Carter's agents were in agreement about the president's personality and character.

Missing from Kessler's story about the metal Zero Halliburton briefcase containing launch codes for nuclear weapons are the accounts of how other presidents had also been remiss in their handling of this vital piece of gadgetry. When Gerald Ford arrived at an economic summit in Paris the 'football' was left on board Air Force One. On occasion, Reagan left his aide carrying the case behind and in March 1981, after he was shot by John Hinckley, the FBI confiscated Reagan's wallet which had the nuclear missile launch codes printed on a business-size card. The wallet remained in limbo at FBI headquarters for 48 hours. There is no evidence Vice President Bush had a copy. In 1973, after Nixon presented Soviet leader Leonid Brezhnev with a Lincoln Continental at Camp David, Brezhnev unexpectedly drove away with Nixon leaving the president's detail behind and separating him from the football and his security agents for nearly 30 minutes.[38] Presidents Ford, Bush 41 and Clinton were also separated from the 'football' during their time in office.[39]

There were numerous occasions when Carter would socialise with his agents. It contradicts Kessler's stories about how Carter appeared to some agents to be 'unsocial' and 'remote'. In September 1980, Jerry Parr was surprised when a 50th birthday party was arranged for him on board Air Force One. Carter organised softball games which included agents as team members (although agent Marty Vencker did say Carter was a 'sore loser').[40]

Former agent Dennis McCarthy believed that some agents' characterisations of the president were made without context. McCarthy believed the 'coolness' arose because of a 'misunderstanding'. 'Carter rarely engaged in small talk with anyone,' McCarthy wrote, 'let alone Secret Service agents.' The agent thought it was a catch-22 situation. Carter thought the agents didn't like him and the agents thought the president didn't like them.[41] Even Marty Vencker, who described Carter as 'remote', sympathised with the president, '. . . we saw the guy when his head was hanging the lowest', Vencker said. 'It made me remember that, for all my bitching about Jimmy, his job was a lot tougher than mine.'[42]

Additionally, Carter's behaviour has, arguably, been misconstrued by some agents who never understood his personality. Both Carter and his wife were always reserved. 'Before 1966 [his first run for governor] [Rosalynn] and I were both very shy,' Carter said. 'It was almost a painful thing to approach a stranger or make a speech.'[43] His friend Red Herzog said Carter was a 'loner' who 'did not need other people's close bond of friendship to support his own ego and personality'; a quality that would appear to make him aloof.[44]

Jody Powell said that as Carter was a relative newcomer to the national political scene he was uncomfortable at first with the constant protection, particularly on walks when he wanted to be left alone. Powell said, 'He did not particularly enjoy bullshit sessions with the boys.' The presidential aide said that Carter did not work at being 'lovable' but did his job and expected everyone else to do theirs 'without a great deal of petting and stroking'.[45] Author Robert Scheer, who interviewed Carter for *Rolling Stone*, said Carter was impatient with 'social chitchat'.[46]

And there were times when Carter would appreciate the companionship of an agent during his walks. 'Carter would walk slowly,' Jerry Parr wrote, 'contemplatively, eyes down'. When Parr asked him why he always looked down Carter replied he was looking for arrowheads and other Cherokee relics. Parr said he enjoyed his walks with Carter on the president's Plains farm as the '. . . musky scent of rich, damp soil awakened my sleeping farmer genes'.[47] 'When I was president', Carter said, '[Secret Service agents] knew when Rosalynn and I preferred to be alone and undisturbed . . .'.[48] Additionally, it is known that Carter and his wife Rosalynn were more comfortable with the African American agents.[49]

Former agent Dan Emmett did not believe that the lack of a personal greeting by a president indicated any animosity or bad feeling. 'The presidents I protected (Bush 41, Clinton, Bush 43)', Emmett wrote, 'had good and bad days at the office and in their personal lives. . . . If the president happened to walk by without speaking . . . we did not feel insulted. We experienced no feelings at all, one way or the other.'[50] Accordingly, Carter's behaviour was not unusual for any president.

For his part, Carter believed his relationship with his detail was based on trust and friendship, although it was always on a level consistent with their professional standing. 'Some of the agents became close companions', Carter said, 'especially those who have run relatively long distances with me or skied across country or down mountain slopes. The younger agents usually serve with us only for about three years, and it is often a sorrowful occasion when their career advancement requires that they may be transferred to other posts.'[51]

Carter became much closer to his detail once he had discarded the burdens of office and allowed his security detail to hunt and fish on his Plains, Georgia farm. It became a choice assignment.

* * *

Carter was once asked if he ever discussed the possibility of assassination with his wife. He said he was not afraid of death and he had already made a commitment to face death when he volunteered for the submarine force. He didn't worry about his decision to seek the presidency. 'There is a certain element of danger in running for president', Carter said, 'borne out by statistics on the number of presidents who have been attacked, but I have to say frankly that it's something I never worry about.'[52]

Carter told author Larry J. Sabato that he had faced at least three home-grown assassination attempts since he left the presidency and was constantly warned by the Secret Service of personal threats during his frequent overseas travel. 'I have had two or three threats to my life after I came home from the White House. When I go on an overseas trip almost invariably, I get a report from the Secret Service that where I'm going is very dangerous.'

Carter also told Sabato, 'Sometimes they [Secret Service] ask me not to go, and I go anyway. They and I both just laugh about it. So I have been more concerned about my safety in doing the Carter Centre's business overseas than I ever was in the White House.'[53]

Carter said he did not '. . . remember being afraid in the White House, or I never have cancelled a trip, but . . . I would make a hasty withdrawal and not stop, shake hands and so forth, when the Secret Service convinced me that it was necessary.'[54]

As president, Carter was the subject of numerous threats to assassinate him; many of which involved manhunts and car chases.[55] However, the most dangerous threat to Carter came from the man who went on to shoot President Reagan in March 1981. The incident occurred during Carter's 1980 re-election campaign.

By late September 1980 John Hinckley began tracking the movements of President Carter in newspaper accounts. He travelled to Dallas, Texas, to buy two revolvers and then flew to Washington DC and stayed at a hotel only three blocks from the White House. During his stay he sent a postcard to his sister describing the executive mansion as 'Carter's Fortress'.

Hinckley read about the president's planned trip to Dayton, Ohio, on 2 October for a campaign rally.[56] When he arrived at the rally he stood a short distance away from the president as Carter shook hands with his supporters. Later Hinckley confessed he had 'wilted' when a Secret Service agent looked him in the eye.[57] According to Hinckley, he came to the rally unarmed and only wished to find out whether or not he could get close enough to the president to shoot him. However, Hinckley did express regret he had not taken his gun with him when he discovered how easy it would have been.[58]

On 7 October Hinckley flew to Nashville, Tennessee, to prepare for Carter's visit there later in the week for a campaign rally at the Grand Ole Opry. On 9 October, the day Carter was due to arrive, Hinckley was arrested at Nashville Airport with three handguns in his suitcase. A security officer had spotted the guns as his baggage went through the airport's X-Ray machine. The guns were confiscated and Hinckley was allowed on his way after appearing before a judge who fined him $62.50.

It was at about this time that the media began reporting a likely Reagan victory in the presidential election, and Hinckley had persuaded himself that killing a candidate who was about to lose an election would rob him of the notoriety he craved.[59]

* * *

In 1980 the Carter re-election campaign was unquestionably aided by the Iran hostage crisis. Exactly one year before the presidential election followers of Iran's Ayatollah Khomeini, who had toppled the Shah of Iran in 1978, stormed the US Embassy protesting the shah's admittance to the United States for treatment of an ultimately fatal cancer condition. Dozens of Americans who were inside were taken hostage. Some were later released, but more than fifty remained hostages throughout 1980, despite an abortive rescue operation ordered by Carter.

Voters rallied around the president during the ongoing crisis. His main challenger for the Democrat nomination was Ted Kennedy. However, Kennedy victories in a number of key states, including New York and California, were unable to save the candidate from taking the Democrat presidential nomination away from Carter. Ultimately Carter was re-nominated at a fractious Democratic convention in New York City.

During the 1980 campaign the president travelled to over sixty towns and cities across the nation. He often took risks and sometimes ignored the advice of his agents when he would exit his limousine to greet crowds of supporters.

During a campaign event in New Orleans he was advised not to 'work the rope line' as the Secret Service had received a report from New Orleans local law enforcement that two men had been observed carrying guns. Carter agreed but as soon as his limousine came to a stop he climbed onto the roof waving to the crowd. Carter repeated his risky tactics in Kentucky. Agent Jerry Parr was so concerned about Carter he held the president by the belt with his left hand and kept his right hand free in case he had to draw his gun.[60]

During his final day of campaigning Carter travelled across the country – from the Midwest to Missouri and Michigan and on to Portland and Seattle before flying back to Plains. He was guarded by head of detail Jerry Parr, Assistant Special Agent in Charge Bob Horton and eight agents.

Carter could not compete with the rising popularity of Republican Party presidential candidate Ronald Reagan. Reagan won the election in a landslide. Although Carter would likely have lost the election because of the economy and inflation, a Reagan landslide would not have occurred if Carter had been able to free the hostages before the day of the election on 4 November 1980.

Carter found the defeat 'incomprehensible'. He returned to Plains to discover that his peanut business had failed and he was a million dollars in debt. However, the former president went on to develop a reputation as one of the nations 'best ex-presidents' as he campaigned around the world for human rights. He was awarded the Nobel Peace Prize in 2002, 'for his decades of untiring effort to find peaceful solutions to international conflicts, to advance democracy and human rights, and to promote economic and social development'.[61]

Chapter 11

The Last Brother

'For years Democrats had thought, "Well, he's the third Kennedy on the scene, and he'll be our standard bearer sooner or later".'

Presidential candidate Senator George McGovern

'Secret Service agents are with those they protect all the time. Agents see politicians in ways that no others do. . . . Sometimes the view is tragic.'

Secret Service agent Dan Emmett

'He knew what was expected of him. He knew, reluctantly, that he probably had to go forward and do this [1980 run for the presidency], but he knew too it was dangerous.'

Melody Miller, Assistant to Senator Edward Kennedy

'I'm somewhere between happiness and sadness, and life and death.'

Senator Edward Kennedy

After his brother Robert's death, Ted Kennedy mused he was not afraid to die. He said, 'If someone's going to blow my head off [I want] just one swing at him.'[1] On another occasion he said he was not frightened of dying, 'What will be, will be. What God will ordain will happen', he said. But he did not want to be killed 'from behind'.[2] At times he allowed dark humour to conceal those fears. His aides Richard Burke and Dick Drayne once told Kennedy that when they walked beside him he should wear a placard sporting a large X. They, in turn, would carry signs with an arrow pointing to the Senator.[3]

Kennedy told a Congressman who wanted him to take Bobby Kennedy's place and run for president in 1968 that although he was not frightened of dying, 'I'm too young to die'. He would try and explain to friends, 'Do you know what it's like to have your wife frightened all the time?'[4]

Kennedy's wife Joan once burst into tears during an interview at her McLean, Virginia, home:

> I'm scared, scared something will happen to him. There may be a person out there trying to make a clean sweep of the Kennedy brothers. Look at us. We're naked! My God! Someone can come down that road out there and come here. There's no name on the mailbox, but that doesn't hide us. The cab drivers know where we are, and every newspaper has printed where we live.[5]

Additionally, Kennedy had constantly to reassure his children that their father would not suffer the same fate as their uncles. Every day he would telephone his children from his Senate office just so they could hear his voice and know he was safe.[6]

Kennedy was never able to reconcile what an assassination attempt on his life would do to his family and his mother. He did not want them to suffer a third time what they had endured in 1963 and 1968.[7] He told his aide Dun Gifford, 'I can't let go. We have a job to do. If I let go, Ethel [Kennedy] will let go and my mother will let go, and all my sisters.'

Senate aide and secretary Melody Miller explained how Kennedy felt every time he took a step outside of his house:

> . . . he never knew whether there was going to be somebody behind a tree trying to knock off the last Kennedy brother. He fully expected it to happen. He told me once . . . that he didn't want to live his life looking over his shoulder, so he made a decision to simply go forward, not to be surrounded by security, because that just reminded him of this problem.[8]

Each time Kennedy was mentioned as a future presidential candidate – in 1968, 1972, 1976, 1980, 1984 and 1988 – his struggle to cope with his own personal failings and the constant fear of assassination became monumental. He frequently found solace in liquor and womanising, living life on the edge. Many years later, long after the Senator's death, his son would say that his father '. . . should, in my view have been in therapy after his brothers were killed. He suffered tremendously. He self-medicated, drank a lot to medicate this post-traumatic stress.'[9]

Often Kennedy's fears would provoke a visible reaction from the Senator when he thought his life was in danger. On one occasion reporter Jack Newfield had lunch with him at a Washington cafeteria. When a lunch tray was dropped by a waitress Newfield witnessed Kennedy throwing his hands to his head.[10] A friend of Kennedy's said that when the Senator appeared in a public place he was always on the lookout for a potential assassin, often changing the sides of the street he happened to be walking along, looking over his shoulder. Melody Miller recalled how he would react to a car backfire and she would '. . . see him dive down and throw his briefcase over his head'.[11]

In March 1970, nearly two years after Robert's assassination, he attended a St Patrick's Day parade in Chicago. Halfway through the march someone in the crowd set off a loud firecracker. Kennedy's legs buckled and his body flinched. His face turned ashen and his eyes clouded. The aides who acted as his bodyguards described protecting Kennedy as a 'mission impossible'. They nervously watched police scanning upper windows along the route hoping to spot a would-be assassin aiming a rifle.[12]

The first sign of Kennedy's inability to cope with the tragedies of his brothers' deaths began in the winter of 1968/69 during one of his frequent visits to his father's Palm Beach mansion. Family chauffeur Frank Saunders was awakened by Kennedy in the middle of the night banging on his door. 'Ted had been drinking all night,' Saunders said. Kennedy told him his car had become 'stuck' and he had driven off the road. He wanted Saunders to 'take care of it'. Kennedy walked home along North Ocean Boulevard as Saunders drove to the scene of the accident. Kennedy's car had crashed not far from his father's house where a straight road took a sharp turn. He had missed the turn and driven over a curb into a shrubbery just short of a cement wall. The car had become bogged down in sand so Saunders called a tow company he knew were discrete. Saunders concluded that Kennedy's car 'had to be speeding to miss the turn'.[13]

Then, in April 1969, when Kennedy was flying back from a congressional trip to inspect the living conditions of poor Indians in Alaska he began drinking heavily, voicing fears he would become a target for fanatics 'just like his brothers'. It was a journey planned by his brother Robert in 1968 to inspect the wretched living conditions of 55,000 Indians, Eskimos and Aleuts but cancelled after the assassination of Martin Luther King.

A hard-drinking Kennedy pelted aides and reporters with pillows and walked up and down the aisles of his plane chanting 'Eskimo power'. He also rambled incoherently about his brother's assassination. 'They're going to shoot my ass off the way they shot Bobby . . .' he said.[14]

Three months after Kennedy's Alaska trip his reckless behaviour resulted in a tragedy on the island of Chappaquiddick on 18 July 1969. Kennedy drove his Oldsmobile off an island bridge, sending young RFK secretary Mary Jo Kopechne to her death and damaging his chances of ever getting to the White House. The accident placed him in a compromising position with an attractive young woman and, most probably, a reckless use of alcohol.

However, despite repeated accusations of a cover-up no evidence has been presented to show that Kennedy's story of the accident – driving down Dike Road, meeting a dog-leg turn, accidently driving off the bridge, attempting to rescue Mary Jo and suffering shock and concussion which led to erratic behaviour – was anything but true.[15]

* * *

Shortly after the George Wallace shooting on 15 May 1972, the Senate Democratic Majority Leader, Mike Mansfield, introduced and got passed legislation providing Kennedy with Secret Service protection.[16] Simultaneously, President Nixon ordered Secret Service protection for other Democrat presidential candidates including Representative Shirley Chisholm and Representative Wilbur D. Mills. Kennedy accepted the offer, and agents were assigned, guarding his McLean, Virginia, home and accompanying him on his campaign travels.[17]

Nixon had mixed motives in agreeing to Secret Service protection for Kennedy. He worried about being blamed if a third Kennedy was shot while not having official bodyguard protection. 'You understand what the problem is,' Nixon told aide Bob Haldeman and John Ehrlichman on 7 September 1972. 'If the son of a bitch gets shot they'll say we didn't furnish it [protection]. So you just buy his insurance.'[18] Nixon said he wanted Kennedy covered 'on the basis that we pick the Secret Service men . . . and not that son of a bitch [Secret Service Director James J.] Rowley'. A 'full force' of forty men was eventually assigned.

Nixon also had an ulterior motive in wanting Kennedy protected. He wanted the Secret Service to keep tabs on him. Before Kennedy's detail was appointed, Nixon asked his aide John Ehrlichman if he knew of anyone he could 'get to . . . [and] . . . one that can cover him around the clock, every place he goes'. Nixon then asked his aides to, 'Plant two guys on him. This could be very useful. We might just get lucky and catch this son-of-a-bitch, ruin him. . . . it's going to be fun.' The president had been making reference to Kennedy's reputation as a 'womaniser'.[19]

The president said he wanted it made 'damn clear' that Kennedy requested the coverage 'because of threats'. Nixon then spoke of getting lucky and ruining Kennedy for '1976'.

Nixon approved hiring a Secret Service agent, Robert Newbrand, whom Nixon's chief of staff, Bob Haldeman, knew well.

Newbrand had once worked on Nixon's vice-presidential detail. Haldeman said Newbrand had spoken to him and said, 'With what you've done for me and what the President's done for me, I just want you to know, if you want someone killed, if you want anything else done, any way, any direction . . .'. Haldeman told Nixon Newbrand would '. . . do anything that I tell him to . . . He really will.'[20]

Secret Service agent Clint Hill remembered receiving a call from the White House with instructions about the appointment and realised Nixon wanted to 'spy' on Ted Kennedy. Hill refused to appoint Newbrand as head of the detail but after receiving another call from the White House he was told, 'Either you put that man in the job, or your job is on the line.' Hill had no other option but to do as he was told. He told his superior Jim Burke about it. Burke promised to '. . . take care of it right now'.[21]

However, Newbrand, who worked in the New York City Field Office, informed his superiors of what was going on and there is no evidence the agent turned into an informer. Newbrand was upset that Nixon could believe he would betray the Secret Service under political pressure. He said, 'I'll lie to them and provide plenty of useless information.' Newbrand also said he would use the opportunity to 'have a little fun with Nixon's aides'.[22]

On 5 June 1972 Secret Service protection was discontinued at Kennedy's request. However, in September during the general election campaign, Nixon wanted Kennedy protected again. Kennedy, who was campaigning for George McGovern, willingly accepted.

* * *

Following Nixon's resignation in August 1974 polls showed that Kennedy led all the likely Democrat and Republican candidates for the 1976 presidential election. However, although Kennedy was confident he could beat Nixon's successor, Gerald Ford, he worried about the effect his candidacy would have on his family. He ruled himself out in the early stages of the campaign to deal with family troubles, including his son Ted Jr's loss of a leg to bone cancer.

Kennedy said he had 'thought it all out' about running for president in 1980. 'Maybe I'm wrong,' he said. 'Maybe it will be a lot worse than I think.' Friends told *TIME* reporters that Kennedy was 'fatalistic' about his life and 'the special danger' in running. One unnamed family member said, 'It's really scary.' Kennedy thought, 'I know how they feel. That's why it's a very personal decision.'[23]

After years of indecision, Kennedy finally decided that he wanted the presidency and announced his candidacy in a speech at Faneuil Hall, Boston, on 7 November 1979. However, his attempt to take away the Democrat nomination from a sitting president, Jimmy Carter, quickly turned into a doomed campaign. Democrats rallied behind Carter making Kennedy's campaign an uphill struggle.

During the campaign Kennedy came to terms with the inherent danger. When a friend attempted to talk him out of running by telling him, 'Somebody out there is waiting for you', Kennedy responded by saying, 'They could be waiting for me even if I weren't running for President.'[24]

Kennedy's Secret Service protective detail was the largest of all the candidates who entered the 1980 presidential election campaign. He had three teams working to guard him consisting of five or six agents in each team. One team did advance work. The second team travelled with him and a third team worked with local law-enforcement officials to block roads and traffic so Kennedy's motorcade could rush through lights and stop signs. He also travelled with an aide, Lawrence Horowitz, who was a licensed physician, and a nurse skilled in trauma, especially for gunshot wounds. Kennedy was given the Secret Service codename 'Sunburn'.

Kennedy's detail worked hard to ensure the Senator was not lost on their watch. A Secret Service official said, 'If it were left to us, we would put these guys behind bulletproof shields all the time. We are trying to get maximum security, and they are trying to get maximum exposure.'[25]

Although Kennedy agreed with historian James McGregor Burn's advice that he should run a campaign via the medium of television, radio, newspaper editorial offices and well-policed arenas, he soon abandoned the idea and began plunging into crowds. At one crowded event Kennedy grabbed Secret

Service agent Patrick Caldwell's arm and pulled him to the front, ducked behind him and used him as a 'medieval shield'.[26]

At the time of the 1980 campaign the Secret Service had on their 'active file' 400 people who were believed to be capable of making an attempt on Kennedy's life. As the threats against him were higher than those for other candidates, diplomacy had to take second place to serious protective measures. The Kennedy detail's zealous behaviour in protecting their candidate often caused tension with local officials. Frequently, fist fights broke out.[27]

As Kennedy trailed behind President Carter in the polls he began to campaign more vigorously, often exposing himself to danger. On one occasion, during the Democrat primary campaign in Illinois, Kennedy decided he would participate in the St Patrick's Day parade in Chicago with his family. His Secret Service detail was displeased with the decision. It was the first time in the presidential campaign when Kennedy would expose himself in such a manner and was extremely risky. The agents argued against it but Kennedy had made his mind up. When the day of the parade arrived agents were met with snow and freezing rain which made their protective mission more complicated. Kennedy arrived at the start of the march in a limousine accompanied by his wife Joan, daughter Kara and sons Patrick and Teddy Jr as well as his sister Eunice and his niece Maria Shriver.

As the family walked behind Chicago Mayor Jayne Byrne the area around them was guarded by the agents as well as Chicago police officers and state police. A SWAT team stood nearby and a police helicopter hovered overhead. As Kennedy and his entourage marched down State Street sounds of gunfire echoed around the area. Kennedy's legs buckled from fear as agents rushed to surround him. Within a short time agents were able to identify 'the shooter' as a reveller with a green dyed beard who had set off a string of firecrackers. Kennedy composed himself and continued shaking hands and marching down the street. However, no sooner had the agents returned to their protection duties one of the detail spotted someone with a camera and long telephoto lens leaning out of a window of a high building. Agents reacted by directing Kennedy to the opposite side of the street.[28]

During the 1980 presidential campaign Kennedy used aide Richard Burke's residence to rendezvous with girlfriends. It was the responsibility of the Secret Service to check out any places the Senator visited to assess the risk factors. The agents swept Burke's house for surveillance bugs and supplied buttons to staff to identify them to agents on duty. The security coded colours were changed frequently. If Kennedy brought a woman to Burke's home for a 'staff meeting' wearing a security button, agents would assume she was on the Senator's staff. The ruse was used throughout Kennedy's campaign. According to Burke, the agents were not fooled and indicated so to Burke.[29]

However, although Kennedy's detail was no more than 'amused' by the Senator's 'ploys', they did respond to a far more serious breach of security protocol. Agents had provided Kennedy with two versions of a bulletproof vest – a trench coat for inclement weather and a heavy vest designed to be worn under his shirt when he was wearing a jacket. Kennedy did not like it as it was uncomfortable and affected his weak back which he had injured in a light plane accident in 1964. The agents acquiesced to Kennedy's complaints and issued him with a lighter jacket. However, Kennedy still balked at wearing it.

Ted Kennedy's campaign was poorly organised and plagued by questions about his behaviour at Chappaquiddick. And despite late victories in the California and New York primaries, the race was never close. In fact, Kennedy's finest moment came in defeat, in a speech to the Democratic National Convention at Madison Square Garden, when he promised the Kennedys would still figure in national politics. 'For me, a few hours ago, this campaign came to an end,' he said to convention delegates. 'For all those whose cares have been our concern, the work goes on, the cause endures, the hope still lives, and the dream shall never die.'

Although Kennedy had little respect for President Carter, he agreed to campaign for him in the general election. Carter felt the Senator remained in danger and instructed the Secret Service to continue protecting him, although the detail was reduced in size.

* * *

Kennedy continued to be touted as a future president following his 1980 defeat. However, he still faced the same dilemmas of the past. His family were against his run for the presidency in 1984 and his mother was vehemently against it.

Additionally, following Kennedy's divorce in 1981, a lawyer close to the Kennedy family told journalist Ed Klein that Kennedy's political legacy was falling apart because of the Senator's erratic personal life. He was '. . . close to being suicidal . . . drinking himself to death', the lawyer said.[30]

Although Kennedy had eschewed the idea of running for president in 1984 and 1988, he continued to support Democrat candidates including the 1984 Democratic Party nominee Walter Mondale and campaigned for him throughout the country. During the final thirty days of the campaign President Reagan directed that Kennedy receive Secret Service protection and signed an 'order of protection' in October of that year. Kennedy's detail was to protect the Senator until the end of the campaign on election day.[31]

Secret Service agent Dan Emmett volunteered to serve with Kennedy's detail. The assignment was 'tough', 'hectic' and 'demanding' for the fifteen agents selected, according to Emmett. They were worked the thirty straight days without a day off. Often Kennedy would visit several cities in one day. Emmett's shift began at midnight and ended at 8.00 am when he was relieved by the day shift.[32]

According to Emmett, Kennedy always cooperated with his bodyguards as he had been well aware of Secret Service protocol since the time of his brother's presidency in the early 1960s. And he always informed his bodyguards of his itinerary so they could plan carefully.

During the campaign Emmett learned that a friendly crowd was just as demanding as a hostile one. Kennedy's popularity, Emmett said, provoked a 'wave-like' reaction in and around him when he appeared to give his campaign speeches. The large crowds seemed oblivious to the rope lines around the speaking platforms and frequently Emmett and his four fellow agents had to form a human barrier around the Senator. During one speech, Emmett recalled, a group of 'older women' grabbed Kennedy's son Patrick rumpling his clothes and taking his PT-109 tie clasp, a cherished 'war hero' symbol of his Uncle Jack's campaign for the presidency.

Although Kennedy did not like to fly in small planes, especially after the 1964 plane crash which damaged his back, he was frequently compelled to use them for campaigning as there simply was no other way to visit all the places on his itinerary. Some campaign stops in small communities were just not accessible by other means. When he flew in an old DC-3 during the campaign, his agents noticed how afraid he was.

On the final afternoon of the 1984 campaign Ted Kennedy gave a party for his bodyguards at his Cape Cod home. The Senator interacted socially with them and was 'the perfect host', according to Emmett. Kennedy gave the agent and another two colleagues a tour of JFK's house in the Kennedy compound. Emmett spent his time there looking at all the political memorabilia in the house which the agent said was like a time capsule, 'everything in

place as it had been when JFK lived there'. When the Senator was finished
he handed the key to Emmett and asked him to lock up.

Dan Emmett was also struck by Kennedy's demeanour. The Senator still
grieved the loss of his brothers, Emmett said, '. . . a man tormented by the
tragedies that had occurred in his life. Secret Service agents are with those
they protect all the time. Agents see politicians in ways that no others do.
Sometimes the view is tragic.'[33]

* * *

Kennedy aide Melody Miller was privy to many of the threats Ted Kennedy
received over the decades she worked for him. Miller said, 'Whenever he
was Presidential and that was being talked about – every one of those four
years, from '68 on – then he was in the centre of the bull's-eye, and our death
threats and death mail would pick up.'[34]

The threats originated from multiple sources, including individuals,
anonymous persons and members of radical groups such as the Ku Klux
Klan, Minutemen organisations and the National Socialist White People's
Party. A typical oral or written threat would be, 'I'm gonna kill Kennedy,
and I really mean it.' Some threats were specific in regard to timing including
a threat to kill Kennedy '. . . on Oct. 25, 1968. The Kennedy residence must
be well protected on that date.' Numerous threats were passed on to the FBI
and the Secret Service, local police departments and Kennedy himself.

The FBI investigated many threats they considered to be 'serious'. One
threat concerned allegations that Robert Kennedy's assassin, Sirhan Sirhan,
had attempted to hire a fellow prisoner to kill him. The prisoner told the FBI
he was offered $1 million and a car but declined.[35]

The mail was 'vicious', Miller said, 'along with vicious phone calls'. She
once kept a threatener on the phone for 45 minutes so the FBI could trace the
call. He was eventually caught by the Secret Service.[36]

Miller made calls to the FBI and Secret Service and turned over threatening letters to the agencies 'on numerous occasions over the years', she said:

> I have given them chapter and verse of everything I could get out
> of somebody on the phone. I've sent them to various homes all over
> the country where people have called and made threats against
> him. . . . There's nothing that I have not heard in my left ear in
> terms of profanity and hate spewed at him, from jealousy or as a
> result of Chappaquiddick . . .[37]

Whenever the FBI, Capitol police or Secret Service considered the threats particularly dangerous two detectives would arrive and guard Kennedy's Washington office, Suite 431 of the Old Senate Office Building. They sometimes stayed weeks at a time. The threats spiked during Kennedy's failed bid for the presidency in 1980, but continued for the rest of his life.

Kennedy was always appreciative of the work the FBI did in investigating the threats. In 1974 there was an unspecified threat against 'Kennedy children'. Following their investigation, he wrote to FBI Director Clarence Kelley, thanking him for, 'The Bureau's advice and guidance . . . [which] was of great comfort to all of us, particularly my sister-in-law Ethel Kennedy'. Kennedy singled out two agents for praise including Special Agent Frank Leonard who conducted the investigation. It is not known if the perpetrator was arrested and convicted.[38]

Over the years Fairfax County plain-clothes police would turn up at Kennedy's house in Mclean, Virginia, whenever a threat was deemed to be 'serious'. The police usually parked at the gate at such times. On one occasion Kennedy's staff had police cars sit in the driveway of Kennedy's home until a would-be assassin was 'tracked down' and arrested.[39]

Kennedy was also the victim of stalkers who gained access to his house at 636 Chain Bridge Road in McLean, Virginia, a short distance from Washington DC.

During the summer of 1979, when Kennedy was considering whether or not to challenge President Carter for the Democrat presidential nomination, police responded to a burglar alarm. Kennedy was at his Squaw Island Cape Cod home at the time of the incident. When the police arrived at his home they found a disoriented and rambling woman on the lower floor of the house. She was taken away for 'observation' and later released. However, the woman returned to the house a few nights later and once again the burglar alarm sounded. She was arrested and later appeared in court where the judge decided she was a stalker and needed to be institutionalised.[40] A second stalker broke into Kennedy's house and managed to reach as far as Kennedy's bedroom before police caught her hiding under the bed.[41]

One stalker investigated by the FBI was a '. . . young man, possibly a student who was in his early 20s'. A Kennedy staffer informed FBI Special Agent Bowers that a 'pest' had become a 'nuisance'. He had called the Senator's office and claimed he had met Kennedy on a plane and been hired to join his staff. At various times he contacted the office to repeat his claims.

On 3 August 1968 the stalker arrived at Kennedy's home and gained access by telling the caretaker he was on the Senator's staff. Kennedy's secretary ejected him. Later that day he called the office seeking an invitation to a private party for staff members.

On 4 August the stalker attempted to board a commercial flight and when told there was no space on the plane he once again claimed to be a member of Kennedy's staff and demanding someone be taken off the plane to make room for him. The airlines called Kennedy's office to report the incident. Subsequently, the stalker called the office on a number of occasions to request a Senate car to pick him up and meet him at the airport. Kennedy's staff was informed by the FBI that the information about the 'pest' did not constitute a violation of federal law within FBI jurisdiction. However, Capitol police were alerted and asked to keep an eye out for him. No further incidents were reported.[42]

There were also a number of unnamed armed individuals who were arrested during the 1980 presidential election campaign. In a scene from the film *In the Line of Fire* the Secret Service raided a flat in Philadelphia and found photos of Ted Kennedy and plans of motorcade routes plastered over the walls as well as documents alluding to 'getting Edward Kennedy'. Some threateners were captured on the edges of crowds during the campaign, according to Melody Miller. They had weapons on them, she said, and the Secret Service 'got them'.[43]

Miller said she practically ran a 'mental health clinic' in Ted Kennedy's Senate office, a warren of four small rooms and a larger one, 20 by 30ft, for the Senator. She talked to 'disturbed visitors', listened to them and tried to give them empathy and 'an understanding ear'. Miller also had to deal with 'numerous phone calls threatening the senator'. She did not call the police about many of the mentally unstable people because she was able to calm them down. She believed the solution to handling the problem was to simply listen to them for a period of time and hoped that venting their frustrations about the Senator would calm them down. Most of them did, Miller said.[44]

However, there were three mentally disturbed visitors who entered the Senator's Capitol Hill office whose behaviour she considered to be particularly dangerous.

The Capitol police knew that Miller and the rest of the staff would usually defuse situations and would not 'over-react'. Just in case, however, a 'panic button' was installed. It was an intercom which would alert the Capitol police officers. The codename to be used in such circumstances was, 'The books are ready in 431'. The Capitol police were aware that Miller would not 'cry wolf' and if the alarm was raised they knew that a serious incident was in the making.

The first incident involved a woman who entered Kennedy's office in 'a rage'. A mentally disturbed African American woman, a graduate of Berkeley, began to pay visits to Kennedy's office asking to meet the Senator. She had been organising a welfare programme for the underprivileged in the DC neighbourhoods and was having some difficulties in putting the programme together. She believed Kennedy could sort out the problem. Each time she had visited the office she had '. . . gotten more and more volatile every time she came', Miller said. One day she entered the office and complained that Miller would not allow her to see Kennedy. The woman threatened the Kennedy aide, vowing to 'get her' and 'get Kennedy'.

When Miller pushed the 'panic button' two Capitol police officers, who happened to be in the hallway, ran in. As the distraught woman tried to enter Kennedy's private office Miller hurried to lock the connecting door. As she was getting ready to lock it, the door flew open. The woman had broken away from the police 'and came tearing right through and into the Senator's private office. I caught up with her on the threshold and tackled her; we both landed on the floor . . . the Senator was at his desk'.[45]

'Here I was, rolling around, getting myself between this woman and the Senator,' Miller said. 'She was yelling, and the police were, and the Senator got up and just started talking very softly.' Kennedy responded by lowering his voice almost to a whisper, 'so that everybody had to be quiet to hear him'. Miller said Kennedy's actions were 'very smart, because he immediately defused the loud anger in the room, and . . . quietly got this woman calmed down'. Kennedy arranged for the woman to meet with staffer Bob Bates who discovered that the enraged woman's 'welfare program' was 'just like feathers' which 'wouldn't come together. It was all kind of spacey.'

Some years later Miller once again began to receive death threats from the woman. They were taken seriously enough for plain-clothes police officers to be detailed to guard her until the woman was found and taken to a mental health facility. Miller said:

> Every day the police [in] plainclothes met me at my car, sat in the
> reception room, stayed with me all day long, lunch and dinner, so

I had a sense of what it's like to be covered by the Secret Service the way the senator was. I understand that it does give you a sense of vulnerability and it is frightening. That then stays with you and you can't live normally and think normally about life, so I could empathize even more with him.[46]

The second serious incident occurred shortly after Ted Kennedy announced his candidacy for the 1980 Democrat presidential nomination. Susan Osgood was a 38-year-old woman who lived in Boston. She had attended Wheaton College in Norton, Massachusetts, and coincidently one of her classmates had been Esther Newberg, part of the group of young woman at the Kennedy cook-out on the night of the Chappaquiddick tragedy. Osgood had a long history of emotional problems and had been hospitalised for a schizophrenic condition at McLean Hospital in Belmont, Massachusetts, and at various hospitals in New York, New Jersey and New Hampshire. Throughout her life she had attempted suicide three times. During summer 1978 she was hospitalised in a Nashua hospital and evaluated in New Hampshire State Hospital. Doctors determined she was not dangerous to herself or others. Although Osgood's mother, Anne, said her daughter had no interest in politics or the Kennedys, the *Boston Globe* reported that notes found in Osgood's apartment indicated she was a supporter of President Carter and Vice President Mondale.

On 28 November 1979, following a trip to Ireland, Osgood entered Kennedy's Senate office shortly before 10.00 am brandishing a 5in hunting knife. One of Kennedy's receptionists, Mary Ann Mikulich, said, 'I was sitting at my desk when a woman came in with a big hunting knife, just yelling at the top of her voice. She didn't say anything.'

Joseph Meusburger, one of several Secret Service agents on duty in Kennedy's office, grappled with Osgood and was able to subdue her but not before he suffered a light cut on his left wrist in the process. Kennedy, who had been working in a nearby office, was not informed of the attack until Osgood had been handcuffed and taken away. Kennedy later praised 'the obvious courage' of his Secret Service agents and added, 'I am grateful that there was no serious injury to any people in my office.'[47]

Osgood was arraigned in the Federal District Court on a charge of assaulting a Federal officer and remanded to St Elizabeth's Mental Hospital until 1 April 1980 then transferred to the District of Columbia Detention Facility.

When Osgood arrived at the jail she refused to say why she attempted to attack Kennedy and offered no information about her background or any explanation for the attack. She did, however, inform jail staff that, as a Christian Scientist, she would not accept medical or psychiatric treatment or examination. She told staff she adhered to the tenets of her faith which rejected the use of medical and psychiatric science in the 'healing process'.

During the time Osgood was treated at the detention facility she was belligerent and hostile to medical staff. She frequently spat at people and generally behaved 'abusively'. On 4 April she was seen by a forensic psychiatrist, Dr Norman L. Wilson, and she 'screamed insults' at him and his staff and threatened she would 'kill him and the staff members if she could'. Her behaviour led to medical staff injecting her with a psychotropic drug, Haldol, to calm her down so she could not harm herself.

Osgood was sentenced on 16 October 1980 after a jury trial. She denied threatening anyone at the jail but did admit she screamed verbal insults at Wilson and threatened to sue him for 'violating her constitutional rights'. She later sued the authorities but the case was dismissed.[48]

Ted Kennedy's second serious brush with death came a year after Osgood's assassination attempt. In December 1980 four months before his attempt on the life of President Reagan, 25-year-old John Hinckley arrived in the reception room of Kennedy's Senate office. As the Senator had twenty-seven aides at the time with additional clerical workers the office was extremely busy.

Hinckley sat down in a wooden armchair and when he was approached by a Kennedy secretary, he told her he '. . . wanted a moment with the senator'. However, as Ted Kennedy had a busy schedule that day, the secretary told Hinckley the Senator was unable to see him. Hinckley said he was in no hurry and would wait. He was armed with a loaded pistol and his plans were to shoot Kennedy the moment the Senator returned to his office.

Fortunately for Kennedy, Senate business forced him to overrun his schedule. After a 3-hour wait Hinckley gave up and left. Three months later, on 31 March 1981, he shot President Reagan as he was leaving the Washington Hilton Hotel.[49]

* * *

Following the 1984 campaign, stories about Kennedy's reckless behaviour increased. According to police officer Steven E. Dekelbaum, Kennedy went through a red light and nearly ran him down. 'He was speeding,' Dekelbaum said. 'I jumped out of the way. . . . he stopped. I approached the car. He reeked [of liquor].' Dekelbaum removed Kennedy's car keys but a senior officer took them and returned them to the Senator after apologising to him. Capitol police officer Rodney C. Eades also observed Kennedy driving recklessly round the Capitol building nearly running over a Congressman. As Eades put his hand out to stop Kennedy, the Senator shouted, 'You know you are a stupid son of a bitch.' Another Capitol police officer said Kennedy would often arrive drunk at his office in the early hours of the morning.[50]

The 1980s were to prove the worst time for Kennedy's public image. He became mired in scandal ranging from the William Kennedy rape trial to tabloid headlines chronicling his affairs and drinking problem. However, in the early 1990s he turned his life around when he met the woman who was to become his second wife, Victoria Reggie. They were married in 1992. At the time Kennedy offered a mea culpa for his well-publicised behaviour. 'I recognise my own shortcomings,' he said in a speech, 'the faults in the conduct of my private life. I realise that I alone am responsible for them, and I am the one who must confront them.'[51]

Chapter 12

Jesse Jackson's Perilous Campaigns

'. . . of the 200 million-plus people in this country, there are a considerable number who, to put it mildly, dislike Jesse Jackson. To put it less mildly, they hate him. . . . Some hear strange voices in their heads, which is why a rock star can be killed outside his home. Others believe it is their duty to save their country or race from some threat that festers in a dark corner of their brains, which is why presidents, aspiring presidents and civil rights leaders have been shot.'

Chicago journalist Mike Royko

'Nothing can ever save you from ambush, if somebody [is going to] do it. Never know when it might come, and [nothing] you can do about it when it does. Coward dies a thousand deaths. I'd already died a million times by now if I thought like that. Thing is, don't be careful, be prayerful. But if tomorrow should be my day, it won't find me over in some corner cowering. If tomorrow is my day, will find me still out there carrying on the work I have all my life. Be out there marching.'

Jesse Jackson, 1995

During the 1960s Jesse Jackson, an ordained Baptist minister and Civil Rights activist, was an aide to the Reverend Martin Luther King and was selected by the Civil Rights leader to head Operation Breadbasket, a charity based in Chicago. The operation challenged major corporations not only to hire more African Americans but to expand opportunities for them to own automobile dealerships, fast-food franchises and provide goods and services to Fortune 500 companies. When King was killed in Memphis, Ralph Abernathy succeeded King as president of the Southern Christian Leadership

Conference (SCLC), but it was Jackson who assumed the mantle as Black America's top Civil Rights leader.

However, King and many of his aides in the SCLC considered Jesse Jackson to be an 'upstart' who used 'race baiting' to further his career as a Civil Rights leader. Despite his official inclusion on King's staff, King soon found himself unimpressed with aspects of Jackson's personality. He was especially troubled how Jackson often escalated encounters with government officials, police departments and innocent bystanders.[1]

According to Jackson biographer Kenneth Timmerman, the author of *Shakedown: Exposing the Real Jesse Jackson*, King became profoundly suspicious of 'Jackson's taste for self-promotion'. King's SCLC team, Timmerman added, 'mistrusted [Jackson's] ambition, his audacity, and his refusal to be a team player'. They also became distressed when, a week after Martin Luther King was assassinated, Jackson claimed he was the last to speak to the assassinated Civil Rights leader and cradled him in his arms as he lay dying on the balcony of Memphis' Lorraine Motel. In reality Jackson was in the parking lot below. Appearing on television the next day, Jackson wore a blood-stained turtleneck shirt.[2]

In November 1983 Jackson announced he was running for the 1984 Democrat presidential nomination at the Washington Convention Centre Hall. His campaign focused on constructing a coalition between African Americans and white working class people.

On the dais with the candidate, in addition to his wife, Jacqueline, and their 5 children, and 1972 presidential candidate Shirley Chisholm, were 110 aides to the Jackson campaign, representing the coalition he was building – Mexican Americans from the Southwest, native American leaders, a representative of the National Farmers Alliance, a black feminist, a bishop of the African Methodist Episcopal Church, black members of Congress, black business people and representatives of student groups.

During his campaign Jackson travelled throughout the nation frequently greeted at every stop by African Americans with the enthusiastic chant 'Run Jesse, run!' For the first time in US history, the black community was inspired by a real chance to win.

Even though Jackson considered himself a moral and peaceful leader like his mentor Martin Luther King, some of his Democrat colleagues associated him with militant black nationalists. The underlying belief was that Jackson's loyalty was solely with African Americans, not Democrats. Even though Mondale, the front-runner, had a decent Civil Rights record of his own he could not afford to be tied too closely with radical black nationalists. Republicans were not impressed with Jackson's candidacy. Carlyle Gregory, a Republican strategist, commented, 'Jesse Jackson is driving white voters into the Republican Party.'[3]

The excitement of having the first viable African American presidential candidate run for the Democratic Party nomination soon turned sour. During his campaign Jackson praised Castro and the Sandinistas and the Salvadorian communist guerrillas. Worst of all, he accepted black Muslim leader Louis Farrakhan's support for his presidential campaign.

Jackson's Civil Rights group Operation PUSH and Farrakhan's Nation of Islam both had national headquarters on Chicago's South Side. They had known each other long before Jackson's presidential run. Thomas N. Todd, a Chicago lawyer who had been friendly with Farrakhan and other black nationalists, was also a close friend and associate of Jackson. Todd took over as acting president of PUSH after Jackson announced his presidential candidacy, and one of his first orders of business was to invite Farrakhan and other black nationalists to speak at the weekly PUSH forum held on Saturday mornings. Between 200 and 2,000 people attended the meetings on any given Saturday. At about the same time Jackson and Todd learned that Farrakhan was considering actively supporting the Jackson candidacy.

The son of a Baptist minister, Farrakhan was born Louis Wolcott, and became a black Muslim in the 1950s when, as a calypso singer in Boston, he was recruited into the Nation of Islam by its best-known leader, Malcolm X. He took the name Louis X and later changed that to Louis Farrakhan. Farrakhan said he was '. . . the voice of God to America and the voice of God to 30 million black people in America and the millions of black people throughout the world'.[4]

The Nation of Islam was an extremist religious sect founded in Detroit in 1930 by Elijah Muhammad. He was judged by his followers as a prophet. Over the years the organisation developed into a movement that attracted as many as 500,000 members and operated a newspaper, a fish importing business, bakeries, restaurants and supermarkets. Louis X quickly moved up through the ranks, first in the Boston mosque, then in New York City. He wrote and recorded a song, 'A White Man's Heaven is a Black Man's Hell', which became a hit among black nationalists throughout the country.

By 1984 the apostle of black nationalism was a nationally known figure. Farrakhan also embraced unpopular Arab leaders while publicly expressing hatred for Jews. In one speech Farrakhan described Judaism as a 'dirty religion'.[5]

On 11 March 1984, the day he publicly endorsed Jackson, Farrakhan said, 'Some white people are going to live . . . but [God] don't want them living with us. He doesn't want us mixing ourselves up with the slave masters' children, whose time of doom has arrived.'[6] Accordingly, Jackson's friendship with the Nation of Islam leader tarnished the candidate's credibility.

Farrakhan provided members of his security force, the Fruit of Islam, as bodyguards for the candidate. He also accompanied Jackson to churches and other campaign stops and travelled to Syria with him to win the release of a captured US flier. Jackson also met with Fidel Castro to organise a similar prisoner release deal. The *New York Times* editorialised that Jackson's '. . . prisoner deals demonstrated no diplomatic skills. . . . on the contrary they confirm his lack of it. . . . How much skill does it take . . . to flatter the interests and views of another government against those of your own and this to cadge a favour from a dictator?'[7]

In his efforts to build a large black political base, Jackson pragmatically concluded it was in his best interest to remain allies with Farrakhan because the Nation of Islam leader had a large black following. Robert F. Kennedy Jr said Jackson's '. . . love affair with Louis Farrakhan and his Jewish xenophobia are . . . unforgivable'.[8]

During the 1984 campaign, when Farrakhan praised Adolf Hitler, calling him 'a very great man', it set off a storm of protest from the United States' Jewish community. Farrakhan also frequently blamed the US government for conspiring to destroy black people with AIDS and addictive drugs. It reminded many Americans of Jackson's allegations in the 1970s that the CIA had conspired to flood African American communities with crack cocaine in order to suppress their populations.

During his campaign Jackson was also accused of being anti-Semitic because of his public embrace of Palestine Liberation Organization leader Yasser Arafat, and partly because of his own comments about Jews. During a Middle East trip Jackson told Phil Blazer, editor and publisher of *Israel Today*, 'I'm sick and tired of hearing about the Holocaust and having Americans being put in the position of a guilt trip. We have to get on with the issues of today and not talk about the Holocaust.' Jackson is also reported to have said, 'The Jews do not have a monopoly in suffering.' However, Jackson's biggest political blunder during the campaign occurred when he used the term 'Hymies' to refer to Jews and 'Hymietown' to refer to New York City.[9]

The 'Hymietown' incident worsened when Farrakhan publicly threatened Milton Coleman, the African American journalist who first reported his 'Hymietown' comment. Jackson's competitors in the primary elections, former Vice President Walter Mondale and Senator Gary Hart, took Jackson to task for his equivocal position on Farrakhan. Jackson had disassociated himself from Farrakhan's remarks but did not repudiate him, referencing New Testament scriptural sources to justify his position. In the end, however, Jackson had no other choice but to publicly denounce Farrakhan's beliefs and actions as 'reprehensible and morally indefensible'.[10]

Notwithstanding the controversy Jackson created, he went on to win five primaries and caucuses and more than 18 per cent of votes cast. But the momentum of the Jackson campaign ended in the state of New York. Walter Mondale's nomination was secure and by the time the Democrat convention began in San Francisco, Jackson had the fewest delegates of the final three candidates.

Between 1984 and 1988 Jackson ran a permanent campaign for the presidency, raising money and travelling abroad. He was the head of the National Rainbow Coalition, which had developed from Jackson's PUSH organisation. The Rainbow Coalition strove to unite people of all colours to create better conditions for the United States' poor.

Jackson's campaign for the 1988 Democrat presidential nomination became much more credible due to his successes in 1984. He was also better financed and better organised. Although most people did not seem to believe he had a serious chance at winning, Jackson once again exceeded expectations and he more than doubled his previous results.

After winning 55 per cent of the vote in the Michigan Democratic caucus, Jackson was considered the front-runner for the nomination, as he surpassed all the other candidates in total number of pledged delegates at the time. But Jackson's campaign suffered a significant setback less than two weeks after a United Auto Workers endorsement when he narrowly lost the Colorado primary to Michael Dukakis and was defeated the following day by Dukakis in the Wisconsin primary. Jackson's showing among white voters in Wisconsin was significantly better than in 1984, but was also noticeably lower than pre-primary polling had predicted.

The back-to-back victories established Dukakis as the front-runner and the Massachusetts Governor went on to win the party's nomination. However, Dukakis lost the general election in November to Vice President George H.W. Bush.

Jackson believed that his campaigns for the presidency helped to bridge the United States' racial divide. He said he could 'feel the conventions of race that had defined American politics tearing'. Reminiscing about the elections, he recalled falling asleep in a car in Columbia, Missouri, and waking up to find himself surrounded by white men wearing sacks over their heads. They were farmers who supported him but couldn't publicly show it. He was successful in gaining the support of nearly 7 million votes and 11 states during the 1988 primaries.[11]

* * *

Jackson was already familiar with bodyguard protection. A number of people in his Chicago organisation had acted as bodyguards and travelled with him to speaking engagements across the country. Additionally, during local community events in Chicago, he usually relied on the presence of at least two armed off-duty Chicago police officers.

One of his personal bodyguards left his post as a union organiser to guard Jackson. He called himself a 'general factotum' and would run errands for him. He was often blamed for minor irritations like failing to collect Jackson's suit bag. The bodyguard put up with the complaints because '. . . [Jackson was] the best we got out there – only real one out there'.

One of the bodyguards Jackson hired turned out to be a 'spy'. Chicago Mayor Richard J. Daley did not trust Jackson and the feeling was mutual. In 1970 Daley arranged for an undercover police officer to act as a bodyguard for Jackson and to report '. . . every move he made'.[12] Daley had been suspicious of Jackson's links to a Chicago gang leader and drug pusher, Jeff Fort, who had a close relationship with Jackson's brother, Noah Robinson. Mayor Daley's son, a county state attorney, investigated financial corruption involving Fort and Robinson in 1983. Fort ended up appearing on the FBI's 'Most Wanted' list after failing to appear for sentencing on drug charges.[13]

Jackson's use of private bodyguards also attracted criticism from the gun lobby. Jackson spoke out in favour of gun control while relying on armed bodyguards. 'Jackson goes nowhere without armed bodyguards while preaching against gun ownership for the "little people" like you and me,' one pro-gun advocate said.[14]

During the initial phase of Jackson's 1984 presidential campaign Farrakhan furnished Jackson with bodyguards before the candidate qualified for Secret Service protection. The suited and bow-tied bodyguards filled some supporters with apprehension because of the reputation their leader had built on his racist language and his condemnation of 'white devils'.

Jackson became the first of eight Democratic announced candidates to receive Secret Service protection in November 1983. He was given the protection under a special ruling following reported threats against his life. The agents had planned to start guarding him on 1 February 1984 but Treasury Secretary Donald Regan ordered the protection earlier for Jackson after receiving a request from his campaign manager, Preston Love. Jackson's detail was the largest of all the candidates.

Many of the agents assigned to Jackson's detail were 'not looking forward to it', according to former agent Dennis V.N. McCarthy. In the beginning, however, agents found Jackson's campaign staff 'easy to work with' and judged Jackson to be 'likeable'. The detail expressed their appreciation for the way Jackson contacted the agents' families on Christmas Day 1983 to apologise for keeping the agents away during the holidays.

However, the relationship between the agents and Jackson's campaign staff soon deteriorated. Agents recognised that the staff had no experience when it came to running a national campaign. Impulsive changes to the candidate's schedule also created tension. 'No security detail can be effective under such circumstances', McCarthy said, 'and a constant battle between agents and Jackson's staff members developed.' When Jackson organised a trip overseas to bolster his foreign affairs credentials impulsive changes to the list of countries he was to visit created security problems with the agency.[15]

As agents attempted to protect Jackson during his walkabouts and scheduled events, many of his supporters complained the agents were 'trying to keep people away'. Some of Jackson's aides attempted to 'acclimate black folk' to the Secret Service. Several agents, according to Jackson aide Eric Easter, 'had a problem with seeing so many black folks every day telling them what to do, while none of us had ever really personally dealt with the Secret Service before'. There were also complaints the government had assigned the weakest agents to protect the candidate. In a small church in East Texas a supporter was overheard to say, 'They [are] all wearing hearing aides.'[16]

Frustrations came to a head when one of the agents on Jackson's detail became involved in a fist fight with a Jackson campaign worker. The agent was swiftly removed from the detail. His colleagues considered emulating the agent so they, too, could be taken off the detail.[17]

Jackson aide Eric Easter confirmed that tensions between Jackson's staff and Jackson's detail led to 'actual fistfights between staff people and a couple of Secret Service people on a couple of trips'. Easter thought the problems arose because agents could not adjust, '[From] protecting presidents to guarding some black guy, and spend your days in black churches, with poor black folks kind of shouting, it was just a complete shock to a lot of the Secret Service. And they to us. It was strange to be walking out of Jackson's hotel room and seeing Uzis leaning against the wall out there.'[18]

Easter became suspicious of the Secret Service agents believing they 'might as well be the FBI' and thought they were '. . . really there to listen to [Jackson's] phone calls. There was just a real distrust of the government being that close. And if he got shot, it was probably going to be one of them.'[19]

Another Jackson aide, Hermene Hartman, complained that one agent had knocked her back with his elbow when she greeted Jackson at Chicago airport following his candidacy announcement in Washington. She was 'stunned' at how the agent had mishandled her. When she began to cry Jackson comforted her as she told him, 'Jesse, what is this? He hurt me.' Jackson said the situation was 'different now . . . it's another ball game. I've got all these people around me now who are strangers. But I need you. You gotta help me. Don't leave me. Not now, I really need you now.' Hartman said she was 'startled' when she felt Jackson's bulletproof vest.[20]

In 1983 Jackson told reporters after a speech to a convention of black elected officials that death threats against him had increased since he announced his candidacy.[21] The prospect he might be assassinated like his mentor Martin Luther King had always been present in Jackson's thoughts. One year after King's assassination a plot to assassinate Jackson had been discovered. Another plot to assassinate him occurred in 1974. By 1984 when he ran for the presidency the plots and threats had increased a hundred-fold.

Jackson often spoke about the possibility of being assassinated. During one campaign tour in Texas when he was giving support to other Democrat candidates and did not have Secret Service protection, he left a church and headed for his car. The church was positioned near woods and as he approached his vehicle he said to an aide, 'Right next to these trees! Damn, who was the genius that figured this out?'[22]

When Jackson was asked about the potential danger and how he psychologically prepared himself he said:

> Well, I absorb it – most of the time, and move on. I know that we live our lives daily thinking that life is certain and death is uncertain. The fact is, death is certain – and life is uncertain. I try to face the facts of my finitude. I am sustained, not by my facts, nor am I limited because of my finitude. I am sustained by my faith.[23]

For his 1984 campaign Jackson was given the Secret Service codename 'Thunder' and asked to wear a bulletproof vest. Ever fearful of an assassination attempt, Jackson's agents began urging reporters to group around him closely, especially those tall enough to block a sniper's view. During the campaign Jackson paid tribute to the Secret Service for doing 'a good job' in protecting him. (During his 1984 campaign he was briefly without US protection, from 2 January. Syrian security agents refused to allow the Secret Service to accompany the candidate to a meeting with President Hafez al-Assad in Damascus.)

Jackson said the low point of his unsuccessful campaign for the presidency in 1984 was the threats made against his life. 'Early on,' he said, 'when we lived under constant threat many of my friends and leaders – Dr King, Bobby Kennedy, Malcolm X – were assassinated.'[24] Jackson said:

> We would get constant reports about threats. I received 311 threats officially, according to the Secret Service, more than anyone who has ever run before. Once the 14th person had actually been arrested there came a point where my staff had to convene members of my family and I had to face my children face to face about the implications of operating on a journey so dangerous and so treacherous . . . So that was a low, perhaps the lowest of all, because one would think in a society as free as ours one would not be faced with those options.[25]

However, Secret Service spokesman Jack Smith said Jackson's statement about threats was incorrect. He said that agency records indicated only nine people, not fourteen, had been arrested because of threats made to the candidate.[26]

Following his appearance at the 1984 Democratic convention, Jackson had asked to retain protection indefinitely but the Reagan administration rejected his request because protection had never been provided to a private citizen. Treasury Secretary Regan said he had consulted both with his staff and the White House senior staff in making the decision.[27]

In 1988 Jackson was given the Secret Service codename 'Pontiac'. Some commentators said the name was 'racist' simply because it had been used as a nickname for a vintage car. Jackson was asked by the Secret Service if he wanted it changed but he said there was no racist slur intended.[28]

During his 1988 presidential campaign Jackson spoke frequently of assassinated leaders Malcolm X, Martin Luther King Jr and Robert F. Kennedy. He said:

> Those who would be peacemakers, ambassadors of hope . . . attract the meanest, sickest elements. Yet the dreamers must outdistance the dream-busters . . . I absorb the blows of various forms of violence every day: verbal violence, threat of physical violence. In my own maturity and spirituality, I perceive and affirm my anxieties with courage. I'm determined to pursue this mission, and I will not surrender.[29]

Jackson's aide Ken Bode said that on one occasion during the 1988 campaign he had accompanied the candidate to a rally in Illinois. Riding in Jackson's car, Bode noticed how his overcoat was so thick it looked like it was made of stiff wooden boards. It was Jackson's blue bulletproof raincoat. Jackson told Bode about the 'seriousness of the threats against him'. Jackson's youngest son Yusef was 17 at the time and had asked his father what would happen to him and the family if he was killed. Jackson replied he was going to continue with his campaign despite the presence of what he described as 'dream busters' waiting for the chance to shoot him.

Bode also expressed dismay about the state of the nation when he observed Jackson putting on a bulletproof vest in a back room at the US Capitol as he waited with Senators to deliver a speech. Jackson took off his coat and strapped on his vest. 'What the hell are we watching?' Bode thought to himself. 'This man putting on a bullet-proof vest to speak at the Capitol of the United States!'[30]

The 1988 campaign was no different from his 1984 run when it came to threats against his life. By May 1988 he had already received at least 100 threats. One of the most serious assassination plots occurred in that month when Londell Williams, a 30-year-old carpenter living in Missouri, 40 miles west of St Louis, and his wife, 27-year-old Tammy, were arrested for plotting to kill the candidate. They conspired to kill Jackson on the Fourth of July with a Colt AR-15 rifle 'because he was getting too close to being President of the United States'. They were members of The Covenant, the Sword and the Arm of the Lord, a white supremacist group. This organisation, tied to the Ku Klux Klan, was one of several extreme right-wing groups that had been under investigation by the FBI. The groups shared violently anti-Semitic and anti-black teachings of sects referred to collectively as the Christian Identity Movement. They held, for example, that Jews were the offspring of Satan. Federal investigators say the Covenant is also. The Covenant had a 224-acre compound in central Arkansas. It was the site of a four-day standoff in April 1985 with Federal and state officers. The group's founder, James Ellison, and five others subsequently pleaded guilty to charges of conspiracy and illegal possession of automatic weapons. Inside the Covenant camp police found an arsenal that included submachine guns, grenades, an antitank rocket and plastic explosives.

In May 1988 an informant had led sheriff's deputies to a wooded area in Franklin County where they found an AR-15 Colt rifle and a bag that the informer said belonged to Williams. The rifle, originally a semiautomatic, had been altered so that it was fully automatic, to fire like a machine gun. At the request of the Secret Service, the informant agreed to wear a concealed tape recorder and meet and talk with Williams. They met on 10 May and had a 45-minute conversation. During the discussion, Williams bragged that he was a member of the white supremacist group and that the organisation was planning to assassinate Jackson on the Fourth of July. 'Refrigerating Jackson is what it's all about.', Williams said. Williams also said in the taped conversation that the supremacist group had given him a rifle but that the group wanted it returned because the gun had been used to kill a law-enforcement officer.

The Missouri couple began to suspect the informant was cooperating with the police. On 11 May 1988, Tammy saw him in a blue van parked near her apartment. She went outside and hid near the van in an attempt to observe his activities. Later in the day a note was discovered at the informant's apartment which read, 'Say cop, live like a dog, die like a dog'. Believing it was

Tammy and Londell who left the note, the informant then went to Londell's apartment where an argument broke out. Tammy and Londell accused the informant of 'bringing in the law'.

Police investigators believed the informant's life was in danger and decided it was time to arrest the couple. They were arrested at their apartment on 13 May. Londell Williams pleaded guilty to threatening to kill and inflict bodily harm on a major candidate for the office of President of the United States and possession of an unregistered firearm. His wife, Tammy, pleaded guilty to possession of an unregistered firearm.[31]

The morning the couple was arrested and charged with threatening to kill Jackson the Secret Service said that threats against Jackson were always 'unusually numerous' and had been increasing during the summer of 1988. It caused the agency 'increased concerns' for Jackson's safety.

When he heard of the arrests Jackson told reporters, 'We know the threats are constant. This is a clear and more documented case. Death threats are running very high now.' Jackson termed those who threaten him 'dream busters' and vowed to continue his efforts to 'make America better every day I live' but was not nervous or concerned about the possibility of an assassination attempt. 'The stakes are too high in the campaign,' he said. Jackson paid tribute to the Secret Service for doing 'a good job' in protecting him.[32]

The next day Jackson received a long-distance call from his 12-year-old daughter Jacqueline, who had been frightened by the news about her father. She wanted to be reassured that everything was all right, Jackson said, 'The pain is how it does affect one's family. It calls one out of campaigning into parenting rather quickly.'

However, even though Jackson said he 'recognized the risks', the threat did not prevent him from plunging into crowds as his agents nervously sprinted after him. He said the 'danger factor' was part of the 'baggage that his campaign had to carry'. Jackson treated the dangers philosophically. He felt 'very spiritual, very philosophical' about the threats, he said.

Newsweek responded to the plot to kill Jackson by editorialising, 'Racial tensions are only one reason . . . He is also more electrifying than most politicians. Historically, assassination attempts have tended to be directed at public figures who connected emotionally (both positively and negatively) with the American People.'

However, Jackson also used the arrests as an opportunity to spread the blame for the assassination plot. He told reporters, 'I cannot just focus on the two people arrested in St Louis. The climate for this antagonism and violence, of course, has been set by many irresponsible public leaders [whose] attacks based on race have set a divisive and dangerous climate . . .'[33]

Within a short time, the Secret Service's anxiety was once again raised when a 9mm bullet was found in Jackson's campaign plane at a stop in Fresno, California. Reporters' bags were searched before the candidate's agents announced the next day that the bullet was actually one of their own.[34]

Shortly after the Missouri arrests the Secret Service had to cancel a prospective trip to Calhoun, Georgia, which Jackson had arranged in order to hold a meeting with one of his advisors, former Carter White House aide Bert Lance. Lance said the Secret Service had called him and said, '. . . one of their informants had overheard somebody talking in a bar [about killing Jackson]. They actually took somebody into custody.'[35]

Losing candidates for presidential nominations generally have to relinquish their detail as soon as the party standard bearer is chosen. Therefore, Jackson technically had exhausted his right to such protection on 22 July 1988, the day after the end of the Democratic National Convention in Atlanta. As Jackson planned to campaign for Democratic nominee Michael Dukakis he requested an extension of the cover. This was granted and President Reagan extended Jackson's protection for thirty days to give him time to arrange private security against death threats he had received.

Jackson received some criticism for requesting an extension of his Secret Service protection. However, journalist Mike Royko said Jackson was a special case:

It's not solely that Jackson is black, although that's the number one reason. As well as the number two and three reasons. . . . he should receive special treatment because he's a special case. The other candidates don't receive the kind of threats, the crazy letters, the vicious phone calls, that come into Jackson's offices. But of the 200 million-plus people in this country, there are a considerable number who, to put it mildly, dislike Jesse Jackson. To put it less mildly, they hate him. . . . when you have millions of haters, in a country that has millions of privately owned firearms, the law of averages says that you're going to have a certain number of haters who are dangerous. Some hear strange voices in their heads, which is why a rock star can be killed outside his home. Others believe it is their duty to save their country or race from some threat that festers in a dark corner of their brains, which is why presidents, aspiring presidents and civil rights leaders have been shot.[36]

* * *

Jackson chose not to run for the 1992 Democratic nomination. Instead, he wanted to try and influence Democratic Party policy using his large constituency to force radical policies he believed in. However, Bill Clinton, the eventual nominee, did not want to be involved with Jackson and cleverly established that decision early in his campaign. Jackson had invited Clinton to speak at a luncheon that was hosted by his Rainbow Coalition. Also appearing at the luncheon was a rap singer, Sister Souljah, who had previously stated, 'If there are any good white people, I haven't met them.' Clinton responded to her remarks by denouncing her presence at the event and said, 'Where are the good white people? Right here in this room.' The audience responded warmly to Clinton's address but Jackson regarded Clinton's remarks as a personal attack.[37]

Jackson and Clinton soon reconciled after the election and the president invited Jackson to the White House. During the Lewinsky scandal he administered 'spiritual advice' to Clinton. However, at the time the media was unaware Jackson was the father of a daughter born out of wedlock. The former candidate had an affair with one of his aides, Karin Stanford, and the child was born in 1998. Stanford admitted she had received 'hush money' from Jackson and said that his marriage was 'basically . . . political'.[38] The affair was confirmed by one of Jackson's drivers and part-time bodyguard who told journalists that he had ferried Jackson around Chicago several times a week for assignations with various women.[39]

While Jackson declined to run for the US presidency again, he continued to be a force on the political stage, pushing for African American rights and serving as a featured speaker at Democratic conventions. In 1990 he won his first election to public office, when he captured one of two special unpaid 'statehood senator' posts which had been created by the Washington City Council to lobby the US Congress for District of Columbia statehood.

Throughout the next three decades Jackson continued to appear in the news. In March 2003 a controversial email about Jessie Jackson was sent to several Secret Service email accounts, including a Deputy Assistant Director and two other former supervisory agents. Jackson's Secret Service agents came under investigation in 2008 when the allegedly racist and sexually charged emails surfaced. One in particular upset Jackson. It was titled, 'The Righteous Reverend'. In the email agents had joked about the deaths of Jackson and his wife when a missile strikes their plane. The email ends with 'it certainly wouldn't be a great loss and probably wouldn't be an accident either'.[40]

Jackson's son, Jesse Jackson Jr, a member of the US Congress, wasn't convinced it was a one-time event. 'The Secret Service is charged with investigating threats, not initiating them. This gives you some sense, some insight, into what may be taking place there,' he said. 'The Congress of the United States has oversight responsibilities and we're going to be looking very carefully at what's going on there.'[41]

Chapter 13

The Front-Runners, 1984–2004

'Some candidates are bigger targets than others – any transition candidate or change candidate has a higher profile. The evocation of the same excitement surrounding John and Robert Kennedy triggers both negatively and positively.'

Senator Gary Hart

'Boys will be boys but boys will not be Presidents.'

President Ronald Reagan, commenting on
Gary Hart's affair with Donna Rice

On 21 April 1983 Senator John Glenn announced his candidacy for the 1984 Democratic nomination for president and initially led the pack of Democrats set to challenge President Reagan. Glenn was a former test pilot and Marine fighter pilot who flew 149 combat missions in the Second World War and Korean War, never once bailing out. Glenn joined the United States' space programme and became an astronaut. In February 1962 he became the first American to orbit the earth in his tiny Mercury capsule, *Friendship 7*.

When Glenn left NASA he set his sights on the US Senate after encouragement from his friend, Senator Robert Kennedy. In 1964, Glenn entered the Ohio Democratic primary running against incumbent Senator Stephen Young. However, an accident resulting in a concussion forced Glenn to leave the race and put his political career on hold. He was eventually elected as a Senator for Ohio in 1974. As a Senator he was known among his colleagues as a hard-working and conscientious legislator.

When the film *The Right Stuff*, based on Tom Wolfe's 1979 book about Glenn and his fellow Mercury NASA astronauts, was released in 1983 it was believed it would bolster his chances for the presidency. However, as Glenn later wrote in his memoirs, 'Tom Wolfe's . . . book was good. . . . but [the film] could have been entitled "Laurel and Hardy Go To Space". Somehow the movie's lukewarm reception had a chilling effect on the campaign. . . . polls which showed me likely to beat the president also reversed, although I still fared better against him than any other Democrat.'[1]

Glenn was stunned by the results of the Iowa caucuses. He had finished a distant sixth in a crowded field which included two other leading candidates who vied for the top spot – the establishment candidate, former Vice President Walter Mondale, and Senator Gary Hart. Glenn, despite being an historic, iconic figure, had one last chance to keep his presidential ambitions alive – the New Hampshire primary on 28 February 1984. However, Glenn came in third with about 12 per cent of the vote. The surprise winner over Mondale was Hart. Glenn's campaign continued for another month before he withdrew from the race. Media commentators observed that while he probably would have been a successful president, he wasn't that good at being a presidential candidate. Glenn's profile was once again raised during the election when the eventual winner of the Democrat nomination, Jimmy Carter, briefly considered him as his running mate.

There were very few incidents of protest or violence during Glenn's short presidential campaign. Ironically, an attack on him came at a time after he had abandoned any plans to run for the presidency. On 25 October 1989 the 68-year-old Glenn was taping a television interview after a tree-planting ceremony at the Smithsonian Institution in Washington DC. Michael John Breen approached the Senator and punched him on the jaw. Glenn managed to hold on to Breen until guards arrived. Breen was later judged to be suffering from a mental illness. He had experienced a 'dream' in which he saw an earthquake which represented the start of 'Armageddon' which the government allegedly knew about but covered up. He thought an attack on a Senator would publicise his alarm. He was charged with assaulting a member of Congress.[2]

* * *

In just twelve years, from 1972 to 1984, Gary Hart went from being George McGovern's campaign manager to a presidential candidate. He was initially not considered a serious contender in 1984. However, Hart had a respectable showing in the Iowa primary and then defeated former Vice President Walter Mondale in New Hampshire the following February. Hart's success in becoming one of the two front-runners for the Democrat nomination was considered to be a political phenomenon by the media.

However, some observers detected a weakness in Hart. Author Lou Cannon said, 'When you take his picture, there's nothing back there. Nothing bounces off him. There's no emanation from him. Some people have some kind of a psychic arc about them. . . . [they] give off an aura; they give off a glow. Reagan gave off a glow, and there was some glow about him that was always there.'[3]

There were early signs that Hart's behaviour could be problematic if he ever ran for office. In 1972 Hart was George McGovern's campaign manager when Georgia Governor Jimmy Carter's aides approached Hart to canvass for Carter's selection as McGovern's vice-presidential candidate. Aides Jerry Rafshoon and Hamilton Jordan went to see Hart and waited outside the campaign manager's hotel suite to make their pitch. 'We saw three beautiful girls go in, one after another,' Rafshoon said. 'Then, they'd come out 15 minutes later.'[4]

When Hart was managing George McGovern's failed presidential campaign in 1972, Secret Service agent Marty Vencker said Hart '. . . wanted to be [Hollywood star] Warren Beatty' adding, 'He never looked you in the eye. You could see he was an opportunist. To me, he represented the most distasteful part of American liberalism.'[5]

Journalist Matt Bai said Hart hinted back in 1972 that he '. . . considered his oft-troubled marriage to [his wife] Lee more of a political necessity, for both of them, than an enduring commitment to monogamy – and if she didn't expect him to be faithful after all this time, how could anyone else?'[6]

In fact, Hart was not discreet about his womanising. At one point during his 1984 campaign when the media was focused on him as a major contender a 'veteran political mistress he'd been seeing since 1982 was startled to have him turn up on her Washington doorstep,' journalist Gail Sheehy said. 'She could see the Secret Service van parked right down the street. Hart stayed the night and blithely walked out her front door the next morning.' However, Sheehy observed the press turned a blind eye to the antics of presidential candidates in those days.[7]

Four years later, however, the media's attitude to the private lives of candidates changed dramatically. Hart attempted a second try at the presidency in 1988 and announced his candidacy on 13 April 1987. He was far ahead in the polls but he was soon discovered to be having an affair with a young model, Donna Rice.

According to a former Secret Service agent who was on Hart's detail well before his encounter with Rice, the Senator routinely cavorted with stunning models and actresses in Los Angeles, courtesy of Beatty. 'Warren Beatty gave him a key to his house on Mulholland Drive,' the agent said. 'It was near Jack Nicholson's house.' Beatty would arrange to have 20-year-old women – 'tens' as the agent described them – meet Hart at Beatty's house.

The unnamed agent added that Hart would tell him that a guest was expected. 'They would wear bikinis and jump into the hot tub in the back. Once in the tub, their tops would come off. Then they would go into the house. The "guests" stayed well into the night and often left before sunlight. Beatty was a bachelor but Hart was a Senator running for president and was married.' The agent said there were sometimes two or three girls with Hart at a time and he was shocked that Hart did not appear to care. 'He was like a kid in a candy store,' the agent said.[8]

According to journalist Becky Little, the real story was bigger than just one affair. 'It was about Hart's fundamental character, and whether a man like him should be president,' she said.[9] During the 1984 election Hart's '. . . escapades were common knowledge amongst Washington pundits', according to journalist Matt Bai.[10] Gail Sheehy said:

> The wife of a very prominent Duke political scientist told me that he would just take every one of the college girls who volunteered [at the McGovern campaign] to bed. And the next day, she would be hanging on her chance to talk to him, and he would walk right past her as if he'd never seen her before. He did that over and over and over again.[11]

Hart also allegedly sexually harassed at least one female reporter. When journalist Patricia O'Brien went to his hotel room to interview him during his 1984 campaign, he greeted her in a short bathrobe then 'got huffy' when she asked him to put some clothes on. 'We almost elected a compulsive sexual predator as president in 1988,' Sheehy said, 'but we didn't because he got himself caught.'[12]

* * *

During the 1984 campaign when his polls were high Hart asked one of his agents that if he was elected president would he be able to escape the confines of being guarded around the clock. Could he take a trip back home to Colorado and walk around by himself? The agent informed Hart that it would simply not be possible. When the candidate arrived in San Francisco for the Democratic National Party Convention he soon understood what the agent meant.

The day after Walter Mondale was nominated Hart was staying at the St Francis Hotel. He planned to walk from his hotel to the Meridien Hotel to meet Vice President Mondale. This event was public, but the fact that Hart was going to walk, and shake hands along the way, was not.

Secret Service agent Poggi was assigned to guard presidential candidate Senator Gary Hart on 19 July 1984, in San Francisco. Poggi was the 'lead advance agent' for the detail assigned to protect Hart. As Hart and his agents were descending in the elevator on the Post Street side of the hotel, the side where Sara Jane Moore had taken a shot at Gerald Ford a decade earlier, his head of detail, Steve Ramsey, suddenly stopped the elevator. He reversed its direction and hustled Hart and his wife back into their hotel room without explaining why.

Ramsay had received information from Poggi that he had spotted a young man who he believed bore a resemblance to George Wallace's would-be assassin Arthur Bremer. Poggi thought he looked 'suspicious'. The man was later identified as 25-year-old Robert Carson. According to Ramsay, the suspect 'had a backpack, kept changing positions for a better view and fit the profile [of a potential assassin]'. When agents challenged the man he ran away. However, they caught up with him, showed him their identifications, pushed him down on the ground and searched him. They discovered he had a .38 pistol in his backpack. The suspect was quickly taken to the San Francisco police headquarters and charged with carrying a loaded firearm and a concealed weapon.[13]

A half-hour after returning to his hotel room Ramsay and his agents escorted Hart and his wife to his five-car motorcade and on to Mondale's hotel. During the journey Hart became curious as to why they had to return to their hotel room. Ramsay told him about the would-be assassin. Hart told his head agent, 'Ask your guys to ask the kid if he knows I did not get the nomination.' Ramsay laughed, relayed the message to the police department and 5 minutes later he heard of Carson's response – 'He didn't?'[14]

According to the courts Poggi acted responsibly under his suspicions that Carson looked and acted 'suspicious'. The judge acting in the case noted:

The setting in which the search and arrest of respondent took place was unquestionably one of very high risk. A nationally known candidate for president of the United States was following less than five minutes behind Agent Poggi. . . . the magnitude of the risk to the Senator's life is the issue here . . . this court believes that Senator Hart was in a position of magnified risk at the time Agent Poggi undertook the pat search of respondent.[15]

Many years later, and long after Hart was protected by the Secret Service, he encountered a life-threatening experience unlike any he had faced when he was running for president. During one of his many hikes along Colorado trails he came face to face with a mountain lion. Fortunately for Hart, the lion stared at him for a few moments then slunk away.[16]

* * *

The wisest decision Walter Mondale ever made, he said, was not to run for president in 1976. For two years, the Minnesota Senator tested the waters for a presidential campaign, conducting an extensive fundraising and public relations tour of the country. Concluding that he had neglected his family and his senatorial responsibilities, and that his standing in the polls had not risen, he dropped out of the race in November 1974.

However, after Jimmy Carter secured the Democratic Party's nomination he selected Senator Walter Mondale as his vice-presidential running mate. They were elected President and Vice President of the United States on 2 November 1976. Mondale lost with Carter four years later, and then stood as a presidential candidate in 1984.

Mondale had forty-five agents to protect him and had a 'good . . . professional' relationship with them. 'There's closeness', Mondale said, 'but with . . . professional detachment'. However, he always admired the work they undertook to ensure his safety. 'You've got to admire people who do that,' he said. Mondale laid down one condition for his protection. He said he did not want protection for his children. However, the Secret Service decided this was against their protocols and, ignoring Mondale's instructions, agents would follow the children surreptitiously.[17]

Agents observed that the new vice president was less than discrete when it came to talking about other politicians. On one occasion an agent on Mondale's vice-presidential detail was taken aback when the vice president said within his earshot, 'Nixon is evil, evil.' Former agent Michael Endicott said Mondale 'was the first political person I had been around who expressed such disdain for another politician in my presence'.[18]

During his campaigns for senator, vice president and presidential candidate Mondale said he was not regularly threatened but remembered the few times he was told of concerns agents had about his safety. He was instructed to allow his agents to stay close as he walked through a crowd. They said this would prevent a gunman from getting 'a clear shot'.[19]

Mondale was vice president for four years and during that time the Secret Service investigated a number of threats against his life including:

- On 16 November 1976, Frank J. Barkin, United States Magistrate for the Western District of Texas, received a letter addressed to him from John Wesley DeShazo. The letter contained threats to kill Senator Robert Dole and Senator Walter Mondale who was also vice president-elect. DeShazo was eventually arrested by Special Agent Beatty. DeShazo admitted to Beatty that he had written the letter and posted it. DeShazo stated, however, that he had no intention of harming anyone, and had written the letter because he wanted psychiatric help. Handwriting exemplars were also obtained from DeShazo at that time.

  DeShazo was convicted of violating '18 U.S.C. § 8761 for knowingly and intentionally causing to be delivered by the United States Postal Service a communication containing a threat to injure then Senator Walter Mondale'. DeShazo had been convicted on two prior occasions, 14 March 1968 and 14 September 1972, for threatening Presidents Johnson and Nixon. He was sentenced to five years in prison.[20]

There were also a few 'scares' during his time in office:

- A man was arrested carrying a shotgun and a semi-automatic weapon at a community college in Dearborn, Michigan, shortly before Mondale was due to give a speech.[21]
- In October 1980, during the Carter re-election campaign, 32-year-old Emmanuel M. Sistrunk threw himself and a baby stroller in front of Mondale's limousine in Salem, Oregon, but he was pulled away by agents.[22]

In 1982 after Mondale had left the vice presidency he expressed dissatisfaction about being protected. 'There's something intimidating about that herd of elephants [the Secret Service],' he said. 'It makes it difficult to reach out to people.' However, when he decided to run for the 1984 Democratic Party nomination Governor George Wallace told him he should take the protection provided for him seriously. Wallace said he should always 'listen to the Secret Service'. He also advised Mondale not to make the same mistake he made in 1972 when he ignored the advice given him by the Secret Service by wading into crowds and 'ending up in a wheelchair'.[23]

According to agent Jerry Parr, Mondale attracted few threats in his 1984 campaign.[24] However, the Secret Service did investigate a number which they deemed serious – including one threat in April 1984 from a Rumanian émigré, 29-year-old Jean Paul Gabor. Gabor, a waiter at a San Antonio restaurant, told customers on 20 April that he intended to kill Mondale, who was scheduled to make a campaign visit to the city the following week. When agents were sent to interview him he chased them from his home. He had been drinking, he said, and thought they were 'communist agents'. During the encounter the agents shot Gabor after he began to assault them. Gabor survived but was acquitted of a charge that he threatened to kill Mondale. Nevertheless, he was still found guilty of assaulting the two agents.[25]

* * *

The 1988 Democratic Party presidential nominee Michael Dukakis said he had 'no security . . . in Massachusetts and would not have it' during his time as governor of the state. Dukakis lived in his own house and did his own grocery shopping. He also took a streetcar to work at the State House in Boston. He said he was able to do this because he had 'a wonderful relationship' with his constituents.[26]

Dukakis would spend two or three days at the State House then eventually bristle at his 'confinement'. A frequently held thought was 'Get me out!', he said. As Massachusetts was a relatively small state he was 'out there all the time' and become 'energised' by his constituents. He laid down strict rules about his security. 'There will be no state troopers,' Dukakis said. 'There will be no security. I'm going to be the guy I've always been.'[27]

When Dukakis was given Secret Service protection after successes in the 1988 Democratic Party primaries he had mixed feelings. Although he understood that a national campaign demanded bodyguard protection, he was 'the last guy to say yes to the Secret Service'. Dukakis reasoned that 'once you say yes to the Secret Service and especially once you've won the [party] nomination, forget it. It's the last time you will ever have the opportunity to have the kind of easy, informal relationship with the people . . . the wall goes up from quarter to seven in the morning until the time you walk into that hotel'.[28]

Dukakis hated campaigning for the Democrat nomination and in the general election. 'Up on a plane, down; up on a plane, down; up on a plane, down,' he said. 'There's nothing more boring, let me tell you.' Asked what it was like living the political equivalent of 'Groundhog Day', Dukakis said, 'Boring as hell.'[29]

Dukakis found that being guarded around the clock was 'very unpleasant'. He thought he had lost a lot of the freedom he enjoyed when he was Governor of Massachusetts, especially meeting his constituents in an 'easy and informal way'. However, he admired the work of the Secret Service even though he found it 'rather difficult' in working to their protocols. 'I held off as long as I could because I didn't want to be walled off', he said, 'but their job is to make sure nobody does any harm to you. They're very professional. Yes, you could [still work] the rope line, but the easy spontaneity I could enjoy as governor just went out the window.'[30]

Dukakis said the whole business of protection 'drove me nuts . . . it's hard to describe but there was this wall'.[31] However, he soon realised protection was a necessary part of running for president when he was confronted with '15,000 absolutely insane Greeks in Astoria that almost trampled us to death with their enthusiasm . . .'. His wife Kitty said the supporters at the campaign rally were 'shaking the car with such vigour' she thought they were going to turn it over.[32]

Michael Dukakis had been a successful three-term governor of his state but during the 1988 presidential campaign he came across as cold, academic and overly righteous. However, it was an explicit negative message in a television commercial during the general election campaign against George H.W. Bush that doomed his chances of becoming president. He was accused of being soft on crime by offering furloughs to convicted murderers. Critics cited the case of Willie Horton who committed new felonies, including rape, when he absconded.

However, the real part of the story that proved fatal was not the ad itself, but Dukakis' failure to rebut it. He said:

I made a decision from the beginning that I was going to run a positive campaign. Little ol' me says I'm not going to respond to the Bush attacks. That was a huge mistake. You can't just sit there and let the other guy beat your brains out. And by the time I woke up to the damage that was being done, it was almost all gone.[33]

Dukakis had few threats during his run for the presidency. However, a scandal about the Secret Service became attached to his campaign. In August 1988, after Dukakis won the Democratic Party nomination, two agents in his detail, David Iacovetti and Daniel Porter, were robbed of their .357 Magnum revolvers, radio equipment and identification pins in a burglary at a Boston hotel during a campaign stop-over. The Secret Service and Boston police said they had some leads in their investigation and insisted the theft did not affect the agency's ability to protect the candidate.[34]

Although there were no serious plots to harm Dukakis, the Secret Service investigated an alleged plot to kill his vice-presidential running mate, Senator Lloyd Bentsen. The threat also involved Republican George H.W. Bush's vice-presidential candidate Senator Dan Quayle. In September 1988 the two candidates received identical anonymous letters which had been sent to their respective Senate offices in Washington. The letters contained an Illinois postmark and were decorated with an abstract drawing accompanied by the words 'Prediction: Assassination' in the news soon!' The FBI, with the assistance of the US Capitol Police, eventually found the letter writer in a Chicago suburb after he sent other threatening letters with a return address. However, the Secret Service concluded that the writer was 'not a threat' and closed the investigation.

Joe O'Neill, who was chief of staff of Bentsen's vice-presidential campaign, said, 'I do remember during the campaign with Bentsen hearing of the threat and the Secret Service being totally on top of it. [Bentsen] never gave it a passing thought. It was never a matter of concern to him. The Secret Service was incredibly vigilant.'

Jack Martin, a top aide to Bentsen in the 1970s and 1980s and chief of staff for his 1988 Senate re-election campaign, said, 'It was not uncommon, particularly during campaign years. He just sort of brushed it off.' Martin said security while travelling with Bentsen was low-key. 'It was an aide – usually me – and a rental car,' Martin said. 'He detested entourages. We never had weapons or anything.' Michael Dukakis was not told of the threat.[35]

* * *

Bob Dole was chosen by President Ford to be his vice-presidential running mate in 1976 and the job of informing him was given to Secret Service agent Marty Vencker and a colleague. They tracked him down to the Senate barber shop and told him that Ford intended to phone him as soon as possible. Dole looked 'shocked and thrilled', Vencker said.[36]

Although Ford and his running mate lost the election to Jimmy Carter and Walter Mondale, Dole thought the experience would place him in a good position to secure the Republican Party's presidential nomination in 1980. However, after running a lacklustre campaign he lost out to Ronald Reagan. Dole tried again in 1988 but lost out once more, this time to George H.W. Bush. He spent the next few years as Senate Majority Leader and bided his time. It came in 1996 and he announced his candidacy for the Republican Party nomination in his home town of Russell, Kansas, a typical small town in the heartland of the nation.

Even liberal journalists had a great deal of respect for Dole. Reporter Howard Wilkinson wrote:

> . . . politics aside, I liked Bob Dole as a human being, he was smart, he was funny and he was a genuine American hero, having lost the use of his right arm and suffering from numbness in his left arm when he was severely wounded as a young soldier in the 10th Mountain Division fighting in the Apennine Mountains of Italy in the waning days of World War II. He almost always carried a pen in his right hand so people would not grasp it to shake hands. I think I made a good impression on him when we first met when I extended my left hand to him.[37]

Dole said that once he had won nomination he found being protected by the Secret Service 'frustrating'. 'Anytime I wanted to talk to constituents, buy a suit, buy groceries', Dole said, 'I was walled off by the Secret Service.' He said the experience '. . . drove me up a wall'. When asked his views of what he was getting himself into he quoted his opponent, Bill Clinton, who said the White House was 'the crown jewel of the federal corrections system'. One Dole aide said, 'If it was up to the Secret Service, [the candidate] would be travelling in an iron box with a slit to give speeches out of.'[38]

The Secret Service agents were not the only members of Dole's campaign retinue who looked after the candidate's safety. He was always accompanied by Mike Glassner, a personal travel aide and senior political staffer. Glassner acted as Dole's closest bodyguard, helping the candidate navigate the physical difficulties Dole faced greeting supporters due to the lack of dexterity in his right arm.

Glassner did not carry a weapon. Often he was seen whispering to Dole's head agent when the candidate was about to break out of the Secret Service's controlled perimeter and move into a nearby crowd to shake hands. Glassner accompanied agents on the 'rope line' when the candidate would meet and greet his supporters. 'You work the rope line from the left to right. That is hard and fast', Glassner said, 'because Dole shakes hands with his left hand, you are facing the people. If you go the other way, it is almost as if you are walking backwards.'[39]

During the 1996 campaign there were some observers who thought the Secret Service protection for Dole was less than efficient. *New York Times* journalist Michael Lewis said that it was 'easy to slip past Dole's Secret Service detail; all you [had to do was] cut your hair, put on a blue suit and walk as though you have a pole stuck up your butt'. Lewis surprised Dole on one occasion when he turned up backstage at a campaign rally in Ontario, California, and introduced himself to the Senator.[40]

During the campaign journalist Tucker Carlson said it was difficult working with the Secret Service 'since, in addition to a tendency to paranoia, Secret Service agents are a notorious lot being rude, even threateningly hostile, to just about anyone below the rank of the candidate himself'. One Dole aide cited the case of 'one hulking agent in a crew cut [who] screamed in the face of a 24-year-old Dole volunteer simply for parking a car incorrectly'. The aide said the Secret Service 'think with their guns'.

However, Carlson believed the real culprits who contributed to the disorganisation in Dole's campaign were the 'advance men'. 'Secret Service agents may be suspicious and surly, but at least they have a clear purpose,' Carlson said. 'In the Dole campaign, senior staffs often do not. Many consider their presence on the campaign trail a nuisance and a distraction, even a bad omen.' Carlson quoted one aide as saying, 'As soon as a lot of senior staff and advisers started travelling with the campaign, we started going down in the polls.'[41]

Dole's aides said that an average advance man could spend hours a day arguing with Secret Service agents and on one occasion blamed the agency for demanding that a fake fence remain unsecured. It led to Dole's fall from a stage in Chico, California, during the campaign. However, this one incident in which Dole's Secret Service agents were taken off guard was spun to the candidate's advantage. Dole's press secretary, Nelson Warfield, told reporters: 'This should put to rest the age question once and for all. If Bob Dole can take a tumble like that and hop right back up on his feet and deliver a great speech, he's strong enough to be president and go a couple of rounds with Mike Tyson too.' Dole joked about the mishap. 'Don't be afraid of standing close to the stage,' he said, 'I'm not gonna dive off today. I was trying to do that new Democratic dance, the Macarena. I'm not gonna try that anymore.' Dean of the Annenberg School for Communication at USC Kathleen Hall Jamieson concurred. She saw it as 'an image of triumph, not of tragedy. He fell. . . . He got up. He went on with his day.'[42]

The Secret Service were also criticised for hyper-vigilance. Agents turned up at a New York restaurant during the campaign to investigate an alleged hostile comment directed at Dole. *New Yorker* journalist Sidney Blumenthal was overheard saying that if Dole really wanted to help his party retake the White House, he would drop dead at the convention and pass the mantle to his vice-presidential choice, Jack Kemp. In reality, it was an innocuous remark but the comment was passed on by a patron of the restaurant and resulted in ten Secret Service agents arriving at Blumenthal's hotel then escorting him into a hallway for questioning for 45 minutes.[43]

Years later Dole reminisced about his loss to Bill Clinton. 'I can remember the Secret Service dropping me off on Election Night,' he concludes. 'You know – good-bye! And then you say, "What do I do tomorrow?" But somebody has to win,' he said. 'And somebody has to lose.'[44]

Dole received threats by letter and telephone during his career. Most were found to be the acts of drunks or venting by mentally unstable individuals. One threat he received when he was Senate Majority Leader was typical.

David Jude Leaverton and David Eugene Nicholson were inmates in the State Penitentiary at Lansing, Kansas. Acting in concert, the two mailed an envelope containing a folded greeting card addressed to 'Senator Bob Dole, U.S. Senate Chambers, Washington, D.C. 20204'. On the face of the greeting card, Leaverton had written, 'I'm tired of all the mental games you people play with me so here is something in return by a real freedom fighter'. Nicholson had written, 'This could have blown your [expletive deleted] head off! Think about it . . .'. The postal authorities were tipped off about the mailing of the envelope and intercepted it in Washington DC before delivery to Dole's office. Both men were arrested and found guilty. Leaverton stated that he was angered by Senator Dole's statements concerning capital punishment. Leaverton also stated to the inspector that he had prior experience in making these devices when associated with 'certain paramilitary groups' and that he 'intended for it to explode'. Leaverton was sentenced to six years in prison.[45]

* * *

When Clinton's vice president, Al Gore, ran for president in 2000, he held a front-runner position as voters appreciated how the president had handled the economy well and wasn't embroiled in any major international conflict. Clinton's poll ratings were high despite his impeachment by Congress and the scandal of having lied about his relationship with a White House intern, Monica Lewinsky. Gore's opponent was Republican George W. Bush.

Gore was far more left wing than Bill Clinton and in fact resented the president for not pursuing more liberal policies. When he became vice president in January 1993 he got along well with Clinton but then became disillusioned with him after the Monica Lewinsky scandal. Gore believed Clinton's scandalous behaviour in office had harmed his chances at succeeding him.

Gore also disliked Republicans and spoke openly about them in a disdainful way in front of his Secret Service detail. Agents said they liked Bill Clinton whereas Al Gore and Clinton's wife Hillary had no redeeming features. According to agents interviewed by journalist Ronald Kessler, Gore was very rude and arrogant towards them and he often remonstrated with them for the slightest of infringements. When Gore became angry at his son, Al Gore III, he pointed at his security detail and said, 'Do you want to grow up and be like them?' It was this statement that was the catalyst for Gore's reputation among agents. According to the agents who spoke to Kessler, most of them prayed Gore would not be elected, and they privatively celebrated in a few of their homes after President Bush won the election.[46]

However, Gore's agents did like his wife Tipper. She would often play pranks on them and 'always insisted on male agents', former agent Dennis Chomicki said. 'She didn't want any female agents on the protection squad.'[47] The agents who spoke to Kessler also said Gore was poor at timekeeping and often made agents wait for the simplest of reasons. On one occasion

Gore arrived an hour late for a dinner with the mayor of Beijing. On another occasion a Secret Service helicopter that was to follow him in Las Vegas almost ran out of fuel because he was so late coming out of his hotel. There were occasions when Gore's timekeeping for appointments led agents to seek him out only to find he was engaged in other activities. As an example, agent Dave Saleeba said a '. . . schedule would call for him to leave the vice president's residence at seven-fifteen a.m. At seven-thirty we would check on him, and he would be eating a muffin at the pool.' When Gore was running late due to his tardiness he would ask his agents to 'speed it up, but don't use the lights and sirens? Get me there as fast as you can.'[48]

Secret Service protocol demanded that whenever their vehicles sped through traffic they would turn on lights and sirens. Gore objected so some agents on his detail found a solution. 'The special agent in charge would come on the radio and say, "Yeah, let's move as quick as we can but safely,"' Chomicki said. 'He'd do it just for the entertainment of the vice president.' Pretending to press the submit button another agent would fake talking on the radio. 'Hey, let's go, speed it up,' Chomicki said the ruse satisfied Gore. The agent also criticised Gore for the way he borrowed money from agents but did not pay them back. 'I think he always thought, "I'm the vice president. I don't have to pay for anything,"' Chomicki said.[49]

Like all presidential candidates, Gore received threats against his life during his time as vice president and 2000 presidential candidate. A typical threat Gore received as vice president was made by David Shane Shelby. In separate letters to Clinton and Gore, Shelby wrote, 'I hate you. . . . Turn Charles Manson loose or I will kill you'. He was arrested as he was about to mail a package to President Clinton filled with explosives.[50]

* * *

US Senator John Kerry received Secret Service protection in February 2004 after he won primary elections in sixteen of eighteen state contests. After receiving the Democratic Party nomination for president he chose his main primary election challenger John Edwards, a North Carolina Senator, to be his running mate. Edwards was later involved in a scandal when he ran for president in 2008. He had fathered a child with his mistress, Rielle Hunter, then lied to the press about it.

Edwards had little respect for the man who chose him as his 2004 vice-presidential candidate. '[Kerry] just wasn't all that smart', Edwards told one of his aides. He found Kerry to be aloof and 'too aristocratic in his bearing to succeed as the leader of a party that looks for major support from unions, African Americans and people in big cities'.[51]

According to Kerry, the 2004 campaign was the last presidential campaign where the candidate could conduct a conversation with someone in the 'rope line'. During campaign rallies the Secret Service would erect strong metal barriers and warned the candidates of every likely scenario when the rope line was approached including the possibility that a baseball offered for signing or a mobile phone could be a bomb. Kerry believed that although the majority of people who approached him or attended his rallies 'showed signs of friendliness', he would now and again spot someone in the crowd who had 'a flicker in their eye' or a 'creased forehead' indicating a 'less than friendly attitude'.[52]

John Kerry's agents were well trained to protect a candidate who enjoyed outdoor pursuits, having previously protected runners Bill Clinton and George Bush. As Kerry was an avid skier, his appointed agents were required to train in protecting a candidate on the slopes.[53]

He had just emerged as the front-runner for the Democratic Party's presidential nomination in March 2004 when he took a snowboarding trip to Ketchum, Idaho. On one run down the slopes, Kerry collided with an agent – in full view of his travelling press corps. Unfortunately, he compounded the bad public relations gaffe by insisting to reporters, while prone on his back, 'I don't fall down. That son of a bitch ran into me,' indicating it was the fault of one of his agents. Kerry's aides insisted he was only joking.[54]

The Secret Service had some anxiety in protecting a presidential candidate who owned five US properties not counting the several foreign properties he owned with his wife, a Heinz company heiress. Initially, the concerns centred on the supply of agents to provide security 24 hours a day if he were to win the general election. Each property would have required rotating shifts of agents every 6 hours for the rest of his life – five Secret Service agents per shift, daily every 6 hours, per property. However, the agency maintained the alleged anxieties were not true and that every single residence, whether it be in the United States or abroad, would not be staffed.

During his campaign and his later position as Obama's Secretary of State Kerry faced threats of assassination including threatening letters and emails, but no incidents of violence against the candidate were reported during the 2004 campaign. A typical threat involved a Las Vegas resident, 53-year-old Robert V. Ruppert, who was arrested in April 2004 for threatening Kerry's life. He was charged with 'knowingly and wilfully threaten to kill, kidnap and inflict bodily harm upon Senator John Kerry'.[55] In 2013 Kerry was visiting his wife, Teresa Heinz Kerry, at Spaulding Rehabilitation Hospital in Charlestown when State Department security officers saw a man taking pictures of the window in Kerry's Boston Beacon Hill home. Boston police arrested him and later found a pellet gun in his vehicle.[56]

Chapter 14

Father and Son

'He [George H.W. Bush] was constantly moving and he would move fast and if you were ahead of him you had to be careful if you slowed down because he'd run you right over. He played golf like he played hockey. He was just constantly moving.'

Secret Service agent Roy Scheer

'When I first met George W. Bush I expected a Connecticut Yankee. What I got was a real West Texan.'

Bush aide Andrew Card

Former CIA Director George H.W. Bush ran for president in 1980. After winning the Iowa caucus he claimed he had the momentum over Republican Party presidential front-runner Ronald Reagan. However, following Reagan's victory in the New Hampshire primary and several others he lost the Republican Party nomination.

At first Reagan considered taking former President Ford as his vice presidential nominee. But, Ford demanded what amounted to a co-presidency role in a future Reagan administration. Reagan found the demand unacceptable. Instead, the nominee chose George Bush as his running mate. Reagan and Bush went on to win the November 1980 general election against sitting president Jimmy Carter.

After eight years as vice president Bush entered the race to succeed President Reagan. In the 1988 Republican presidential nomination battle, he unexpectedly finished third in Iowa losing to Bob Dole. Dole was also leading in the New Hampshire polls but ended up losing out to Bush. Bush went on to win the Republican Party nomination for president and won the general election against Democratic Party candidate Michael Dukakis.

During the 1988 campaign Bush had been successful in presenting himself as 'warm, sincere, relaxed and secure. . . . a person most people like', according to polls. A year into his presidency another poll found 80 per cent of the public approved of him 'as a person'.[1] Four years later President Bush lost the presidency to Bill Clinton. 'Frankly', former president Richard Nixon said, 'he was a poor campaigner.'[2] The family's future now resided in Bush's son, George Jr, who won the presidency against Democratic Party nominee and Clinton's vice president Al Gore in the 2000 presidential election.

* * *

When George H.W. Bush ran for the presidency in 1980 he wanted to avoid looking too 'imperial' which is why he eschewed Secret Service protection until after the 1980 Iowa caucuses. According to former agent Marty Vencker, Bush did not want to look like a 'big shot'. He wanted to 'roll up his sleeves and talk with the people'. However, Bush was forced to accept Secret Service protection after his campaign managers persuaded him he would look 'more presidential' if he had agents around him. The managers even included agents in their promotional videos for campaign ads but decided Bush's agents were 'too short' so they used actors instead.[3]

There were also additional reasons why Bush acceded to the wishes of his staff. On 15 March 1980 the Puerto Rican terrorist group FALN (Armed Forces of National Liberation) took over Bush's campaign office in New York for several hours. Other members of the group invaded President Carter's campaign headquarters. The group of armed members tied up Bush staffers. Additionally, Bush's son Jeb had received death threats when he campaigned for his father in Puerto Rico. The terrorist group had detonated more than a hundred bombs in the United States over the past six years killing five people. Both hostage incidents were successfully concluded by local police forces.[4]

During the campaign Bush was described as an 'affable' person who could 'shoot the breeze' with anyone including his Secret Service agents. One staffer described him as having a good sense of humour, 'funny and charming and very relaxed'.[5] Former agent Roy Scheer said the 'main thing' about George Bush was the fact he was 'one of the most decent guys I've ever been around'.[6]

When Reagan and Bush won the 1980 election the agents who protected both candidates were split into two groups. Agent Roy Scheer was chosen to cover Bush. 'He was constantly moving', Scheer said, 'and he would move fast and if you were ahead of him you had to be careful if you slowed down because he'd run you right over. He played golf like he played hockey. He was just constantly moving.'[7]

Following his inauguration as vice president, Bush's agents were so comfortable with the new vice president they felt secure in playing jokes on one another during the long and often tedious hours they spent protecting the Second Family at the vice-presidential residence in Washington DC. One agent, for example, convinced another it was perfectly fine to do his laundry at the residence. When Barbara Bush discovered the agent washing his clothes she simply considered it to be 'amusing'.

A year after Bush was inaugurated as vice president the Secret Service believed they had come under attack when Bush travelled through the streets of Washington DC. Bush was on his way to work at the White House in February 1982 when his detail heard and felt a loud bang emanating from the top of the vice-presidential limousine. As the car pulled up alongside a construction site 150 law-enforcement officers made a door to door search of the area, which was about six blocks from the White House. Several blocks were cordoned off. At first it was believed the 'projectile' was a bullet. Bush said, 'I thought it might have been a shot or something.' However, the FBI determined it was a 'brick or stone' falling from a twelve-storey brick apartment site called Washington Park. Bush said there 'wasn't anything to laugh about [but] there wasn't anything scary about it'.[8]

For the Secret Service 'protecting Bush' also meant protecting his secret private life. During his 1980 presidential campaign Bush had been romantically linked to a staff aide, Jennifer Fitzgerald. The press speculated endlessly about Bush's alleged 'affair' and called it 'The Jennifer Problem'. Bush aides described Fitzgerald as a 'massive pain in the ass to everyone' and a 'barrier between the campaign and the candidate'. Fitzgerald became Bush's 'gatekeeper' in much the same way Bob Haldeman and Sherman Adams fulfilled that role for Nixon and Eisenhower. She was brusque and formal and was sometimes referred to as the 'ice lady'.[9]

During the 1980 primaries Fitzgerald had an important role in deciding where Bush would campaign whether it was at luncheons for business people or factory gates. According to some sources, she had a 'strange power' over her boss. Some staffers queried whether she was a 'martinet or mistress'. Bush's son George Jr insisted the rumours were false. However, there were credible reasons why the press raised the issue. Yale president and former ambassador to the UK Kingman Brewster's biographer Geoffrey Kabaservice said that Bush arranged for Fitzgerald to work for Brewster in London and Bush would visit her there. '[Brewster] was irritated at her frequent absences going to the states to see George,' Kabaservice said. 'Their relationship was no secret to the embassy staff. Everyone knew that she was George's mistress.'[10]

Roy Elson, former aide to Senator Karl Hayden, said he knew Fitzgerald 'very well and there's no question in my mind what her relationship was with George Bush . . .'.[11] Fitzgerald was moved from the Bush campaign but when he became vice president she was once again given a staff position.

However, it was a story involving the Secret Service which appeared to confirm the truth about Bush's extramarital affairs. On 18 March 1981 security personnel accompanying Secretary of State Al Haig and Attorney General William French Smith at Washington's Le Lion d'Or restaurant approached the table of the two cabinet members and informed them of an incident that had taken place in the city. Haig and Smith left the restaurant only to return 45 minutes later 'laughing their heads off'. Vice President Bush had been involved in a traffic accident accompanied by Jennifer Fitzgerald. He had been concerned about negative press publicity so he asked his agents to contact Haig and Smith for assistance. Bush had been concerned that Fitzgerald's name might appear on a police blotter.

According to an editor at *The Washington Post*, Michael Kerner, 'If the accident had made the police blotter, we probably would've had to report it. But if it was just George Bush with another woman we wouldn't have touched it – then.' Kerner recalled another incident when Bush visited a woman who lived on Connecticut Avenue. When a fire broke out Bush's Secret Service agents would not allow the Fire Department to handle the fire in the apartment building until they had removed the vice president from the building. Kerner said, 'We all knew about it . . . but nobody wrote about it in those days. There was a conspiracy of silence about politicians . . . George, like a lot of others, was able to get away with quite a lot'.[12]

When Bush was elected president in 1988 his attitude towards his bodyguards did not change. His detail described him as 'extremely kind, considerate and always respectful'. G. Michael Verden, who was assigned to Bush's detail during his presidency and after, said Bush was '. . . the same person behind the cameras as he was in front of the cameras . . . he treated everybody the same'.

Bush also took great care in making sure the agents' comforts were taken care of. Both Bush and his wife Barbara brought them meals and on occasion Barbara Bush brought warm clothes to agents standing outside their Kennebunkport summer home in Maine. One agent who was given a warm hat tried nicely to say 'no thanks' even though he was obviously freezing. President Bush said, 'Son, don't argue with the First Lady, put the hat on.'

Verden said Bush '. . . treated everyone with respect. He was bipartisan. It didn't matter what party you came from. Whatever job you had at the White House he'd treat everyone the same.' Verden said he was never too familiar with Bush but the president would always make the first move in sparking conversation or enlisting his agents in some activity, especially at his home in Kennebunkport. Verden said that Bush told him that if he was going fishing with him the agent had to fish also. 'Bush was grounded,' Verden said. 'If you look at his background – vice president for eight years, CIA, Ambassador to China – you'd think he might have a bit of arrogance. Absolutely not.'[13]

Uniformed Secret Service agent Gary Byrne recalled how the Bushes came across as genial and friendly with their protectors. Bush had a rapport with the Secret Service, Byrne said, and when the uniformed White House agent first met the First Lady he didn't reply when she said 'Good morning'. However, he soon learned that the Bushes liked to greet agents. Byrne was also surprised to learn the Bushes also liked to socialise with their detail even though the policy of the agency was antithetical to the practice. Agents were often invited to join in during barbecues and family gatherings.

George Bush was constantly 'on the go' and it was difficult for his body-guards to keep up with him especially during the president's jogging sessions. Even on foot many agents had a hard time keeping up with the president. In addition to two agents flanking him a third had to run backwards to provide rear-view security.

Additionally, there were two Bush sporting activities they found risky. Bush liked to play golf on public courses, which was a security issue. Former Secret Service agent Dan Emmett said, 'There is all this open space, and you have other people playing because you cannot just shut down the course.'

Bush's Kennebunkport home was also a challenge for the Secret Service. It was situated in a seaside tourist area, surrounded by water on three sides. Agents had to go through special training as the vice president liked to take out his high-speed cigarette boat. At first agents had struggled to keep up with him but the problem was solved by the bodyguards using a powerful Mirage 36 speedboat with twin 400hp engines.

In the run-up to Bush's re-election campaign an incident occurred which had serious repercussions. It involved Bush's health which alarmed his agents. Bush had suddenly been stricken with fatigue and shortness of breath during a jog at Camp David. His agents took him to the infirmary and from there he was flown to Bethesda Naval Hospital by helicopter. He was suffering from an irregular heartbeat. A week later Bush was diagnosed with Graves' Disease which drained his energy and forced him to take frequent naps. It had an effect on his 1992 re-election campaign.[14]

Another health scare occurred during a twelve-day presidential trip to Australia, Singapore, South Korea and Japan. Bush collapsed during a dinner hosted by the Japanese prime minister and vomited on the premier's lap. Secret Service agents quickly rushed forward as Bush slid to the floor. The president, however, soon recovered.[15]

There were a number of assassination plots during George H.W. Bush's time as vice president and president. During the 1988 presidential election campaign 22-year-old David Russell attended a Bush campaign rally in Kentucky armed with a .45 calibre handgun. As Bush shook hands with supporters Russell took photos of him. The would-be assassin came within 40ft of the vice president. Two days later he wrote a letter to the White House, demanding that Bush drop out of the race and attached a photo he had taken at the rally. Russell threatened to assassinate the vice president if he refused. Russell was arrested and charged. He later admitted in court that he had acted 'stupidly'. The judge concluded that he 'intended to carry out his act' and sentenced him to twenty-two months in prison.[16]

John Spencer Daughetee had stalked George Bush since the 1988 presidential election campaign. Following Bush's election, Daughetee waited outside a building in Washington DC where the new president-elect was giving a speech. However, Daughetee could not position himself close enough to get a shot off. In April 1989, Daughetee followed Bush to Hamtamck, a suburb of Detroit, where the president was scheduled to deliver a speech. However, Daughetee's assassination plan was foiled when he was told to go through a magnetometer. He panicked, attempted to find another place in the crowd where he could shoot Bush, but the president had left by the time the would-be assassin had found a suitable place to shoot.[17]

Roger Hines was a 6ft 4in, 457lb, 35-year-old man who had four prior criminal convictions and five hospitalisations for mental problems and had once entered a hospital with an axe and threatened patients and staff. On 13 January 1992, at the beginning of Bush's campaign for re-election, Hines stole a .357 Magnum revolver and fifty rounds of ammunition in Oregon before travelling to Washington DC. On 21 January 1992 Hines took his gun to a school where he believed the president would be making an appearance. However, Hines chose the wrong school. Fortunately, Bush was 45 miles away at the Emily Harris Head Start Centre in Catonsville, Maryland, southwest of Baltimore.

Hines left Washington DC at the end of January and travelled west. On 12 February 1992, he sold the .357 Magnum at a gun shop in San Francisco and four days later, while in Salt Lake City, he posted a letter to Walt Dillman, his state probation officer in Oregon. The letter stated:

> I haven't kill(ed), but I could and will if I need to. I am on my way back east again. . . . the first time I went back was to kill President Bush and was so close to doing so. I was at Fort Mead and he was at a kid's day-care centre preschool. I was within 30 feet of him and I had that .357 in my hand in the pocket. I wanted to be known as someone in this U.S.A. . . .

The letter triggered a nationwide manhunt for the potential assassin. Hines was tracked down by the Secret Service, arrested and found guilty of threatening Bush.

On 28 February 1992, Hines was arrested at a bus depot in Portland, Oregon. When he was searched police found a butcher's knife, a hunting knife and a handwritten diary. Hines told agents that he would 'kill President Bush some other time'. He also admitted sending postcards and letters threatening to kill Bush and while in custody he also confessed his assassination plans to a local television station. He said he would do it again in a 'hart [*sic*] beat' if he could get out of jail. He explained he wanted to kill President Bush to get attention. Hines also sent a letter to a female acquaintance and wrote, '. . . I was on a killing roll and you could have been next. I was going to rob you and cut you up into parts . . . you should hope I don't get out of jail for about ten years, because you could be next'.[18]

On 1 June 1992, Hines pleaded guilty to making threats against the president and being a felon in possession of a firearm. The court noted Hines' 'extraordinarily dangerous mental state' and 'significant likelihood that he will commit additional serious crimes'. The court sentenced Hines to 100 months' imprisonment for being a felon in possession of a firearm and a concurrent 60 months for making threats against the president, followed by 3 years of supervised release.[19]

During Bush's re-election campaign Deborah Butler, a 32-year-old legal secretary who lived in Denver, Colorado, wrote in her diary of her admiration for President Ford's would-be assassin Sara Jane Moore and her plan to kill President Bush. Although Butler had no previous psychotic episodes in her life, she had lately been having mental problems. She decided to shoot the president 'to draw attention to herself and her need for help'.

On 15 September 1992, Butler drove to Englewood, a Denver suburb, for a Bush re-election campaign rally held in Inverness Business Park. She concealed a .32 revolver in the back waistband of her trousers before joining a campaign crowd awaiting Bush's motorcade. Butler was ready to take a shot at the president but her attention was diverted long enough for Bush's motorcade to drive past her.

Butler intended approaching Bush's speaking platform but saw that she would have to go through a metal detector. Instead, she sat on a small hill nearby. Arapahoe County Sheriff Pat Sullivan saw Butler and thought she looked suspicious. He ordered one of his deputies to keep an eye on her. 'Place yourself between her and the presidential motorcade,' Sullivan told one of his deputies. 'I poked him in the chest to make sure he had a bullet-proof vest on,' the sheriff said. The deputy approached Butler and searched her backpack during a routine sweep but returned it to her after finding nothing suspicious.

Butler drove home. After she told her husband of her aborted assassination attempt he took her to a psychiatric hospital. She told staff at the hospital she 'had just tried to shoot the president'. After the staff informed the FBI of her plans Butler was taken into custody. Police found her diary which detailed her assassination plans.[20]

On 8 December 1992 Butler was found competent to stand trial. She pleaded guilty to threatening the president and in January 1993 was sentenced to twenty-seven months in prison and ordered to receive psychiatric treatment. She apologised to the court and said, 'I'm very sorry for what happened and all the trouble that I caused and I thank everyone for their help and consideration in dealing with me.' She was also fined $2,000 and put on probation for three years after she had served her term at the federal penitentiary in Rochester, Minnesota.[21]

* * *

When Bush's son George W. Bush ran for the 2000 presidential election he was serving as Governor of Texas. Following his victory against Democratic Party candidate Al Gore both President George W. Bush and his father George

H.W. Bush became known as 'Bush 41' and 'Bush 43'. The unofficial titles were given by the Secret Service and later the monikers were picked up by the press.

Bush had decided to run for Governor of Texas in 1993 as the Republican Party candidate. His bid was a long shot, with even his own mother telling him that he could not win against the popular, charismatic incumbent Democratic Governor Ann Richards. However, Bush came across to voters as very personable and the Bush name no doubt was a large influence in his election victory.

The protective detail provided for Bush when he was Governor of Texas was a contingent of police officers from the Department of Public Safety. The agency provided security for the governor and his family and also provided those services to visiting governors from other states and to members of the state legislative and judicial branches when assigned.

When Bush took office he took daily bike exercise usually on Austin's Town Lake Trail. Wearing a hat and sunglasses, he would be accompanied by two officers and a third officer on foot. On the campaign trail Bush understood the importance of pacing himself, making sure he put aside time for exercise, getting a good night's rest, keeping a focus on the 'big picture' and not worrying about the day-to-day analysis of campaigning. He always preferred to have a small entourage when he travelled. Often he was accompanied by a personal aide, his spokesman and two or three of his 'best officers'.[22]

Governor Bush ran for re-election as Governor of Texas in 1998 and won with a record 69 per cent of the vote. As his successful campaign attracted national attention, he decided to run for the presidency in 2000. Bush formally announced his candidacy for the Republican presidential nomination in June 1999 in a speech in Cedar Rapids, Iowa. Eventually he raised $40 million for the campaign which made him the front-runner. By the end of 2000 he had received more than $193 million in donations.[23] His main opponent in the primary elections was Senator John McCain.

Bush's behaviour and actions in his younger days, particularly as they related to alcohol, raised some questions during his campaigns for governor and later when he ran for president. He famously responded that he was 'young and irresponsible' when he was 'young and irresponsible'.[24] However, his former sister-in-law Sharon Bush challenged Bush's excuses and said he had 'done coke' at Camp David during his father's presidency.[25]

Just prior to Election Day in November 2000, the story about his drunk driving as a young adult appeared in the press. Bush admitted that he had been convicted of drunk driving in September 1976. A state trooper saw

Bush's car swerve onto the shoulder, then back onto the road. He failed a road sobriety test and blew a .10 blood alcohol, pleaded guilty, was fined and had his driver's licence suspended. He said that he had drunk 'several beers' at a local bar before the arrest. Bush was 30 at the time. During the presidential campaign he said that he stopped drinking when he turned 40 because it became a 'problem'.

Bush's campaign for the Republican Party nomination began by travelling across the country guarded by his officers and a group of Texas Rangers. His security detail was given the added assignment of handling press passes for state events out of the campaign office.[26]

Bush also had the services of 6ft 4in Joe Allbraugh, a crew-cut bodyguard who labelled himself as Bush's 'campaign manager' but in reality he acted as the governor's 'enforcer', according to the *Austin Chronicle*. Allbraugh usually wore cowboy boots and looked 'more like a Marine drill instructor or an Oklahoma state trooper than a political operative'. He was nicknamed 'Sergeant Rock'. In fact, Allbraugh admitted his role as a bodyguard when he told a reporter, 'There isn't anything more important than protecting him and the first lady [of Texas]. I'm the heavy, in the literal sense of the word.'[27]

When Bush received Secret Service protection he was given the codename 'Trailblazer'. Immediately, Bush endeared himself to his detail by being unpretentious, often serving his bodyguards meals, sharing jokes and enlisting them in sporting activities. During time on his Texas ranch he would wear cowboy regalia, cowboy boots, jeans and a checked work shirt. Andrew Card, Bush's chief of staff, said that when he first met the 33-year-old Bush at Kennebunkport he '. . . expected a Connecticut Yankee. What I got was a real West Texan.' Card said Bush was a 'tell-it-like-it-is person. He's from the rough and tumble world of Midland, Texas [where] your word means more than a contract there. He accepts people who can be with him or against him but it's the people who are with him and against him at the same time that he has trouble with.'[28]

The Secret Service was appreciative of the way Bush worked with the agency during the 2000 campaign. He treated his agents with respect and always accepted their advice when it came to safety protocols. The Bushes made sure their entire administrative and household staff understood they should respect and be considerate of the agency. Agents appreciated the fact that Bush was always punctual and they were surprised at how the president's public face differed from his private one. Agent Evy Poumpouras believed Bush did not have any 'pretensions', was 'consistent and genuine' and 'remained authentic in any situation'. The female agent compared Bush with other Washington politicians who 'tried to impress you by projecting a fabricated version of themselves'.[29]

Agents told author Ron Kessler they 'were always amazed at the difference between Bush in person and the way he came across at press conferences'. An agent assigned to Bush said that although he seemed awkward in front of the microphone that he was 'funny as hell' and had an incredible sense of humour. An agent told Kessler that Laura Bush had 'the undying admiration of almost every agent', and that he had not heard anything negative about her. Former agent Tim Wood, a supervisor on Presidential Protection Detail during the first two years of President George W. Bush's first term in office, said Laura Bush was 'one of the nicest First Ladies, if not the nicest and she never had any harsh word to say about anyone'.[30]

Bush's Crawford, Texas, ranch served as the 'Western White House' during his eight years as president. He spent nearly every vacation there. The detail was a prime assignment because agents liked the Bush ranch and loved to accompany the president when he chopped wood there. He would also occasionally host barbecues for his security detail and helped serve their meals. He ate with them, sat with them and talked with them, asking about their families, the names of which he always remembered. He also knew each agent by their first name, and called them by their first name. Agents believed his personality was genuine and consistent.[31]

The Secret Service guarded the 1,600-acre property. Part of the overnight protection assignments was to stand for a 12-hour shift in cabins situated throughout the ranch. The cabins were nothing more than 'shabby wooden boxes', according to Poumpouras. Constantly on alert for intruders and wildlife, particularly wildcats, Agent Poumpouras hated that particular duty but enjoyed the daylight shifts on the ranch when it was 'beautiful, peaceful and quiet' with mature oaks and elm trees and 'waves of Buffalo grass, white prickly poppies and more than 40 miles of hike trails'.[32]

Many agents volunteered to accompany Bush on his jogs and Secret Service supervisors always attempted to choose the best runners for his detail so they could keep up with him. Bad knees eventually caused him to switch to a bicycle. However, although his detail considered the president to be in excellent shape for his age, they were always concerned about his safety as they considered his bike rides to be hazardous in light of the fact he was not really an excellent cyclist, falling off on numerous occasions.

Agents did not have any time to relax because Bush liked to hack new paths on the hiking trails around his ranch and 'pull fish out of the Brazos River'. Bush would often attempt to outpace his agents during the mountain bike trail rides around the ranch, and Poumpouras said 'he was fast' and agents 'frequently fell out' in the middle of these impromptu races. Agents would jump into the back of the Secret Service follow-up vehicle. Bush found it amusing as other agents were forced to peddle even harder to keep up with him. Some agents never volunteered to ride with Bush, recognising how difficult it would be keeping up with him.

After Bush became president their respect for him increased when he waded into a crowd during a visit to Chile to rescue one of his agents. The incident occurred at an international summit in Chile. The fracas arose when Chilean police refused Secret Service entry to an official function in Santiago. The lead agent approached the line of Chilean security men and demanded to be allowed through. Within a few seconds, the confrontation began to escalate with voices being raised and shoving in all directions. The president reached over two rows of Chilean security guards, grabbed his lead agent by the shoulder of his suit jacket and began to pull, yanking the agent out. Bush was said to be 'not amused' by the incident.[33]

Although agents worked well with Bush's vice president, Dick Cheney, they did not always have respect for him. Cheney had a long history of alcohol abuse, including two convictions for driving under the influence when he was younger. In 2006 Secret Service agents guarding him reported he was 'clearly inebriated' when he accidently shot Texas lawyer Harry Whittington during a hunting party in Texas. The agents said Cheney and several members of the hunting party, including the vice president, consumed alcohol before and during the hunting expedition. Cheney exhibited 'visible signs' of impairment agents said, including 'slurred speech and erratic actions'. The agents and others reported Cheney had consumed far more than the 'one beer' which the vice president claimed he had drunk. The lawyer survived the shooting after receiving medical care.[34]

* * *

In 2003, Bush received 500 death threats every month, more than any predecessor up to that time. Although many were instantly discounted, between twenty-five and forty each month were taken seriously enough to have made him the most protected president in history. For example, on a trip to London in 2008 Bush's security entourage included on the 904 civilian staff from the Department of Defense, 600 from the Armed Services, 250 Secret Service officers, 205 White House staff, 103 US Information Agency staff, 44 Department of State staff, 30 more from the Departments of Agriculture, Commerce, Labour, Transportation and Treasury, 18 Senior Advance Office staff, 16 members of Congress and 12 sniffer dogs.[35]

John Liebech, a thirty year veteran from the US Defense Department and former Advance Team member, said:

> If they could the Secret Service would have the President arrive after dark at a military airport, stick him in a tank and make him stay the night in the vault at the Bank of England. As far as [the Secret Service are] concerned, on every balcony there lurks an Oswald, on every street corner a Hinckley, in every crowd a Sarah Jane Moore or Lynette Fromme [both of whom tried to shoot President Gerald Ford]. No one wants to be known for losing the President on their watch.[36]

Traditionally, both major party presidential candidates are briefed about the state of US national security prior to the general election. In 2000, during the period when Bush was nominated as the Republican Party candidate and the general election the following November, the CIA thought up a ruse to make him understand the realities of a terrorist threat. Four agency officials, headed by Acting Deputy CIA Director John McLaughlin, visited the candidate at his Texas ranch on 2 September 2000. Working with the Secret Service, CIA Deputy Director of the CIA's Counterterrorism Centre, Ben Bonk, planted a briefcase in Bush's ranch house. It contained a bomb the CIA had built which was based on a design seized from a Japanese terrorist cult that had been used to kill thirteen Japanese citizens. However, the 'bomb' did not contain the deadly poison gas used in the original design. When Bonk told Bush about the briefcase he predicted there would be a definite terrorist attack within the coming four years.

Bonk opened the briefcase and Bush watched the red digits counting down. Bonk said the 'bomb' was harmless but it had the desired effect on the candidate. Bush was shocked.[37]

One of the most serious threats that alarmed the Secret Service was a telephone call reporting that Air Force One was the next target after the attacks on New York's Twin Towers and the attack on the Pentagon. The threatener had allegedly used the codename for the president's plane – 'Angel' – making the threat more credible. However, the codename had not been used by the threatener but by an intelligence officer who had erroneously reported the codename had been used.[38]

Throughout Bush's eight years as president he was targeted by terrorist organisations like al-Qaeda and individuals who had an extreme animus towards him. He was the victim of an assassination attempt in the republic of Georgia when an assassin threw a hand grenade at him. He also received threats from Jay Bradley Gilgert, who had been investigated numerous times by the Secret Service; Jonathan Lincoln, a prison inmate who tried sent a threatening letter to Bush shortly after the September 11 terrorist attacks; Charles Fuller, who was serving a forty-six-month sentence in Terre Haute, Indiana, for sending three letters threatening President Clinton in 1998; Ahmed Omar Abu Ali, a man living in Virginia who was sentenced to life in prison for joining al-Qaeda and plotting to assassinate Bush; Miami Cuban ex-convict Catalino Lucas Diaz, who hurled a black cylinder onto the White House's northeast lawn; and Aleksander Aleksov, who asked uniformed officers outside a White House gate if they worked for the Secret Service and told them that he wanted to kill the president.[39]

However, during his re-election campaign in 2004 Bush faced one of the most unusual assassination plots ever conceived. It came from a Buffalo, New York, man, 56-year-old Darrel David Alford, who told acquaintances he wanted to equip one of his model airplanes with a bomb then take it to an arena or stadium where Bush was to make an appearance. Alford intended to detonate the bomb as his plane flew over the platform where Bush was to give his speech. Darrel pleaded guilty to making threats against the president.[40]

Bush received threats to his life long after he left the presidency. In 2014 44-year-old Benjamin Smith threatened to 'kill, kidnap and inflict bodily harm' on him. He was arrested in Manhattan as he sat in his car armed with a loaded .38 calibre rifle, two boxes of ammunition, a container of gasoline and a machete. He professed a love interest in one of the former president's twin daughters, Barbara. 'Bush will get his,' he shouted as he was arrested. When asked about his marital status, Smith said, 'I'm divorced and not currently seeing anyone, but I am working on a relationship with Barbara Bush.' Smith's mother had alerted authorities when she found a note in their home in Pittsford that read, 'I have to slay a dragon and then Barbara Bush is mine . . . America is finished. Obama, Etc.' The Secret Service was able to track Smith down through his mobile phone.[41]

Chapter 15

The Comeback Kid

'These guys [Secret Service] are almost like a suit. They are that close. They hear everything.'

Harold Ickes, Clinton's former deputy chief of staff

'. . . there is a larger point in the case of Clinton that goes well beyond any moral or ethical judgment about – or prurient interest in – his private life. When sources come forward of their own volition to describe how Clinton's private activities have caused lies to be told, threats to be made, and cover-ups to be undertaken, an issue of public integrity is raised, and the public's right to know outweighs a public figure's claim to privacy or journalistic discretion.'

Journalist David Brock

'[Clinton is] so thoroughly corrupt it's frightening.'

Bob Herbert, *New York Times*

'He's sick, he's got an addiction. He needs treatment.'

Former President Gerald Ford commenting on Clinton's womanising

In 1992, Democrat Arkansas Governor Bill Clinton, in a better-than-expected second-place finish in New Hampshire, had salvaged his campaign after scandalous revelations involving his extramarital affairs. He went on to win the Democratic Party's presidential nomination and in the general election campaign against President George H.W. Bush was elected president with a 43 per cent plurality. However, in the end he was mired in political and personal scandal. He humiliated his wife and daughter and was suspended from the practise of law after becoming only the second president to be impeached.

When Bill Clinton became president he was reportedly unhappy about the intrusive nature of the Secret Service. Walking on to the South Lawn to play with Socks, the White House cat, he was immediately surrounded by three agents. It was probably that moment when he realised his protection as president would be very different from when he was Governor of Arkansas. 'The White House is the crown jewel of the federal corrections system,' Clinton said.

There were frictions with the Secret Service shortly after Clinton was sworn in. 'It was a cross-cultural thing,' a former aide said, '. . . The Clintons were unused to the close presence of the agents and also wanted to handpick them, fearing that after 12 years of Republicans in the White House, the agents in place might not be loyal to them.'

Like presidents before him, it took a while before Clinton realised that everywhere he went he would be followed. 'They are that close. They hear everything,' Clinton's former deputy chief of staff, Harold Ickes said. 'These guys are almost like a suit.' Another Clinton aide said that when the president left the White House grounds the agents became 'much more intrusive'. When he stayed overnight in a hotel, there were agents in the halls, in the elevators and outside the doors of his suite. 'I talk openly in front of them', the aide said, 'and the president talks openly in front of them . . .'.

His friend, Arkansas State Police Captain Buddy Young, who was Clinton's security chief for a decade during his governorship said, 'I don't think he likes all this Secret Service business. It's just such a circus.'[1] While the Clintons kept agents out of the two top floors of the residential quarters of the White House, the detail was virtually everywhere else, except inside the Oval Office.

* * *

During Clinton's time as Governor of Arkansas (11 January 1983–12 December 1992) he was guarded by state troopers. The governor's security detail also protected Clinton's family as well as the gubernatorial mansion in Little Rock. During the six terms that Clinton was in office the troopers acted as chauffeurs, butlers, bodyguards and frequently shopped for the family. They did everything for the Clintons. The troopers said the Clintons' relationship was a 'political partnership' and more a business relationship than a marriage.

Having spent so much time with Clinton they knew him well. Nearly a year after Clinton was inaugurated as president five troopers were interviewed by journalist David Brock. The result was a shocking portrayal of a man who would arguably not have been elected president if their stories had been published during the presidential election campaign. Following the troopers' revelations, 'Clinton made a personal plea for journalistic forbearance,' according to author Robert M. Entman. '[It was] not widely reported and, arguably withholding these facts meant censoring data that the public should have known . . .'. Entman suggested the media's stifling of the troopers' stories and lack of scrutiny of Clinton's behaviour lowered the standards of the journalistic profession.[2]

The five troopers interviewed were L.D. Brown, Larry Patterson, Danny Ferguson, Roger Perry and Ronnie Anderson. They questioned how Clinton was able to present himself to the voters as 'someone he was clearly not'. They said Clinton had the skills of a great actor who managed to provide empathy with the voter by coming across as 'one of them'.

The troopers also had positive views of Clinton describing him as a communicator, conciliator, a man who liked to be liked and a personable man who was easy to get along with. They saw him as a charismatic politician who sometimes saw himself as a kind of 'movie star'. The troopers had many private conversations with Clinton often on long journeys for speaking engagements. During one journey Clinton admitted that if he had to leave politics he wouldn't know what to do with himself.

However, the troopers also witnessed Clinton's fiery temper and frequent outbursts if something went wrong. Trooper Larry Patterson, the senior member of the group, accompanied Clinton to the 1988 Democratic convention where the governor was asked to give a speech. Unfortunately, things went wrong with a teleprompter which urged delegates to shout for Jesse Jackson. Clinton was clearly embarrassed and thought the nominee Michael Dukakis was responsible in a bid to disable him as a political competitor. When Clinton received a call from Dukakis during the general election campaign the Arkansas governor began to use epithets denouncing the Democrat Party nominee. Eventually, Clinton agreed to campaign for Dukakis.[3]

Larry Douglas (L.D.) Brown was the trooper who developed the closest relationship with Clinton. Brown started his career in law enforcement as a guard at the notorious Tucker prison in Arkansas. When he joined the Arkansas State Police he was assigned to the security detail of then-Governor Bill Clinton between 1982 and 1985.

Brown was once described as 'Clinton's soul mate'. During his time as a state trooper Brown's speciality was undercover narcotics and he had been trained by the DEA school in Miami. Clinton helped Brown gain admission to the Central Intelligence Agency where he witnessed cocaine smuggling that led to his breakup with Clinton. After leaving the CIA and the Arkansas State Police, Brown earned a Ph.D. degree then operated a consulting firm in Little Rock, Arkansas. A father of four, he was married to Chelsea Clinton's babysitter, Becky McCoy.[4] Christopher Hitchens interviewed Trooper Brown who showed him documents given to him in Clinton's own handwriting. The documents revealed that an off-the-record airport in the Ouachita mountains of Arkansas was used to ship illegal weapons to the Nicaraguan Contras. 'The returning planes were stuffed with cocaine, partly to finance the gun-running and partly to pay off (and also to implicate and silence) those who took part in it,' Hitchens wrote.[5]

Following Clinton's inauguration two of the troopers who were on Governor Clinton's security detail, Larry Patterson and Roger Perry, decided to go on the record about the governor's extramarital affairs, which they admittedly facilitated. Two other troopers, Danny Ferguson and Ronnie Anderson, confirmed the allegations about Clinton but decided against going public at that time. Two of the troopers were persuaded by Brock to go on the record because they were enraged at the lies Clinton told.

The core allegations the troopers made were that, while on official duty, they:

- Scouted women and asked them for their phone numbers to give to the governor. The troopers described it as running a 'procurement service'.
- Secured motel rooms and other assignation points.
- Drove Clinton in state vehicles to these assignation points and kept watch while Clinton was inside.
- Lent Clinton their own state cars to make his escapades less noticeable.
- Delivered gifts to the women.
- Informed Clinton about where his wife was and lied to his wife about where he was. The troopers said Clinton would leave the mansion late at night after his wife was sleeping for meetings with girlfriends occurring several times a month. Hillary was a heavy sleeper, they said. Alternatively, the troopers would sneak

women into the governor's mansion then mount a 'Hillary Watch'.

- The trooper's confirmed former Miss Arkansas Sally Purdue's story of how Clinton's security detail would take the governor to Purdue's home in Little Rock. 'They'd pull up in a wooded area about 30 feet from the house and wait there,' Purdue said. 'When Bill was ready to come out he would signal using my patio lights, flicking it off and on.' During the 1992 primary campaigns a Clinton aide, Ron Tucker, threatened her and told her not to talk about her affair with the candidate. She discovered her car had been vandalised and she also received hate mail and threatening phone calls.[6]

Brown was a witness to almost all of the offences allegedly committed by Clinton when he was Governor of Arkansas: misuse of state funds for sexual liaisons, campaign fundraising and bribery, as well as cocaine use. Through his cooperation with prosecutors and congressional investigators, Brown was later called as a witness in Robert Fiske's and Kenneth Starr's investigations into the Clintons and he also appeared in congressional hearings. Most of what he had to say to investigators was told under the penalty of perjury.

Brown said he arranged meetings with women for Clinton over 100 times, admitting he was no saint himself and that he participated in the 'residuals'. Larry Patterson and Roger Perry also admitted they had colluded in at least a half-dozen long-term affairs and 'hundreds of random sexual encounters' while assigned to Clinton's detail.[7] Since 1987 the bodyguards said Clinton had affairs with a staffer in the governor's office, the wife of a prominent judge, a local reporter, an employee at Arkansas Power and Light and a cosmetics clerk at a Little Rock department store. Patterson and Perry said Clinton's extramarital encounters took place at least two or three times a week. Each girlfriend had been assigned a designated state trooper whose job it was to call her and find out when Clinton could see her. Often he would meet up with them during his jogging sessions.[8]

Brown said, 'I would talk to them personally, sometimes give them my business card. If they were from out of town, I would find out where they were staying. If we were out of town and/or in town anywhere in Arkansas, I would try to get their telephone number and introduce them subsequently to the Governor.' Clinton would meet women when he went jogging and asked Brown to pick him up.[9]

Many years later Brown would expand on his information about the Clintons. On one occasion he was guarding then Arkansas Governor Clinton and his wife while they dined in a private dining room with two other couples at a Little Rock restaurant. Brown said there was 'a diagonal swap . . . bolstered by booze'. Brown watched Hillary and Vince Foster as they 'kissed and fondled each other, while Foster's wife looked on'. Brown said Bill watched them kissing and hugging the wife of a third couple, whom Brown described as a 'beautiful, gleaming Kewpie doll with brains'.[10]

When the couples left the restaurant, Brown said Hillary and Foster were 'drunk, kissing passionately'. Foster had 'his hand on Hillary's rear and is just squeezing it all to hell'. Brown also said both Bill and Hillary had admitted to him that they had an 'open marriage'. The governor also confided in Brown their decision. 'We need to be happy, satisfied', Clinton allegedly said, 'some people are satisfied in different ways.' Brown's observations were confirmed years later when Clinton became president. One of their agents saw Hillary Clinton and Vince Foster 'locked in a passionate embrace'.[11]

Vince Foster became a White House presidential aide following Clinton's inauguration. He committed suicide in May 1993 in Fort Macy Park, a short drive from the executive mansion, after he was criticised by the media for his handling of the 'Travelgate' scandal; a scandal in which employees of the White House Travel Office were replaced by friends of Bill and Hillary Clinton. Many years later Starr would confirm that shortly before Foster's suicide the presidential aide had a bitter argument with Hillary Clinton.

Brown's deposition was made during a court case in which 24-year-old Paula Jones, an attractive young woman who Clinton noticed when she was working on the registration desk at a conference given by the Arkansas Industrial Development Commission, alleged that Governor Clinton had sexually harassed her and exposed himself. The conference was held at the Excelsior Hotel in Little Rock on 8 May 1991. At this time Clinton was busily preparing for his attempt to win the Democratic Party nomination for president and compete in the upcoming 1992 primaries.

Within a short time, one of Clinton's bodyguards, Trooper Danny Ferguson, arrived at the desk and asked Jones if she would like to meet the governor. Ferguson had been instructed by Clinton to approach Jones and tell her he found her attractive. If she responded favourably, she was to be taken to a hotel room where Clinton would be waiting. It was standard practice, Ferguson said.

Jones was flattered and agreed to go to Clinton's hotel room. She believed if Clinton liked her she might be offered a job in the governor's office. However, it soon dawned on Jones that Clinton had other things in mind. After meeting her, Clinton praised her 'curves' and ran his hand up her leg. 'His face was red and I'll never forget that look,' she said. 'I tried to move away. I thought if I started asking about his wife he'd get the message.' She told him she was 'not that kind of girl'. Paula left Clinton's suite and shortly afterwards she was in a state of 'embarrassment, horror, grief, shame, worry and humiliation', according to her friend Pamela Blackard, who was stationed with Jones at the registration desk. Later that day she recounted the whole unedifying experience to her best friend, Debra Ballantine.[12]

In 1998, Clinton was forced to pay $850,000 to settle a sexual harassment lawsuit brought by Jones. It is a matter of record that Clinton offered jobs to the state troopers in an effort to get them to maintain their silence. It is also a matter of fact that those first articles in 1993 led to the disclosure of Paula Jones' name, which led ultimately to Clinton's impeachment.[13]

* * *

Former presidential candidate Bob Kerrey knew long before the general public that Bill Clinton wanted to be president. He said:

> The moment I remember is discovering that Bill Clinton *wanted* to live in 1600 Pennsylvania Avenue. He had intentionally overnighted there when Jimmy Carter was president. He knew where the living spaces were. He knew what they looked like. He had a feel for what that experience was going to be, and it made him feel good. Whereas when I got to thinking about living at 1600 Pennsylvania Avenue, it gave me the chills.[14]

For years Clinton had set his sights on the presidency. Eschewing standing as a presidential candidate in 1988, after his aide Betsy Wright brought up the problem of his alleged adulterous nature, Clinton decided his best bet was to run for president in 1992.

Clinton's candidacy was nearly doomed from the start after one of his mistresses, Gennifer Flowers, called a press conference at the beginning of the primary campaign and said she had conducted a twelve-year affair with the Arkansas Governor. Flowers appeared at the press conference armed with audio tapes which clearly revealed she knew Clinton intimately. Clinton denied he had an affair even though Flowers' mother confirmed the allegation. After Clinton won the presidency her allegations were confirmed by Clinton's state troopers.

And it was not until years later, during Clinton's forced testimony in the Paula Jones sexual harassment case, six years later, that he admitted the affair with Flowers. Flowers called the governor's mansion 'frequently' the troopers said, asking for 'Bill'. If Hillary was not at home, he would take the call. But if she was there, the troopers were told to tell Flowers he would call back. Larry Patterson would often drive the governor to Quapaw Towers in Little Rock where she lived. Patterson would wait in the parking lot for up to 2 hours for Clinton to return.

To combat the revelations, or 'bimbo eruptions' as Betsy Wright called them, Clinton agreed to appear on CBS' *60 Minutes* alongside his wife. The interview appeared on national television directly after the 'Super Bowl', guaranteeing a huge audience. Using well-rehearsed lines, Clinton told the CBS reporter he did indeed have problems in his marriage 'causing some pain' but he was innocent of any wrongdoing. A few days later, Clinton came in second in the New Hampshire primary election after former Senator Paul Tsongas. Clinton hailed himself as the real winner and the 'Comeback Kid'.

According to White House FBI liaison Gary Aldrich, it was White House aide Lloyd Cutler who convinced Hillary Clinton to support her husband when the Flowers scandal erupted. She told Cutler her demands if she was to do that. Hillary wanted to take over a 'significant portion of the Executive Branch'. It was termed 'Hillary's Deal'.[15]

The Clintons began a campaign of 'trashing' any woman who had the temerity to expose Clinton's affairs. Their motives were questioned calling their stories 'trash for cash'. There were some critics of the Clintons who wondered how the Arkansas Governor could have survived being mired in scandal. Author John Dickerson believed the press felt so guilty about destroying presidential candidate Gary Hart's chances of becoming president in the previous presidential election they were shamed for exposing Hart's extramarital affairs. Consequently, Clinton did not face intense press scrutiny when Flowers made her allegations.[16]

When Clinton defeated Bush in the presidential election the former president gave Clinton advice about the Secret Service, 'Don't get on the wrong side of the Secret Service,' Bush advised. 'They can make life miserable.'[17]

After Clinton took office he had the idea he could bring his state troopers to Washington to supplant the Secret Service. The troopers would be in a better position to ensure his 'privacy'. Clinton even believed state troopers would be able to carry the 'football, the nuclear device which could launch missiles'. That idea was never followed up mainly because the president-elect was unaware of the protocols involving presidential protection.[18]

During Clinton's term in office Secret Service agents saw him as disingenuous, false, polite but not kind and that he did nothing without a motive that in some way would enhance his image and political career. They believed he was only nice because he wanted everyone to like him. However, although many agents 'detested' Hillary Clinton, they were not so condemning of her husband and recognised he did, in fact, have charisma and was 'more cordial', 'friendlier' and 'less demanding'. He was also described as 'easy-going' and 'amiable'.[19] Occasionally he would smile at or shake hands with agents even though they knew he had an obvious air of superiority towards them. But they did not particularly like or trust him.[20]

Secret Service agents and those who knew him when he was in the White House corroborated the claims made by Clinton's state troopers that he had a 'bad temper'. Former Carter White House aide Lloyd Cutler, who met Clinton on a number of occasions, said his temper was well known to 'a lot of people'. 'Clinton has this volcanic temper', Cutler said, '. . . I guess one of the things that I wonder about is, what is that like? What kind of environment is that like, when you have to deal with a person who has such an enormous temper?'[21]

A former aide to Spiro Agnew said the Clintons were 'a trial' for the Secret Service. The Clintons were contemptuous of and often berated them in public for any slight infraction of the rules including getting too close to them during their protective duties.[22] Clinton's secretary, Betty Currie, said Clinton heard complaints the Secret Service made about the president's timekeeping or lack of. She said:

> I only heard complaints about time, I didn't hear – that's all I heard was about time. I never heard the Secret Service complain. If he

wanted to venture out to a crowd, sometimes he would ask them. When they told him no, he usually listened to them. Usually. But as someone said, he's never met a hand he didn't want to shake . . . I think he liked all the agents because they were very close. They risked their lives for him and he knew that, so he would be very concerned.[23]

During his 1992 campaign, Bill Clinton began to run as a form of exercise and as a way to meet voters. One way to do this was to run in public places, where the people were. This presented a big challenge to the candidate's detail. Agents were required to run as far as 3 to 4 miles with Clinton, while holding a pistol and a radio. All had to possess not just the endurance to finish but also had the added problem of responding to an impending attack on the candidate. It was a frustrating situation for the Secret Service. Former agent Dan Emmet called it a 'nightmare . . . the worst thing for the Secret Service is to take a sitting president into public when no one has been swept, and anyone could be out there'.[24]

Clinton continued to jog when he was elected president in November 1992. And the exercise also continued to create difficulties for the Secret Service. Prior to Clinton's election the presidential detail had not really taken part in any fitness activities with presidents. Even though Clinton jogged at a moderate pace, agents were not in great shape at first and soon had to up their own levels of fitness.

To keep Clinton safe during his jogs, the Secret Service tried to get the president to run on a track or on military bases, but he refused. To Clinton, the jogs meant he could be seen by voters throughout the streets of Washington DC and other cities.

It wasn't until many years later that one reason for Clinton's jogs became clear. According to Gary Byrne, a uniformed member of the White House Secret Service, Clinton would go jogging around the White House lawns just to pick up women. Byrne said he first became aware of the 'jogging list' early into Clinton's first term. When President Clinton was jogging outside, he said:

Women who were dressed as if they were going clubbing or working out, started showing up at the southeast gate. The agents . . . would get the women's names, and run them to see who they were.

If the women wouldn't cooperate, they would be ushered out of the jogging group. Agents . . . insinuated that this list was used by President Clinton to try to meet these women.[25]

Byrne's other claims included:

- Conformation of a long-time rumour that Clinton carried on an affair with Eleanor Mondale, the daughter of former Vice President Walter Mondale. Byrne once caught the pair in a 'compromising position'. Byrne described White House intern Monica Lewinsky as having an emotional outburst when she was outside the White House gates and discovered the reason a Secret Service agent would not give her access to the president was because he was 'screwing with Eleanor in the Oval Office'.
- Clinton would routinely sneak out to visit his 'well known and less well known mistresses' in Washington DC. Such trips were known as 'Off the Record', or OTR, a privilege normally reserved for occasions like visits to the families of dead servicemen. But Clinton supposedly began to use them for his secret assignations which left the Secret Service outraged. Agents were 'dejected, disappointed, bewildered and shocked', according to Byrne, as well as being 'past fury'.
- Byrne says he walked into a room where the president was 'involved inappropriately with a woman'. He said he once threw out a White House towel stained with a woman's lipstick – and the president's 'bodily fluids'.
- Byrne describes an environment in which secret agents and White House staff knew about Bill Clinton's 'many' affairs and were forced to help cover them up.
- Agents also took care never to have Hillary run into any of her husband's mistresses.[26]

Secret Service agents on Clinton's detail had other embarrassing moments apart from keeping watch during Clinton's extramarital excursions including incidents involving foreign heads of state.

One incident occurred during Russian president Boris Yeltsin's 1995 visit to the United States. It nearly created an international crisis. Yeltsin had been drinking late at night at Blair House, across the street from the White House, when Secret Service agents found the Russian president clad only in his underwear, standing alone on Pennsylvania Avenue and trying to hail a cab. Words slurring, he told them he wanted a pizza. The next night, Yeltsin eluded his security detail when he climbed down the back stairs of Blair House. A building guard took Yeltsin for a drunken intruder until Russian and US agents arrived on the scene and rescued him.[27]

However, a more serious incident involving Yeltsin occurred during the times Clinton met with White House intern Monica Lewinsky. Clinton's phone calls to her were monitored by British, Russian and Israeli intelligence through 'scooping up microwaves off the top of the White House', according to journalist Daniel Halper. Halper said Yeltsin admitted as much in his memoirs.[28]

There were also occasions when Clinton's detail became apprehensive about meetings with foreign leaders who were protected by heavily armed bodyguards. During a private meeting in Syria's presidential palace between President Clinton and President Hafez al-Assad agent Dan Emmett was instructed that if for any reason the Syrian bodyguards drew their Skorpion fully automatic pistols with magazines holding between ten and twenty rounds:

> I would per my training shoot each of them twice with my Sig Sauer pistol until the threat was neutralized, I had expended all ammunition, or I was out of the game. I repositioned myself a bit in order to ensure that President Clinton and Assad would not be in my line of fire. . . . It would be catastrophic beyond imagination if a Secret Service bullet from my pistol struck either POTUS or Assad.[29]

The dangers to Clinton's life were rammed home by the head of his Secret Service detail, Lewis Merletti. When Clinton worked the 'rope line' he had accepted mobile phones from well-wishers to speak to their relatives. Merletti knew it was a dangerous practice and warned the president not to do this. Clinton didn't listen to him so Merletti decided to show him photographs of a dead terrorist assassinated by Israel's Mossad. The Israelis had used a mobile phone filled with explosives. Merletti said after that experience Clinton never again accepted a phone unless it was given to him by one of his agents.[30]

During his time in office Clinton was the victim of numerous assassination plots, threats and assassination attempts. In November 1996, shortly after he was re-elected, he was targeted by al-Qaeda. He was saved by an instinctive decision made by his detail leader, Lewis Merletti. President Clinton was in Manila for an Asia-Pacific Economic Cooperation summit and had on his agenda a visit with a local official. He was running late and impatient to get going. Moments before the motorcade was about to move, agents using a special intelligence-gathering capacity picked up radio chatter mentioning the words 'wedding' and 'bridge'. Terrorists had used these words to signify a terrorist attack. Merletti changed the route, which happened to include a bridge. Clinton was angry at the decision but did not override it. When agents arrived at the bridge, they found explosives – had Clinton taken the prescribed route, he very likely would have been killed. An investigation revealed that the plot was masterminded by a Saudi terrorist living in Afghanistan named Osama bin Laden.[31]

* * *

In 1998 Bill Clinton became the second president to be impeached for abuses of power. The origins of the impeachment began years before with allegations that the Clintons had engaged in an illegal land deal when Clinton was Governor of Arkansas. An independent prosecutor was appointed to investigate. The investigation was first headed by Robert Fiske and later by Kenneth Starr. The media named it the 'Whitewater' investigation after the parcel of land in Arkansas which the Clintons had purchased.

Attorney General Janet Reno approved the expansion of Starr's investigation. As the years passed the independent prosecutor was unable to find any guilt 'beyond a reasonable doubt'. However, there were other issues that arose during the investigation that eventually led to Clinton's impeachment. The investigation eventually took four years to complete and cost over $48 million.

The tangential issue which eventually led to Clinton's impeachment was not Whitewater but his lying under oath about his relationship with White House intern Monica Lewinsky.

In 1998 the Monica Lewinsky affair became the United States' No. 1 scandal. It began with an affidavit in the Paula Jones sexual harassment case. A friend of Lewinsky's who worked in the Pentagon, Linda Tripp, told independent prosecutor Kenneth Starr's office that she had tape-recorded conversations with her friend Monica. Events soon took off – in a sworn deposition connected to the Paula Jones case Clinton told lawyers that he had never spent time alone with Lewinsky in the Oval Office, except perhaps on brief occasions; Clinton's denial at a press conference that he did not have sexual relations with 'that woman, Monica Lewinsky'.

Starr quickly announced his intention to subpoena Secret Service agents in the White House detail and to question them about their daily observations as they worked next to the president. The Treasury Department which was responsible for the agency fought Starr, saying agents must maintain a code of silence in order to do their job effectively. White House lawyers concurred saying that any president should be able to trust agents if they were to do their job protecting him. Secret Service Director Lewis Merletti met with Starr and attempted to persuade the prosecutor that involving Secret Service agents in the investigation might very well damage the protective mission and the relationship between the president and the men and women responsible for his life.

On 10 February 1998 former agent Lewis Fox claimed in a television interview in Pittsburgh that Lewinsky had spent at least 40 minutes in the Oval Office with Clinton in late 1995. Three days later the Justice Department and the Treasury Department (which at the time was responsible for the Secret Service) decided to allow limited questioning of Fox by Starr and his team of lawyers. The concession failed to satisfy Starr who then subpoenaed an agent on active duty. In response the Justice Department filed a sealed brief on 21 February claiming a protective function privilege that would defend agents from forced disclosure. In response Starr called the 'protective function privilege' a 'phantom doctrine' which had never been recognised 'under American law'. Starr said that '. . . not even Richard Nixon's lawyers had come up with such a bizarre notion'.[32]

During March and April the pressure on the agents became more intense. On 3 April Starr signed a sealed motion to compel and asked Clinton's lawyers to waive privilege. The case was heard on 13 May and after appeals Starr won. The Court's ruling held that the protective function privilege enjoyed no support in law.

Accordingly, Starr's team of prosecutors eventually interviewed two-dozen members of the White House Protective Detail including White House uniformed agents Keith Williams, Larry Cockell, Brent James Chinery and Gary Byrne. They were compelled to repeat under oath what they knew about the president's relationship with Lewinsky. It became a legal battle between independent counsel Kenneth Starr and the Clinton administration. Starr wanted agents assigned to Clinton's detail to testify about whether Clinton was ever alone with Monica Lewinsky in the Oval Office and whether the two were observed engaging in sexual acts.

In the end the agents' testimonies were not required because by then Starr and his prosecutors had built an airtight case. The independent prosecutor's report was despatched to Congress for judgment. On 12 December 1998 the House of Representatives voted for impeachment. In February 1999 a trial was held in the US Senate. Clinton was cleared of all charges as senators believed the charges against the president did not rise to the level of high crimes and misdemeanours.

According to author Emmett Tyrell, Monica Lewinsky was not the only White House intern Clinton had a relationship with. 'During the Lewinsky scandal', Tyrell wrote, 'my researchers at the American Spectator gathered a list of seven White House staffers, five of them interns, whom Clinton used as comfort women. None would go public.'[33]

In 2014 investigative journalist Daniel Halper revealed, after gaining access to a never-before-seen Lewinsky lawyer's dossier, that Clinton had committed a sexual attack when he returned to the United States following his time in England as a Rhodes Scholar, in about 1970. He met a young woman in San Francisco who was a student at a California university. Clinton dated the woman then asked her to meet him in San Francisco's Golden Gate Park. Clinton allegedly pushed her to the ground and attempted to rape her. The woman defended herself and managed to run off. 'No charges were ever filed,' Harper wrote. Decades later, however, when Clinton was running for president he contacted her. She believed it was a 'blatant attempt' to discover if she was going to say anything about the encounter to the press.[34]

In the years that followed Clinton's presidency the former president attempted to provide a mea culpa for the way he behaved in the White House. He told Taylor Branch the Lewinsky affair began because 'I cracked; I just cracked.'[35]

When he engaged in a conversation with White House aide General Hugh Shelton in his final days in office Shelton said the president looked at him and said, 'You know, you and I are cut out of different pieces of cloth, but I want you to know how much I admire and respect what you stand for. If I've caused any embarrassment to the men and women in uniform, I sincerely regret it.' Shelton saw tears running down Clinton's face. 'He really felt deeply that he owed it to me to say that, which I really appreciated,' Shelton said. 'To be candid, I've never told anybody about that side of him.'[36]

After he left office Clinton's extracurricular excursions continued to cause problems for his protective detail. His visits to New York nightclubs and restaurants even shocked the New York Police Department's Dignitary Protective Unit which scouted public accommodations before the ex-president's visits. Sources within the unit said he was an 'ongoing problem' for them particularly in his meetings with 'fast women' and 'drug users'. The unit issued warnings to Clinton but these were ignored.[37]

And, nearly twenty years after Clinton's presidency, the former president continued to court scandal – a scandal that involved his Secret Service detail – or rather a lack thereof.

Clinton said that in 2002 and 2003 he took a total of four trips on disgraced billionaire Jeffrey Epstein's aeroplane. The billionaire later worked out a deal in 2008 with federal prosecutors, including President Trump's Labour Secretary Alexander Acosta, that allowed Epstein to avoid ten years in prison on charges of sexually abusing minors as young as 14 and having some of his victims recruit other girls in exchange for serving thirteen months in jail and paying restitution to victims. The trips Clinton took on Epstein's plane included one to Europe, one to Asia and two to Africa, which included stops in connection with the work of the Clinton Foundation. Supporters of the Foundation, and his Secret Service detail travelled on every leg of every trip, he said through one of his spokespersons.

However, when the details of the flights were scrutinised by the *Washington Examiner* in 2019 investigative reporters revealed Clinton took twenty-seven flights on Epstein's private jet during at least six different trips. The six Clinton-Epstein trips included a Miami to Westchester trip, two Asia trips, a trip to Europe in February 2002 and two trips to Africa in July 2002 and late September to October 2002.

On the first Asia trip, the logs show Clinton and Epstein were joined by top Clinton aide Doug Band, wealthy socialite and Epstein's onetime girlfriend Ghislaine Maxwell, former Epstein assistant Sarah Kellen, women listed only as 'Janice' and 'Jessica' and a few others.

Most importantly, there were no Secret Service agents on Clinton's trip with Epstein to Africa in late September and early October 2002, where the investigation revealed they were joined by actor Kevin Spacey and comedian Chris Tucker. Epstein's former masseuse said that on almost every trip she went on 'there were young girls around'.[38]

Chapter 16

Evergreen

'[The Clintons] were almost totally dependent on each other. . . . every step of the way. Hillary Clinton was a contributing and enabling partner.'

Historian William H. Chafe

'[The political rise of the Clintons was] strategic cleverness, reckless gambles, and an unquenchable thirst for political power.'

Journalist Daniel Halper

'As for Bill and Hillary Clinton, the citizens of the United States deserved better. Talented they were, to be sure, but deeply flawed, fundamentally dishonest, contemptuous of law and process.'

Kenneth Starr, Independent Prosecutor

During her time as 'First Lady of Arkansas' Hillary Clinton became frustrated that her husband's philandering would damage 'The Plan', as the couple called their pursuit of power. 'The Plan' was developed during the 1970s when the young couple delineated their career paths. Bill was to run for Governor of Arkansas followed by an attempt to become president. Bill's career would then take second place to Hillary's. Eventually, they reasoned, she would become the first female President of the United States.

However, 'The Plan' had to withstand the years of conflict between Hillary Clinton and her husband, according to Clinton bodyguard Larry Patterson. The state trooper recalled how Hillary's role as First Lady of Arkansas was fraught with arguments between herself and her husband. He told journalist David Brock:

> I remember one time when Bill had been quoted in the morning paper saying something she didn't like. I came into the mansion

and he was standing at the top of the stairs and she was standing at the bottom screaming. She has a garbage mouth on her, and she was calling him motherf***er, c***sucker, and everything else. I went into the kitchen, and the cook, Miss Emma, turned to me and said, 'The devil's in that woman'.[1]

Hillary was standoffish with her state trooper bodyguards. When she left the mansion she said nothing to the troopers about where she was going or for how long. In fact, she avoided speaking to them as much as possible. She would give instructions about her protection through her husband. They saw Hillary as the more 'gutsy' of the two, always playing the role of decision-maker. Troopers Patterson and Roger Perry believed Hillary was more obsessed with Bill's political success than her husband. She would fight tooth and nail during Bill's campaigns.

Hillary, as described by the troopers, pursued power incessantly and she had few friends outside politics. Trooper Roger Perry said:

Everything was politics with Hillary. They wouldn't go out to dinner with friends the way you or I would . . . If they were invited to a private party, and there were only going to be eight or ten people there, she would say, 'We're not going to waste time at that thing. There aren't enough people there.' I never saw Hillary just relax and have a good time.[2]

Hillary took out her frustrations on the couple's state trooper security detail calling them 'shit-kickers', 'rednecks', 'hicks' and 'white trash'. She was contemptuous and dismissive of them at one time referring to their pistols as 'phallic symbols'. Resenting their constant presence, Hillary would reply to their greetings with 'F*** off'. She instructed Trooper Larry Patterson not to say a word to her when they were out in public. She was not interested in the people of Arkansas, the troopers agreed. She was only interested in getting her husband elected. Otherwise she was contemptuous of the voters.[3]

Hillary's temper was so bad she sometimes acted deranged. One day as she left the mansion by car troopers observed how a short time later she returned, stopped her car 'violently, tires squealing', screaming, 'Where is the goddamn f***ing flag?' Patterson explained that it was early so the troopers had not had time to put up the flag. Hillary responded, 'I want the goddamn f***ing flag up every f***ing morning at f***ing sunrise.'[4]

One veteran state trooper, Ralph Parker, was one of the few members of the security detail to risk alienating Hillary. Once, when she received the 'Mother of the Year' award at the governor's mansion, Parker said, within range of Hillary's staff, that the award should have been, 'motherf***** of the year award'. Parker was aware that Hillary had spent little time with her daughter Chelsea.[5]

Larry Patterson also saw the Clinton's call each other 'Jew bastard' and 'Jew mother******'. He had heard Hillary make anti-Semitic remarks 'at least 20 times'. Hillary's anti-Semitism was confirmed by Paul Fray who had managed Bill Clinton's unsuccessful bid for Congress in 1974.[6]

The troopers said Hillary Clinton was well aware of her husband's affairs. Clinton friend and political operative Dick Morris said that Bill Clinton had 'hundreds of women' as the result of a 'sex addiction' and that Hillary had 'boxed off' her knowledge of the affairs in the interests of the Clinton political partnership. Clinton's secret encounters with women continued after he received Secret Service protection as a presidential candidate. Agents moved into the Little Rock mansion during the 1992 campaign.[7]

Hillary Clinton's affair with her Rose Law firm colleague Vince Foster was widely known. White House Director of Security Craig Livingstone was a close friend of the Clintons; 'extremely close', according to FBI agent and White House liaison officer Gary Aldrich. Aldrich believed that one important conversation he had with Livingstone confirmed the rumour of the affair. Livingstone told Aldrich, 'You remember when Bill and Gennifer [Flowers] were doing their thing? Vince and Hillary were doing their thing.' The affair was also known 'to a person' by 'everyone in the Arkansas Democrat-Gazette newsroom', according to the newspaper's editor.[8]

The Vince Foster/Hillary Clinton affair was confirmed by Jim McDougal, an Arkansas friend of the Clintons who brought the Clintons into the Whitewater land deal (much later the deal would be investigated by a federal independent prosecutor but no evidence of corruption was found). McDougal told author Christopher Andersen before his death in 1998, 'Everybody knew about Hillary and Vince . . . But Bill was not really in a position to object, now was he?'[9]

When Bill Clinton was elected president, Foster moved to Washington to work in the Clinton White House as Deputy White House Counsel. He believed that if his affair with Hillary was revealed it would ruin his life, his reputation and his marriage. 'He was worried sick about it,' Gary Aldrich said. Additionally, Daniel Halper discovered, investigative reporters were '. . . examining the relationship in the days before his suicide'.[10]

On 20 July 1993, after working for only a few months in the White House, Foster drove to Fort Macy Park, a short distance from the executive mansion, put a pistol to his head and fired. Media stories at the time blamed Foster's depression and his inability to deal with the brutal realities of Washington politics for his death. A week before he took his own life, FBI agents investigating the death learned Foster had received a dressing down from Hillary Clinton in front of staff. It triggered his suicide, agents believed. Author Ronald Kessler wrote, 'During the White House meeting, Hillary continued to humiliate Foster mercilessly . . .'.

'Hillary put him down really, really bad in a pretty good-size meeting. She told him he would always be a little hick town lawyer who was obviously not ready for the big time,' former FBI agent Coy Copeland said. Former FBI supervisory agent Jim Clemente said Foster was 'profoundly depressed, but Hillary lambasting him was the final straw because she embarrassed him'. Hillary told Foster, 'You're not protecting us' and 'You have failed us,' Kessler wrote. 'After the meeting, Foster's behaviour changed dramatically, the FBI agents found. Those who knew Foster said his voice sounded strained, he became withdrawn and preoccupied, and his sense of humour vanished. At times, Foster teared up. He talked of feeling trapped.'

Kenneth Starr omitted the revelations about Hillary and Foster from his independent prosecutor's report (which led to President Clinton's impeachment) because he 'did not want to inflict further pain' on Hillary by revealing how her humiliation of Foster had pushed him over the edge.[11]

Foster's suicide would lead to allegations he was murdered by the Clintons. However, in his definitive account of the tragedy, *A Washington Tragedy: Bill & Hillary Clinton and the Suicide of Vincent Foster*, investigative journalist Dan Moldea successfully debunked the malicious accusations which were deliberately spread by right-wing groups.

Later, when Bill became president-elect, troopers continued to guard the couple and also smuggled women into the governor's mansion through the outer security cordon by telling Secret Service agents they were staff members or family members. Three times during the period after Clinton was elected and his inauguration Larry Patterson called one of Clinton's girlfriends, a judge's wife, to see if she was available for Clinton. On the day Clinton left the governor's mansion to travel to Washington for his inauguration he asked Patterson to bring her to the airport for the send-off. When Hillary Clinton saw the woman she became enraged. She turned to Patterson and said, 'What the f*** do you think you're doing? I know who that whore is. I know what she's doing here. Get her out of here.'[12]

Edward Klein quoted Hillary instructing Ivan Duda, a private detective, in the 1980s, 'I want you to do damage control over Bill's philandering . . . Bill's going to be president of the United States . . . I want you to get rid of these bitches he's seeing . . . I want you to give me the names and addresses and phone numbers, and we can get them under control.'[13]

The stories provided by Patterson and Klein have been cited as proof that Hillary Clinton knew about her husband's affairs. However, it was an incident that occurred in the 1970s that provided the strongest indication that not only did Hillary know about her husband's affairs but 'enabled them'. It came from Juanita Broaddrick. She met Clinton during the 1978 gubernatorial election race at a fundraiser. She said Clinton raped her. It wasn't until years later that Broaddrick revealed her traumatic experience to her son after having lived with the memory for years. Shortly after the rape incident, at another campaign fundraiser, Hillary Clinton had offered her hand to Broaddrick and said, 'I just want you to know how much Bill and I appreciate what you do for him.' Shortly before Bill Clinton ran in the 1992 presidential primaries he approached Broaddrick and said, 'Juanita, I'm so sorry for what I did. I'm not the man I used to be. Can you forgive me?' She told him to go to hell.[14] The story was given added credibility when Broaddrick was interviewed for the documentary *The Clinton Affair*, broadcast in 2018.[15]

* * *

When Bill and Hillary Clinton entered the White House in January 1993 Hillary was considered to be the strongest personality of the two. They settled into what could be described as a co-presidency, with Hillary exercising an influence on her husband's presidential policies and personal decisions no previous First Lady ever had. According to White House aide George Stephanopoulos, Hillary '. . . established a wholly owned subsidiary within the White House, with its own staff, its own schedule and its own war room [which was] called the "Intensive Care Unit".'[16]

In her book *Living History*, Hillary Clinton wrote of her gratitude to the White House staff including her agents. However, one agent said she never voiced the appreciation to the agents. 'Hillary did not speak to us,' he said. 'We spent years with her. She never said thank you.' Former agents who were interviewed by Washington investigative journalist Ronald Kessler said they disliked Hillary from the time she became First Lady and thereafter. 'They consider it a form of punishment to be assigned to her detail,' he said, adding that the agents said she was rude and 'disconnected from the little people'.[17]

In Arkansas Hillary Clinton would send her bodyguards to run errands and carry her bags. When she arrived in Washington she discovered that such behaviour did not go down well with the Secret Service. Protocol dictated agents were required to keep their hands free in case their protectees were attacked. When some agents refused to carry her bags they were quickly reassigned to other duties.[18]

The Clintons soon became close to Senator Edward Kennedy during the Clinton presidency. The Senator gave her advice on how to deal with the Secret Service. He told Hillary he had made the mistake of allowing his Secret Service agents, in the years he was a leading presidential candidate, to provide such protection as to prevent him from making close contact with voters. He advised her not to make the same mistake.[19] Hillary took Kennedy's advice – and more.

In fact, Hillary Clinton wanted as little contact as possible with her protective detail. She was also so contemptuous of her agents she used profanity to intimidate them. Chelsea Clinton said her parents referred to the Secret Service as 'pigs'.[20] According to author Emmett Tyrell, 'many agents' asked to be removed from the Clintons' security detail.[21]

Hillary also liked to elude her agents if she could get away with it. On one occasion in Little Rock she drove away in her car without notifying them. She was gone for several hours and when the Secret Service finally contacted her she would not tell them where she was. She made light of her escapade saying, '. . . I enjoyed a marvellous sensation of personal freedom'.[22]

Hillary Clinton had an equal hatred and open disdain for anyone in uniform including police officers and the military. Publicly, Hillary courted law-enforcement organisations, but she did not want police near her. 'She did not want police officers in sight,' a former agent told Ronald Kessler. 'She did not want Secret Service protection near. She wanted state troopers and local police to wear suits and stay in unmarked cars. People don't know police are in the area unless officers wear uniforms. If they are unaware of a police presence, people are more likely to get out of control.'[23]

Hillary's temperament with regard to her treatment of the state troopers, and later Secret Service agents, was confirmed by others including security officers who protected her when she was President Obama's Secretary of State. She was protected by the Secret Service and State Department security staff. In an FBI interview a former State Department official said her 'treatment of DS [Department of State] agents on her protective detail was so contemptuous that many of them sought reassignment or employment elsewhere'. The State Department security officer added, 'Prior to Clinton's tenure, being an agent on the Secretary of State's protective detail was seen as an honour and privilege reserved for senior agents. However, by the end of [her] tenure, it was staffed largely with new agents because it was difficult to find senior agents willing to work for her.'[24]

Air Force Staff Sergeant and K9 handler Eric Bonner, who was involved in protection duties for the Clintons, said in July 2016, 'I got to do a few details involving "Distinguished Visitors". One of my last details was for Hillary when she was Secretary of State. I helped with [electronic] sweeps of her . . . quarters and staff vehicles.' According to Bonner, Clinton told him, '"Get that f****** dog away from me." Then she turns to her security detail and berates them up and down about why that animal was in her quarters.' Bonner added, 'Hillary doesn't care about anyone but Hillary.'[25]

Hillary's attitude was also corroborated by a United Airlines pilot who, while in the military, flew many Special Air Missions for the White House. He flew four presidential support missions in the C-141 out of Dover Air Force Base in Delaware. The pilot said Hillary Clinton was 'arrogant and orally abusive to her security detail' and 'forbade her daughter, Chelsea, from exchanging pleasantries with them'. He said Chelsea was not pleased with her mother's attitude and 'mean-spiritedness' and ignored her mother's instructions. The pilot saw Chelsea as a 'nice, kind-hearted, and lovely young lady'. He added that Hillary's agents all wanted to be on a different detail. The pilot also witnessed Hillary's behaviour towards her husband and saw agents 'cringe' when she lashed out at him.[26]

However, there were some members of the White House staff who did feel empathy and compassion towards the First Lady. Kate Andersen Brower said that at the height of the Monica Lewinsky scandal several staffers told her that they said they felt sorry for her because she craved privacy and couldn't get it. Brower said White House usher, Worthington White, told her he moved tourists out of the White House and kept her Secret Service agents at bay so that she could enjoy a few short hours of solitude by the pool.[27]

Another member of the White House staff, maid Betty Finney, told Brower she enjoyed helping Hillary Clinton. It 'meant the world' to her. Finney added that she liked the high level of security in the White House. It helped make the people who work there feel safe, she said. 'You know the snipers are up there to protect you. Why not feel at home?' Former Secret Service agent Evy Poumpouras said Hillary was 'one of the most prevailing women . . . I have ever seen. . . . in every situation she was like a mountain standing tall and strong in a blizzard . . .'.[28]

Although there is no real evidence that Hillary engaged in extramarital affairs when she was a presidential candidate, there is some evidence her bodyguards did. Journalist Amy Chozick reported how agents, along with Clinton staff members, often 'hooked up' during the 2008 campaign. The Secret Service's motto, she said, was 'Wheels Up, Rings Off' and 'Secret Service guys were ducking into reporter's hotel rooms'.[29]

* * *

Hillary, who was given the Secret Service codename 'Evergreen', the same codename the agency used when she was First Lady, ran for the presidency on two occasions – 2008 and 2016. Both times many voters found it difficult to understand exactly why she was running. Her responses to questions by the media echoed Senator Ted Kennedy's garbled answer to a television reporter when he was asked why he wanted to be president. However, she did have experience in government, she was a woman and she believed it was her turn.

Although she believed it was 'her time' in 2008, she didn't count on a charismatic African American politician taking the nomination away from her. After a number of wins in the 2008 Democrat presidential primaries she eventually lost to Barack Obama.

During the run-up to the 2016 presidential primaries Hillary Clinton became the presumptive 'next president of the US' and the prospective 'first woman President of the United States', according to many sources in the media. Throughout her 2016 primary election campaign for the Democratic Party presidential nomination she fought off challenges by her major opponents, Bernie Sanders and Elizabeth Warren, to emerge victorious at the convention which was held in Philadelphia in July 2016.

Even though voters were well aware she had a long history of being eco-
nomical with the truth and polls showed the American public distrusted her,
that did not stop her from winning the nomination. The first word people
associated with Clinton was 'liar' and the number of voters who were either
'undecided, sceptical or antagonistic to her were huge'.[30]

When Hillary announced her decision to run it was once again not
immensely clear to many of her aides, let alone the public, 'why her, why
now?' Additionally, her campaign was damaged by long memories of her husband's scandal-ridden presidency. Moreover, when Hillary was diagnosed
with pneumonia by her doctor during the campaign, it brought into question
her fitness for the presidency.

Before the second nationally televised debate with Donald Trump, her
Republican opponent, she was placed in an embarrassing position. She
berated Trump for 'rating' women's attractiveness. 'We have seen him insult
women. We've seen him rate women on their appearance, ranking them from
one to ten,' Hillary said.

Hillary's comments about Trump did nothing except remind her audience
of her husband's same habit of rating women. In court testimony Bill Clinton's
favourite state trooper bodyguard, L.D. Brown, said, '. . . as degrading as it
may sound, [it] is something that [Bill Clinton] and I both would do'. Brown
made the comments while he was being deposed in the Paula Jones sexual
harassment lawsuit against Bill Clinton, on 10 November 1997. '. . . pretty
much every pretty woman that we would see, eight, nine, ten, seven, six,
whatever,' Brown said.[31]

To counteract the claims Trump held a press conference with women who
had been dismissed and discredited by the Clintons and their allies over
the years. Sitting in the audience for the second debate were some of the
women who had been described by Clinton associates as 'bimbos', 'floozies'
and 'stalkers' when they spoke out about Bill Clinton's sexual harassment and
affairs. The line-up included Paula Jones, Juanita Broaddrick and Kathleen
Wiley. A fourth woman was present. She was Kathy Shelton who at the age
of 12 was raped by a man Hillary defended at a trial in Arkansas in 1975.[32]

During the general election campaign her lead over Donald Trump in the
opinion polls led many in the media to conclude she would win the election
as polls placed her well ahead of her opponent. Many states leaned her way
in the Midwest, and she was ahead in North Carolina and Florida, two states
that were vital to victory in the Electoral College. Yet within two months

everything was lost. An already close race saw one important deciding factor in the race. It came in October when the FBI launched an investigation into the Clinton staff's use of a private server for their emails. Clinton fell 3–4 per cent in the polls instantly, and her campaign never had time to rebut the investigation or rebuild her momentum so close to Election Day. Some commentators said the FBI lost her the race.

However, there may have been another important decisive factor which lost her the election and it came in the form of a book written by a member of the Secret Service. In his 2016 book former White House uniformed Secret Service agent Gary Byrne said that Hillary Clinton was arrogant and orally abusive to her security details throughout her time as First Lady and later as a US Senator.

Byrne said during her time as First Lady she had a 'Jekyll and Hyde' personality that left White House staffers scared stiff of her explosive temper. He described her temperament as 'erratic, uncontrollable and occasionally violent', that she acted friendly one moment, then raged the next. 'What I saw in the 1990s sickened me,' he said.

Often the Secret Service agents would be embarrassed to hear the verbal attacks Hillary inflicted on her husband, Byrne said. Even behind closed doors Hillary Clinton would scream and holler so loudly that everyone could hear what she was saying. Agents spoke of how they felt sorry for President Clinton and most wondered why he tolerated it instead of just divorcing his 'attack dog' wife. It was clear to the agents, Byrne said, the Clintons did not like or respect each other even before the Monica Lewinsky scandal. It was a 'marriage of convenience', Byrne said, confirming what others had previously written about the couple and their pursuit of power.

The many other revelations about the Clintons and Hillary in particular included:

- Byrne said agents had discussions about the possibility that they would have to protect Bill from his wife's physical attacks.
- A paranoid Hillary Clinton tried to have the Secret Service banned from the White House and once tried to ditch her security detail.
- Byrne arrived for work one day in 1995 following a loud fight between the Clintons the night before. The dust-up, he said, left a light blue vase 'smashed to bits' and Bill sporting a 'real, live, put-a-steak-on-it black eye'.

- Hillary threw a Bible at a Secret Service agent hitting him in the back of the head.
- An assignment to protect Hillary Clinton 'was a form of punishment handed down by passive-aggressive middle management'.
- Byrne describes the former first lady as being prone to all-consuming bouts of rage behind closed doors.
- Hillary repeatedly swore at Secret Service agents: 'She'd explode in my face without reservation or decorum.' She is reported to have told a Secret Service agent to 'Go to hell.' In another instance, a uniformed officer said Mrs Clinton had told him to 'Go f*** yourself' when he bid her good morning.

Critics of Byrne's book, *Crisis of Character*, noted that as a uniformed Secret Service officer, the lowest level of security at the White House, Byrne would not have had the close access to the Clintons that protective agents do. 'Operationally, one who has the working knowledge of how things are done there would realise that certain of those statements do not coincide with the operational plan,' Jan Gilhooly, the group's president and a former Secret Service agent said.[33]

The board of directors of the Association of Former Agents of the US Secret Service took exception to Byrne's revelations. The public condemnation of the book was an extraordinary move by the group, which has largely remained out of the political fray since its founding in the 1970s. The organisation issued a statement which read in part, 'There is no place for any self-moralising narratives, particularly those with an underlying motive.'[34]

However, the well-documented evidence supporting Byrne is difficult to ignore. In fact, Hillary Clinton's history of unhinged abuse against those who worked for her spanned decades and was reported by many authors and journalists as well as Secret Service agents.

Former Secret Service agent Dan Emmett, who served under Clinton, said Hillary treated officers like 'hired help'. FBI agent Gary Aldrich reported that Hillary told an agent, 'Stay the f*** back, stay the f*** away from me!' She screamed at her Secret Service agents, 'Don't come within ten yards of me, or else! Just f***ing do as I say, okay!!?'[35] Edward Klein also reported Hillary shouting at her agents and using expletives.[36]

Gary Aldrich, FBI liaison officer inside Clinton's White House, said Hillary called her agents 'personal, trained pigs'. He said:

Hillary had a clear dislike for the [US Secret Service] agents, bordering on hatred . . . Two Secret Service agents heard Hillary's daughter Chelsea refer to them as 'personal, trained pigs' . . . The agent on the detail tried to scold Chelsea for such disrespect. He told her . . . he believed that her father, the president, would be shocked if he heard what she had just said to her friends. Chelsea's response? 'I don't think so. That's what my parents call you.'[37]

Sally Bedell Smith also explored the Clintons' marriage and Bill's multiple affairs in her book *The Clintons at the White House*:

Their marriage has been dogged by Bill's tomcat tendencies since before they exchanged vows in 1975. In Arkansas, where he was governor, his extramarital activities nearly broke the marriage twice . . . Hamilton Jordan, then a prominent Democratic Party worker, recalled that when Bill lost his first re-election for governor in 1980 he sought consolation by 'recklessly chasing women' . . .[38]

Author Christopher Andersen, in his book *American Evita*, published in 2005, supports many of the stories Byrne provided in 2016. The Secret Service detail assigned to protect the president-elect was shocked by the Clintons' behaviour, Andersen said. When an agent explained to Hillary that the agents could not perform the tasks state troopers did, such as carry baggage, caddy or go on shopping errands, she told him, 'If you want to remain on this detail get your f****** ass over here and grab those bags.' Agent William Bell said Hillary threw a briefing book at her husband when the couple were arguing in their limousine. She missed and the book hit the agent who was driving the car on the back the head.[39]

The Secret Service was also dismayed at the way the Clintons hired staff. The president and his wife overruled the agency by hiring personnel who had been rejected by the Secret Service as unsuitable because of their 'criminal records'. Twenty-one staffers who were asked to take a drug test failed.[40]

Contradicting critics who alleged Byrne held no position that would place him in proximity to the president, Byrne responded by saying he was assigned to guard the Oval Office for three years during the Clinton presidency and would never have been subpoenaed to testify before a grand jury during the Monica Lewinsky scandal if the critics were correct.

Byrne's book was also given credibility by author Ronald Kessler whose books about the Secret Service featured many unflattering stories given to him by former agents. They corroborated earlier allegations of mistreatment of Secret Service personnel by Hillary. Kessler said:

> My Secret Service sources tell me that Gary Byrne was a respected Secret Service uniformed officer who can be trusted to tell an honest story. Byrne's accounts tracks completely with the material in my book . . . the agents portray Bill as being like an abused child, treated by Hillary as nastily as she treats her Secret Service agents.[41]

In 2016, following criticisms by the media, Byrne refused to retract any of his allegations and repeated his reasons for writing about them in his book:

> Hillary Clinton is now poised to become the Democratic nominee for president of the United States but she simply lacks the integrity and temperament to serve in the office. . . . From the bottom of my soul I know this to be true. And with Hillary's latest rise, I realize that her own leadership style – volcanic, impulsive, enabled by sycophants, and disdainful of the rules set for everyone else – hasn't changed a bit.[42]

* * *

Hillary Clinton had a long period of protection as First Lady and a US Senator. In 2009 she was appointed Secretary of State by President Obama and due to her status in that position her Secret Service detail was increased. When she left office in 2013 her detail was reduced to normal levels. When she became a 2016 presidential candidate the detail was once again increased.

During Hillary's 2016 presidential campaign the Secret Service became embroiled in a controversy when the agent in charge of the Denver Field Office, Kerry O'Grady, announced she was part of the 'resistance'. It meant she was a supporter of Hillary Clinton. O'Grady also said she would 'not take a bullet' for Donald Trump. It was a clear violation of Secret Service rules that stipulated agents should be non-partisan.[43]

The Secret Service were also accused of doing little to investigate more than a half-dozen social media threats against her life after Donald Trump announced in a speech the idea that 'Second Amendment people' could act against her. Trump's comment sparked a storm of controversy. Addressing a crowd in Wilmington, North Carolina, in August 2016 he said that if Clinton won the election she would get to 'pick her judges. . . . Nothing you can do, folks. Although the Second Amendment people – maybe there is, I don't know,' Trump said.

The agency did not appear to take any of the social media comments posted on Twitter, Facebook and YouTube seriously, according to media critics. The agency responded by announcing that agents did not locate or speak with any of the individuals who made the threats because their social media profiles did not reveal personally identifiable information. However, no attempt was made by the Secret Service to contact Twitter, Facebook or YouTube for help in identifying the people who made the threats. The Secret Service closed all the cases within a few days of opening them.[44]

However, the agency did track down and speak with one person who made a threatening statement about Clinton. The alleged 'threat' was made by Al Baldasaro, a New Hampshire State Representative who served as an informal adviser to Trump on veterans' issues. During an appearance on a conservative radio show, Baldasaro said, 'Clinton should be put in the firing line and shot for treason.'[45]

Hillary was also the target of animal rights protestors during her campaign. In August 2016 Secret Service agents rushed to protect Hillary at a Las Vegas rally after protesters approached her as she delivered a speech on stage. It was the first time agents from Clinton's detail rushed the stage to protect her. The protesters held signs and chanted to protest the treatment of animals, prompting four agents to encircle Clinton, who never appeared to be in danger.[46]

And it was Hillary's agents who saved her when she collapsed on a pavement during the 2016 campaign. Hillary had left a September 11 remembrance event in New York and as she walked to her van she stumbled avoiding injury when agents caught her and placed her in the vehicle. The incident called her health into question and became an important issue in the campaign. To offset stories about her health she staged a photo-op outside her daughter Chelsea's New York apartment in which she ordered her agents to stand far away from her. She also refused to wear her bulletproof vest for sartorial reasons.[47]

Hillary also insisted on using a non-bulletproof vehicle that was unsuitable in many ways for adequate protection. Double doors opened in different directions, it did not have an armoured engine and was not fast enough to evade attackers.

During her election campaigns for senator in 2000 and for president in 2008 and 2016 Hillary Clinton was the target of many plots and assassination threats including:

- In December 2000, shortly after Clinton was elected as a Senator for New York, a 30-year-old Canadian man, Colin McMahon, was arrested and charged with threatening to kill her. Clinton and her daughter, Chelsea, were targeted as well as Canada's prime minister, Jean Chretien. 'His intentions in our opinion were clear,' Sergeant Steve Saunders of the Royal Canadian Mounted Police said. 'The threat was to assault the prime minister and the threat was to kill Hillary Clinton and to kill Chelsea Clinton.'[48]
- In 2007 a 19-year-old Baton Rouge LSU student, Richard Ryan Wargo, was arrested by the Secret Service for threatening to assassinate Hillary Clinton. On campus Wargo started making threats against Clinton. He said he was interested in committing an act of terrorism that would be 'a national event'. Wargo planned to carry out his act of terrorism whenever Mrs Clinton visited Baton Rouge during a primary.[49]
- In 2016 Trump supporter Dan Bowman thought Hillary Clinton should be assassinated. 'If she's in office, I hope we can start a coup. She should be in prison or shot,' he said of a possible Clinton presidency. 'We're going to have a revolution and take them out of office if that's what it takes. There's going to be a lot of bloodshed. But that's what it's going to take.' Activist Deray Mckesson threatened violence if Clinton was elected. He said, 'Hillary needs to be taken out. If she gets into power, I'll do everything in my power to take her out of power, which if I have to be a patriot, I will.' When asked whether he was making a physical threat against Clinton, the Trump supporter responded, 'I don't know, is it?'[50]
- A man from Green Bay, Wisconsin, said he worried there would be another Revolutionary War if Clinton takes office. 'People are going to march on the capitols. They're going to do whatever needs to be done to get her out of office, because she does not belong there,' 25-year-old Jared Halbrook said, warning that if 'push comes to shove', Clinton '. . . has to go by any means necessary, it will be done'.[51]

Threats continued after Hillary lost the 2016 presidential election:

- In October 2018 Cesar Sayoc sent a pipe bomb intended for Hillary Clinton. This was one of a few sent to both the Clintons and Barack Obama in the same week.[52]
- In 2019 69-year-old Larry Hopkins, a right-wing militia leader who arrested illegal immigrants trying to cross the border from Mexico, became an informant for the FBI. He told the agency his group was planning to assassinate former President Obama, Hillary Clinton and Democrat donor George Soros. Hopkins was head of the United Constitutional Patriots. Hopkins was arrested and charged with possession of a firearm as a felon. He had three felony convictions in Michigan and Oregon, including for impersonating a police officer, and nine guns were seized from his home in 2017. The heavily armed Militia members stopped migrants near the border in New Mexico. The United Constitutional Patriots claimed they were assisting law enforcement in enforcing US immigration laws. They claimed they had captured thousands of migrants who had illegally entered the country.[53]
- In April 2020, 37-year-old Jessica Prim, who lived in Illinois, was arrested outside Pier 86 in Manhattan by USS *Intrepid* security. The Secret Service was there because the agency had put out an alert on Prim after she allegedly posted threatening messages about Joe Biden and Hillary Clinton on Facebook earlier that day. Among her posts in recent days were several pro-Trump messages and QAnon conspiracy theories about Democrats: 'Hillary Clinton and her assistant, Joe Biden and Tony Podesta need to be taken out in the name of Babylon! I can't be set free without them gone. Wake me up!!!!!' Secret Service agents reported observing her to be 'in possession of several cutting instruments, blunt objects and alleged marijuana'. She was found to be carrying eighteen knives and other weapons in her vehicle after she threatened Joe Biden, Hillary Clinton and other Democrats online.[54]

Chapter 17

Obama's Challengers

'[2008 Republican presidential candidate] John McCain may believe that he's not as polarizing a figure as Hillary or Obama, but that's not the point. . . . The primary motivator of would-be assassins is not the dislike of the candidate. It's wanting to go out in a big way and make a name for yourself.'

> Former Secret Service agent Andrew O'Connell

'[Before Secret Service protection was provided] threats [occurred] almost daily, and our security company said it was getting to the point where they could not guarantee safety.'

> Aide to 2012 Republican presidential candidate Mitt Romney

When Senator Barack Obama announced his intentions to run for president there was an outpouring of anger from far-right extremists who did not wish to see him become the first African American president.

As a response to the mounting threats, Obama was approved for Secret Service protection by the secretary of Homeland Security on 2 May 2007; marking the first time in history a presidential candidate received protection almost two years prior to the presidential election. At the same time, his presumptive opponent, Senator John McCain, did not receive protection until almost a year later.

During his campaign there were numerous threats made against Obama's life. Most threateners were racists and extremists angered at how an African American might become president or they were mentally imbalanced individuals who developed a strange fascination with guns and weaponry becoming fixated on killing. This type of Obama threatener included Collin McKenzie-Gude, Jerry Michael Blanchard and Raymond H. Geisel who were arrested, charged and found guilty of threatening a presidential candidate. White supremacists Daniel Cowart, Paul Schlesselman, Shawn

Robert Adolf, Tharin Robert Gartrell and Nathan Dwaine Johnson were not charged as it was believed there was no probable cause to support any charges of attempting to assassinate a presidential candidate.

Collin McKenzie-Gude, aged 20, wanted to kill Barack Obama during the 2008 presidential campaign by planting roadside bombs. Jerry Blanchard was indicted for threatening to kill Senator Obama during a 15 July 2008 breakfast at a Charlotte Waffle House. Two customers witnessed Blanchard saying, 'Obama and his wife are never going to make it to the White House. He needs to be taken out and I can do it in a heartbeat.' Raymond H. Geisel, threatened to use a military sniper rifle to assassinate the president and also threatened to put a bullet in the head of then President George Bush.[1]

Every threat was fully investigated by the Secret Service; arrests were made and court trials followed. The threats continued throughout Obama's presidency, although they subsided to 'normal' levels after his inauguration.[2]

Agents said that were treated with respect by both Barack Obama, and his wife Michelle. Obama's agents had twice been invited to dinner, both times at his home. The relationship between the Obamas and their Secret Service details was so cordial Michelle insisted that agents call her by her first name. Obama said he had a 'pretty terrific crew' of agents assigned to guard him. He was also grateful for 'all the sacrifices they make on my behalf and on my family's behalf'.[3]

In his early days in the White House, Obama looked to the Bush administration veteran agents for guidance. Obama once stopped in front of one of the formal White House rooms, hesitated, and then asked a Secret Service officer nearby if he was allowed to enter. 'Yes, sir,' said the officer. 'You can go wherever you want.'[4]

Obama would also sometimes confide in the men and woman who protected him. On one occasion he turned to Secret Service agent Evy Poumpouras after a conversation with a Congressman who was a guest at a White House function. Obama was respectful and amiable with the politician but after he left the president appeared to be 'disheartened' and said, 'That's the same man who has been publicly berating me since my first day in office.' Poumpouras said that instead of avoiding the White House guest 'he extended nothing but magnanimity to his critic. Instead of settling the score, he settled his sentiments.'[5]

Although Obama was known for his 'tardiness', all that changed when he began to receive Secret Service protection. Agents were experts at timekeeping and Obama never remonstrated with his agents when they reminded him to keep on schedule.

However, Barack Obama was yet another president who bristled under the tight confines of Secret Service protection. On one occasion he told his agents he needed a haircut. They told him they would have to 'case the place' before he was allowed to enter the barbershop. 'Why can't I just go to my barber', he complained, 'I've been going to him for years!'[6]

For their part the Secret Service was frustrated by Obama's unpredictability, specifically his unscheduled forays away from the heavily guarded White House grounds. His impulsiveness was described as 'the bear gets loose'. Obama admitted that, '. . . every once in a while I'm able to sneak off . . . What I've said to my team is, "Get me out of Washington".' His press secretary said that what Obama missed the most was 'the ability to walk down the street and talk to people'.[7]

Obama did acknowledge his unorganised walks and trips to restaurants made his detail nervous. During a trip to Austin, Texas, he said, 'I got about probably a mile, mile and a half and then some people started spotting me so that by the time Secret Service got nervous, and then by the time we got back, there was a big rope line and there was all the fuss.'[8]

Former Secret Service agent Dan Emmett said Obama's 'off the record' walks posed a 'unique challenge' for the president's security team, 'There's a huge challenge in that you have virtually no time to put it together,' Emmett said. 'The biggest worry is wandering random crime in progress, or if you happen to run into the random crazy guy – the people walking down the street talking to themselves who could be armed somehow.'[9]

Emmett said the proliferation of smart phones and social media, which allow any individual to instantly broadcast the president's whereabouts, only heightened the risk of trips outside the bubble. 'Word gets around quickly – everybody has an iPhone,' he said.

However, former assistant director of the Secret Service Mickey Nelson said that the unscheduled trips had benefits, 'We use the element of surprise to our advantage,' Nelson said. 'If we don't know we're going there to the last minute, the adversary certainly doesn't know it.'[10]

There was one occasion when Obama mused to one of his agents about the dangers of unstable people who inhabited the crowds of supporters on his campaign stops. The idea of assassination stayed with Obama during his presidency. During one campaign speech for the 2014 mid-term elections a man in the crowd, standing less than 50ft away, interrupted him with loud cries. 'Antichrist!' the man yelled. 'You'll be destroyed!' As his agents moved towards the heckler, Obama realised that he had been heckled by the same man before and made a joke about it, 'He needs to update his material,' Obama said. In fact, the president took the threat seriously. 'That man would kill me,' he told his agents.[11]

The Obama presidency coincided with a number of well-publicised scandals surrounding the Secret Service. Some of the scandals affected the trust Obama and his family had in the agency.

The report found 143 instances in which intruders entered secure spaces from 2005 to 2015 including White House 'fence-jumpers' and unauthorised people getting close to the president. The report concluded that the Secret Service was 'an agency in crisis'.[12]

The report examined a 2011 White House shooting episode, the misconduct of agents in Colombia where they cavorted with prostitutes and an incident involving Secret Service supervisors driving into a crime scene after attending a drinks party. The report also claimed that over the course of a single month security lapses led to one incident when an uninvited guest at the White House went backstage to speak to the president.[13]

Some media commentators argued that scandals proliferated during the Obama years because the agency declined in competence after September 11 when new agents were hired and not given enough training. Up until 2003 the Secret Service existed under the control of the Department of the Treasury and agents operated efficiently. When the agency was then relocated to the Department of Homeland Security an unintended consequence of September 11 resulted in the hiring of hundreds of new agents in a very short amount of time, which ultimately sacrificed its rigorous standards.

Obama received numerous threats during his presidency. 'What we're looking for are changes in behavioural patterns,' former Secret Service agent Jonathan Wackrow said. 'Everybody who makes a threat against the president doesn't get arrested, but we keep track of them and many times that's what keeps them from transcending into physical action.'[14] The threats included:

- In April 2009, during the United Nations Alliance of Civilizations summit in Istanbul, Turkey, a man of Syrian origins was discovered carrying forged Al Jazeera TV press credentials. He confessed his plan to murder Obama with a knife and claimed there were three alleged accomplices.[15]

- In November 2011 Oscar Ramiro Ortega-Hernandez open fired on the White House with several rounds from a semi-automatic rifle. A window was broken, but no injuries resulted.[16]

- In April 2013 a letter laced with ricin was sent to Obama.[17]

- In February 2015 three men from New York City were arrested and charged in a terrorist plot that included joining ISIS, killing President Obama, hijacking an aeroplane and bombing Coney Island. One of the three men, Abdulrasul Hasanovich Juraboev, an Uzbekistan national, wanted to become a martyr by killing the president. Both men were arrested and charged. Another accused, Kazakh national Akhror Saidakhmetov, plotted to travel to Turkey with an informant and proposed finding an excuse to gain access to the pilot's cabin and diverting the plane to the Islamic State, so that the Islamic State would gain a plane. He was arrested at JFK airport while attempting to board a 12.30 am flight to Ukraine en route to Turkey, where he allegedly planned to sneak across the border into Syria and join ISIL.[18]

- In July 2015 a 55-year-old Tomah, Wisconsin, man, Brian D. Dutcher, told a security guard at a La Crosse library, 'The usurper is here and if I get a chance I'll take him out and I'll take the shot,' referring to Obama, who was in Wisconsin to give a speech. Dutcher confirmed in an interview with the Secret Service that he made the remarks to the security guard. Dutcher posted on Facebook on 30 June, 'That's it! Thursday I will be in La Crosse. Hopefully I will get a clear shot at the pretend president. Killing him is our CONSTITUTIONAL DUTY!' Dutcher also told a La Crosse detective that his threat was serious and that 'he would not have said what he said if he didn't intend to carry it out'.[19]

- In 2016, the US Secret Service accused 36-year-old Jonathan Smead of phoning a death threat to the president and referencing past assassins, including Lee Harvey Oswald and John Wilkes Booth. Smead also threatened to kill Hillary Clinton. A judge sentenced Smead to five years of probation, requiring no federal prison sentence.[20]

* * *

As Barack Obama campaigned through the Democrat primaries in 2008 the Republican candidates were competing for the Republican Party nomination. Initially, in 2007, John McCain was struggling among Republican Party contenders, so he decided to skip Iowa and concentrate on New Hampshire (the same primary where he had unexpectedly triumphed in 2000, eventually losing out to George W. Bush). McCain's win rejuvenated his presidential campaign and he eventually became the 2008 Republican Party presidential nominee.

McCain was reluctant to campaign accompanied by Secret Service agents because, he said, it would inhibit his contact with voters. Historically speaking, McCain was not alone in shunning security. Billionaire Ross Perot declined Secret Service protection during his third-party 1992 presidential bid. Others have applied for protection but been turned down.

McCain had private bodyguards who accompanied him to events. When he travelled on charter planes, reporters and staffers were screened and checked for weapons by private security each time they boarded the plane. Additionally, a police bomb-sniffer dog would sweep through the press bus before reporters were allowed to board McCain's JetBlue charter plane. However, the security paled in comparison with the protection at Hillary Clinton's and Barack Obama's 2008 campaign events, where Secret Service agents were always very visible, staying close to the Democrat candidates at rope lines with voters.

Before he received Secret Service protection McCain told reporters, 'It's my intention, if we win this nomination, to reject Secret Service. . . . Why do I need it?' At the time, McCain even dismissed the need for official protection should he become president. 'The day that the Secret Service can assure me that if we're driving in the motorcade and there's a guy on a rooftop with a rifle, that they can stop that guy, then I'll say fine,' he said. 'But the day they tell me, "Well, we can't guarantee it," then fine, I'll take my chances.'[21]

While McCain seemed to enjoy the relative freedom of delving into unscreened crowds and riding Amtrak trains unencumbered by an entourage during the spring of 2008, there were some who worried he was a sitting target for an assassin. Journalists accompanying McCain's campaign declined to report his actions publicly out of a concern that disclosure might inspire would-be assailants. His reluctance to receive protection inspired criticism from former agents who said he was putting others at risk and from the *Arkansas Democrat Gazette*, which published a 7 April editorial warning that the decision to go without Secret Service protection was 'John McCain's big mistake', one that threatened the 'stability of the political system'.

Former Secret Service agent Andrew O'Connell, who helped protect Presidents George H.W. Bush and Bill Clinton, said McCain is taking an unnecessary risk. 'I don't think it's a wise move,' said O'Connell. 'John McCain may believe that he's not as polarizing a figure as Hillary or Obama, but that's not the point. . . . The primary motivator of would-be assassins is not the dislike of the candidate. It's wanting to go out in a big way and make a name for yourself.'[22]

Frank O'Donnell, who supervised the Secret Service's Los Angeles Field Office, said he watched television and became alarmed as he saw McCain speaking at huge rallies. O'Donnell said he was 'just holding my breath, hoping there wasn't another Arthur Bremer out there'.[23]

The dangers made McCain's wife Cindy uneasy. 'I'm looking at the faces and sometimes I'm spotting troublesome spots,' she said. McCain was criticised by former agents for his reluctance to accept Secret Service protection. Barbara Riggs, who protected President Reagan, said, 'One of the reasons that Congress decided that candidates should receive protection is so that our democratic process isn't altered by the hand of one individual, in the case of an assassination. When an individual chooses not to take it, it's just an individual choice. Certainly, having Secret Service protection impacts people's lives.'[24]

After months of resisting Secret Service protection, McCain finally relented. On 27 April 2008 he was assigned a detail and given the code-name 'Phoenix'. McCain was typically assigned agents who set aside their field-office jobs investigating counterfeiting and fraud, the Service's other charge, for three-week shifts on protective detail. At public events and in motorcades, additional plain-clothes agents from the nearest field office and uniformed local police beef up security and help the candidate's entourage move smoothly through the streets.

Mark Hughes and Billy Callahan were in charge of McCain's details – each crew alternated weeks with the candidate. Hughes was accustomed to McCain's chafing at the restrictions on the candidate's movements and schedules but it came as a surprise to other agents.[25]

Unlike Obama, Secret Service agents said McCain was 'irritable, impatient, and displayed his famous temper over trivial annoyances'. Agents said McCain was 'really hard to work with. He's always complaining, just making comments. We knew from the start that he wasn't a big fan of ours. We get in his way. We impede his ability to meet the people.' On the other hand, Cindy McCain, who was given the codename 'Parasol', 'was a pleasure to work with and has a good sense of humour,' agents said.[26]

Throughout his campaign McCain appeared to be the victim of few threats. However, he received a number death threats before he declared his candidacy from people who disliked his liberal approach to illegal immigration. 'I have never seen an issue that has inflamed the passions of the American people the way the issue of immigration reform has ever', McCain said at the time, 'including Iraq. I have never heard such rhetoric. We have never received death threats before . . . like I received.'[27]

The threats McCain received during his 2008 campaign included one by a jail inmate, Marc Harold Ramsey. On 23 August 2008 he was arrested after sending a threatening letter laced with white powder that triggered a security scare at the Colorado campaign office of John McCain. Ramsay was pinpointed within hours because the envelope's return address included his name, his inmate number and the location of the jail where he was incarcerated. The letter, addressed to McCain and opened by a campaign staffer, arrived in the post at the Senator's suburban Denver campaign office. It led to the office's evacuation. Several campaign workers went to the hospital as a precaution, and more than a dozen others underwent decontamination procedures at the scene, but no one was injured.[28]

McCain's vice-presidential running mate, Sarah Palin, also received death threats after she was nominated and in the weeks and months following the threats escalated. 'She doesn't belong to the NRA [National Rifle Association] to support the right of each citizen to have weapons in an aim of self-defence, but just to support the right of every Southern white citizen to shoot all non-white people legally!', one sender identified as Dominique Villacrouz wrote, adding, 'Sarah Palin MUST BE KILLED'. In another message dated 12 September 2008, a resident in Antwerp, Belgium, also called for Palin to be shot, saying that 'only on that moment justice will be accomplished'.[29]

In November 2008, McCain's Secret Service agents offered to accompany him back to his ranch in Sedona, but McCain insisted on saying his farewell as soon as he conceded the election to Barack Obama. The next morning, he was seen driving his own car to shop for groceries.

The Arizona Senator continued to receive threats long after he ran for president. Brandon Ziobrowski, of Cambridge, Massachusetts, was arrested by the FBI's Joint Terrorism Task Force in New York City after threatening Immigration and Customs Enforcement agents on social media. Ziobrowski tweeted he was willing to 'give $500 to anyone who kills an ICE agent'.[30]

When John McCain died in 2018 the Secret Service paid tribute to him using his old codename from when he was the 2008 presidential nominee. 'It was an honour to protect [Senator John McCain] during his candidacy for President. Phoenix – May you Rest In Peace,' the agency said from its official Twitter account.

* * *

According to one of his aides, former Massachusetts Governor Mitt Romney was not eager to have Secret Service protection as it 'created a distance between a candidate and the voters that we were not eager to have'. However, the campaign staff relented as there were 'threats almost daily, and our security company said it was getting to the point where they could not guarantee safety'.[31]

Accordingly, Romney's staff welcomed the offer of official Secret Service protection in January 2012, as polling gave him 'front-runner' status. The Secret Service gave him the codename 'Javelin'. It was the day after he won the 2012 Republican Party Florida primary by a fourteen-point margin over Republican presidential candidate Newt Gingrich. Previously, Romney's campaign had paid a company, US Safety and Security headed by a former agent Joseph Funk, to provide security at his events. But as the 2012 Romney campaign attracted increasing crowds it became progressively more difficult for his team to ensure his safety.[32]

Romney's detail consisted of fifteen agents. Agents who spoke to journalist Ronald Kessler said that Romney and his wife Ann 'treated them like family', often inviting them to lunch and dinner. Because of strict protection protocols the agents 'usually declined' the invitations.[33]

Romney described his experiences as a presidential candidate as 'a heady thing'. He said:

[The Secret Service was] only the icing on the adulation cake. Day after day, thousands of people were shouting my name, investing in me their hopes for victory. The day before the election, Kid Rock electrified a packed arena in New Hampshire for me, and when we were introduced, the crowd cheered for Ann and me for three solid minutes before we could speak.

During a visit to Denver for his first presidential debate of 2012 with his opponent President Obama, Romney's motorcade was led by 'thirty or so police motorcycles and vehicles flashing their red and blue lights' en route to the debate venue. He was accompanied by 'not only the detail of agents that surrounded Ann and me in our bulletproof SUV but also the tactical unit that followed, armed with machine guns and sitting with an open tailgate, facing any vehicle that might come from behind us'. He was amazed that 'the miles of interstate expressway from my hotel to the auditorium were closed to all traffic – for me'.

Romney also expressed some concern during his campaign when he was informed by 'one of our national security agencies' that all his emails were being closely read by a 'foreign government'. In fact, the same was true for all the people who had emailed him, he said, including his family, staff and friends. 'Their emails were also being monitored by that government.'[34]

There were some mistakes made by Romney's detail that led to negative publicity both for his campaign and the Secret Service. One agent on the detail left a gun unattended in the bathroom of a plane carrying the candidate to Indiana. The chartered aircraft was carrying Romney, campaign staff and journalists from Tampa, where the Republican National Convention was being staged, and Indianapolis, where Romney addressed the American Legion. After a reporter found the gun in the lavatory, a Secret Service agent quickly retrieved the weapon. The gun appeared to have been left behind accidentally while the agent was using the restroom, and Romney did not appear to be in any danger. When the agent was reassigned Romney felt 'distressed', believing the dangers were 'minimal'. The candidate put in a request that she not be removed from the detail to the Director, Mark Sullivan. Not wishing to set a precedent which might undermine the agency's management, the Director declined Romney's request.[35]

During campaign rallies Romney's staff wanted the Secret Service to use rope to provide a barrier between the supporters and Romney. The agents wanted to install bike racks which would have made it much more difficult for Romney to greet the crowd and shake hands. A compromise was agreed – if a crowd consisted of 100 or more people bike racks would be used.

A Secret Service agent assigned to Romney's detail during the 2012 presidential campaign revealed details of President Obama's campaign schedule to Romney aides while drinking with members of the Romney campaign team, 'unprompted and in an apparent attempt to impress an aide toward whom the agent had made advances'. The agent reportedly also provided joyrides in his Secret Service vehicle with the lights flashing.[36] Other problems with Romney's campaign included the fact that not enough magnetometers were provided for the candidate's Secret Service detail for use during Romney's campaign appearances.

During the 2012 presidential campaign a reporter alleged that the Secret Service foiled a number of assassination attempts on Barack Obama and Mitt Romney. However, when challenged about the evidence supporting his claims, he said his story was not about death threats. The story, which was written by Marc Ambinder, was about Mitt Romney saying farewell to his Secret Service detail in which he mentioned 'assassination plots'. Ambinder did not elaborate beyond saying the 'several' plots were thwarted.

However, Secret Service spokesman Edwin Donovan said the agency did not participate in the story and wasn't sure where Ambinder was getting his information. 'We didn't work with Marc Ambinder on that article, so I don't know what his sourcing is,' Donovan said. Ambinder responded by tweeting, 'Press folks, please stop bothering the Secret Service. If there are/were other plots, they sure as hell didn't tell me about them.'[37]

However, it is also true that by the time Romney received official protection there was at least one threat per day either by phone or by mail. None of the threats appeared to rise to the level of serious 'plots' and most of them turned out to be little more than 'venting'. But others were taken seriously and a number of people were arrested for issuing threats including hundreds of online death threats. A typical threat online read, 'Give me a rifle I'll assassinate both Romney and Obama'.[38]

No sooner had Romney begun his campaign the dangers of running for president were made explicit when a spectator at a campaign rally in Eagan, Minnesota, threw a cup of glitter at Romney. The cup could easily have been filled with acid. And within a short time the incident was repeated in Denver. The 'attackers' were arrested and charged with disturbing the peace.

Fox News host Sean Hannity commented on the threats during one of his broadcasts. 'There has been a dramatic increase in the number of death threats to Governor Romney,' Hannity said. 'This seems to have begun after the first [presidential] debate.' Responding to Hannity's remarks, former Secret Service agent Dan Bongino said, 'What people don't realize is that it takes away valuable resources because the Secret Service doesn't have the luxury not to investigate each death threat.' Bongino continued, 'You see all these threats, all the threats on twitter, and each one needs to be investigated and these aren't simple investigations, they're very time consuming.'[39]

The many threats against his life that Romney received included:

- William Thomas Driscoll, aged 66, was arrested in New Orleans for making threats against Romney and former president George W. Bush. Driscoll 'self-committed' himself to Seaside Behavioural Center on 28 February 2012. The next day a psychiatrist there alerted the Secret Service that Driscoll allegedly had said he wanted to kill Bush and Romney. Agents went to the hospital and interviewed Driscoll on 1 March and he allegedly told them he planned to take the lives of Bush and Romney once he got out of the hospital and could travel to Alabama to obtain a gun. Driscoll has been on the Secret Service's radar going back to 1982 when he 'made statements that he heard voices which told him to kill then President Ronald Reagan'. Between 1982 and 1993 Driscoll made multiple threats against President Reagan, President George H.W. Bush and President Bill Clinton. The Secret Service arrested him in 1984 and 1985.[40]
- In February 2006 Daniel Tavares threatened to kill Mitt Romney and other Massachusetts public officials when he was released from prison. Romney said the convicted killer should never have been released from prison.[41]
- Julia Rodriguez, a Democrat delegate from New York, was investigated by the Secret Service after she told a reporter at the Democratic National Convention that she would like to 'kill' GOP presidential candidate Mitt Romney. In a video, Rodriguez explained that she was born in Puerto Rico, but currently lived in the Bronx. Responding to a question from a

reporter, Rodriguez went on to say that she believed 'Romney will destroy this country' and that she 'would like to kill him' if she saw him.[42]

• A convicted sex offender was arrested and charged with making death threats against President Barack Obama and Republican presidential candidate Mitt Romney. Brandon Britton, 51, of Akron, was arrested by Secret Service agents. Britton was recorded as saying that he was '. . . anti-government and going to kill President Obama and Governor Romney'.[43]

Romney lamented after losing the election to Obama, 'The cheers were gone as well, replaced by the agonizing reappraisal by others of what had gone wrong. I was back to driving my own car, filling my own gas tank, and buying groceries at Costco, just like I had been doing for several decades before.' Romney said that what he and his wife remembered about the campaign was not the pomp and popularity but the friends they made. 'We became very close with a number of the Secret Service agents,' Romney said. '. . . In fact, as we prepared to go onto the stage to concede the victory to President Barack Obama, more than one of those agents fought back tears. We miss them as friends – not as power candy.'[44]

Chapter 18

Protecting Trump and Biden

'I want to thank the Secret Service; these guys are fantastic.'

Donald Trump

Most US presidents served in elected office before being elected president. Many served as governors or US Senators first and a few were members of the US House of Representatives before being elected president. Some presidents who lacked political experience had strong military backgrounds; they include Presidents Dwight Eisenhower and Zachary Taylor. However, only two presidents, Donald Trump and Herbert Hoover, had neither political nor military experience.

In his first months in office Trump faced an exodus of his advisers and failed to get through most of his major reforms – repealing Obamacare, tax cuts and appropriations for the US/Mexico wall – having been blocked repeatedly by a recalcitrant Congress. However, during his presidency he had many successes including the installation of 3 Supreme Court justices and 220 judges overall to the federal bench, the institution of a 'Space Force', tax reform and reform of the criminal justice system, all for lifetime appointments. Amy Coney Barrett became Trump's third Supreme Court justice shortly before the 2020 election day.

Trump's withdrawal from the Iranian Nuclear Deal had mixed responses from national and international politicians. But he also had some foreign policy successes. He moved the US Embassy in Israel from Tel Aviv to Jerusalem, launched a missile strike on Syria, withdrew from the Trans-Pacific Partnership trade agreement, increased pressure on North Korea to end its nuclear missile programme and brokered a peace agreement between Israel and Morocco and Israel and the United Arab Emirates. He also defeated the terrorist group ISIS and killed its leader, Abu Bakr al-Baghdadi.

However, during his one term in office Trump was surrounded by scandal including allegations he had cheated on his taxes and colluded with Russia during the 2016 election. Other scandals he survived included revelations of an affair with porn star Stormy Daniels and lying about 'paying her off' and a comment he had made years earlier about mistreating women in a sexual manner. His presidency was often described as 'dysfunctional'.

Trump was impeached by the House of Representatives for allegedly pressuring Ukraine to dig up damaging information on one of his main Democratic Party challenger, Joe Biden and Biden's son Hunter. He was tried in the Senate and acquitted. However, his handling of the coronavirus pandemic seriously damaged his re-election chances in 2020 and he lost the election. (By the time of the election more than 130 Secret Service agents had contracted the virus and were forced to quarantine.) He was the third commander-in-chief to be impeached and one of eleven incumbent presidents to fail to win re-election.

* * *

During Trump's 2016 presidential campaign he was faced with governing a country that was split in a way not seen since 1968, when the political fabric of the country seemed to tear apart from race riots, anti-Vietnam War demonstrations, political assassinations and a widening gap between young and old Americans.

In many ways Trump's 'divisive' campaign was reminiscent of the presidential campaigns of Robert and Edward Kennedy, two politicians who provoked intense love and hatred in equal measure. Like Trump, Robert Kennedy was aware of the profound emotions, many negative, his campaign had incited. 'I'm pretty sure there'll be an attempt on my life sooner or later', Kennedy said, 'not so much for political reasons . . . plain nuttiness, that's all. There's plenty of that around.'[1] In 1968 many reporters following RFK's primary campaigns believed the candidate was extremely vulnerable to attack. In 1979 reporters following Edward Kennedy's campaign to secure the Democratic Party nomination for president called it the 'death watch'. The candidate inspired millions of Americans but also attracted extreme opprobrium. The threat of assassination attempts had been partially responsible for Kennedy's decisions to forego presidential candidacies in 1968, 1972 and 1976. When he eventually threw his hat into the ring for the 1980 Democrat presidential nomination threats to his life increased.

Trump had asked for Secret Service protection in October 2015 after his announcement he intended to seek the Republican nomination for president. As his popularity increased, along with the crowds at his rallies, his Secret Service detail was appointed in early November.

During the 2016 Republican primary elections Trump overwhelmed his Republican opponents by winning victory after victory. Establishment Republicans were startled to see the size of Trump rallies and the enthusiasm his speeches engendered. However, Trump also attracted hate in equal measure which became a major anxiety for the Secret Service. Because of heightened tensions and the hatred Trump attracted among young militant voters on the left the agency was fully aware that of all the candidates in the race it was Donald Trump who would most likely be targeted by a potential assassin.

Initially, the vitriol and hatred against the candidate took the Secret Service by surprise. The agency had to deal with an unprecedented campaign of threatening messages on social media, casually and cavalierly advocating the murder of the president of the United States. Incensed threateners never realised, or simply did not care, that the First Amendment did not shield individuals who promoted assassination. Secret Service offices around the country spent numerous man-hours investigating the threats.

In the 2016 presidential election, out of the over twenty candidates in the primaries only Donald Trump, Ben Carson and Bernie Sanders received Secret Service protection. Hillary Clinton maintained a Secret Service protective detail as a former first lady, which was increased for the campaign. Only one candidate, Senator Ted Cruz, was eligible for Secret Service protection but declined it due to not wanting that 'wall' between him and the voters.

Trump's Secret Service bodyguard was augmented by local police as well as other government agency security teams including the Transportation Security Administration. Private security firm XMark said it provided personal security for Trump across the US until the election, when it was relieved by the Secret Service. His Secret Service detail was limited to keeping Trump safe during the campaign and the venues where he spoke secure.

Trump's own private security force was led by Keith Schiller, a retired New York City police officer who was first hired in 1999 as a part-time bodyguard. His security team included retired FBI agents Eddie Deck, Gary Uher and

Michael Sharkey as well as Ron Jurain, a New York police officer, and 6ft 4in, 275lb Burt Mentor, 'who had been shot a couple of times'.[2]

When Trump was elected president he kept his personal security team. It represented a major break from tradition. All modern presidents and presidents-elect have entrusted their personal security entirely to the Secret Service, and their event security mostly to local law enforcement. Additionally, there was no other example of a president-elect continuing with any private security after Election Day – when Secret Service protection expands dramatically for the winner. In fact, most candidates in the past dropped their outside security the moment they were granted Secret Service protection.

The 58-year-old, 6ft 4in-tall Schiller was issued with a Secret Service-issued perimeter pin and was often misidentified as a member of Trump's Secret Service detail. A native of New Paltz, New York, and father of two, Schiller had been director of security for the Trump organisation since 2004. During the campaign Schiller never strayed from Trump's side and it was Schiller who decided who got through the protective detail to meet the candidate. Additionally, Schiller provided more than just security. At times, Trump asked Schiller's opinion on all manner of subjects.[3]

It was Schiller who was in charge of Trump's security when the billionaire visited Moscow in 2013 for the Miss Universe pageant. Schiller had been approached by a suspected Russian intelligence agent who said he would supply 'girls' for Trump when the evening's entertainment show ended. Schiller told the suspected agent in strong terms that would not happen. Schiller went as far as stationing a security guard outside Trump's hotel room and two men who guarded the front and rear entrances to the hotel. Later, allegations would surface during the 2016 election campaign that a 'dossier' existed which included compromising film footage of Trump consorting with prostitutes at the hotel. Trump strongly denied the accusation.

There were critics of Trump's security arrangements. 'It's playing with fire,' said Jonathan Wackrow, a former Secret Service agent who worked on President Barack Obama's protective detail during his 2012 re-election campaign. Having a private security team working events with Secret Service 'increases the Service's liability' he said, 'it creates greater confusion and it creates greater risks. You never want to commingle a police function with a private security function.' He added, 'If you talk to the guys on the detail and the guys who are running the rallies, that's been a little bit difficult because it's so abnormal.' However, Wackrow understood the difficulty in challenging Trump's arrangements for his own security. 'What are they going to do, pick a fight with the president-elect and his advisers?' he said. 'That's not a way to start a romance.'[4] However, by the time Trump took the oath of office his personal private security team had been stood down and the Secret Service arranged all of the president's protective measures.

During the campaign Donald Trump had been vilified as arrogant, obnoxious, racist and a megalomaniac. However, a number of agents went on the record to challenge these views. They revealed Trump's personality was in direct contradiction to the negative image portrayed in the media. He treated agents 'respectfully' and unlike Hillary Clinton, he regularly chatted with them. A family member of an agent who had protected all the major candidates during the election campaign said, 'Pretty much all Secret Service agents liked him . . . [in part because] he was very respectful and grateful to them'. Another unnamed friend of a Secret Service agent said Trump '. . . treats the agents respectfully, and seems to genuinely want them to be well taken care of'. And, unlike former President Bill Clinton, Trump was punctual. This was critical for his bodyguards as candidates who ran late often increased stress levels substantially.[5]

For their part, Secret Service agents appeared to extend their appreciation by helping Trump to cheat at golf. He asked them to move his mishit balls. He 'cheats like a mafia accountant', sportswriter Rick Reilly said. 'Trump even tried to get one over on Tiger Woods. He cheats at the highest level. He cheats when people are watching, and he cheats when they aren't.'[6]

Trump also relied on his agents to supervise his meals. According to author Michael Wolff, Trump 'had a long-time fear of being poisoned, one reason why he liked to eat at McDonald's – nobody knew he was coming and the food was safely premade'.[7]

Trump often expressed his appreciation for his agents. At a special ceremony to celebrate the 152nd anniversary of the founding of the Secret Service in July 2017 Trump said:

> As President of the United States, I am honoured to recognize the men and women of the Secret Service for their hard work and dedication. Melania and I are especially thankful for those who selflessly stand by our side to safeguard our family every day. We are privileged to benefit from the unfailing professionalism and skill of these extraordinary men and women.[8]

In November 2016, Trump won the election but without winning the popular vote. It provoked many on the liberal left to accuse him of having 'stolen' the election. Hard-core supporters of his presidential opponent, Hillary Clinton, could not come to terms with a man who they labelled in the campaign as a misogynist and racist.

Trump found the demands of the presidency onerous. Soon after he took the oath of office he expressed misgivings about his new job. He thought that being the president of the United States would be 'easier' and he felt restricted. He said he missed 'being behind the wheel. I like to drive – I can't drive anymore'. The president said he 'loved' his previous life. 'I had so many things going,' he said. 'This is more work than in my previous life. I thought it would be easier.' Trump lamented how little time he had to himself under his 24-hour Secret Service protection. 'You're really into your own little cocoon', he said, 'because you have massive protection that you really can't go anywhere.'[9] He was clearly overwhelmed by the protection in place when he became president. When he first entered the White House he put a lock on his second-floor bedroom. His agents insisted he have it removed and the president acquiesced to their wishes.[10]

Under the Trump administration, forty-two people, including eighteen members of the Trump family, received Secret Service protection. When Barack Obama was in office thirty-one people were under protection.

* * *

For Donald Trump the threat of an attempt on his life first became a reality six months into the 2016 Republican primary campaigns. A 19-year-old mentally disturbed British man was arrested in Las Vegas after he tried to take a police officer's gun inside a theatre where Trump was to speak. Michael Sanford confessed he drove to the rally from California intending to kill Trump. He later pleaded guilty to related federal charges.

In January 2015 Sandford had made a two-week trip to New York City in the United States, during which time he had a mental breakdown and was sectioned overnight. Later that year, he returned to the United States, ostensibly to visit a US girl he had begun a relationship with while she had been visiting the United Kingdom who had since returned to the United States and been imprisoned on drugs charges.

On 16 June 2015, when Donald Trump announced that he intended to run for President of the United States, Sandford decided that '. . . if Trump was elected, it would change the world . . . somebody had to stand up for

America'. Following his arrest Sandford told his father of his anger about Trump and his policy of building a wall on the US–Mexico border. He was also angered by Trump's intended policy of halting Muslim immigration, believing Trump was a 'racist'. Additionally, the would-be assassin had been showing signs of mental disturbance. He said he was 'hearing voices' telling him to 'kill Donald Trump'.

On 16 June 2016, Sandford drove to Las Vegas and visited 'Battlefield Vegas', a shooting range and practised shooting live ammunition using a rented 9mm Glock pistol. This was the first time he had fired a gun. This, in itself, was illegal as he was an illegal alien.

On the evening of 17 June 2016, Sandford joined a queue at the Treasure Island Hotel and Casino for the following day's Trump campaign rally. At 9.00 am the following morning, as Trump was speaking, Sandford noticed that Ameel Jacob, a police officer with the Las Vegas Metropolitan Police Department who was providing security for the event, appeared to have his 9mm Glock 17 pistol unlocked in its holster. Sandford approached Jacob, who was positioned approximately 30ft from the stage where Trump was speaking and engaged him in conversation. He told the guard he wanted Trump's autograph. Within seconds Sandford seized Jacob's pistol with both hands but was unable to remove it from its holster due to the retention security. Jacob immediately subdued him assisted by other security personnel. No shots were fired.

Following his arrest Sandford was interrogated by Secret Service agents and confessed his intention to assassinate Trump. He told them he believed he would be killed in the process. Sandford also told them he would attempt to kill Trump again if he was given the opportunity.

Sandford was charged with three felonies: two counts of being an illegal alien in possession of a firearm and one count of impeding and disrupting the orderly conduct of government business and official functions. On 13 September 2016, he pleaded guilty saying, 'I tried to take a gun from a policeman to shoot someone with, and I'm pleading guilty.'

Despite his offences, which carried a maximum sentence of ten years, he was given a twelve-month jail sentence after his lawyers defended him on the basis of his suffering from Asperger's syndrome. Sandford apologised for his actions and said, 'I know saying sorry is not enough. I really do feel awful about what I did. I wish there was some way to make things better. I have cost taxpayers so much money. I feel terrible.' He subsequently claimed to have no memory of the assassination attempt despite his confession to Secret Service agents.[11]

Responding to the assassination attempt, Trump praised his security detail. 'I can tell you this,' he said, 'we have tremendous Secret Service and we have tremendous police throughout this country, and I think they did a fantastic job.' The following month Trump again sang the praise of the agents who guarded him. 'I'm the best thing that's ever happened to the Secret Service', Trump said, 'because I go around . . . saying how great they are. They are great. These are great, great people.'[12]

Following his election as president the Secret Service continued to investigate the growing menace of hate campaigns voiced through social media. Accordingly, the agency was forced to interview a number of liberal/left celebrities who attempted to boost their careers by threatening Trump. Many called for his 'assassination'. But the agency cautioned that, although it would investigate all social media postings containing credible threats, there was a difference between someone saying they are planning to kill the president and someone suggesting that someone else should attempt an assassination. The agency was also aware that mere threats did not necessarily constitute an 'assassination threat'. Generally, the Secret Service took the position that indirect threats were not prosecuted, and their investigators would 'prioritise' them before determining their credibility.

In January 2017 a typical assassination threat came from Dominic Joseph Puopolo Jr who posted a video on Twitter saying he intended to use a high-powered rifle to carry out the assassination attempt at President-elect Donald Trump's inauguration. Puopolo posted a video on Twitter saying, 'This is the 16th of January 2017. I will be at the review/inauguration and I will kill President Trump, President-elect Trump today with a high powered rifle.' When Puopolo appeared in court he claimed he was 'Jesus Christ'.[13]

In May 2017 President Trump appointed a new Secret Service Director, Randolph 'Tex' Alles. Alles acknowledged that providing 24-hour-a-day protection at Trump's residence in New York and his Mar-a-Lago resort in Florida, as well as protecting members of the Trump family, added to demands on the agency. He also said that the Secret Service was investigating 'about the same number' of threats against Trump as it did 'against the last several presidents'. The actual figure, Alles said, was around 'six to eight threats per day' and came 'in the form of e-mails and social media posts, as well as reports of suspicious activities and statements', but in most cases threateners were 'lacking in serious intent', some to the point of even 'walking back' on their threats. However, details of the more serious cases were forwarded to the US Attorney for prosecution.

Like presidents before him, Trump was also the target of stalkers. Even before he became president Trump had been stalked by 46-year-old Frank Monte, who lived in New Jersey. Monte had a history of violence. He had previously been released from a four-year term in prison in 2012 for threatening to kill two people with a loaded gun in Miami. Monte was arrested on charges that he had stalked Trump through Manhattan. However, as he had spent nearly three-and-a-half years behind bars pending his trial, he was released in May 2017 because he had already been held in jail longer than any prison sentence he could possibly receive.[14]

Attempts to gain illegal access to the White House did not diminish during Trump's presidency. Less than two months after his 20 January 2017 inauguration the president's bodyguards arrested four individuals who were considered a threat. On 10 March, a man jumped over a bike rack in an attempt to scale the White House fence. He was immediately apprehended before reaching the fence. He said he wanted to deliver a letter to someone in the Trump administration.[15] In the second incident a man appeared outside the White House claiming to have a bomb in his car and was arrested without incident.[16]

However, one of the most serious incidents which put Trump in danger occurred when 26-year-old Jonathan Tran scaled three barriers, one of them being an 8ft vehicle gate, and then spent quarter of an hour walking around the grounds of the White House while Trump was inside even though he had set off multiple alarms. Tran, who was carrying two cans of mace when he was spotted by Secret Service officers, even 'jiggled the door' to the executive mansion.[17] Trump responded to the incident by saying that the Secret Service were doing a 'fantastic job' and said the suspect was 'troubled'.

Former Secret Service agent Dan Bongino said the breaches of security meant that President Trump was not safe inside the White House and that even the Secret Service would not be able to protect him during a terror attack. 'The Secret Service cannot even keep one person off the grounds,' Bongino said. 'What will they do if 40 terrorists charge the White House? And believe me the terrorists are already thinking about that.'[18]

Trump also faced the dangers of assassination by Islamic jihadists. In November 2017 Islamic terrorists attempted to assassinate him when the president was in the Philippines but the attempt was foiled by Secret Service agents. The Philippines became an attraction for ISIS after jihadis were forced out of Middle-Eastern countries.

Trump's visit was for the Association of South East Asian Nations' ASEAN 50 Summit, where he met with Philippines President Rodrigo Duterte. Days before the president's visit, ISIS issued a series of threats via video that featured a picture of the President filled with bullets, and a message urging jihadists to 'lie in wait' and 'ambush' him. Agents tracked a man who was heading in the direction of the president's hotel after posting on Twitter, 'Gonna be in Manila the same time as Trump . . . I'll take one for the team,' the tweet announced. Agents also visited Manila's Luneta Park after identifying a known ISIS operative who was meeting with an associate there. They also located another suspect, an ISIS operative, known to be in the city. Philippines police officers arrived at the park and the suspects were arrested. Trump was about 20 minutes from landing in the country on Air Force One.[19]

* * *

The 2020 presidential election promised to be as dangerous for President Trump as the 2016 election. It was one of the most violent and confrontational elections in US history. Over a hundred cities across the US erupted in violence following the death of African American George Floyd during his arrest by Minneapolis police officers. Demonstrators were also joined by radical left groups like Extinction Rebellion who were opposed to Trump's conservative policies.

In May 2020 Trump's Secret Service detail was so alarmed by a 1,000-strong crowd of anti-Trump demonstrators outside the White House they strongly advised him to be taken to the special secure room in the basement of the executive mansion for his safety. Trump acceded to their wishes.

During the riots that took place across the US Trump praised his agents. When rioters threatened to storm the White House Trump said his agents showed great tolerance for the protestors. Trump tweeted:

> [The Secret Service] let the 'protestors' scream and rant as much as they wanted but whenever someone got too frisky or out of line they would quickly come down on them hard. Nobody came close to breaching the fence. If they had they would have been the most vicious dogs and the most ominous weapons I've ever seen. That's when people would have been really badly hurt. Many Secret Service agents [are] just waiting for action.[20]

Trump's opponent in the 2020 presidential election was Democrat Joe Biden. Biden had been a US Senator since 1973 when he was chosen as Barack Obama's vice presidential running mate in 2008. He served two terms as vice president.

Biden's political success has been undercut by personal tragedy. Within two months of being elected in 1972, he lost his wife, Neilia, and his young daughter in a tragic car accident. He also suffered two brain aneurysms and, in 2015, lost his son Beau to brain cancer. He said he had the 'gravest doubts [about God] for about a year' after he lost his wife and daughter, 'but [my Catholic faith] came back, and it blossomed, but there was a period of time where I could not fathom that there could be a God and that could happen'.[21]

Throughout his career in politics Biden built a reputation for career-threatening gaffes and miscues. During his run for the presidency in 1988 he was discovered to have plagiarised a speech by British Labour party leader Neil Kinnock which destroyed his candidacy. Other 'gaffes' included the time when Biden was criticised for allegedly divulging potentially classified security protocols in 2009. Biden told dinner guests at a Gridiron Club event the existence of a secret bunker under the vice president's Washington DC mansion which used to be the old US Naval Observatory. The bunker is believed to be the secure, undisclosed location where former Vice President Dick Cheney remained under protection in secret after the September 11 attacks. It lies behind a massive steel door secured by an elaborate lock with a narrow connecting hallway lined with communications equipment.[22]

In 2013 the vice president also faced criticism for his comments about gun ownership. In a Facebook post he said that he had advised his wife, Jill, to fire a shotgun in the air from their Delaware home's porch if she was concerned for her safety. 'I said, "Jill, if there's ever a problem, just walk out on the balcony here, walk out and put that double-barrel shotgun and fire two blasts outside the house,"' Biden said. 'You don't need an AR-15 – it's harder to aim,' he added, 'it's harder to use, and in fact you don't need 30 rounds to protect yourself. Buy a shotgun. Buy a shotgun.' However, Delaware law would have likely made his suggestion illegal unless the shots were fired in self-defence in a 'truly life-threatening situation'. The Wilmington police department responded to Biden's post by saying that city residents were not allowed to fire guns on their property and are also not allowed to shoot trespassers. They said that if Jill Biden took her husband's advice she could have been charged with aggravated menacing, a felony, and reckless endangering in the first degree.[23]

In 2020 Biden also faced severe criticism when politicians on the left of the Democratic Party raised issues about his previous calls for mass incarceration, tax cutting for the rich, cuts to social security and other safety net programmes, imperialism, NAFTA and against any form of universal healthcare.

* * *

Biden was familiar with Secret Service protection as vice president. He began his vice presidency by promising to do his best 'not to get trapped in the bubble. . . . if I work hard at it I can still be available and approachable'.[24] However, the heavy security – there were sometimes as many as twenty agents for a large public event – forced Biden to make changes to his lifestyle. As a senator he always enjoyed driving himself around his home town of Wilmington, Delaware. He now had to change to the Secret Service driving him everywhere in his limousine. He still travelled home from Washington by train giving him the nickname 'Amtrak Joe' but when he became vice president he cut the number of journeys as they were considered by his agents to be too risky. Agents guarding the vice president were amazed at how train passengers would engage Biden and treat him as a normal commuter.

The Secret Service had grown exponentially since the time of JFK. When Joe Biden took office he was protected not only by his personal contingent of bodyguards but a whole phalanx of protection squads including the counterassault team, or CAT, a heavily armed tactical unit assigned to the president, vice president, foreign heads of state, or any other protectee, such as a presidential candidate, deemed to require extra coverage. In the event of an attack, the CAT's mission is to divert the attack away from a protectee, allowing the working shift of agents to shield and evacuate the individual.

Biden's agents described the presidential candidate as a man who treated them 'with respect'. One agent said the vice president '. . . got a kick out of schmoozing with agents', often buying them food.[25]

There were some dissenters. Biden would impulsively decide to fly home to Delaware, disrupting any plans the agents might have had. This turned their 'personal lives into nightmares' one agent said. 'It's tough on people's family lives and marriages.' Another agent added, 'Biden likes to be revered as everyday Joe, and that's his thing. But the reality is no agents want to go on his detail because Biden makes agents' lives so tough.'[26] Another agent said that although Biden is known for his well-publicised support for the average working-class American and the 'underdog', he does not appear that way to agents.[27]

Iowa Democratic Party activist Jim Williams corroborated that observation. William's met Biden a number of times during election campaigning in
the state:

> [I] met just about all who ran starting in about 1990 on the
> Democratic ticket. [I] met very closely . . . Joe Biden. . . . Going
> back a few years [I found Biden] was quite impolite to what I call
> service people – drivers, bellboys, waiters, and always wanted to
> be treated as a 'big shot'. The last time I spoke with him was this
> past Labour Day [2019] at a union picnic – boy, has he aged and his
> speech was faulty.[28]

There were times when Biden would be criticised by the press over his
security arrangements. He was accused of endangering himself and members
of his protective detail by insisting that his motorcade kept sufficient distance
that it did not disturb his neighbours in Delaware. However, the instructions
to his agents meant his military aide and doctor had to follow a mile behind
his limousine. Journalist Ronald Kessler quoted an unnamed agent as saying,
'What's going to happen is either you're going to have a dead vice president
in Delaware or you're going to have agents killed in Delaware because Secret
Service management refused to stand up to [Biden].'[29]

In 2016 Gina Cherwaty filed a lawsuit over a car accident involving a Joe
Biden vice-presidential motorcade. She was injured in October 2016 when
Secret Service agent James Hall ran a red light in Wilmington and struck
several cars, including hers. Government lawyers denied negligence by
Hall, while not specifically addressing whether he ran a red light. A Secret
Service official claimed that Hall's vehicle was operating its emergency lights
and siren and had slowed to a near stop. Cherwaty's lawyer said witnesses
reported no lights or siren. The case was been resolved in mediation.[30]

Biden's agents were also involved in controversy during his time as vice
president. According to police logs, notes and reports one incident involving
his detail occurred when the vice president and his family were spending
their 24 November 2011 Thanksgiving on the island of Nantucket. The
agents engaged in a bar room brawl in the island's Rose and Crown nightclub.
It was one of at least two fights in and around Martha's Vineyard involving
Secret Service agents and other members of Obama's and Biden's security
details that police investigated that year.

The fight 'caused visible damage to both parties'. It involved Secret Service agent Jonathan Dawes and Massachusetts State Police bomb technician Eric 'Bomb Squad' Gahagan. Both men were assigned to Biden. The men fought with three Air Force officers who had just been assigned to the same detail. Gahagan accused the Air Force men of taking photos of him dancing with female Secret Service agent Yumi Kim. The Air Force officers, John Tran, Michael Valeich and Lucas Wiemer, suffered black eyes, head contusions and a chipped tooth. At first they believed their assailants were local police officers. Gahagan and Dawes knew the airmen were part of the Biden detail.[31]

One of the most publicised 'scandals' that occurred during Biden's vice presidency was the revelation he enjoyed 'skinny-dipping' in the pool of the vice-presidential mansion. According to Ronald Kessler, 'Agents say that, whether at the vice president's residence or at his home in Delaware, Biden has a habit of swimming in his pool nude . . . female Secret Service agents find that offensive'.[32] However, it is arguable that Biden's behaviour was somewhat innocuous as previous presidents had also engaged in the practice without criticism. Past examples of 'presidential skinny-dipping' included President John Quincy Adams, who frequently swam naked in the Potomac River, causing no fuss. President Teddy Roosevelt, an avid outdoorsman, swam naked in the Potomac. Billy Graham was one of many White House guests who swam naked with President Lyndon Johnson in the White House pool.

There were moments when Biden's detail believed the vice president was in danger including an incident in his home town of Wilmington. In 2015 several gunshots were fired from a speeding vehicle outside Biden's Delaware home just outside Wilmington in the quiet neighbourhood of Greenville. Biden and his wife Jill were not home and no one had been injured. The incident occurred at night when agents posted outside the Biden home heard gunshots and one saw a vehicle speed away on the public road outside the secure perimeter. Police searched the area for suspects and damage but found neither. Within an hour, however, police detained a man who attempted to pass an officer as he secured an outer perimeter. The man was detained for resisting arrest and questioned but was not charged in relation to the shooting.[33]

* * *

Biden announced his candidacy for the 2020 Democratic Party presidential nomination in 2019. Initially believed to be a candidate with no chance of winning, he soon proved the doubters wrong by sweeping the presidential primary sweepstakes in the all-important 'Super Tuesday' elections. Biden's momentum came after the former vice president decisively won the South Carolina primary and then received endorsements from three former 2020 candidates, Pete Buttigieg, Minnesota Senator Amy Klobuchar and former Texas representative Beto O'Rourke. Following his nomination as the 2020 Democrat presidential candidate he chose California Senator Kamala Harris as his running mate and the Secret Service gave her the codename 'Pioneer'.

Biden presented himself during the election as 'working class Joe' from Scranton, Pennsylvania (where he originally came from). To blacks Biden was the loyal vice president of the first black US president. To women he presented himself as the man who would 'bring dignity back to the Oval Office'. To the radical left, however, he became the weak president-to-be who would easily give in to their socialist demands.

At first, Trump was favoured to win re-election. However, Biden attacked the 'egregious tactics' of federal officials who had been sent to Portland by President Trump to protect federal buildings from Black Lives Matter and ANTIFA (anti-fascist) protestors. Despite risking a backlash from middle-class Americans who saw the protestors as 'rioters', Biden's polls kept on rising as he embarked on his campaign – a campaign that had been severely limited by the coronavirus crisis.

Throughout the summer of 2020 the 77-year-old Biden had to content himself with campaigning from the confines of his Wilmington home. When he eventually ventured forth to campaign in late September his critics attacked him as unfit for the presidency because he was too old and showed 'signs of dementia'.

Former vice presidents receive protection for six months after they leave office, which meant Biden's Secret Service protection ended in mid-2017. During the initial stages of the 2020 primary campaign trail, Biden hired private security, assisted by local police departments.

At the beginning of the campaign, however, Biden's security depended on his staff and one bodyguard – a former Secret Service agent named 'Jim', according to *New York* magazine. He was 'tall and official-looking. He greets the world chest-first, his hands resting in a dignified clasp, his expression even, his mouth unmoving. Most people assume that he's a Secret Service agent. Which he was.'[34]

After two protestors rushed the stage at a Biden campaign rally in New Hampshire in March 2020 it was widely believed that the candidate's protection was lacking. A security guard pulled one of the protestors away as Jill Biden grabbed the second protestor by the wrists and pushed her away from her husband. Once both protesters were escorted off the stage, the crowd began to chant 'Let's go Joe! Let's go Joe!' Biden reassured everyone that they were unharmed. 'I wasn't scared for me,' Biden said, 'I was worried for Jill. She's incredible.' The incident provoked calls for better protection for the presidential candidates. Biden said he was tired of protestors interrupting his campaign speeches and called for Secret Service protection.[35]

Some members of Congress put pressure on the Department of Homeland Security to dispatch Secret Service protection to the remaining 2020 presidential candidates earlier than usual, citing such incidents and calling for improved protection for presidential candidates.

Biden concurred and said he would welcome Secret Service protection. Memories of the Robert Kennedy assassination were voiced by some commentators.

Accordingly, Biden made an official request for US Secret Service protection. Biden's request was approved by the Candidate Protection Advisory Committee. The group made the recommendation 'to inform the decision' of the Department of Homeland Security.[36]

This was the second formal petition for government-funded security Biden had made during the Trump administration. The first came in 2017 when his requisite six-month protective detail after leaving the White House expired. (Former vice presidents are given such protection after a new president is elected and they leave office.) That request was denied.

Biden was soon provided with a Secret Service detail and assigned the codename 'Celtic', which was first used when he was vice president. It came much later in the election cycle than Trump and presidential candidate Ben Carson received in the 2016 race.

After serving as vice president, Biden knew what he was getting into when it came to the logistical limitations and inconvenience of 24/7 Secret Service protection. 'Campaigns aren't always in a hurry to get protection because when they do, everything changes,' former uniformed Secret Service agent Gary Byrne said. 'Sometimes it's not as great as it sounds. The Secret Service is very intrusive in everybody's lives.' But the protection also provided travel convenience and the prestige of an expensive motorcade ensemble with the level of security only government can provide. Asked if he thought Biden was in danger, Byrne replied, 'They absolutely are in my opinion. But there's a whole history of presidential candidates running without protection.'[37]

According to Byrne, Biden was well known among agents and officers as being very hard to protect. Byrne said:

> I still have friends who have served on his detail and they just hated it, he's a pain in the backside. He was reckless, slipping out of the house sometimes without warning. And just kind of cantankerous around the house – not wanting to follow directions. You can't say, 'I'll get along with the Secret Service as long as they do what I tell them.' Once the tail starts wagging the dog like that, that's not Secret Service protection, that's armed Uber.

However, Byrne agreed that the need for protection was obvious after both Biden and presidential candidate Bernie Sanders experienced protesters rushing them on stage. In Sanders' case, his Twitter followers often incited other critics online, and some of those episodes included threats of violence. Byrne recalled that many presidential candidates, such as John McCain, avoided having Secret Service protection as long as they could because it made their logistics less cumbersome and they could employ private, tight-knit security details they could better control.[38]

When Joe Biden was vice president, and later after he left office, he received numerous threats against his life including:

- Minnesotan Barry Ardolf, who pleaded guilty to six charges of computer hacking and child porn in December 2010, was involved in a dispute with his neighbour the following year. He hacked into his neighbour's Wi-Fi, set up Yahoo email accounts in his neighbour's name and then sent an email to Biden reading in part, 'I swear to God I'm going to kill you'. Ardolf pleaded guilty to threatening the vice president two days into his trial.[39]
- In 2018 Joe Biden was one of the targets of the 'MAGA Bomber' who sent sixteen mail bombs to thiteen people around the United States. Each bomb device consisted of roughly 6in of PVC pipe, a small clock, a battery, some wiring and 'energetic material', which is essentially potential explosives and material that gives off heat and energy through a reaction to heat, shock or friction. None exploded before being found and no injuries were sustained. The investigation ranged from New York to

Delaware to Maryland to the District of Columbia to Florida and California resulting in the arrest of Cesar Sayoc, an avowed Donald Trump supporter.

Sayoc lived in the Miami suburb of Aventura and had an extensive arrest record, including charges for theft, battery, domestic violence and other offences. In August 2002, he was found guilty of making a bomb threat to a utilities worker. He worked as a booking agent for a live-events company and was a former wrestler and cage fighter.

Sayoc's arrest took place at an auto-parts shop in the city of Plantation. His white van was covered in stickers celebrating Republicans and denouncing Trump's opponents. He had been linked by a fingerprint to a package sent to the California Congresswoman Maxine Waters. His other targets were former President Obama, former Secretary of State Hillary Clinton, actor Robert De Niro, financier George Soros, CNN, former Attorney General Eric Holder, former CIA Director John Brennan, Senators Cory Booker, Kamala Harris and former Director of National Intelligence James Clapper. Sayoc was sentenced to twenty years in prison.[40]

Biden was the target of two separate kidnapping and assassination attempts during the 2020 election campaign:

- In October 2020 42-year-old James Dale Reed was 'upset at the political situation' when he wrote a threatening letter. A door camera captured video of a person resembling Reed leaving the letter on his neighbour's doorstep early on the morning of 4 October. The neighbour said he didn't know Reed but had supported the 2020 Democrat candidates for president and vice president. The letter threatened violence against Democrats and said that 'Grandpa Biden' and Harris would both be attacked and executed.
  An anonymous tip to police led to the Secret Service investigating his offence of threatening a presidential candidate. Reed initially denied leaving the letter but was arrested two days later after he admitted writing and delivering it to his neighbour. The Secret Service said that Reed was 'known to' the Secret

Service for making a threatening statement against an unidentified person under the agency's protection in 2014.[41]

- In April 2020 Alexander Hillel Treisman posted on the
  meme-sharing platform iFunny 'Should I kill joe biden?'
  In May, he planned his attack on the presidential candidate
  by travelling to within 4 miles of Biden's home in Delaware,
  and at about same the time he bought an AR-15 rifle in New
  Hampshire. He wrote a checklist note ending with the word
  'execute'.

On 28 May, police in Kannapolis, North Carolina, who
were responding to a report of an abandoned van in a bank
parking lot, looked through the vehicle's window and saw an
AR-15-style rifle, a box for a .380 calibre handgun, a canister
'of the explosive material Tannerite' and a box of 5.56 calibre
ammunition. After the van was seized, a search of the vehicle
found about '$509,000 in U.S. currency, books (about survival,
bomb-making, improvised weapons and Islam), drawings of
swastikas and planes crashing into buildings', along with a Sig
Sauer AR Rifle, a 9mm Luger, a Kel-Tec Sub-2000, a .22 calibre rifle and a Russian Mosin Nagant M91/30 bolt-action rifle.

Treisman arrived at the bank later that day in a Honda Accord
and asked about the seized van. Police went to the bank after
employees contacted them and took Treisman into custody. A
search of the Honda revealed two more handguns, a .380 calibre
and a 9mm Luger, 'found concealed in a clothes hamper'.[42]

* * *

Joe Biden became president-elect nearly a week after a contentious election in
which President Trump refused to accept defeat citing ballot-rigging by the
Democrats. Trump's handling of the coronavirus pandemic, with 300,000
more deaths than normal at the time of the 3 November vote, had been a
major factor in his defeat. Although Trump's lawyers challenged the legit-
imacy of the election in the courts and refused to accept defeat, the Secret
Service had no such doubts and provided Biden with a full presidential detail
long before the news media called the election for him.

It was not long before the threats to assassinate the new President-Elect
began. On 12 January, ten days before Biden was due to be sworn into office
45-year-old Louis Capriotti threatened to assassinate him on the steps of the

US Capitol. Capriotti made the threat on 29 December 2020 in a voicemail to a US House member from New Jersey in which he said that if Biden thought he was '. . . going to put his hand on the Bible and walk into that f***ing White House on January 20th, they're sadly f***ing mistaken . . . We will surround the mother***ing White House and we will kill any mother***ing Democrat that steps on the mother***ing lawn.' Capriotti was arrested and charged with transmitting a threat in interstate commerce. Capriotti's arrest came less than a week after a mob of President Trump's supporters stormed the US Capitol as Congress began formally counting the Electoral College votes to certify Biden's win. Five people died in the riot.[43]

Following Biden's inauguration a threatener was arrested after he phoned the White House and threatened to 'kill Biden' and 'chop the heads off White House staff'. David Kyle Reeves was arrested on a charge of threatening the president between late January and 1 February.

In February 2021 66-year-old Sylvia Hall claimed to be delivering a letter to President Biden at the White House. She and an unidentified man carrying a BB gun approached Secret Service agents outside a security checkpoint close to the White House complex. She was arrested and was found to be carrying a loaded gun in her car. Hall was charged with carrying a pistol without a licence, possession of an unregistered firearm and possession of unregistered ammunition.[45]

President Biden also faced threats of a different nature as soon as he was sworn into office. His son Hunter was accused of having alleged 'conflicts of interest' involving overseas work – including in China and Ukraine – while his father was vice president. The purported scandal began when Hunter Biden left his laptop in a computer shop and failed to collect it. The computer revealed Hunter's debauched lifestyle which involved prostitutes and drugs and contained evidence of criminal activity by Hunter and his associates including drug trafficking and prostitution. It also contained messages referring to his financial records. The computer ended up in the hands of the FBI. The records on the computer raised questions about how much Hunter's dealings were mingled with his father's. (It was later revealed, in August 2021, that Hunter had 'lost' another laptop when he bought drugs from a Russian drug dealer.)[46]

Six months into his presidency concerns about Biden's health, which his supporters and his critics alike voiced during the election campaign, were resurrected when his agents spoke of concerns about the president's cognitive abilities. At times he seemed to be confused by the instructions given to him by his agents and there were calls for the president to undergo cognitive tests.[47]

* * *

The siege of the Capitol on 6 January 2021 and the Antifa and Black Lives Matter riots that took place throughout the United States in 2020 shocked and appalled the Secret Service who saw them as a harbinger of the challenges to come. 'Violence is violence,' Stephen P. Monteiro, a member of President Bill Clinton's detail said, 'There is violence on the left and violence on the right. We don't differentiate between the origins of violence.'[48]

Former agent J.J. Hensley said, '. . . you're going to be looking at social media and seeing what's out there on open source . . . They still have the old threats, and now they have the new threats: We're worried about everything from a switchblade to a drone, which could have explosives on it.'[49]

Vic Erevia, the special agent in charge of President Barack Obama's detail from 2011 to 2013, said:

I worry, frankly . . . how the last four years may have impacted . . . culture . . . This current period feels distinctly more dangerous than at any time during my lifetime. I believe the challenges it presents will persist. Travel will bring new tests for the protective details as they deal with emboldened actors armed to the teeth. You can't launch the National Guard every time the president goes somewhere . . .[50]

Notes

Chapter 1

1. Robert Scheer, *Playing President: My Close Encounters with Nixon, Carter, Bush I, Reagan, and Clinton – and How They Did Not Prepare Me for George W. Bush* (Acashic Books, 2006), 16.
2. George Rush, *Confessions of an Ex-Secret Service Agent – The Marty Vencker Story* (Donald I. Fine, 1988), 50.
3. Diablo Gazette.com, 'Inside the Secret Service – A Former Agent's Stories', June 28, 2016, http://www.diablogazette.com/2016/06/inside-the-secret-service-a-former-agents-stories/.
4. Rush, *Confessions of an Ex-Secret Service Agent*, 150.
5. Jennifer Senior, 'The Politics of Personality Destruction', *New York*, 1 June 2007, https://nymag.com/news/politics/32864/.
6. Marlene Cimons, 'A President and His Protectors: Clinton is a challenge for the Secret Service, but agents are used to it', *Los Angeles Times*, 12 January 1993, https://www.latimes.com/archives/la-xpm-1993-01-12-mn-1307-story.html.
7. Mark Morgenstein, 'Florida police, community mourn officer killed in presidential motorcade', CNN, September 10, 2012, https://edition.cnn.com/2012/09/10/us/florida-motorcade-officer-dies/index.html.
8. *San Bernardino Sun-Telegram*, 'Presidential Hopefuls Reaping All the Benefits of Security', 23 October 1975, A15, https://cdnc.ucr.edu/cgi-bin/cdnc?a=d&d=SBS19751023.1.14&e=-------en--20--1--txt-txIN--------1.
9. John F. Kennedy Presidential Library, Statement by James J. Rowley, 29 March 1976, https://www.jfklibrary.org/sites/default/files/archives/JFKOH/Rowley%2C%20James%20J/JFKOH-JAJR-01/JFKOH-JAJR-01-TR.pdf.
10. Rush, *Confessions of an Ex-Secret Service Agent*, 128.
11. J. Gerald Harris, 'Georgia Baptist Jim Cool recalls years with Secret Service', *Christian Index*, July 5, 2007, http://www.tciarchive.org/3397.article.
12. Massie Ritsch, 'Candidates and Their Protectors Play an Endless Tug of War', *Los Angeles Times*, 23 April 2000.
13. Ibid.
14. Anthony Summers, *The Arrogance of Power: The Secret World of Richard Nixon* (W&N, 2000), 247.
15. *US News and World Report*, 'Bill Clinton's Running Habit: A Secret Service Nightmare', 29 February 2012.
16. Ibid.
17. Ritsch, 'Candidates and Their Protectors Play an Endless Tug of War'.
18. *The Missorian*, 'The Adventures of a Secret Service Agent', www.emissourian.com/.
19. Ritsch, 'Candidates and Their Protectors Play an Endless Tug of War'.
20. Dan Emmett, 'What it's Really Like Being a Secret Service Agent', *The Wall Street Journal*, 1 October 2014.
21. Pam Dixon, 'Guarding Bush', *KPLC*, March 13, 2003.

22. Rush, *Confessions of an Ex-Secret Service Agent*, 71.
23. Jake Rosen, '14 Secrets of Secret Service Agents', *Mental Floss*, 6 April 2017.
24. Joseph Petro, *Standing Next to History – An Agent's Life Inside the Secret Service* (Thomas Dunne Books, 2005), 234.
25. Clare Crawford, 'In a Presidential Year, the Chief of the Secret Service Worries About Protection, Not Politics', *People* magazine, 22 March 1976.
26. *Huff Post*, 'How Has Secret Service Protection Evolved from JFK to Donald Trump?', 1 March 2017.
27. Gerald Blaine, *The Kennedy Detail* (Gallery Books, 2010), 399.
28. Ritsch, 'Candidates and Their Protectors Play an Endless Tug of War'.
29. Ibid.
30. Crawford, 'In a Presidential Year, the Chief of the Secret Service Worries About Protection, Not Politics'.
31. Brad Koplinski, *Hats in the Ring* (Presidential Publishing, 2000), 494.
32. Rush, *Confessions of an Ex-Secret Service Agent*, 73.
33. Petro, *Standing Next to History*, 23.
34. Ed Hinman, 'What Kim Jong Un's Crazy Elite Bodyguards Teach Us About Threat Deterrence', *Task and Purpose*, 15 May 2018, https://taskandpurpose.com/opinion/kim-jong-uns-crazy-elite-bodyguards-teach-us-threat-deterrence/.
35. *TIME*, 'Secret Service: New Boss for a Troubled Team', 26 November 1973.
36. Mike Royko, 'Jesse Jackson Deserves His Bodyguards', *Chicago Tribune*, 27 July 1988, https://www.chicagotribune.com/news/ct-xpm-1988-07-27-8801170948-story.html.

Chapter 2

1. Merle Miller, *Lyndon – An Oral Biography* (Ballantine Books, 1980), 346.
2. Tom Leonard, 'JFK's White House Harem', *Daily Mail*, 12 March 2020, 34.
3. Seymour M. Hersh, *The Dark Side of Camelot* (Little, Brown and Company, 1997), 323.
4. Elise Cooper, 'A Secret Service Agent Remembers', *American Thinker*, 7 June 2016.
5. *The National Herald*, 'Secret Service Agent Giannoules Guarded JFK on Eve of Assassination', 17 October 2014.
6. Amy Davidson Sorkin, 'Mimi and the President', *New Yorker*, 10 February 2012, https://www.newyorker.com/news/amy-davidson/mimi-and-the-president.
7. Hersh, *The Dark Side of Camelot*, 21, 228–39.
8. Ibid., 240–1.
9. Ibid., 229.
10. JFK Library, Oral History Interview, Kate Thom Kelley, 9 April 2003, https://www.jfklibrary.org/asset-viewer/archives/JFKOH/Kelley%2C%20Kate%20Thom/JFKOH-KTK-01/JFKOH-KTK-01.
11. Hersh, *The Dark Side of Camelot*, 234.
12. Don Fulsom, 'The President and the Prostitute', *Crime Magazine*, http://www.crimemagazine.com/president-and-prostitute-jack-kennedy-and-ellen-rometsch.
13. Ronald Kessler, 'Secret Service Describes JFK as Reckless', *Newsmax*, 13 February 2012, https://www.newsmax.com/Newsfront/Secret-Service-JFK-Alford/2012/02/13/id/429282/.
14. JFK Library, Don S. Hewitt, Oral History Interview, 10 August 2002, https://www.jfklibrary.org/asset-viewer/archives/JFKOH/Hewitt%2C%20Don%20S/JFKOH-DSH-01/JFKOH-DSH-01.

15. JFK Library, Samuel H. Beer, Oral History Interview, 11 July 2002, http://www.jfklibrary.org/Asset-Viewer/Archives/JFKOH-SB-01.aspx.
16. *The Sydney Morning Herald*, 'Armed Men Seized at US Rally – Near Sen. Kennedy', 6 November 1960.
17. *Wilmington NC Star News*, 'President – 50-50 Chance Assassination might Kill Him', 26 July 1962, 15.
18. Mel Ayton, *Hunting the President – Threats, Plots and Assassination Attempts – From FDR to Obama* (Regnery Publishing, 2014), 55–70.
19. Blaine, *Kennedy Detail*, 63.
20. Allen Rich, 'Former Secret Service agent gives personal account of Kennedy assassination', *Front Page*, 25 August 2009, www.northtexashistorycenter.org.
21. Theodore H. White, *In Search of History* (Harper & Row, 1st edn 1978), 521.
22. Peter Sheridan, 'Five Presidents and Me: The story of a US secret service agent', *Daily Express*, 30 May 2016.
23. Rich, 'Former Secret Service agent gives personal account of Kennedy assassination'.
24. *The Report of the U.S. President's Commission on the Assassination of President John F. Kennedy*, 427, and twenty-six accompanying volumes of Hearings and Exhibits published by the US Government Printing Office in 1964. Also *The Warren Report* (Doubleday, 1964), without supporting volumes and forward by Louis Nizer and afterword by Bruce Catton.
25. Ibid., 445.
26. Ibid., 454.
27. US Congress, *House Select Committee on Assassinations Report*, 228–37. Investigation of the Assassination of President John F. Kennedy, conducted by the Select Committee on Assassinations of the US House of Representatives, published by the US Government Printing Office in 1979.
28. Mike Cochran, 'Living, working through four hectic days that changed the world forever', *Fort Worth Star-Telegram*, 15 November 2013.
29. Susan Cheever, 'Could the Secret Service Have Saved JFK?', *Vanity Fair*, 17 October 2014, https://www.vanityfair.com/news/politics/2014/10/secret-service-jfk-assassination.
30. Ibid.
31. Kessler, 'Secret Service Describes JFK as Reckless'.
32. Cheever, 'Could the Secret Service Have Saved JFK?'.
33. '"JFK's Secret Service agents were too hung over to react in Dallas", says author, by Irish Central Staff', *Irish Central*, 18 November 2018, https://www.irishcentral.com/roots/history/jfk-secret-service-agents-too-hungover-to-react.
34. Ibid.
35. Cheever, 'Could the Secret Service Have Saved JFK?'.

Chapter 3
1. *The Free Lance Star*, 'Views Are Same: LBJ and Goldwater Shun Secret Service Guard', 17 August 1964, 5.
2. Rufus W. Youngblood, *20 Years in the Secret Service – My Life With Five Presidents* (Simon & Schuster, 1973), 63.
3. Dwight D. Eisenhower Presidential Library, Interview with Jack M. Woodward, https://www.eisenhowerlibrary.gov/sites/default/files/research/oral-histories/oral-history-transcripts/woodward-jack-512.pdf.

4. Vince Devlin, 'Former Secret Service agent kept watch over presidents and their families', *The Missoulian*, 29 April 2007.

5. Youngblood, *20 Years in the Secret Service,* 150.

6. LBJ Presidential Library, Oral History Interview, Cartha Delaoch, 18 February 1992, http://www.lbjlibrary.net/collections/oral-histories/deloach-d.-cartha. html.

7. Michael Beschloss, *Taking Charge – Johnson White House Tapes 1963–1964* (Simon & Schuster, 1998), 441.

8. Michael Beschloss, 'L.B.J.'s Bravado and a Secret Service Under Scrutiny', *New York Times*, 2 October 2014.

9. Michael Beschloss, 'Lyndon Johnson on the Record', *Texas Monthly*, December 2001, https://www.texasmonthly.com/politics/lyndon-johnson-on-the-record/.

10. Cooper, 'A Secret Service Agent Remembers'.

11. Melissa Sartore, 'What it's Actually Like to Guard the President, According to Former Members of the Secret Service', https://www.ranker.com/list/ stories-from-secret-service-members/melissa-sartore.

12. Robert Dallek, 'Three New Revelations About LBJ', *The Atlantic Monthly*, April 1998, 42–4.

13. Sheridan, 'Five presidents and me: The story of a US secret service agent'.

14. Youngblood, *20 Years in the Secret Service*, 147.

15. Sartore, 'What it's Actually Like to Guard the President, According to Former Members of the Secret Service'.

16. Dwight D. Eisenhower Presidential Library, Interview with Jack M. Woodward, p. 28, https://www.eisenhowerlibrary.gov/sites/default/files/research/oral-histories/ oral-history-transcripts/woodward-jack-512.pdf.

17. Sheridan, 'Five Presidents and Me: The story of a US secret service agent'.

18. '60 Minutes, Clint Hill Interview', 8 December 1975, https://www.metacritic.com/ tv/60-minutes/season-8/episode-12-december-7-1975---secret-service-agent-9.

19. Youngblood, *20 Years in the Secret Service*, 85.

20. Ibid., 89.

21. Dallek, 'Three New Revelations About LBJ'.

22. Philip H. Melanson, *The Secret Service – The Hidden History of an Enigmatic Agency* (Basic Books, 2005), 289.

23. Youngblood, *20 Years in the Secret Service*, 166.

24. LBJ Presidential Library, Oral History Interview of Margaret Chase Smith and William Lewis, 20 August 1975, http://www.lbjlibrary.net/collections/oral-histories/ oral-history-collection.html#s.

25. Youngblood, *20 Years in the Secret Service*, 168.

26. Beschloss, 'L.B.J.'s Bravado and a Secret Service Under Scrutiny'.

27. Ibid.

28. John F. Kennedy Presidential Library, Statement by James J. Rowley, 29 March 1976, https://www.jfklibrary.org/sites/default/files/archives/JFKOH/Rowley% 2C%20James%20J/JFKOH-JAJR-01/JFKOH-JAJR-01-TR.pdf.

29. Youngblood, *20 Years in the Secret Service*, 230.

30. Harry Stein, 'The Goldwater Takedown: Media coverage of the 1964 presidential campaign was a precursor to today's partisan journalism', *City Journal*, Autumn 2016, https://www.city-journal.org/html/goldwater-takedown-14787.html.

31. Ibid.

32. Ibid.

33. Justia.com, Barry M. Goldwater v. Ralph Ginzburg, Warren Boroson, 18 July 1969, https://law.justia.com/cases/federal/appellate-courts/F2/414/324/84727/.
34. United States Congress, *Review of Secret Service Protective Measures, Senate Committee on Appropriations* (US Government Printing Office, 1975), 46.
35. Youngblood, *20 Years in the Secret Service*, 166.
36. *The Free Lance Star*, 'Views Are Same: LBJ and Goldwater Shun Secret Service Guard', 17 August 1964, 5.
37. The American Presidency Project, 'The President's News Conference', 15 August 1964, https://www.presidency.ucsb.edu/documents/the-presidents-news-conference -1021.
38. United States Congress, *Review of Secret Service Protective Measures*, 46.
39. Internet Archive, Barry Goldwater, 'Memo From J. Edgar Hoover to Clyde Tolson (et al.), 16 September 1964', https://archive.org/details/BarryGoldwater.
40. Theodore H. White, *The Making of the President 1964* (Harper Perennial, 2010), 203.
41. Ibid.
42. Richard H. Rovere, 'The Campaign: Goldwater', *The New Yorker*, 25 September 1964, https://www.newyorker.com/magazine/1964/10/03/the-campaign-goldwater.
43. *New York Times*, 'Miller Suggests Secret Service Provide a Guard for Goldwater; Says "Serious Consideration" is Being Given to Chance of Campaign Violence', 12 August 1964.
44. Youngblood, *20 Years in the Secret Service*, 166.
45. Rovere, 'The Campaign: Goldwater'.
46. Internet Archive, FBI Files, 'Memo From J. Edgar Hoover to Clyde Tolson (et al.), 16 September 1964', https://archive.org/details/BarryGoldwater.
47. United States Congress, *Review of Secret Service Protective Measures*, 49.
48. Youngblood, *20 Years in the Secret Service*, 168.
49. United States Congress, *Review of Secret Service Protective Measures*, 46–7.
50. Internet Archive, FBI Files, 'Memo to J. Edgar Hoover from SAC, Phoenix, 29 October 1958', https://archive.org/details/BarryGoldwater.
51. Internet Archive, FBI Files, 'Senator Barry Goldwater – Request For Protection Mr. Mohr to C. D. Deloach, 22 November 1963', https://archive.org/details/ BarryGoldwater.
52. *Desert Sun*, 'Federal Guards Seen for Barry Threat Against Senator May Bring Secret Service Action', 20 August 1964, https://cdnc.ucr.edu/?a=d&d= DS19640820.2.4&srpos=14&e=-------en--20--1--txt-txIN-PRESIDENTIAL+CA NDIDATES%2c+SECRET+SERVICE-------1.
53. Internet Archive, 'FBI Memo, Louis Samuel Weiner, Pheonix, Arizona, 21 July 1964', https://archive.org/details/BarryGoldwater.
54. Internet Archive, 'FBI Memo, Alleged Threat to Assassinate Senator Barry Goldwater A Rosen To Mr Belmont, 6 July 1964 – FOIPA Request, Subject: Goldwater, Barry Morris Sr', https://archive.org/details/BarryGoldwater.
55. Internet Archive, 'FBI memo, Information Concerning Threat to Assassinate Senator Barry Goldwater, Los Angeles, 23 June 1964', https://archive.org/details/ BarryGoldwater.
56. United States Congress, *Review of Secret Service Protective Measures*, 46.

Chapter 4

1. *The Ogden Standard*, 15 July 1915, 1.

2. Scott Miller, *The President and the Assassin – McKinley, Terror, and Empire at the Dawn of the American Century* (Random House Trade Paperbacks, 2013), 310.
3. *Butler Weekly Times*, 'Man Attempts to Shoot Fairbanks – Blacksmith Tries to Kill Vice President Before Vast Michigan Throng', 15 June 1905, 1.
4. Ibid.
5. *The San Francisco Call*, 'Fairbanks Attacked by Anarchist', 8 June 1905, 3.
6. Carl Solberg, *Hubert Humphrey – A Political Biography* (Minnesota Historical Society Press, 2003), 227.
7. Michael Brenes, 'The Tragedy of Hubert Humphrey', *New York Times*, 23 March 2018.
8. Neil Mehler, 'Humphrey Won't Run In 1976', *Chicago Tribune*, 23 April 1974.
9. Hubert Humphrey, *The Education of a Public Man – My Life and Politics* (University of Minnesota Press, 1991), 309.
10. Jerry Parr with Carolyn Parr, *In the Secret Service – The True Story of the Man Who Saved President Reagan's Life* (Tyndale, 2013), 95.
11. Petro, *Standing Next to History*, 108.
12. Parr, *In the Secret Service*, 123.
13. United States Congress, *Review of Secret Service Protective Measures*, 41.
14. Clint Hill, *Five Presidents: My Extraordinary Journey with Eisenhower, Kennedy, Johnson, Nixon, and Ford* (Gallery Books, 2017), 319.
15. Rush, *Confessions of an Ex-Secret Service Agent*, 145.
16. Youngblood, *20 Years in the Secret Service*, 203.
17. Dennis V.N. McCarthy, *Protecting the President – The Inside Story of a Secret Service Agent* (Dell Publishing Co., 1985), 257.
18. Youngblood, *20 Years in the Secret Service*, 202.
19. Ibid., 210.
20. Parr, *In the Secret Service*, 104.
21. Sartore, 'What it's Actually Like to Guard the President, According to Former Members of the Secret Service'.
22. United States Congress, *Review of Secret Service Protective Measures*, 50.
23. UPI, 'Hubert Humphrey lived under the threat of assassination', 11 August 1984, https://www.upi.com/Archives/1984/08/11/Hubert-Humphrey-lived-under-the-threat-of-assassination-around/3127461044800/.
24. Ibid.
25. Carolyn Miller Parr, 'I Was Married to the Secret Service Agent Who Saved Reagan', *USA Today*, 24 August 2017, https://eu.usatoday.com/story/opinion/2017/08/24/secret-service-agents-grueling-job-deserves-good-pay-reasonable-hours-column/596951001/.
26. Cimons, 'President and His Protectors: Clinton is a challenge for the Secret Service, but agents are used to it by'.
27. James Lileks, '1947 assassination attempt on Hubert H. Humphrey', *Star Tribune*, 15 March 2018, https://www.startribune.com/minnesota-moment-1947-assassination-attempt-on-hubert-h-humphrey/477003703/.
28. FBI Files, The Vault, 'Memo From [redacted] to Mr Rosen, 30 August 1968, Prediction Concerning Killing of Vice President Hubert H Humphrey, Threats Against the President', https://vault.fbi.gov/hubert%20h.-humphrey/hubert-h.-humphrey-part-24-of-32.
29. FBI Files, the Vault, 'Threat to Hubert Humphrey', https://vault.fbi.gov/hubert%20h.-humphrey.
30. *New York Times*, 'Threat to Humphrey Holds Man', 28 October 1964.

31. Washington Capital News Service, 3 December 1964, 1.
32. United States Congress, *Review of Secret Service Protective Measures*, 41.
33. FBI Files, The Vault, 'Hubert H. Humphrey, Memo, dated 16 July 1965', https://vault.fbi.gov/hubert%20h.-humphrey.
34. FBI Files, The Vault, 'Hubert H. Humphrey, Anonymous Telephone Call on 3/21/67 From Unidentified Male Indicating a Threat to Shoot Vice President Hubert H Humphrey', 21 March 1967, https://vault.fbi.gov/hubert%20h.-humphrey.
35. FBI Files, The Vault, 'Threat to Hubert Humphrey', https://vault.fbi.gov/hubert%20h.-humphrey.
36. FBI Files, The Vault, 'Unknown subject: Threat to Kidnap Vice President Hubert H. Humphrey, Palo Alto, California, 20 February 1967', https://vault.fbi.gov/hubert%20h.-humphrey.
37. United States Congress, *Review of Secret Service Protective Measures*, 44.
38. *Chicago Tribune*, 'Two Eggs Tossed at Humphrey; Just Miss Him', 2 April 1967.
39. *Chicago Tribune*, 'Brussels Gang Throws Eggs at Hubert, Misses', 10 April 1967.
40. *Lodi News Sentinel*, 'Leftists Plot to Kill Humphrey in West Berlin', 6 April 1967, 1.
41. Jillian Becker, *Hitler's Children – The Story of the Baader-Meinhof Terrorist Gang*, (Authorhouse, 2014), 28.
42. FBI Files, The Vault, 'Hubert H. Humphrey, Memo Director to LA Office, 31 October 1968', https://vault.fbi.gov/hubert%20h.-humphrey.
43. *The Atlantic*, 'Chicago's Blackstone Rangers', May 1969.
44. *Herald Journal*, 'Murder Target Humphrey Says', 1 September 1968, 1.
45. *The Milwaukee Sentinel*, 'Humphrey Was Target of Threats', 13 August 1968, 10.
46. Parr, *In the Secret Service*, 131.
47. Bill Lynch, 'Baton Rouge Plot to Kill HHH Revealed', 24 July 1967, https://archive.org/details/nsia-ThreatsAgainstHumphreyHubertH/mode/2up.
48. John McAdams, The Kennedy Assassination website, 'Joe Cooper Saved Vice President From Assassination But Wound Up Dead After Investigating JFK's Murder' by John Moulder, 8 June 1975, http://mcadams.posc.mu.edu/weberman/jcooper.htm.
49. FBI Files, The Vault, 'Hubert H. Humphrey, Files, Memo from Deloach, Intelligence Division, 8 February 1965', https://vault.fbi.gov/hubert%20h.-humphrey.
50. FBI Files, The Vault, 'Memo from Cartha DeLoach to Mr Mohr, 1 April 1965', https://vault.fbi.gov/hubert%20h.-humphrey.
51. Stephen Spignesi, *In the Crosshairs: Famous Assassinations and Attempts from Julius Caesar to John Lennon* (Barnes & Noble Books, 2004), 52.
52. Parr, *In the Secret Service*, 102.

Chapter 5

1. *Santa Cruz Sentinel*, 'I Play Russian Roulette Every Morning', 6 June 1968, https://cdnc.ucr.edu/?a=d&d=SCS19680606.1.6&srpos=14&e=-------en--20--1--txt-txIN-Nelson+Rockefeller%2c++bodyguards-------1.
2. Ibid.
3. David C. Heymann, *RFK – A Candid Biography* (William Heineman, 1998), 464.
4. J. Randy Taraborrelli, *The Kennedy Heirs* (Griffin, 2020), 475.
5. Neal Gabler, *Catching The Wind – Edward Kennedy and the Liberal Hour 1932–1975* (Crown, 2020), 547.
6. Evan Thomas, *Robert Kennedy – His Life* (Simon & Schuster, 2002), 68.
7. Anthony Summers, *Goddess – The Secret Lives of Marilyn Monroe* (Phoenix Paperback, 2012), 307.

8. Larry Tye, *Bobby Kennedy – The Making of A Liberal Icon* (Random House, 2016), 191.
9. Richard Burton and Chris Williams (ed.), *The Richard Burton Diaries* (Yale University Press, 2013), 301–2.
10. Piers Morgan, 'I Turned Down Bobby Kennedy . . .', *The Mail on Sunday*, 3 January 2021.
11. Jerry Oppenheimer, *The Other Mrs. Kennedy: Ethel Skakel Kennedy: An American Drama of Power, Privilege, and Politics* (St Martin's Press 1994), 157.
12. Frank Saunders, *Torn Lace Curtain*, with James Southwood (Holt, Rinehart and Winston, 1982), 309.
13. *Irish America*, 'Those We Lost, Robert Kennedy and Bill Barry hit it off they met in the FBI office in New York', November/December 2018, https://irishamerica.com/2018/11/those-we-lost-51/.
14. Louden Wainwright, 'Suddenly, A Mass of Screaming Men and Women', *LIFE*, 22.
15. Bill Dwyre, 'The 1984 Olympics had Rafer Johnson to light the way', *Los Angeles Times*, 28 July 2009.
16. Jeffri Chadiha, 'How Robert F. Kennedy's life and death galvanized an NFL star', 4 June 2018, https://www.nfl.com/news/sidelines/rosey-and-bobby.
17. Ibid.
18. Lisa Fedararo, 'A Security Adviser, and Friend, to the Kennedys', *New York Times*, 18 May 1991.
19. John F. Kennedy Presidential Library, Oral History, William Barry, https://www.jfklibrary.org/asset-viewer/archives/RFKOH/Barry%2C%20William%20G/RFKOH-WGB-03/RFKOH-WGB-03.
20. Wainwright, 'Suddenly, A Mass of Screaming Men and Women'.
21. The Undefeated.com, 'How Rosey Grier and Rafer Johnson Became Friends With Robert Kennedy by Jerry Bembry', 5 June 2018, https://theundefeated.com/features/how-rosey-grier-and-rafer-johnson-became-friends-with-robert-kennedy/.
22. See Mel Ayton, *The Forgotten Terrorist – Sirhan Sirhan and the Assassination of Robert F. Kennedy* (University of Nebraska Press/Potomac Books, second edn 2019), Chapter 3, Sirhan and Palestine.
23. Robert A. Houghton, *Special Unit Senator: The Investigation of the Assassination of Senator Robert F. Kennedy* (Random House, 1970), 181.
24. Francine Klagsbrun and David C. Whitney (eds), *Assassination: Robert F. Kennedy, 1925–1968* (Cowles, 1968), 109.
25. FBI Kensalt Files, Interviews, 7 June 1968, Inglewood, Ca LA 56- 156 and 8 June 1968, Corona, Ca LA-56-156.
26. John Seigenthaler, *A Search for Justice* (Aurora, 1971), 254.
27. Jules Witcover, 85 *Days – The Last Campaign of Robert Kennedy* (Ace Publishing Corporation, 1969), 218.
28. Houghton, *Special Unit Senator*, 165.
29. Robert Blair Kaiser, *RFK Must Die: A History of the Robert Kennedy Assassination and Its Aftermath* (E.P. Dutton, 1970), 165.
30. Godfrey H. Jansen, *Why Robert Kennedy Was Killed – The Story of Two Victims* (Third Press, 1970), 138–9.
31. Houghton, *Special Unit Senator*, 231–2.
32. Kaiser, *RFK Must Die*, 270.
33. Ayton, *Forgotten Terrorist*, Appendix.
34. Houghton, *Special Unit Senator*, 246.

35. Ibid., 262.
36. FBI Files, 'Robert F. Kennedy Assassination – (Summary) – Report consisting of the Los Angeles County Board of Supervisors Independent Investigation by Special Counsel Thomas F. Kranz, 4', https://vault.fbi.gov/Robert%20F%20Kennedy%20%28Assassination%29%20.
37. LAPD Summary Report, 9.
38. Ibid.
39. Joseph E. Mohbat, 'Assassination expected to change campaign styles of candidates', *Santa Cruz Sentinel*, 6 June 1968, https://cdnc.ucr.edu/?a=d&d=SCS19680606.1.6&srpos=14&e=-------en--20--1--txt-txIN-Nelson+Rockefeller%2c++bodyguards-------1.
40. Daryl F. Gates, *Chief: My Life in the LAPD* (Bantam Books, 1993), 148.
41. Ibid., 150.
42. Heymann, *RFK*, 493.
43 LAPD Summary Report, 37.
44. LAPD Summary Report, 5.
45. Houghton, *Special Unit Senator*, 173–5 and 284–6.
46. Ibid.
47. Heymann, *RFK*, 464.
48. Fred Bernstein and Richard Natale, 'Director John Frankenheimer's the Manchurian Candidate Plays to a Full House After 26 Years', *People*, 16 May 1988, https://people.com/archive/director-john-frankenheimers-the-manchurian-candidate-plays-to-a-full-house-after-26-years-vol-29-no-19/.
49. Dan Moldea, *The Killing of Robert Kennedy* (Norton, 1995), 210.
50. Warren Rogers, 'Not Again!, Eyewitness to the Killing of RFK', *The Washington Post*, 23 May 1993.
51. *New York Times*, 'Sirhan Felt Betrayed by Kennedy', Associated Press, 20 February 1989.
52. See John McAdams, 'The Kennedy Assassination' and Mel Ayton, 'The JFK and RFK Assassinations and the Bogus "Manchurian Candidate" Theories', 2007, https://mcadams.posc.mu.edu/Manchurian.html.
53. Ron Kessler, 'Expert Discounts RFK 2nd Gun Theory', *The Washington Post*, 19 December 1974.
54. Frank Buckley, 'Vincent DiPierro, RFK Assassination Witness', *KTLA*, 5, 3 January 2018, https://ktla.com/podcasts/frank-buckley-interviews/vincent-dipierro-rfk-assassination-witness/?share=email.
55. Moldea, *Killing of Robert Kennedy*, 201. See also Moldea's fiftieth anniversary edition of *The Killing of Robert Kennedy*, 'The Cesar Polygraph Test', 216–24.
56. See Ayton, *Forgotten Terrorist*, Moldea, *The Killing of Robert Kennedy* and Mel Ayton, 'The Robert Kennedy Assassination – The Final Truth', *Crime Magazine*, 19 March 2021, http://crimemagazine.com/robert-kennedy-assassination---final-truth
57. Rush, *Confessions of an Ex-Secret Service Agent*, 56.
58. Petro, *Standing Next to History*, 22.
59. David Greenberg, 'After the Assassination: How Gene McCarthy's Response to Bobby Kennedy's Murder Crippled the Democrats', *Slate*, 4 June 2008.

60. Dominic Sandbrook, *Eugene McCarthy: The Rise and Fall of Postwar American Liberalism* (Foder's Travel Publications, 2005), 206. See also Kathleen Hughes, *The Monk's Tale: A Biography of Geoffrey Dickmann, OSB* (Liturgical Press, 1991), 293.

Chapter 6

1. H.W. Brands, *Reagan: The Life* (Doubleday, 2015), 137.
2. Curtis Patrick, *Reagan – What Was He Really Like?*, Vol. 1 (Morgan James Publishing, 2011), 223.
3. Ibid.
4. *Newsweek*, 'Safety First', 25 December 1967, 13.
5. Patrick, *Reagan*, Vol. 1, 39. Author's Note: Later, in 1978, Van Court came under FBI investigation for his relationship with a convicted con man that had ties to organised crime. However, he remained friends with Reagan and visited the Reagan ranch after being invited to join the annual Reagan ranch picnic. Justice Department officials eventually approved his appointment as a federal marshal (US Congress, Nomination of Edwin Meese III – Hearings before the Judiciary Committee).
6. *San Bernardino Sun*, 'M.P. Guard Officials', 30 October 1970, 2.
7. Curtis Patrick, *Reagan – What Was He Really Like?*, Vol. 2 (Morgan James Publishing, 2018), 24.
8. Michael A. Endicott, *Walking with the President – Stories Inside the Perimeter* (Booksurge Publishing, 2009), 42.
9. Ronald Reagan, *An American Life – The Autobiography* (Threshold Editions, 2011), 172.
10. Patrick, *Reagan*, Vol. 2, 224.
11. Reagan, *An American Life*, 173.
12. Scheer, *Playing President*, 163.
13. Reagan, *An American Life*, 45.
14. *Courier Herald*, 'Buckley resident relives years with Secret Service', 6 July 2009.
15. Endicott, *Walking with the President*, 50. Author's Note: According to a later interview with Endicott the agent said the attackers actually lit the bombs and threw one of them before escaping. 'As it turned out, they tried to firebomb Reagan's home with all manner of weapons. I'll never forget it. I was on the point and I saw one of the attackers in the car lighting a Molotov cocktail and then tossing it toward the house. Those were the kind of times that we lived in and lived through,' he said. Reagan said the attackers were beneath his window '. . . in the act of lighting a Molotov cocktail'.
16. Ibid.
17. Endicott, *Walking with the President*, 54.
18. Ibid.
19. Reagan, *An American Life*, 175.
20. Patrick, *Reagan*, Vol. 2, 224.
21. *San Bernardino Sun*, 'Guard Protecting State Officials', 30 October 1970, 1.
22. Alex Ray, *Hired Gun: A Political Odyssey* (University Press of America, 2008), 63.
23. Kieran K. Skinner (ed.), *Reagan In His Own Hand* (Free Press, 2001), Introduction.
24. *C-Span*, 'Mr. LeBlanc talked about his friendship with Ronald Reagan and his work on the Reagan ranch', 5 December 1999, https://www.c-span.org/person/?dennisleblanc.

25. Christy Armstrong, 'Mason shares experiences as guard of four presidents', *Cleveland Banner*, 2 April 2016, http://clevelandbanner.com/stories/mason-shares-experiencesas-guard-of-four-presidents,31314.
26. John R. Barletta, *Riding With Reagan – From the White House to the Ranch* (Citadel Press, 2005), 128.
27. *C-Span*, 'Mr. LeBlanc talked about his friendship with Ronald Reagan and his work on the Reagan ranch'.
28. Petro, *Standing Next to History*, 56.
29. Rush, *Confessions of an Ex-Secret Service Agent*, 117.
30. Petro, *Standing Next to History*, 66.
31. Rush, *Confessions of an Ex-Secret Service Agent*, 117.
32. Ibid., 123.
33. Ronald Kessler, 'Secret Service Says President Reagan Was Sharp', *Newsmax*, 27 January 2011, https://www.newsmax.com/ronaldkessler/secret-service-president-ronaldreagan/2011/01/27/id/384169/.
34. *TIME*, 'Former Reagan Aide Says He Saw a Gun in the President's Briefcase', https://time.com/3923183/ronald-reagan-gun/.
35. Barletta, *Riding With Regan*, 199.
36. Ibid., 177.
37. *TIME*, 'Former Reagan Aide Says He Saw a Gun in the President's Briefcase'.
38. Rush, *Confessions of an Ex-Secret Service Agent*, 117.
39. *The Evening Independent*, 'Candidates Keep Secret Service "Over-Extended"', 21 November 1975, 3A.
40. Rick Pearlstein, *The Invisible Bridge* (Simon & Schuster, 2015), 550.
41. Justia.com, United States of America v. Michael Lance Carvin, July 18, 1977, https://law.justia.com/cases/federal/appellate-courts/F2/555/1303/184340/.
42. *The Evening Independent*, 'Police Say Carvin Jumped Bond', 4 June 1976, 3A.
43. *Spartanburg Herald-Journal*, 'Stalker Gets Heavy Jail Time for Threats', 16 January 1999, A2.
44. Pearlstein, *The Invisible Bridge*, 550.
45. Craig Shirley, *Reagan's Revolution* (Thomas Nelson Publishers, 2009), 97.
46. Ibid.
47. Gale Holland, 'Jerry Parr, Secret Service agent credited with saving President Reagan's life, dies at 85', *Los Angeles Times*, 9 October 2015.
48. Ibid.
49. Courtney Jolley, 'As Secret Service agent, alumnus may have saved Reagan', Loyola.edu, 22 July 2011, https://www.loyola.edu/explore/magazine/stories/2011/alumnus-may-have-saved-reagan.
50. Holland, 'Jerry Parr, Secret Service agent credited with saving President Reagan's life, dies at 85'.
51. Ronald Kessler, 'Secret Service Enabled Reagan Shooting', *The Washington Times*, 9 October 2014.
52. *The Modesto Bee*, 'Secret Service Worried About "Copycat" Threats', 7 April 1981, A6.
53. Rush, *Confessions of an Ex-Secret Service Agent*, 232.
54. Peter Baker, 'Starr vs. Secret Service: Two Definitions of Duty', *The Washington Post*, 15 May 1998, page A1.

55. Justia.com, United States of America v. Mary Frances Carrier, Decided 20 May 1983, https://law.justia.com/cases/federal/appellate-courts/F2/672/300/330941/.
56. Ayton, *Hunting the President*.
57. Scott MacFarlane, 'Officials Failed to Assess Potential Risk Posed by Freed Reagan Shooter John Hinckley', *NBC News*, 10 May 2018, https://www.nbcwashington.com/news/local/officials-failed-to-conduct-risk-assessment-of-freed-reagan-shooter-john-hinckley/2028507/.

Chapter 7

1. Tumbit.com, 'Road Trip: Richard Nixon's Election Day Escape', 14 March 2004, https://deadpresidents.tumblr.com/post/79570845554/road-trip-richard-nixons-election-day-escape.
2. U.E. Baughman, *Secret Service Chief* (Harper and Brothers, 1961), 245.
3. Baughman, *Secret Service Chief*, 244–5.
4. Ibid., 244.
5. Youngblood, *20 Years in the Secret Service*, 251.
6. *The National Herald*, 'Secret Service Agent Giannoules Guarded JFK on Eve of Assassination'.
7. Youngblood, *20 Years in the Secret Service*, 249.
8. Ibid., 250.
9. Vince Devlin, 'Former Secret Service agent kept watch over presidents and their families', *The Missoulian*, 29 April 2007.
10. *Washington Independent Review of Books*, Clint Hill with Lisa McCubbin, *Five Presidents: My Extraordinary Journey with Eisenhower, Kennedy, Johnson, Nixon, and Ford*, reviewed by Joseph A. Esposito, 13 June 2016, http://www.washingtonindependentreviewofbooks.com/index.php/bookreview/five-presidents-my-extraordinary-journey-with-eisenhower-kennedy-johnson-ni.
11. Hill, *Five Presidents*, 332.
12. Ibid., 344.
13. Gerald R. Ford Oral History Project, Larry Buendorf, 22 June 2010, https://geraldrfordfoundation.org/centennial-docs/oralhistory/wp-content/uploads/2013/05/Larry-Buendorf-.pdf.
14. Bill Gulley, *Breaking Cover* (Simon & Schuster, 1980), 238.
15. McCarthy, *Protecting the President*, 250.
16. Summers, *Arrogance of Power*, 277.
17. Merriman Smith, 'Observant Reporter Finds GOPers In Miami', *Madera Daily Tribune*, 30 July 1968, 3.
18. Peter Sheridan, 'Five presidents and me: The story of a US secret service agent', *Daily Express*, 30 May 2016.
19. Rush, *Confessions of an Ex-Secret Service Agent*, 42.
20. Summers, *Arrogance of Power*, 246.
21. Ronald Kessler, *The First Family Detail* (Crown Forum, 2014), 50.
22. *Esquire*, '13 Intimate Stories About U.S. Presidents, "Deep Throat? I have no idea"', by Esquire Editors, 10 October 2015, https://www.esquire.com/news-politics/a38229/presidents-1015/.
23. Seymour M. Hersh, *Reporter* (Allen Lane, 2018), 203.
24. Youngblood, *20 Years in the Secret Service*, 235.

25. The Miller Center Foundation and the Edward M. Kennedy Institute for the United States Senate, Interview with George McGovern, 2016, https://www.emkinstitute.org/resources/george-mcgovern.

26. Christy Armstrong, 'Mason shares experiences as guard of four presidents', *Cleveland Daily Banner*.

27. Endicott, *Walking with the President*, 376.

28. Rush, *Confessions of an Ex-Secret Service Agent*, 185.

29. Kate Andersen Brower, *The Residence – Inside the Private World of the White House* (Harper Paperbacks, 2016), 156.

30. *New York Post*, 'Racy New Tell All Uncovers Prezes' Secret Servicing', 4.

31. Richard Nixon Presidential Library and Museum, Stephen Bull Oral History, https://www.nixonfoundation.org/wp-content/uploads/2019/06/Steve_Bull_Oral_History.pdf.

32. Endicott, *Walking with the President*, 494.

33. Sartore, *What it's Actually Like to Guard the President, According to Former Members of the Secret Service*.

34. Edwin Chen, 'Nixon Plot to Tie McGovern to Wallace Attack Reported', *Los Angeles Times*, 7 December 1992, https://www.latimes.com/archives/la-xpm-1992-12-07-mn-1225-story.html.

35. Summers, *Arrogance of Power*, 470.

36. Rush, *Confessions of an Ex-Secret Service Agent*, 186.

37. Richard Nixon Presidential Library and Museum, Stephen Bull Oral History, https://www.nixonlibrary.gov/sites/default/files/forresearchers/find/histories/Steve_Bull.pdf.

38. Crawford, 'In a Presidential Year, the Chief of the Secret Service Worries About Protection, Not Politics'.

39. Ben A. Franklin Special to *The New York Times*, 'Kennedy Guarded by Secret Service', 16 May 1972, https://www.nytimes.com/1972/05/16/archives/kennedy-guarded-by-secret-service-senator-kennedy-accepts-nixons-of.html.

40. *St Petersburg Times*, 'Veteran is Charged in Threat on Nixon', 12 August 1972, 1.

41. Hill, *Five Presidents*, 334.

42. Ibid., 352.

43. Fred Blumenthal, *Spiro Agnew: Best-Protected Vice President*, JFK Hood, http://jfk.hood.edu/Collection/Weisberg%20Subject%20Index%20Files/S%20Disk/Secret%20Service/Item%2007.pdf.

44. *The Times News*, 'Agnew Unhurt After his car is Bombed', 1 January 1970.

45. The Miller Center, The Presidential Recordings, Program, Richard M. Nixon, John D. Ehrlichman and H.R. 'Bob' Haldeman on 20 July 1971, https://millercenter.org/the-presidency/secret-white-house-tapes/smoking-gun.

46. Chen, 'Nixon Plot to Tie McGovern to Wallace Attack Reported'.

47. Rich Butler and staff, 'Truth or Fiction? Secret Service Agents Perspective of U.S. Presidents', 17 March 2015, https://www.truthorfiction.com/secret-service-presidents/.

48. Cimons, 'A President and His Protectors, Clinton is a challenge for the Secret Service, but agents are used to it'.

49. Parr, *In the Secret Service*, 134.

50. Ibid., 188.

51. Ibid., 138.

52. Ibid., 139.

53. *The National Herald*, 'Secret Service Agent Giannoules Guarded JFK on Eve of Assassination'.
54. *The Southeast Missourian*, 'Rude's The Mood', 4 November 1970, 6.
55. Parr, *In the Secret Service*, 137.
56. *The National Herald*, 'Secret Service Agent Giannoules Guarded JFK on Eve of Assassination'.
57. Justin P. Coffey, *Spiro Agnew and the Rise of the Republican Right* (Praeger, 2015), 206.
58. Endicott, *Walking with the President*, 131.
59. Spiro T. Agnew, *Go Quietly . . . or Else* (William Morrow, 1980), 186–92.
60. Haaretz.com, 'The late Vice President Spiro Agnew requested money in 1980 from Saudi Arabia to "continue to fight" against U.S. Zionists', 22 February 2019, https://www.haaretz.com/us-news/former-vp-spiro-agnew-in-1980-asked-saudi-leader-for-money-to-fight-us-zionists-1.6959767.
61. Rush, *Confessions of an Ex-Secret Service* Agent, 58.
62. Agnew, *Go Quietly . . . or Else*, 164.
63. *The Chicago Herald*, 'Threat to Kill Spiro Agnew', 16 January 1970, 1.
64. The FBI Files, The Vault, 'Alleged Plot to Assassinate Vice President Agnew, East Side Crazies, New York City, 10 October 1970', https://vault.fbi.gov/Spiro%20Agnew.
65. The FBI Files, The Vault, 'Possible Shots Fired, Rancho Mirage, California; Possible Assault of Vice President of the United States, 1 October 1973', https://vault.fbi.gov/Spiro%20Agnew.
66. The FBI Files, 'Unsub: Attempt to Assault Vice President Spiro Agnew During Demonstration, Columbus, Ohio, 9 May 1972', https://vault.fbi.gov/Spiro%20Agnew.
67. The FBI Files, The Vault, 'Threat Against Vice President, 30 September 1973', https://vault.fbi.gov/Spiro%20Agnew.
68. The FBI Files, The Vault, 'Threat Against the Former Vice President, 25 January 1974', https://vault.fbi.gov/Spiro%20Agnew.
69. The FBI Files, 'Unsubs: Camilla Hall II Symbionese Liberation Army, Richard Nixon et al, 16 July 1974', https://vault.fbi.gov/Spiro%20Agnew.
70. Ronald Kessler, *Inside Congress* (Gallery Books, 2013), 233.

Chapter 8

1. Alex Cohen, *RFK Assassination Sparked Secret Service Change*, NPR, 4 June 2008, https://choice.npr.org/index.html?origin=https://www.npr.org/templates/story/story.php?storyId=91122836.
2. Linda Greenhouse, 'For Nearly a Generation Nelson Rockefeller Held the Reins of New York State', *New York Times*, 28 January 1979.
3. *Newsweek*, 'Safety First', 25 December 1967, 13.
4. *San Bernardino Sun*, Vol. 74, 'L.A. Tightens Security For Rocky's Visit Today', 12 June 1968, https://cdnc.ucr.edu/?a=d&d=SBS19680612.1.9&srpos=6&e=-------en--20--1--txt-txIN-Rockefeller%2c+SECRET+SERVICE-------1.
5. Holmes Alexander, 'How Secret Service Keeps Tabs on Rocky', *Desert Sun*, 24 June 1968, 12.
6. FBI Files, 'FBI Memo, To Director, Albany, Little Rock, Los Angeles, New York, Threat Against Rockefeller Family, 28 February 1967', https://altgov2.org/wp-content/uploads/fbi_posse-comitatus1of2.pdf.

7. The FBI Files, 'Memo Acting, Director FBI To US Secret Service, Threat Against The President, 13 June 1973', https://altgov2.org/wp-content/uploads/fbi_posse-comitatus1of2.pdf.
8. Eugene V. Gallagher and Michael Ashcraft (eds), *Introduction to New and Alternative Religions in African American Diaspora* (Greenwood, 2006), 183.
9. Rush, *Confessions of an Ex-Secret Service Agent*, 22.
10. United States Congress, *Review of Secret Service Protective Measures*, 118.
11. Cohen, 'RFK Assassination Sparked Secret Service Change', 4 June 2008.
12. Justia.com, US Court of Appeals for the Sixth Circuit, United States v Carlos Alberto Valle, Dec. 9, 1982, https://law.justia.com/cases/federal/appellate-courts/F2/697/152/11021/.
13. George Lardner, 'Nixon Ordered Spy Placed in Sen. Kennedy's Secret Service Detail', *The Washington Post*, 8 February 1997, A6.
14. Cohen, 'RFK Assassination Sparked Secret Service Change'.
15. *Business Insider*, 'Woodward and Bernstein Reveal Shocking New Details About Richard Nixon', 12 January 1976, 40.
16. *The Philadelphia Enquirer*, 'Muskie's Tears How the Press' Perception Can Change History', 8 March 1987.
17. Ronald Kessler, *Inside the White House* (Pocket Books, 1995), 76.
18. United States Congress, *Review of Secret Service Protective Measures*, 53.
19. Ibid., 59.
20. FBI Files, The Vault, 'Muskie Threats', www.archive.org/details/EdmundMuskie.
21. FBI Files, The Vault, 'Threat to Assassinate Senator Edmund Muskie and Governor George Wallace by the Black Military Underground for Revolutionary Action, From FBI Boston to FBI Director, 29 February 1972', www.archive.org/details/EdmundMuskie.
22. The Miller Center Foundation and the Edward M. Kennedy Institute for the United States Senate, Interview with George McGovern, 2016.
23. Ed Pilkington, 'The White House Losers', *The Guardian*, 29 March 2008, https://www.theguardian.com/politics/2008/mar/29/uselections2008.usa.
24. United States Congress, *Review of Secret Service Protective Measures*, 55.
25. Ibid., 56.
26. Walter Rugaber, 'Secret Service Says Aide Gave Out McGovern Data', *The New York Times*, 17 August 1973.
27. The Miller Center Foundation and the Edward M. Kennedy Institute for the United States Senate, Interview with George McGovern, 2016.
28. Justin William Moyer, 'In Confession to Historian George McGovern Revealed He Had a Secret Child', *Democratic Underground*, 30 July 2015, https://upload.democraticunderground.com/10141162165.
29. Bob Collins, 'Nixon Knew of McGovern "Illegitimate" Child', *MPR News*, 27 July 2015, https://www.mprnews.org/story/2015/07/27/fbi-files-nixon-knew-of-mcgovern-illegitimate-child.
30. Rush, *Confessions of an Ex-Secret Service Agent*, 63.
31. Ibid., 62.
32. John Meroney, 'How to elect a president: Jimmy Carter, two South Georgia political novices, and the unpredictable road to the White House', *Atlantic Magazine*, 9 March 2020, https://www.atlantamagazine.com/great-reads/how-to-elect-a-president-jimmy-carter-two-south-georgia-political-novices-and-the-unpredictable-road-to-the-white-house/.
33. Endicott, *Walking with the President*, 129.

34. Ibid., 131.
35. FBI Files, The Vault, 'Sargent Shriver', https://vault.fbi.gov/robert-sargent-shriver-jr.
36. FBI Files, The Vault, 'Senator McGovern Alleged Threat Against Member of Congress, 10 February 1973, From Minneapolis, to Acting Director', https://www.scribd.com/doc/272615863/Threats-to-McGovern-in-1972-McGovern-FBI-files.
37. FBI Files, 'Teletype NY Plains to Acting Director, Unidentified Male Voice, Threat To Kill Senator George S McGovern at Americana Hotel NYC 4 October 1972, Congressional Assassination Statute, 11 October 1972', https://www.scribd.com/doc/272615863/Threats-to-McGovern-in-1972-McGovern-FBI-filesn.
38. FBI Files, The Vault, 'FBI Atlanta, 16 November 1972, Threat Against Presidential Candidate George S McGovern, 8 November 1972', https://www.scribd.com/doc/272615863/Threats-to-McGovern-in-1972-McGovern-FBI-files.
39. FBI Files, The Vault, 'Unsub: Threat to Assassinate Senator George S McGovern, Protection of Presidential Candidates, To: Acting Director FBI From Oklahoma City FBI, 16 May 1972', https://www.scribd.com/doc/272615863/Threats-to-McGovern-in-1972-McGovern-FBI-files.
40. *The Sun*, 'Arrests on Gun Charges Made at McGovern Hotel', 15 July 1972, 1.
41. FBI Files, The Vault, 'FBI Philadelphia 20 October 1972 Unknown Subject, Threat to Bomb Senator George S McGovern, Cheney State College, Cheney, Pennsylvania, 19 October 1972', https://www.scribd.com/doc/272615863/Threats-to-McGovern-in-1972-McGovern-FBI-files.
42. Michael Klinski, 'Threats in N.C.: McGovern FBI files', *Scribd*, 26 July 2015, https://www.scribd.com/doc/272616412/Threat-in-1972-McGovern-FBI-files.
43. FBI Files, 'Threats to Senator George McGovern', https://www.scribd.com/doc/272615863/Threats-to-McGovern-in-1972-McGovern-FBI-files.
44. FBI Files, The Vault, 'Memo from Mr B.H. Cooke to Mr Gallagher Information Concerning Alleged Plot to Assassinate Senator George S McGovern Greensboro North Carolina, 19 October 1975, 20 October 1975', https://www.scribd.com/doc/272615863/Threats-to-McGovern-in-1972-McGovern-FBI-files.
45. The Edward M. Kennedy Institute for the United States Senate, Interview with George McGovern, 2016.

Chapter 9

1. Jack Nelson, *Scoop: The Evolution of a Southern Reporter* (University Press of Mississippi, 2012), 131.
2. Dan T. Carter, *The Politics of Rage* (LSU press, 2000), 316.
3. Brian Lyman, '"Stand up for America" – George Wallace's chaotic, prophetic campaign', *USA Today*, 15 December 2019, https://eu.usatoday.com/story/news/nation-now/1968-project/2018/08/16/stand-up-america-george-wallaces-chaotic-prophetic-campaign/961043002/.
4. 'Safety First', *Newsweek*, 25 December 1967, 13.
5. Nelson, *Scoop*, 130.
6. Merriman Smith, 'Observant Reporter Finds GOPers in Miami', *Madera Daily Tribune*, 30 July 1968, 3.
7. Philip Shabecoff, 'Bodyguard a Wallace Volunteer and U.S. Secret Agent Also Shot', *The New York Times*, 16 May 1972.
8. Nelson, *Scoop*, 130.
9. Ibid.
10. Carter, *Politics of Rage*, 340.

11. Shabecoff, 'Bodyguard a Wallace Volunteer and U.S. Secret Agent Also Shot'.
12. Deseret.com, 'Shooter of Wallace in 1972 leaves prison, shuns publicity', 10 November, 2007, https://www.deseret.com/2007/11/10/20052690/shooter-of-wallace-in-1972-leaves-prison-shuns-publicity.
13. Ben A. Franklin, 'Kennedy Guarded by Secret Service', *The New York Times*, 16 May 1972.
14. Stephan Lesher, *George Wallace – American Populist, Addison Wesley* (Addison Wesley, 1994), 479.
15. Ibid., 480.
16. Rush, *Confessions of an Ex-Secret Service Agent*, 47.
17. Wikipedia, Arthur Bremer's diary, March/early April 1972, https://en.wikipedia.org/wiki/An_Assassin%27s_Diary.
18. Ed Hinman, *'What Kim Jong Un's Crazy Elite Bodyguards Teach Us About Threat Deterrence'*, *Task and Purpose*, 15 May 2018, https://taskandpurpose.com/opinion/kim-jong-uns-crazy-elite-bodyguards-teach-us-threat-deterrence/.
19. Homer Bigart, 'Bremer Diary Details Effort to Kill Nixon, 4 August, *The New York Times*, 1972.
20. Justia.com, Bremer v. State of Maryland, July 6, 1973. https://law.justia.com/cases/maryland/court-of-special-appeals/1973/583-september-term-1972-0.html.
21. Ronald Kessler, *In the President's Secret Service – Behind the Scenes with Agents in the Line of Fire and the Presidents They Protect* (Crown Publishers, 2009), 22.
22. Aaron Kraut, 'George Wallace's assassination attempt: FBI agent reflects, 40 years later', *The Washington Post*, 9 May 2012.
23. Lawrence Meyer, 'Gun Still Firing as Bystander Wrestled Suspect to the Ground', *The Washington Post*, 16 May 1972, Section A, p. 1.
24. Leada Gore, 'George Wallace shot 45 years ago today: Where are they now? Arthur Bremer, Cornelia Wallace', Al.com, 15 May 2017, https://www.al.com/news/2017/05/george_wallace_assassination_a.html.
25. Lawrence Meyer, 'Gun Still Firing as Bystander Wrestled Suspect to the Ground'.
26. Justia.com, Bremer v. State of Maryland, July 6, 1973.
27. Kraut, 'George Wallace's assassination'.
28. Luke A. Nichter, 'Caught on Tape: The White House Reaction to the Shooting of Alabama Governor and Democratic Presidential Candidate George Wallace', History News Network, http://historynewsnetwork.org/articles/45104.html.
29. Justia.com, Bremer v. State of Maryland, July 6, 1973.
30. Catherine Skipp, 'Arthur Bremer is Alone', *Newsweek*, 10 November 2007.
31. David Montgomery, 'Arthur Bremer Shot George Wallace to be Famous. A Search for Who He is Today', *The Washington Post*, 3 December 2015.
32. *San Bernardino Sun*, untitled, 28 April 1974, 124.
33. Nelson, *Scoop*, 134.
34. Kraut, 'George Wallace's assassination attempt: FBI agent reflects, 40 years late'.
35. Drummond Ayres Jr, 'Wallace Isolated by Tight Security', *New York Times*, 1 February 1976.
36. Gore, 'George Wallace shot 45 years ago today: Where are they now? Arthur Bremer, Cornelia Wallace'.
37. AP News, 'Trooper Shot With Wallace Dies in Suicide', 16 December 1989.
38. Montgomery, 'Arthur Bremer Shot George Wallace to be Famous. A Search for Who He is Today'.
39. Nelson, *Scoop*, 137.

Chapter 10

1. Gilbert King, 'A Halloween Massacre at the White House', Smithsonian.com, 25 October 2012, https://www.smithsonianmag.com/history/a-halloween-massacre-at-the-white-house-92668509/.
2. Petro, *Standing Next to History*, 105.
3. Peter Sheridan, 'Five presidents and me: The story of a US secret service agent', *Daily Express*, 30 May 2016.
4. Rush, *Confessions of an Ex-Secret Service Agent*, 122.
5. Gerald R. Ford Oral History Project, Larry Buendorf Interviewed by Richard Norton Smith, 22 June 2010, https://geraldrfordfoundation.org/centennial-docs/oralhistory/wp-content/uploads/2013/05/Larry-Buendorf-.pdf.
6. Ibid.
7. Matt Bai, *The Front Runner* (HarperCollins, 2019), 28.
8. Clare Crawford, 'In a Presidential Year, the Chief of the Secret Service Worries About Protection, Not Politics', *People* magazine, 22 March 1976.
9. Gerald R. Ford Oral History Project Larry Buendorf Interviewed by Richard Norton Smith 22 June 2010.
10. Ibid.
11. Justia.com, United States of America v. Sara Jane Moore, December 16, 1975, https://law.justia.com/cases/federal/appellate-courts/F2/599/310/114403/.
12. Ibid.
13. *Spartanburg Herald-Journal*, 'Sara Moore Hoped to Expose System', 8 May 1976, 1.
14. *TIME*, 'Part of the Job', 13 April 1981, 23.
15. US Senate, Inquiry into the Matter of Billy Carter and Libya, 6 August 1980, https://www.intelligence.senate.gov/sites/default/files/961015.pdf.
16. *New York* magazine, Vol. 5 (1972), p. 49.
17. Grant Hayter-Menzies, *Lillian Carter – A Compassionate Life* (McFarland, 2014), 153.
18. John Meroney, 'How to elect a president: Jimmy Carter, two South Georgia political novices, and the unpredictable road to the White House', *Atlantic Magazine*, 9 March 2020.
19. The Miller Center Foundation, Interview with Jimmy Carter, 2003, https://miller-center.org/the-presidency/presidential-oral-histories/jimmy-carter.
20. Hayter-Menzies, *Lillian Carter*.
21. Rush, *Confessions of an Ex-Secret Service Agent*, 124.
22. *San Bernardino Sun*, 'Abortion Foes Jostle Carter', 8 September 1976.
23. Cimons, 'President and His Protectors: Clinton is a challenge for the Secret Service, but agents are used to it'.
24. Rush, *Confessions of an Ex-Secret Service Agent*, 111.
25. University of Georgia, James Earl 'Chip' Carter III interviewed by Bob Short, 23 June 2008, http://ohms.libs.uga.edu/viewer.php?cachefile=russell/RBRL220ROGP-036.xml.
26. Parr, *In the Secret Service*, 200.
27. Harris, 'Georgia Baptist Jim Cool recalls years with Secret Service'.
28. Rush, *Confessions of an Ex-Secret Service Agent*, 129.
29. Jimmy Carter Library, Exit Interview with Sylvia Ehrhardt, 2 January 1980, https://www.jimmycarterlibrary.gov/assets/documents/oral_histories/exit_interviews/Ehrhardt.pdf.
30. Michael McNutt, 'Former Presidential Bodyguard Glad to be Home', *The Oklahoman*, 22 September 1985.

31. Rush, *Confessions of an Ex-Secret Service Agent*, 127.
32. Ibid., 40.
33. McNutt, 'Former Presidential Bodyguard Glad to be Home'.
34. Kessler, *In the President's Secret Service*, 70.
35. Kessler, *First Family Detail*, 87.
36. Rush, *Confessions of an Ex-Secret Service Agent*, 124.
37. Gerald Ford Foundation, Oral History, Larry Buendorf, Interviewed by Richard Norton Smith, 22 June 2010.
38. Jim Byron, 'Town Car Diplomacy – 40 Years Ago', Richard Nixon Foundation, 26 June 2013, https://www.nixonfoundation.org/2013/06/town-car-diplomacy-40-years-ago/.
39. BBC News, 'Clinton drops nuclear football', 26 April 1999, http://news.bbc.co.uk/1/hi/world/americas/328442.stm.
40. Rush, *Confessions of an Ex-Secret Service Agent*, 126.
41. McCarthy, *Protecting the President*, 170.
42. Rush, *Confessions of an Ex-Secret Service Agent*, 150.
43. Scheer, *Playing President*, 92.
44. Jonathan Alter, *His Very Best – Jimmy Carter, A Life* (Simon & Schuster, 2020), 61.
45. Jody Powell, *The Other Side of the Story* (William Morrow, 1986), 207.
46. Scheer, *Playing President*, 60.
47. Parr, *In the Secret Service*, 201.
48. Jimmy Carter, *White House Diary* (Picador, 2011), 306.
49. Alter, *His Very Best*, 322.
50. Dan Emmett, *I Am A Secret Service Agent* (St Martin's Press, 2017), 198.
51. Carter, *White House Diary*, 307.
52. Scheer, *Playing President*, 93.
53. Paul Bedard, 'Book: Jimmy Carter targeted by US and foreign assassins', *Washington Examiner*, 24 July 2013.
54. Coursera, 'Jimmy Carter – Part Two, The Kennedy Half-Century', University of Virginia, https://www.coursera.org/lecture/kennedy/president-jimmy-carter-part-two-WVI5J.
55. See Ayton, *Hunting the President*, Chapter 8, 'Deacon'.
56. Del Quentin Wilber, *Rawhide Down* (Picador, 2012), 70.
57. Rush, *Confessions of an Ex-Secret Service Agent*, 205.
58. Ibid., 251.
59. James W. Clarke, *On Being Mad or Merely Angry: John W. Hinckley Jr and Other Dangerous People* (Princeton University Press, 1990), 41.
60. Parr, *In the Secret Service*, 209.
61. Jimmy Carter Library, President Carter, Chief Agent Bill Bush Plains Secret Service Detail Oral History interview, 6 December 1990, https://www.jimmycarterlibrary.gov/research/oral_histories.

Chapter 11

1. Edward Klein, *Ted Kennedy – The Dream That Never Died* (Three Rivers Press, 2010), 77.
2. David Lester, *Good Ted, Bad Ted: The Two Faces of Edward Kennedy* (Citadel Press, 1993), 199.
3. Jules Witcover, *Marathon* (Viking Press, 1977), 123.
4. Burton Hersh, *Shadow President* (Steerforth Press, 1997), 7.

5. Lester, *Good Ted, Bad Ted*, 199.
6. Klein, *Ted Kennedy*, 132.
7. Randy Taraborrelli, *After Camelot* (Grand Central Publishing, 2012), 231.
8. Miller Center, Presidential Oral Histories, Edward M. Kennedy Histories, Melody Miller Oral History, July 2008, https://millercenter.org/the-presidency/presidential-oral-histories/melody-miller-oral-history-072008.
9. *The Kennedys – A Fatal Ambition*, produced by Elen Capurro, Executive producer Jeff Anderson, Viacom Int. Studios Production for Channel 5, 2020.
10. Lester, *Good Ted, Bad Ted*, 188.
11. Miller Center, Presidential Oral Histories, Edward M. Kennedy Histories, Melody Miller Oral History, July 2008, https://millercenter.org/the-presidency/presidential-oral-histories/melody-miller-oral-history-072008.
12. Hersh, *Shadow President*, 7.
13. Saunders, *Torn Lace Curtain*, with James Southwood, 336.
14. *Newsweek*, 'Snow Job?', 21 April 1969, 8.
15. See Mel Ayton, 'What's Wrong with "Chappaquiddick" the Movie?', *History News Network*, 9 April 2018.
16. Gabler, *Catching the Wind*, 594.
17. Ben A. Franklin, 'Kennedy Guarded by Secret Service', *The New York Times*, 16 May 1972.
18. *'Teddy': In His Own Words*, http://nixontapes.org/emk.html.
19. Klein, *Ted Kennedy*, 120.
20. *'Teddy': In His Own Words*, http://nixontapes.org/emk.html.
21. Blaine, *Kennedy Detail*, 376.
22. Hill, *Five Presidents*, 390.
23. *TIME*, 'The Kennedy Challenge', 5 November 1979, 19.
24. *TIME*, 'Somebody's Waiting For You', 5 November 1979, 26.
25. Ibid.
26. Garry Wills, *Under God – Religion and American Politics* (Simon & Schuster, 1991), 180.
27. Craig Shirley, *Rendezvous with Destiny* (Intercollegiate Studies Institute, 2014).
28. Richard Burke, *The Senator* (St Martin's Press, 1992), 249.
29. Ibid., 236.
30. Klein, *Ted Kennedy*, 163.
31. Emmett, *I am a Secret Service Agent*, 72.
32. Ibid.,
33. Ibid., 79.
34. Miller Center, Melody Miller Oral History, July 2008, https://millercenter.org/the-presidency/presidential-oral-histories/melody-miller-oral-history-072008.
35. FBI Files, The Vault, 'Senator Edward Moore "Ted" Kennedy', https://vault.fbi.gov/Senator%20Edward%20Kennedy and Newsweek, Another Kennedy Death Threat, 24 August 1981, 8.
36. Miller Center, Presidential Oral Histories, Edward M. Kennedy Histories, Melody Miller Oral History, July 2008, https://millercenter.org/the-presidency/presidential-oral-histories/melody-miller-oral-history-072008.
37. Ibid.
38. FBI Files, The Vault, 'US Senate, Letter from Edward Kennedy to FBI Director Clarence M. Kelley, 27 September 1974', https://vault.fbi.gov/Senator%20Edward%20Kennedy).

39. Miller Center, Presidential Oral Histories, Edward M. Kennedy Histories, Melody Miller Oral History, July 2008, https://millercenter.org/the-presidency/presidential-oral-histories/melody-miller-oral-history-072008.
40. Burke, *Senator*, 194.
41. Burton Hersh, *Ted Kennedy – An Intimate Biography* (Counterpoint, 2011), 443.
42. FBI Files, The Vault, 'FBI Memo From M.A. Jones to Mr Bishop 6 August 1968', https://vault.fbi.gov/Senator%20Edward%20Kennedy.
43. Miller Center Melody Miller Oral History, July 2008.
44. Hersh, *Ted Kennedy*, 443.
45. Miller Center, Melody Miller Oral History, July 2008.
46. Ibid.
47. B. Drummond Ayres Jr, 'Woman Wielding a Hunting Knife Subdued in Kennedy Senate Office', *The New York Times*, 29 November 1979, https://www.nytimes.com/1979/11/29/archives/woman-wielding-a-hunting-knife-subdued-in-kennedy-senate-office-she.html.
48. Justia.com, Osgood v. District of Columbia, July 5, 1983, https://law.justia.com/cases/federal/district-courts/FSupp/567/1026/1454401/.
49. Lester, *Good Ted, Bad Ted*, 197.
50. Kessler, *Inside Congress*, 19.
51. *The Independent*, 'A hero for his time: The fall and rise of Edward Kennedy', 27 August 2009, https://www.independent.co.uk/news/people/profiles/a-hero-for-his-time-the-fall-and-rise-of-edward-kennedy-1777659.html. Author's Note: I met Senator Kennedy on two occasions at the Capitol Building in Washington DC, in August 1989 and August 1994. I was introduced to the Senator by a mutual friend, a Congressional police officer. For the first meeting Kennedy was outgoing, ebullient and friendly, his booming voice echoing around the Senate Reception Room. However, after I mentioned his brothers Jack and Bobby he looked down, lost in his thoughts and unable to respond to my comments. He seemed one moment to be full of life, smiling and gregarious, but the next to be transported somewhere else and lost in his own thoughts. I instantly realised the impact of my words. I thought of the funerals he had attended and of the hundreds if not thousands of people who had mentioned his brothers. Books, television documentaries, films and magazines must have brought it all back, forcing him to relive the many tragedies in his life. It was quite evident that the suffering had not abated and had become a constant presence in his life.

Chapter 12

1. American Free Press, 'Why Martin Luther King Distrusted Jesse Jackson', 26 February 2018, https://americanfreepress.net/why-martin-luther-king-distrusted-jesse-jackson/.
2. Ibid.
3. Lance Michael Young, 'Creating community through symbolic discourse: An analysis of Jesse Jackson Jesse Jackson's rhetoric at the Democratic National Conventions, 1984–2000', University of Nevada, Las Vegas, 1 January 2003, https://digitalscholarship.unlv.edu/cgi/viewcontent.cgi?article=2522&context=rtds.
4. R. Shipp, 'Muslim From Chicago Known for Fiery Views, *New York Times*, 17 April 1984, https://www.nytimes.com/1984/04/17/us/muslim-from-chicago-known-for-fiery-views.html.
5. Roger Bruns, *Jesse Jackson – A Biography* (Greenwood, 2005), 80.
6. Ibid., 79.

7. Kenneth R. Timmerman, *Shakedown: Exposing the Real Jesse Jackson* (Regnery Publishing, 2002), 167.
8. Isabel Vincent and Melissa Klein, 'Diary bombshell: RFK's slams against Al Sharpton, Jesse Jackson and Gov. Cuomo', *New York Post*, 9 September 2013, https://nypost.com/2013/09/09/diary-bombshell-rfks-secret-slams-against-al-sharpton-jesse-jackson-and-gov-cuomo/.
9. Ronald Smothers, 'The Impact of Jesse Jackson', *New York Times*, 4 March 1984, https://www.nytimes.com/1984/03/04/magazine/the-impact-of-jesse-jackson.html.
10. Marshall Frady, *Jesse: The Life and Pilgrimage* (Simon & Schuster, 2006), 355.
11. GunsSaveLife.com, 'Lessons learned from Jesse Jackson, Dan Gross, Father Pfleger', 7 June 2015, http://www.gunssavelife.com/chucks-guns-protest-il-lessons-learned-from-jesse-jackson-dan-gross-father-pfleger-etc/.
12. Rush, *Confessions of an Ex-Secret Service Agent*, 281.
13. Timmerman, *Shakedown*, 163.
14. GunsSaveLife.com, 'Lessons learned from Jesse Jackson, Dan Gross, Father Pfleger'.
15. McCarthy, *Protecting the President*, 181.
16. Frady, *Jesse*, 333.
17. McCarthy, *Protecting the President*, 182.
18. Frady, *Jesse*, 334.
19. Ibid.
20. Ibid., 331.
21. Desert Sun, 'Jesse Gets First Guards', 11 November 1983, 5.
22. Frady, *Jesse*, 395.
23. Myra MacPherson, 'Jesse Jackson: The Fire and the Faith', *The Washington Post*, 22 May 1984.
24. Rosanna Greenstreet, 'Q and A The Rev. Jesse Jackson', *The Guardian*, 13 April 2012, https://www.theguardian.com/lifeandstyle/2012/apr/13/rev-jesse-jackson-us-politician.
25. UPI, 'Jackson received 311 death threats', 28 December 1984, https://www.upi.com/Archives/1984/12/28/Jackson-received-311-death-threats/5079473058000/.
26. Ibid.
27. Santa Cruz Sentinel, 'Jackson Loses Secret Service', 22 July 1984, A7, https://cdnc.ucr.edu/?a=d&d=SCS19840722.1.7&srpos=172&e=-------en--20--161--txt-txIN-PRESIDENTIAL+CANDIDATES%2c+SECRET+SERVICE-------1.
28. Rita Beamish, 'Secret Service Says Jackson Doesn't Think "Pontiac" Code is Racist', 24 June 1984, *AP*, https://apnews.com/ff325bb8163ec60d77cafdc26141e27d).
29. Frady, *Jesse*, 394.
30. Ibid., 395.
31. Justia.com, United States of America v. Londell Williams, US Court of Appeals for the Eighth Circuit, Decided July 20, 1989, https://law.justia.com/cases/federal/appellate-courts/F2/879/454/438560/.
32. James Coates, 'Missouri Pair Indicted on Threat to Jackson', *Chicago Tribune*, 20 May 1988, https://www.chicagotribune.com/news/ct-xpm-1988-05-20-8803180558-story.html.
33. *Jet magazine*, 'Jackson Blames "Divisive" Climate for Recent Plot by Couple to Kill Him', 6 June 1988, 53.
34. Gwen Ifill, 'Jackson Philosophical About Threats', *The Washington Post*, 22 May 1988, https://www.washingtonpost.com/gdprconsent/?next_url=https%3a%2f%2fwww.washingtonpost.com%2farchive%2fpolitics%2f1988%2f05%2f22%2fjackson-philosophical-about-threats%2f5f9fd59e-d6c4-48cf-99f7-56ef8463fc76%2f.

35. Frady, *Jesse*, 394.
36. Royko, 'Jesse Jackson Deserves His Bodyguards'.
37. Edward Klein, *Blood Feud* (Regnery Publishing, 2014), 37.
38. Christopher Andersen, *American Evita* (William Morrow, 2004), 168.
39. Timmerman, *Shakedown*, 391.
40. Cryptome.org, Reginald G Moore, et al. V. Michael Chertoff, Secretary, US Department of Homeland Security, 5 September 2008, http://cryptome.org/usss-racism.pdf.
41. Geoffrey Gardner, 'Rev. Jesse Jackson Requests Secret Service Files', *NPR*, 15 May 2008, https://www.npr.org/sections/newsandviews/2008/05/rev_jesse_jackson_requests_sec.html.

Chapter 13

1. John Glenn, *John Glenn – A Memoir* (Bantam Books, 1999), 349.
2. R. Eric Petersen and Jennifer E. Manning, 'Violence Against Members of Congress and Their Staffs', Congressional Research Service, 17 August 2017, https://fas.org/sgp/crs/misc/R41609.pdf.
3. Richard Nixon Presidential Library and Museum, Lou Cannon Oral History, 21 February 2008, https://www.nixonlibrary.gov/sites/default/files/forresearchers/find/histories/cannon-2008-02-21.pdf).
4. John Meroney, 'How to elect a president: Jimmy Carter, two South Georgia political novices, and the unpredictable road to the White House', *Atlantic Magazine*, 9 March 2020, https://www.atlantamagazine.com/great-reads/how-to-elect-a-president-jimmy-carter-two-south-georgia-political-novices-and-the-unpredictable-road-to-the-white-house/.
5. Rush, *Confessions of an Ex-Secret Service Agent*, 62.
6. Bai, *Front Runner*, 81.
7. Becky Little, 'How Gary Hart's Sex Scandal Betrayed His Character', *History.com*, 7 November 2018, https://www.history.com/news/gary-hart-scandal-front-runner.
8. Kessler, *In the President's Secret Service*, 54.
9. Little, 'How Gary Hart's Sex Scandal Betrayed His Character'.
10. Bai, *Front Runner*, 81.
11. Little, 'How Gary Hart's Sex Scandal Betrayed His Character'.
12. Ibid.
13. Justia.com, People v. Carlson, June 24, 1986, https://law.justia.com/cases/california/court-of-appeal/3d/187/supp6.html.
14. *The New York Times*, 'Close Calls by Gary Hart', 28 August 2008, https://www.nytimes.com/2008/08/29/opinion/29hart.html.
15. Justia.com, People v. Carlson, June 24, 1986, https://law.justia.com/cases/california/court-of-appeal/3d/187/supp6.html.
16. Bai, *Front Runner*, 196–8.
17. Endicott, *Walking with the President*, 307.
18. Ibid., 303.
19. Kathleen Hennessey and Christi Parsons, 'For Secret Service, A Delicate Dance of Guards and Guarded', *Los Angeles Times*, 3 October 2014, (http://www.latimes.com/nation/la-na-obama-secret-service-20141004-story.html.
20. Court Listener, United States v. John Wesley Deshazo, January 4, 1978, https://www.courtlistener.com/opinion/350680/united-states-v-john-wesley-deshazo/.

21. *Luddington Daily News*, 'Secret Service Arrest Man Prior to Mondale Appearance', 7 November 1978, 3.
22. *Lakeland Ledger*, 'Jobless Cook Jailed in Mondale Incident', 5 October 1980, 5.
23. *Times Daily*, 'Huntsville Woman Top Secret Service Agent in State', 6 June 2000, 21.
24. Parr, *In the Secret Service*, 194.
25. Reuters, 'Texan, Charged with Threat to Kill Mondale, is Acquitted', https://www.nytimes.com/1984/10/07/us/texan-charged-with-threat-to-kill-mondale-is-acquitted.html.
26. Koplinski, *Hats in the Ring*, 224.
27. Ibid.
28. Ibid.
29. Ed Pilkington, 'The White House Losers', *The Guardian*, 29 March 2008, https://www.theguardian.com/politics/2008/mar/29/uselections2008.usa.
30. Patt Morrison, 'Michael Dukakis, Prof. Politics', *Los Angeles Times*, 30 May 2012, https://www.latimes.com/opinion/la-xpm-2012-may-30-la-oe-0530-morrison-dukakis-20120530-story.html.
31. Koplinski, *Hats in the Ring*, 225.
32. Jennifer Senior, 'The Politics of Personality Destruction', *New York* magazine, 1 June 2007, http://nymag.com/news/politics/32864/.
33. Ibid.
34. UPI, 'Secret Service rooms burglarized', 9 August 1988, https://www.upi.com/Archives/1988/08/09/Secret-Service-rooms-burglarized/7926587102400/.
35. *Fort Worth Star-Telegram*, 'Bentsen, Quayle got death threats in 1988', 5 August 2012, https://www.houstonchronicle.com/news/houston-texas/article/Bentsen-Quayle-got-death-threats-in-1988-3764558.php.
36. Rush, *Confessions of an Ex-Secret Service Agent*, 120.
37. Howard Wilkinson, 'The Best Day of Bob Dole's Life in Politics, and I was There', WVXU.org, 5 October 2018, https://www.wvxu.org/post/two-days-october-1996-when-bob-dole-had-about-all-ohio-he-could-take.
38. Michael Lewis, *Losers – The Road to Everyplace but the White House* (Vintage Books, 2000), 242.
39. Blaine Harden, 'Dole's Right-Hand Man', *The Washington Post*, 3 August 1996, https://webcache.googleusercontent.com/search?q=cache:q7L4AT9PcKkJ:https://www.washingtonpost.com/archive/politics/1996/08/03/doles-right-hand-man/1d0e297c-1535-421e-8d8e-e082e87f2ede/+&cd=2&hl=en&ct=-clnk&gl=uk.
40. Lewis, *Losers*, 161.
41. Tucker Carlson, 'The Quixotic Quest for the Perfect Dole Picture', 20 October 1996, *Washington Examiner*, https://www.washingtonexaminer.com/weekly-standard/the-quixotic-quest-for-the-perfect-dole-picture.
42. Maria La Ganga and John Broder, 'Dole's Tumble Sends His Aides Spinning', *Los Angeles Times*, 20 September 1996, https://www.latimes.com/archives/la-xpm-1996-07-27-mn-28418-story.html.
43. *Washington Examiner*, 'Let's hear it for the Secret Service', 25 August 1996, https://www.washingtonexaminer.com/weekly-standard/lets-hear-it-for-the-secret-service.
44. Jennifer Senior, 'The Politics of personality Destruction', 1 June 2007, *New York* magazine, http://nymag.com/news/politics/32864/.

45. Law Resource.org, United States Court of Appeals, David Jude Leaverton, 11 December 1987, https://law.resource.org/pub/us/case/reporter/F2/835/835. F2d.254.86-2590.html.

46. Peter Kot, 'Secret Service: Al Gore Was a Dick', *Nashville Scene*, 6 August 2009, https://www.nashvillescene.com/news/article/13029601/secret-service-al-gore-was-a-dick.

47. Kessler, *In the President's Secret Service*, 148.

48. Ibid.

49. Massie Ritsch, 'Candidates and Their Protectors Play an Endless Tug of War', *Los Angeles Times*, 23 April 2000, https://www.latimes.com/archives/la-xpm-2000-apr-23-mn-22577-story.html.

50. Matt Brown, 'Man Arrested for Allegedly Threatening President; Explosives Seized', *AP*, 26 January 1995, https://apnews.com/article/be875160283543b195dcf4fe5060425f.

51. Andrew Young, *The Politician* (Thomas Dunne Books, 2010), 119.

52. John Kerry, *Every Day is Extra* (Simon & Schuster, 2018), 288.

53. Ibid.

54. Michael Crowley, 'Kerry's Career Marked by Physical and Political Mishaps', 1 June 2015, *Politico*, https://www.politico.com/story/2015/06/john-kerrys-career-marked-by-physical-and-political-mishaps-118518.

55. *Fox News*, 'Man Arrested After E-Mail Threat to Kerry', 22 April 2004, https://www.foxnews.com/story/man-arrested-after-e-mail-threat-to-kerry.

56. Jaclyn Reiss, 'Police arrest man outside John Kerry's home', *Boston Globe*, 15 July 2013.

Chapter 14

1. Robert Shogan, *The Double-Edged Sword – How Character Makes and Ruins Presidents, From Washington to Clinton* (Westview Press, 2000), 191.

2. Kitty Kelley, *The Family – The Real Story of the Bush Dynasty* (Bantam, 2005), 507.

3. Rush, *Confessions of an Ex-Secret Service Agent*, 51.

4. US Department of Justice, 'National Institute of Justice Terrorism in the United States and the Potential Threat to Nuclear Facilities', by Bruce Hoffman, January 1986, Prepared for the US Department of Energy, https://www.ncjrs.gov/pdffiles1/Digitization/101049NCJRS.pdf.

5. Herbert S. Parmet, *George Bush – The Life of a Lone Star Yankee* (Prentice Hall, 1993), 241.

6. CBS, KSHBTV, 'Local Man Remembers Guarding Bush 41 As President', Roy Scheer, 2 December 2018, https://www.youtube.com/watch?v=1-WVEsvXeCs.

7. Ibid.

8. *Times Daily*, 3 February 1982, 2, https://news.google.com/newspapers?nid=1842&dat=19820203&id=xBMsAAAAIBAJ&sjid=cMgEAAAAIBAJ&pg=1062,321822.

9. Parmet, *George Bush*, 239.

10. Kelley, *The Family*, 353.

11. Ibid., 327.

12. Kelley, *The Family*, 376.

13. *WGN9 News*, Interview with G. Michael Verden, https://www.youtube.com/watch?v=t-kk4LMtTLww&list=PLrDCltVG9udpdNu_QHj0OMp9_G4aGtmJJ&index=3.

14. Kelley, *The Family*, 508.

15. Ibid., 509.

16. See Ayton, *Hunting the President*, 174.

17. Justia.com, United States of America, Plaintiff-appellee, v. John Spencer Daughetee Defendant-appellant, 30 F.3d 140 (9th Cir. 1994) Argued and Submitted 14 April 1994. Decided 5 Aug. 1994, https://law.justia.com/cases/federal/appellate-courts/F3/30/140/471233/.
18. United States Court of Appeals, Ninth Circuit, United States of America v. Roger Leroy Hines, Decided 20 June 1994, http://cases.justia.com/us-court-of-appeals/F3/26/1469/619449/.
19. *The Bulletin*, 'Ex-Felon Pleads Guilty to Plot Against Bush', 20 June 1992, D3.
20. *The Spokesman Review*, 'Legal Secretary Arrested Accused of Stalking Bush', 23 September 1992, A4.
21. *The Free Lance Star*, 'Woman Who Stalked Bush Sentenced', 9 January 1993, A5.
22. Scott McClellan, *What Happened: Inside the Bush White House and Washington's Culture of Deception* (PublicAffairs, 2008), 40.
23. Kelley, *The Family*, 588.
24. Ibid., 579.
25. RealChange.org, 'Bush's Skeleton Closet', http://www.realchange.org/bushjr.htm#drunk.
26. Ross Ramsay, 'A New and Improved Teflon Politician', *Texas Tribune*, 12 July 1999, https://www.texastribune.org/1999/07/12/a-new-and-improved-teflon-politician/.
27. Robert Bryce, 'The Loyal Lieutenants, Bush Applies Litmus Test of Allegiance in Choosing Inner Circle', *Austin Chronicle*, 17 March 2000, https://www.austinchronicle.com/news/2000-03-17/76395/.
28. *Summary: A Matter of Character: Summary and Review and Analysis of Ronald Kessler's Book*, BusinessNews Publishing, https://www.amazon.co.uk/Summary-Matter-Character-Analysis-Kesslers/dp/2512005275.
29. Ibid., 8.
30. Rich Monetti, 'New Rochelle's Nick Trotta Comes Home to Honor After Distinguished Career as Secret Service Agent', Vocal.media, 2017, https://vocal.media/theSwamp/new-rochelles-nick-trotta-comes-home-to-honor-after-distinguished-career-as-secret-service-agent.
31. VansOpinions, 'The Secret Service Views of Past Presidents', 12 December 2018, https://www.vansopinions.com/modules.php?name=News&file=article&sid=186.
32. Evy Poumpouras, *Becoming Bulletproof: Life Lessons from a Secret Service Agent* (Icon Books, 2020), 4.
33. *The Washington Times*, 'In role reversal, president rescues Secret Service agent', Saturday, 20 November 2004, https://www.washingtontimes.com/news/2004/nov/20/20041120-113709-8651r/.
34. Doug Thompson, 'Secret Service Agents Say Cheney Was Drunk When He Shot Lawyer', *Capitol Hill Blue*, 22 February 2006, https://www.opednews.com/articles/opedne_doug_tho_060222_secret_service_agent.htm.
35. Kris Hollington, 'All the President's Men', *Daily Mail*, 7 July 2008, http://www.dailymail.co.uk/home/moslive/article-1031210/All-The-Presidents-Men-The-unimaginable-lengths-needed-George-Bush-alive-.html#.
36. Ibid.
37. Kurt Eichenwald, *500 Days: Secrets and Lies in the Terror Wars* (Touchstone Books, 2013), 152.
38. *Fox News, Fox Across America with Jimmy Fallon*, 'Ari Fleischer Interview', Jimmy Fallon Show, 11 September 2020.
39. See Ayton, *Hunting the President*, 205–20.

40. *The South-East Missourian*, 'Buffalo Man Pleads Guilty to Threatening Bush', 10 January 2005, 3A.
41. Jessica Chasmer, 'N.Y. man arrested for allegedly threatening to kill George W. Bush', *The Washington Times*, 2 February 2014, https://m.washingtontimes.com/news/2014/feb/2/ny-man-arrested-allegedly-threatening-kill-george-/.

Chapter 15
1. Roger Simon, 'Bodyguards Cover President Like a "Suit"', *Chicago Tribune*, 26 April 1998, https://www.chicagotribune.com/news/ct-xpm-1998-04-26-9804260470-story.html.
2. Beth Miller Vonnahme, 'Robert M. Entman (2012). A Review of Scandal and Silence – Media responses to presidential misconduct', *International Journal of Public Opinion Research*, 2 September 2013, 396–8, https://doi.org/10.1093/ijpor/edt018.
3. David Brock, 'Living with the Clintons, Bill's Arkansas bodyguards tell the story the press missed', *The American Spectator*, January 1994, http://www.shwiggie.com/articles/clintons.html.
4. Ambrose Evans-Pritchard, *The Secret Life of Bill Clinton – The Unreported Stories* (Regnery Publishing, 1997), 332.
5. Christopher Hitchens, 'A Hard Dog to Keep on the Porch', *London Review of Books*, 6 June 1996, https://www.lrb.co.uk/the-paper/v18/n11/christopher-hitchens/a-hard-dog-to-keep-on-the-porch.
6. Candice E. Jackson, *Their Lives – The Women Targeted by the Clinton Machine* (World Ahead Publishing, 2005), 43–4.
7. Ibid., 69.
8. Andersen, *American Evita*, 85.
9. *The Washington Post*, 'The Deposition of L.D. Brown', 10 November 1997, https://www.washingtonpost.com/wp-srv/politics/special/pjones/docs/brown031398.htm.
10. Andersen, *American Evita*, 123.
11. Ibid.
12. Evans-Pritchard, *The Secret Life of Bill Clinton*, 358.
13. William C. Rempel and Douglas Frantz, 'Troopers Say Clinton Sought Silence on Personal Affairs: Arkansas: The White House calls their allegations about the President's private life "ridiculous"', *Los Angeles Times*, 21 December 1993, https://www.latimes.com/archives/la-xpm-1993-12-21-mn-4179-story.html.
14. Jennifer Senior, 'The Politics of Personality Destruction', *New York* magazine, 1 June 2007, http://nymag.com/news/politics/32864/.
15. Gary Aldrich, *Unlimited Access – An FBI Agent Inside the Clinton White House* (Regnery Publishing, 1996), 194.
16. John Dickerson, *Whistlestop – My Favourite Stories From Presidential Campaign History* (Hachette, 2017), 57.
17. Simon, 'Bodyguards Cover President Like a "Suit"'.
18. Emmett Tyrell, *The Clinton Crack-Up – The Boy President's Life After the White House* (Nelson Current, 2007), 62.
19. Ibid., 64.
20. VansOpinions, 'The Secret Service Views of Past Presidents', 12 December 2018, https://www.vansopinions.com/modules.php?name=News&file=article&sid=186.
21. White House Interview Program, 'Interview with Lloyd Cutler', 8 July 1999, https://www.archives.gov/files/presidential-libraries/research/transition-interviews/pdf/cutler.pdf.

22. Tyrell, *The Clinton Crack-Up*, 60.
23. Miller Center.org, Interview with Betty Currie, 11–12 May 2006, https://millercenter.org/the-presidency/presidential-oral-histories/betty-currie-oral-history.
24. Dan Emmett, 'What it's Really Like being a Secret Service Agent', 1 October 2014, http://www.wsj.com/articles/whatitsreallylikeinthesecretservice1412177937.
25. Daniel Halper, 'Bill Clinton would jog to meet women and pick up: Secret Service agent', *New York Post*, 25 June 2016, https://nypost.com/2016/06/25/clinton-white-house-was-a-den-of-cocaine-and-mistresses-ex-secret-service-officer/.
26. Daniel Bates, 'How Secret Service busted Bill Clinton on his way to an assignation', *Daily Mail*, 19 December 2017, https://www.dailymail.co.uk/news/article-5192341/Bill-Clinton-snuck-White-House-visit-mistresses.html.
27. Susan Page, 'Secret interviews add insight to Clinton presidency', *USA TODAY*, n.d., https://usatoday30.usatoday.com/news/washington/2009-09-21-clinton-tapes_N.htm.
28. Daniel Halper, *Clinton Inc – The Audacious Building of a Political Machine* (Broadside Books, 2015), 252.
29. Dan Emmett, *Within Arm's Length* (iUniverse, 2012), 2.
30. Annie Jacobsen, *Surprise, Kill, Vanish – The Definitive History of Secret CIA Assassins, Armies and Operators* (John Murray, 2019), 330.
31. Ibid., 331.
32. Kenneth Starr, *Contempt – A memoir of the Clinton Investigation* (Sentinel, 2018), 213.
33. Tyrell, *The Clinton Crack-Up*, 69.
34. Halper, *Clinton Inc*, 250.
35. Susan Page, 'Secret interviews add insight to Clinton presidency'.
36. *The Atlantic*, 'Oral History: The Secret History of the Clinton White House', 10 June 2017, https://www.theatlantic.com/politics/archive/2014/12/the-way-they-remember-it-an-oral-history-of-the-clinton-years/383560/.
37. Tyrell, *The Clinton Crack-Up*, 70.
38. Jerry Dunleavy, 'Flight manifests reveal Bill Clinton travelled with Epstein six times, not the four times he admitted', *Washington Examiner*, 10 July 2019, https://www.washingtonexaminer.com/news/flight-manifests-reveal-bill-clinton-traveled-with-epstein-six-times-not-the-four-times-he-admitted.

Chapter 16

1. David Brock, 'Living with the Clintons, Bill's Arkansas bodyguards tell the story the press missed', *The American Spectator*, 1994, http://www.shwiggie.com/articles/clintons.html.
2. Ibid.
3. Andersen, *American Evita*, 90.
4. Brock, 'Living with the Clintons, Bill's Arkansas bodyguards tell the story the press missed'.
5. Andersen, *American Evita*, 90.
6. Ibid., 187.
7. Ibid., 167.
8. Halper, *Clinton Inc*, 257.
9. Julian Borger, 'Bill Clinton – Book revives Hillary Clinton infidelity story', *The Guardian*, 4 August 1999, https://www.theguardian.com/world/1999/aug/04/clinton.usa.

10. Halper, *Clinton Inc*, 257.
11. Ronald Kessler, 'Ken Starr says Hillary Clinton DID trigger Vince Foster's suicide', *Daily Mail*, 10 April 2019, https://www.dailymail.co.uk/news/article-6903755/Kenneth-Starr-admits-omitted-report-Hillary-Clinton-triggered-Vince-Fosters-suicide.html.
12. Nigel Cawthorne, *#WeToo in the White House* (Gibson Square Books, 2018), 106.
13. Edward Klein, *The Truth About Hillary: What She Knew, When She Knew It, and How Far She'll Go to Become President* (Sentinel, 2006), 98–9.
14. Jackson, *Their Lives*, 225.
15. *The Clinton Affair*, directed by Blair Foster, Executive Producer Alex Gibney et al., A&E Television Network, 2018.
16. Steven F. Hayward, *The Politically Incorrect Guide to the Presidents – From Wilson to Obama* (Regnery Publishing, 2012), 238.
17. Katie Jerkovich, 'Author: Secret Service Hillary Tell-All Should be believed', *Daily Caller*, 9 June 2016, https://dailycaller.com/2016/06/09/author-secret-service-hillary-tell-all-should-be-believed/.
18. Tyrell, *The Clinton Crack-Up*, 67.
19. Tarraborrelli, *After Camelot*, 485.
20. Kate Andersen Brower, *First in Line* (Harper, 2018), 153.
21. Tyrell, *The Clinton Crack-Up*, 64.
22. Aldrich, *Unlimited Access*, 203.
23. Kessler, *In the President's Secret Service*, 169.
24. Deroy Murdock, 'Hillary F. Clinton Curses Those Who Keep Her Safe', *National Review*, 22 October 2016, https://www.nationalreview.com/2016/10/hillary-clinton-security-detail-curses-foul-mouth/.
25. Ibid.
26. VansOpinions, 'The Secret Service Views of Past Presidents', 12 December 2018, http://vansopinions.com/modules.php?name=News&file=article&sid=186&mode=thread&order=0&thold=0.
27. Kate Andersen Brower, 'The Secret Lives of Hillary and Bill in the White House', *Politico*, 7 April 2015, https://www.politico.com/magazine/story/2015/04/clinton-white-house-the-residence-excerpt-116706_full.html.
28. Ibid.
29. Amy Chozick, *Chasing Hillary – Ten Years, Two Presidential Campaigns and One Intact Glass Ceiling* (Harper, 2018), 53.
30. Thomas Goulding, 'Five things we've learned about Hillary Clinton's failed presidential campaign from new inside account', *The Independent*, 4 May 2017, https://www.independent.co.uk/news/world/americas/us-politics/hillary-clinton-failed-us-presidential-campaign-five-things-learn-book-shattered-jonathan-allen-a7715991.html.
31. Alana Goodman, 'Bill Clinton's Bodyguard', *Daily Mail*, 10 October 2016, https://www.dailymail.co.uk/news/article-3831334/Bill-Clinton-s-bodyguard-revealed-former-president-viewed-women-purely-chased-dominated-conquered-graded-scale-one-ten-Hillary-slams-Trump-doing-THING.html.
32. Chozick, *Chasing Hillary*, 326.
33. *South China Morning Post*, 'Ex-colleagues say former Secret Service officer's book attacking Hillary Clinton rings untrue', 22 June 2016, http://www.scmp.com/news/world/united-states-canada/article/1979143/ex-colleagues-say-.

34. Edward-Isaac Dovere, 'Secret Service veterans denounce anti-Clinton tell-all book', *Politico,* 21 June 2016, https://www.politico.com/story/2016/06/hillary-bill-clinton-secret-service-224578.

35. Aldrich, *Unlimited Access*, 139.

36. Klein, *The Truth About Hillary*, 15.

37. Aldrich, *Unlimited Access*, 90.

38. Zachary Stieber, 'Clinton Rumours: Tabloid Says Bill and Hillary Are "Swingers" in "Open Marriage"', *The Epoch Times*, 13 November 2014, https://www.theepochtimes.com/bill-clinton-hillary-clinton-are-swingers-bodyguard-says-couple-admitted-open-marriage_1078994.html 1/4.

39. Andersen, *American Evita*, 120.

40. Ibid., 121.

41. Jerkovich, 'Author: Secret Service Hillary Tell-All Should Be Believed'.

42. Emily Smith, 'Bill, White House Staff Lived in fear of Hillary', *New York Post*, 5 June 2016, https://pagesix.com/2016/06/05/tell-all-book-reveals-hillarys-erratic-uncontrollable-ways-in-the-white-house/.

43. Gary J. Byrne, *Crisis of Character* (Center Street, 2016), 232.

44. *Buzzfeed*, 'This is How the Secret Service Reacted to Threats Against Hillary Clinton', 17 February 2017, https://www.buzzfeednews.com/article/jasonaleopold/this-is-how-the-secret-service-reacted-to-threats-against-hi.

45. Ibid.

46. Theodore Schleifer, 'Secret Service rushes stage to protect Clinton from protesters', *CNN*, 4 August 2016, https://edition.cnn.com/2016/08/04/politics/secret-service-agents-hillary-clinton-animal-rights/index.html.

47. Byrne, *Crisis of Character*, 227.

48. The Globe and Mail.com, 'Man Held for Threats to PM, Clintons', 2 December 2000, https://www.iol.co.za/news/world/canadian-threatened-to-kill-hillary-clinton-54616.

49. Greg Meriwether, 'LSU Student Arrested for Threatening to Kill Sen. Hillary Clinton', *WAFB TV*, 4 May 2007, https://www.wafb.com/story/6470375/lsu-student-arrested-for-threatening-to-kill-sen-hillary-clinton/.

50. Gaby Del Valle, 'Trump Supporters Threaten to Assassinate Hillary Clinton, Overthrow Government', *Gothamist*, 17 October 2016, https://gothamist.com/news/trump-supporters-threaten-to-assassinate-hillary-clinton-overthrow-government.

51. Ibid.

52. CBS NEWS, 'Militia leader allegedly told FBI they were training to assassinate Obama, Hillary Clinton', 23 April 2019, https://www.cbsnews.com/news/militia-leader-larry-hopkins-allegedly-told-fbi-they-were-training-to-assassinate-barack-obama-hillary-clinton/.

53. Ibid.

54. Ben Yakas, 'QAnon Believer Arrested in Manhattan Carrying 18 Knives After Allegedly Threatening Joe Biden & Hillary Clinton', *Gothamist*, 30 April 2020, https://gothamist.com/news/qanon-believer-arrested-manhattan-carrying-18-knives-after-allegedly-threatening-joe-biden-hillary-clinton.

Chapter 17

1. See Ayton, *Hunting the President*, 221–41.

2. Justin Rohrlich, 'Prosecutions for death threats against US politicians spiked last year', *Quartz,* 26 March 2019, https://qz.com/1578862/arrests-for-death-threats-against-us-politicians-rose-in-2018/.
3. Kathleen Hennessey and Christi Parsons, 'For Secret Service, a delicate dance of guards and guarded', *Los Angeles Times,* 3 October 2014, http://www.latimes.com/nation/la-na-obama-secret-service-20141004-story.html.
4. Ibid.
5. Entrepreneur.com, Episode 81: *Evy Poumpouras – Former Secret Service Agent, Host on Bravo TV's Spy Games, Author of Becoming Bulletproof,* https://www.entrepreneur.com/listen/habits-hustle/356194.
6. John Heilemann and Mark Halperin, *Race of a Lifetime* (Viking, 2010), 109.
7. Justin Sink, 'Obama's unpredictability "stresses" the Secret Service', *The Hill,* 13 July 2014, https://thehill.com/blogs/blog-briefing-room/news/212072-obamas-unpredictability-stresses-secret-service.
8. Ibid.
9. Marc Ambinder, 'Inside the Secret Service', *The Atlantic,* March 2011, https://www.theatlantic.com/magazine/archive/2011/03/inside-the-secret-service/308390/.
10. Ibid.
11. Kathleen Hennessey and Christi Parsons, 'For Secret Service, a delicate dance of guards and guarded'.
12. Marisa Schultz, 'Secret Service agents can't stop thinking about their sex lives', *New York Post,* 4 December 2015, http://nypost.com/2015/12/04/secret-service-agents-cant-stop-thinking-about-their-sex-lives/.
13. *CNN,* 'Secret Service Fast Facts', 7 January 2020, https://edition.cnn.com/2016/04/18/us/secret-service-fast-facts/index.html.
14. *US News and World Report,* 'Biden Swims Naked, Upsetting Female Secret Service Agents, Book Claims', 1 August 2014, https://www.usnews.com/news/blogs/washington-whispers/2014/08/01/biden-swims-naked-upsetting-female-secret-service-agents-book-claims.
15. CNN, 'Plot to Assassinate Obama Foiled in Turkey', 6 April 2009, https://edition.cnn.com/2009/POLITICS/04/06/turkey.assassination.plot/.
16. See Ayton, *Hunting the President,* 221–41.
17. BBC, 'Obama "Ricin" Suspect Arrested', 18 April 2013, https://www.bbc.co.uk/news/world-us-canada-22194061.
18. Aaron Katersky and Mike Levine, 'Isis: 3 New York Men Arrested in Alleged Plot to Join Terror Group, Feds Say', *ABC News,* 25 February 2015, https://abcnews.go.com/US/WorldNews/isis-arrested-plot-join-terror-group/story?id=29222291.
19. David Wright, 'Wisconsin man allegedly threatens to kill President Barack Obama', CNN, 4 July 2015, https://edition.cnn.com/2015/07/03/politics/wisconsin-man-threatens-to-kill-obama/index.html.
20. Scott MacFarlane, 'Man Who Threatened to Assassinate President Obama Violated Probation, Disappeared From Authorities', NBC Washington, 3 November 2017, https://www.nbcwashington.com/news/local/man-who-threatened-to-assassinate-president-obama-violated-probation-disappeared-from-authorities/31547/.
21. Christopher Lee and Michael D. Shear, *The Washington Post,* 'Secret Service Says McCain Has No Protection', 3 April 2008, http://voices.washingtonpost.com/44/2008/04/mccain-has-not-requested-secre.html.
22. *CBS News,* 'No Secret Service Protection For McCain', 4 April 2008, https://www.cbsnews.com/news/no-secret-service-protection-for-mccain/.

23. Massie Ritsch, 'Candidates and Their Protectors Play an Endless Tug of War', *The Los Angeles Times,* 23 April 2000, https://www.latimes.com/archives/la-xpm-2000-apr-23-mn-22577-story.html.

24. *ABC News,* 'Which presidential candidate gets Secret Service protection comes down to a few factors', 20 April 2019, https://abcnews.go.com/Politics/presidential-candidate-secret-service-protection-factors-analysis/story?id=62513154.

25. John McCain and Mark Salter, *The Restless Wave: Good Times, Just Causes, Great Fights, and Other Appreciations* (Simon & Schuster, 2019), 12.

26. Kessler, *In the President's Secret Service,* 224.

27. *Denver Post,* 'Trailing McCain jokes about ranking, reveals death threats . . .', 15 August 2007, www.denverpost.com, https://www.denverpost.com/2007/08/15/trailing-mccain-jokes-about-ranking-reveals-death-threats/.

28. Robert Boczkiewiez, 'Jail inmate charged with mail threat to McCain', Reuters, 23 August 2008, https://uk.reuters.com/article/uk-usa-politics-mccain-threat/jail-inmate-charged-with-mail-threat-to-mccain-idUKN2236086420080823.

29. *France 24,* 'Sarah Palin received death threats after 2008 nomination', 11 June 2011, https://www.france24.com/en/20110611-us-white-house-republicans-palin-received-death-threats-after-2008-nomination.

30. *NBC News,* 'Man Arrested in NYC Allegedly Offered $500 to Kill an ICE Agent, Threatened to Slit John McCain's Throat', 9 August 2018, https://www.nbcnewyork.com/news/local/man-arrested-in-nyc-is-accused-of-threatening-ice-us-sen-mccain/1824429/.

31. Kessler, *First Family Detail,* 214.

32. IB Times.com, 'Mitt Romney Gets Secret Service Protection: Why Does He Qualify?', 1 February 2012, https://www.ibtimes.com/mitt-romney-gets-secret-service-protection-why-does-he-qualify-404022.

33. Kessler, *First Family Detail,* 214.

34. Mitt Romney, 'Speeches, Life Lessons From the Front', BYU Edu.com, 18 November 2014, https://speeches.byu.edu/talks/mitt-romney/life-lessons-front/.

35. *The Washington Post,* 'Secret Service agent leaves gun unattended on Mitt Romney's plane', 29 August 2012, http://www.washingtonpost.com/blogs/election-2012/wp/2012/08/29/secret-service-agent-leaves-gun-unattended-on-mitt-romneys-plane/.

36. Shawn McCoy, 'Exclusive: Secret Service Agent Leaked President's Campaign Stops', *Insiders Sources,* 1 October 2014, http://www.insidesources.com/category/politics/.

37. Hugo Gye, 'Revealed: How Secret Service "stopped several assassination plots against Romney and Obama during election campaign"', *Daily Mail,* 9 November 2012, https://www.dailymail.co.uk/news/article-2230594/Secret-Service-stopped-assassination-plots-Romney-Obama.html.

38. Randy Hall, 'Death Threats Against Romney Soar After Second Debate: Will Media Cover?', Newsbusters.com, 19 October 2012, http://newsbusters.org/blogs/randy-hall/2012/10/18/death-threats-against-romney-soar-after-second-debate-will-media-cover#ixzz2ArznGAXK.

39. Sean Hannity, 'The last debate', *Fox News,* 22 October 2012, http://www.hannity.com/show/2012/10/22.

40. Carol Cratty, 'They Might Lose Their Guns', CNN, 21 March 2012, http://articles.cnn.com/2012-03-21/justice/justice_threats-arrest_1_secret-service-mitt-romney-threats?_s=PM:JUSTICE.

41. *Fox News*, 'Romney Condemns Release of Man Who Threatened to Kill Him, But Will Not Apologize for Judge's Decision', 23 November 2007, https://www.foxnews.com/story/romney-condemns-release-of-man-who-threatened-to-kill-him-but-will-not-apologize-for-judges-decision.

42. Greta Van Susteren, 'Secret Service "aware of" DNC's delegate's threat to "kill" Gov. Romney', *The Blaze*, 6 September 2012, http://gretawire.foxnewsinsider.com/video/the-blaze-secret-service-aware-of-dncs-delegates-threat-to-kill-gov-romney/.

43. Emily Valdez, 'Cleveland, Man Accused of Unusual Obama, Romney Threats', Fox 8, 5 October 2012, http://fox8.com/2012/10/05/complaint-akron-man-threatened-to-kill-obama-romney/.

44. Mitt Romney, 'Speeches, Life Lessons From the Front', BYU.edu, 18 November 2014, https://speeches.byu.edu/talks/mitt-romney/life-lessons-front/.

Chapter 18

1. See Chapter 5 and Mel Ayton, 'And Now We Hear that Someone Wants to Kill Donald Trump?', History News Network, 8 March 2016, https://historynewsnetwork.org/article/162217.

2. Corey Lewandowski, *Let Trump be Trump* (Hachette, 2017), 66.

3. Alicia A. Caldwell, 'Trump's language up to him', *Concord Monitor*, 29 March 2016, http://www.concordmonitor.com/Articles/2016/03/From-Archives-2/trump-cmnw-031916.

4. Ibid.

5. Corey Charlton, 'Donald's Defenders: Secret Service Agents Reveal They Love Donald Trump Because He is Punctual and Polite', *The Sun*, 10 November 2016, https://www.thesun.co.uk/news/2159036/secret-service-agents-reveal-they-love-protecting-donald-trump-because-he-is-punctual-and-polite-and-they-get-to-travel-in-luxurious-private-jets/.

6. *The Independent*, 'Trump uses Secret Service agents to help him cheat at golf, book claims', 25 April 2019, https://www.independent.co.uk/news/world/americas/us-politics/trump-golf-cheat-secret-service-book-rick-reilly-a8885901.html.

7. Tim Marcin, 'Trump Eats McDonald's Because He's Afraid of Being Poisoned Elsewhere', *Newsweek*, 3 January 2018, https://www.newsweek.com/trump-eats-mcdonalds-because-afraid-poison-donald-fast-food-obsession-769796.

8. The White House, 'Statement by Donald J Trump on United States Secret Service 152nd Anniversary', 5 July 2017, https://www.whitehouse.gov/the-press-office/2017/07/05/statement-president-donald-j-trump-united-states-secret-service-152nd.

9. Tom Leonard, 'I Thought This Job Would be Easier . . . I Miss My Old Life, Admits Trump', *Daily Mail*, 29 April, 2017, 14.

10. Michael Wolf, 'The Trump Show', *Daily Mail*, 4 November 2020, 8.

11. Danny Collins and Lauren Frue, 'Who is Michael Sandford?', *The Sun*, 9 May 2017, https://www.thesun.co.uk/news/3486914/michael-sandford-brit-who-tried-to-assassinate-donald-trump-2016-voices/.

12. Bianca Padro Ocassio, 'Trump: I am "the best thing that's ever happened" to the Secret Service', *Politico*, 22 July 2016, http://www.politico.com/story/2016/07/trump-secret-service-226022.

13. Zoe Nauman, 'Man charged over threat to kill Donald Trump at inauguration is "family friend of Bill and Hillary Clinton who once donated £16,000 to Democrats"',

The Sun, 18 January 2017, https://www.thesun.co.uk/news/2648945/man-calling-himself-jesus-christ-arrested-for-tweeting-threat-to-kill-donald-trump-at-his-inauguration-with-high-powered-rifle/.

14. Rebecca Rosenberg, 'Alleged Trump Stalker Released From Jail', *New York Post*, 11 May 2017, http://nypost.com/2017/05/11/alleged-trump-stalker-released-from-jail/.

15. *Politico*, 'Protective barrier outside White House breached, drawing Secret Service response', 18 March 2017, http://www.politico.com/story/2017/03/white-house-barrier-breach-236218.

16. *New York Post*, 'Man Claiming to have explosives nabbed outside White House', 19 March 2017, http://nypost.com/2017/03/19/man-claiming-to-have-explosives-nabbed-outside-white-house/.

17. Deroy Murdock, 'Trump Haters Call for Presidential Assassination', *National Review*, 25 March 2017, http://www.nationalreview.com/article/446110/trump-assassination-threats-investigate-prosecute.

18. *India Today*, 'Donald Trump not safe in White House', 18 March 2017, http://indiatoday.intoday.in/story/trump-not-safe-in-wh-says-former-secret-service-agent/1/907013.html.

19. Leah McDonald, 'US Secret Service dealt with assassination threat against Donald Trump in Manila', *Daily Mail*, 15 October 2018, https://www.dailymail.co.uk/news/article-6277667/Special-Agents-foiled-assassination-attempt-Donald-Trump-ISIS-year.html.

20. *Mail on Sunday*, 'Trump Pours Fuel on Flames', 31 May 2020, 26,

21. Wilfred Frost, 'Frost Biden Tapes', *Daily Mail*, 26 November 2020, 3,

22. Jonathan Passantino, 'Biden Reveals Location of Secret VP Bunker', *Fox News*, 18 May 2009, http://www.foxnews.com/politics/2009/05/18/biden-reveals-location-secret-vp-bunker.print.html.

23. Steven Nelson, 'Joe Biden's Shotgun Advice Could Land Jill Biden in Jail', *US News.com*, 20 February 2013, https://www.usnews.com/news/articles/2013/02/20/joe-biden-shotgun-advice-could-land-jill-biden-in-jail.

24. Michael V. Uschan, *Joe Biden* (Lucent Books, 2010), 87.

25. Kessler, *In the President's Secret Service*, 223.

26. AmericanPriority.com, 'Sexual Misconduct Allegations Against Joe Biden Extend to Female Secret Service Agents', 15 May 2020, https://americanpriority.com/news/nolte-sexual-misconduct-allegations-against-joe-biden-extend-to-female-secret-service-agents/.

27. Ronald Kessler, 'Joe Biden's disrespect for the Secret Service, Hillary Clinton was the worst, but Biden would bolt for Wilmington without notice', *Washington Times*, 13 May, https://m.washingtontimes.com/news/2020/may/13/joe-bidens-disrespect-for-the-secret-service/.

28. Iowa Democratic Party campaign consultant Jim Williams, email to the author, 25 April 2020.

29. 'Exposed: the US vice-president and his secret vice Joe Biden enjoys skinny dipping, according to a new book supposedly based on gossip from Secret Service', *The Daily Telegraph*, 1 August 2014, https://www.telegraph.co.uk/news/worldnews/northamerica/usa/11007077/Exposed-the-US-vice-president-and-his-secret-vice.html.

30. Randall Chase, 'Lawsuit over Biden motorcade crash involving Secret Service agent resolved in mediation', *Associated Press*, 12 December 2019, https://eu.delawareonline.com/story/news/2019/09/11/lawsuit-over-biden-motorcade-crash-resolved-mediation/2287457001/.

31. Jana Winter, 'Biden's brawlers: Veep's security team squared off in Nantucket melee', *Fox News*, 21 June 2012, https://www.foxnews.com/politics/exclusive-bidens-brawlers-veeps-security-team-squared-off-in-nantucket-melee.
32. Kessler, *First Family Detail*, 15.
33. *Los Angeles Times*, 'Gunshots fired outside Vice President Joe Biden's Delaware home', 18 January 2015, http://www.latimes.com/nation/nationnow/la-na-nn-shots-fired-joe-biden-home-delaware-20150118-story.html.
34. Olivia Nuzzi, 'Joe Biden is the least formidable front-runner ever. Will it matter?', *New York* magazine, 28 October 2019, https://nymag.com/intelligencer/2019/10/joe-biden-2020-campaign.html.
35. Sam Neumann, 'Joe Biden Calls Recent Protestors "Outrageous" and Said He'd Welcome Secret Service Protection', *People*, 6 March 2020, https://people.com/politics/joe-biden-calls-recent-protestors-outrageous/.
36. Noah Gray, Jim Acosta, Eric Bradner and Arlette Saenz, 'Biden receives Secret Service protection', CNN, 17 March 2020, https://edition.cnn.com/2020/03/17/politics/joe-biden-gets-secret-service-protection/index.html.
37. Susan Crabtree, 'Biden's Late Secret Service Request Raises Protection Issues', *Real Clear Politics*, 13 March 2020, https://www.realclearpolitics.com/articles/2020/03/13/bidens_late_secret_service_request_raises_protection_issues_142656.html.
38. Ibid.
39. *Wired*, 'Biden Death Threat Case: Minnesota Man Says He's Not Guilty Anymore', 22 April 2011, https://www.wired.com/2011/04/ardolf/.
40. Dan Mangan, '"MAGA Bomber" Cesar Sayoc sentenced to 20 years in prison for trying to kill Trump critics, including Obama, Clinton, Biden, Booker, Harris', CNBC, 5 August 2019, https://www.cnbc.com/2019/08/05/cesar-sayoc-sentenced-to-20-years-for-sending-bombs-to-trump-critics.html.
41. Associated Press, 'Maryland man charged with making death threats against Biden and Harris', 21 October 2020, https://www.theguardian.com/us-news/2020/oct/21/joe-biden-kamala-harris-death-threats-maryland.
42. James Beal and Catherine Gioino, 'Two men accused of plotting to assassinate US presidential hopeful Joe Biden', *The Sun*, 23 October 2020, https://www.thesun.co.uk/news/13001891/man-accused-plot-assassinate-us-candidate-joe-biden/.
43. Tamar Lapin, 'Illinois man allegedly threatened to "kill Democrats" at Biden inauguration', *New York Post*, 12 January 2021, https://nypost.com/2021/01/12/illinois-man-allegedly-threatened-to-kill-dems-at-biden-inauguration/.
44. Joshua Rhett Mille, 'North Carolina man vowed to kill Biden, "chop" heads off at White House', *New York Post*, 15 February 2021, https://nypost.com/2021/02/15/nc-man-vowed-to-kill-biden-chop-heads-off-at-white-house/.
45. Tamar Lapin, 'Woman arrested near White House after claiming to have letter for Biden', *New York Post*, 14 February 2021, https://nypost.com/2021/02/14/woman-arrested-near-white-house-claimed-to-have-letter-for-biden/.
46. Steven Nelson, 'Senators ask Secret Service director to explain role in Hunter Biden gun incident', *New York Post*, 26 March 2021, https://nypost.com/2021/03/26/senators-ask-secret-service-director-to-explain-role-in-hunter-biden-gun-incident/.

47. John Varga, '"Clueless" and "lost" Biden sparks ridicule in bizarre gaffe with Secret Service agents', Daily Express, 12 August 2021, https://www.express.co.uk/news/world/1475752/joe-biden-health-us-president-white-house-donald-trump-twitter-ont.
48. Marc Ambinder, 'The Secret Service is bracing for Dangerous Times', *The Atlantic*, 19 January 2021, https://www.theatlantic.com/politics/archive/2021/01/how-secret-service-plans-protect-joe-biden-now/617726/.
49. Ibid.
50. Ibid.

Bibliography

Government Reports

The Secret Service itself prepared two short histories of its law-enforcement role, each of which includes a helpful description of the agency's presidential protective function: *Moments in History, 1865–1990* (US Government Printing Office) and *Excerpts from the History of the United States Secret Service 1865–1975* (US Government Printing Office).

In addition to the records provided by the Secret Service, a number of government reports and scholarly articles were useful in writing this book:

Assassination Records Review Board, Secret Service agents' interviews, January 3, 1978, HSCA, 180-10071-10165, Agency File No.: 007996, January 11, 1996, http://www.fas.org/sgp/advisory/arrb98/part08.htm

FBI Records, *Robert F Kennedy Assassination – (Summary) – Report consisting of the Los Angeles County Board of Supervisors Independent Investigation by Special Counsel Thomas F. Kranz*, https://vault.fbi.gov/Robert%20F%20Kennedy%20%28Assassination%29%20

Fein, R.A., and Vossekuil, B., *Preventing Assassination: Exceptional Case Study Project (ECSP)*, National Institute of Justice US Department of Justice NIJ publication (NCJ 167224), National Criminal Justice Reference Service, 1997

Hoffman, Jay L., MD, 'Psychotic Visitors to government offices in the National Capital', *The American Journal of Psychiatry*, 1943; 99:571-575, http://ajp.psychiatryonline.org/article.aspx?articleid=142391

Kaiser, Frederick M., *Direct Assaults Against Presidents, Presidents-Elect, and Candidates*, Congressional Research Service, The Library of Congress, 7 June 2008

Kirkham, James F., Levy, Sheldon G., Crotty, William J., *Assassination and Political Violence – A Staff Report to the Commission on the Causes and Prevention of Violence*, Bantam/Matrix Books, 1970

Petersen, R. Eric and Manning, Jennifer E., *Violence Against Members of Congress and Their Staffs*, Congressional Research Service, August 17, 2017, https://fas.org/sgp/crs/misc/R41609.pdf

Phillips, Robert T.M., MD, PhD, 'Assessing Presidential Stalkers and Assassins', *The Journal of the American Academy of Psychiatry and the Law*, 2006; J 34:154–64, http://www.ncbi.nlm.nih.gov/pubmed/16844794

Reid Meloy, J. (ed.), *The Psychology of Stalking*, Academic Press, 2001, via http://www.scribd.com/doc/76962424/The-Psychology-of-Stalking

The Report of the U.S. President's Commission on the Assassination of President John F. Kennedy (McGraw-Hill Book Co., 1964), commonly referred to as the Warren Commission Report, contains an excellent historical section regarding presidential security and attacks on chief executives to 1963, the year of the Kennedy assassination.

Sebastian, Joseph A. and Foy, James L., 'Psychotic Visitors to the White House', *The American Journal of Psychiatry*, December 1 1965; 122:679-686, http://ajp. psychiatryonline.org/article.aspx?articleid=150147

'The Secret Service Was Deficient in the Performance of Its Duties', *Final Report of the House Select Committee on Assassinations (HSCA Report)*, 227–37, http://www. archives.gov/research/jfk/select-committee-report/part-1d.html

Treasury Department Foundation of American Scientists, *Public Report of the White House Security Review*, http://www.fas.org/irp/agency/ustreas/usss/t1pubrpt.html

United States Congress, *Inquiry into the Matter of Billy Carter and Libya*, Vols 1–3, by the US Congress Senate Committee on the Judiciary Sub Committee to Investigate The Activities of Individuals Representing the Interests of Foreign Governments, 6 August 1980

United States Congress, *Review of Secret Service Protective Measures*, Senate Committee on *Appropriations* (US Government Printing Office, 1975)

US Congress, *Nomination of Edwin Meese III – Hearings before the Judiciary Committee, United States Senate, Ninety-eighth Congress, Second Session, on the President's Nomination of Edwin Meese III to be Attorney General of the United States, March 1, 2, 5, and 6* (Government Printing Office, 1984)

Presidential Libraries Accessed

Barack Obama Presidential Library and Museum, http://barackobamapre- sidential-library.com/

Dwight D. Eisenhower Presidential Library and Museum, http://www.eisen- hower. archives.gov/

George H.W. Bush Presidential Library and Museum, http://bushlibrary.tamu.edu/ index.php

George W. Bush Presidential Library and Museum, http://www.georgewbush- library. smu.edu/

Gerald R. Ford Presidential Library and Museum, http://www.fordlibrary- museum. gov/

Jimmy Carter Library and Museum, http://www.jimmycarterlibrary.gov/

John F. Kennedy Presidential Library and Museum, http://www.jfklibrary. org/

LBJ Presidential Library, http://www.lbjlibrary.org/

Nixon Presidential Library and Museum, http://www.nixonlibrary.gov/

Ronald Reagan Presidential Foundation and Library, http://www.reagan- foundation. org/

William J. Clinton Presidential Library and Museum, http://www.clintonli- brary.gov/

Books

Agnew, Spiro T., *Go Quietly . . . or Else*, William Morrow, 1980

Aldrich, Gary, *Unlimited Access – An FBI Agent Inside the Clinton White House*, Regnery Publishing, 1996

Alter, Jonathan, *His Very Best – Jimmy Carter, A Life*, Simon & Schuster, 2020

Andersen, Christopher, *American Evita*, William Morrow, 2004

Andersen Brower, Kate, *The Residence – Inside the Private World of the White House*, Harper Paperbacks, 2016

——, *First in Line*, Harper, 2018

Ayton, Mel, *Hunting the President – Threats, Plots and Assassination Attempts – From FDR to Obama*, Regnery Publishing, 2014

——, *The Forgotten Terrorist – Sirhan Sirhan and the Assassination of Robert F. Kennedy*, University of Nebraska Press/Potomac Books, second edn 2019

——, *Plotting to Kill the President: Assassination Attempts from Washington to Hoover*, Potomac Books, 2017

Bai, Matt, *The Front Runner*, HarperCollins, 2019

Barletta, John R., *Riding With Reagan – From the White House to the Ranch*, Citadel Press, 2005

Baughman, U.E., *Secret Service Chief*, Harper and Brothers, 1961

Becker, Jillian, *Hitler's Children – The Story of the Baader-Meinhof Terrorist Gang*, Authorhouse, 2014

Beschloss, Michael, *Taking Charge – Johnson White House Tapes 1963–1964*, Simon & Schuster, 1998

Blaine, Gerald, *The Kennedy Detail*, Gallery Books, 2010

Brands, H.W., *Reagan: The Life*, Doubleday, 2015

Brandus, Paul, *Under This Roof – The White House and the Presidency*, Lyons Press, 2018

Bruns, Roger, *Jesse Jackson – A Biography*, Greenwood, 2005

Bugliosi, Vincent, *Reclaiming History: The Assassination of President John F. Kennedy*, W.W. Norton, 2007

Burke, Richard, *The Senator*, St Martin's Press, 1992

Burton, Richard and Williams, Chris (ed.), *The Richard Burton Diaries*, Yale University Press, 2013

Byrne, Gary J., *Crisis of Character*, Center Street, 2016

Carter, Dan, *The Politics of Rage*, LSU Press, 2000

Carter, Jimmy, *White House Diary*, Picador, 2011

Cawthorne, Nigel, *#WeToo in the White House*, Gibson Square Books, 2018

Chozick, A., *Chasing Hillary – Ten Years, Two Presidential Campaigns and One Intact Glass Ceiling*, Harper, 2018

Churchwell, Sarah, *The Many Lives of Marilyn Monroe*, Granta Books, 2004

Clarke, James W., *American Assassins: The Darker Side of Politics*, Princeton University Press, 1982

——, *On Being Mad or Merely Angry: John W. Hinckley Jr and Other Dangerous People*, Princeton University Press, 1990

——, *Defining Danger – American Assassins and the New Domestic Terrorists*, Transaction Publishers, 2007

Clymer, Adam, *Edward M. Kennedy*, Harper Perennial, 2016

Coffey, Justin P., *Spiro Agnew and the Rise of the Republican Right*, Praeger, 2015

Collier, Peter and Horowitz, David, *The Kennedys*, David, Secker and Warburg, 1984

Dickerson, John, *Whistlestop – My Favourite Stories from Presidential Campaign History*, Hachette, 2017

Edwards, Lee, *Just Right – A Life in Pursuit of Liberty*, ISI Books, 2017

Eichenwald, Kurt, *500 Days: Secrets and Lies in the Terror Wars*, Touchstone Books, 2013

Emmett, Dan, *Within Arm's Length*, iUniverse, 2012

——, *I Am A Secret Service Agent*, St Martn's Press, 2017

Endicott, Michael A., *Walking with Presidents: Stories from Inside the Perimeter*, Booksurge Publishing, 2009

Evans-Pritchard, Ambrose, *The Secret Life of Bill Clinton – The Unreported Stories*, Regnery Publishing, 1997

Exner, Judith, *My Story*, Futura Publications Ltd, 1977

Frady, Marshall, *Jesse: The Life and Pilgrimage*, Simon & Schuster, 2006

Gabler, Neal, *Catching The Wind – Edward Kennedy and the Liberal Hour 1932–1975*, Crown, 2020

Gallagher, Eugene V. and Ashcraft, Michael (eds), *Introduction to New and Alternative Religions in African American Diaspora*, Greenwood, 2006

Gates, Daryl F., *Chief – My Life in the LAPD*, Bantam Books, 1993

Glenn, John, *John Glenn – A Memoir*, Bantam Books, 1999

Gulley, Bill, *Breaking Cover*, Simon & Schuster, 1980

Halper, Daniel, *Clinton Inc – The Audacious Building of a Political Machine*, Broadside Books, 2015

Hayter-Menzies, Grant, *Lillian Carter – A Compassionate Life*, McFarland, 2014

Hayward, Steven F., *The Politically Incorrect Guide to the Presidents – From Wilson to Obama*, Regnery Publishing, 2012

Healey, Thomas S., *The Two Deaths of George Wallace*, Black Belt Press, 1996

Heilemann, John and Halperin, Mark, *Race of a Lifetime*, Viking, 2010

Hersh, Burton, *Shadow President*, Steerforth Press, 1997

——, *Ted Kennedy – An Intimate Biography*, Counterpoint, 2011

Hersh, Seymour M., *The Dark Side of Camelot*, Little, Brown and Company, 1997

——, *Reporter*, Allen Lane, 2018

Heymann, C. David, *RFK – A Candid Biography*, Willaim Heineman, 1998

Hill, Clint, *Five Presidents: My Extraordinary Journey with Eisenhower, Kennedy, Johnson, Nixon, and Ford*, Gallery Books, 2017

Houghton, Robert A., *Special Unit Senator: The Investigation of the Assassination of Senator Robert F. Kennedy*, Random House, 1970

Hughes, Kathleen, *The Monk's Tale: A Biography of Geoffrey Dickmann, OSB*, Liturgical Press, 1991

Humphrey, Hubert, *The Education of a Public Man – My Life And Politics*, University of Minnesota Press, 1991

Jackson, Candice, *Their Lives – The Women Targeted by the Clinton Machine*, World Ahead Publishing, 2005

Jacobsen, Annie, *Surprise, Kill, Vanish – The Definitive History of Secret CIA Assassins, Armies and Operators*, John Murray, 2019

Jansen, Godfrey H., *Why Robert Kennedy Was Killed – The Story of Two Victims*, Third Press, 1970

Kaiser, Robert Blair, *RFK Must Die: A History of the Robert Kennedy Assassination and Its Aftermath*, E.P. Dutton, 1970

Kelley, Kitty, *The Family – The Real Story of the Bush Dynasty*, Bantam, 2005

Kerry, John, *Every Day Is Extra*, Simon & Schuster, 2018

Kessler, Ronald, *Inside the White House*, Pocket Books, 1995

——, *In the President's Secret Service – Behind the Scenes with Agents in the Line of Fire and the Presidents They Protect*, Crown Publishers, 2009

——, *Inside Congress*, Gallery Books, 2013

——, *The First Family Detail*, Crown Forum, 2014

Klagsbrun, Francine and Whitney, David C. (eds), *Assassination: Robert F. Kennedy, 1925–1968*, Cowles, 1968

Klein, Edward, *The Truth About Hillary: What She Knew, When She Knew It, and How Far She'll Go to Become President*, Sentinel, 2006

——, *Ted Kennedy – The Dream That Never Died*, Three Rivers Press, 2010

——, *Blood Feud*, Regnery Publishing, 2014

Koplinski, Brad, *Hats in the Ring*, Presidential Publishing, 2000

Lesher, Stephan, *George Wallace – American Populist*, Addison Wesley, 1994

Lester, David, *Good Ted, Bad Ted: The Two Faces of Edward Kennedy*, Citadel Press, 1993

Lewandowski, Corey, *Let Trump be Trump*, Hachette, 2017

Lewis, Michael, *Losers – The Road to Everyplace but the White House*, Vintage Books, 2000

McCain, John and Salter, Mark, *The Restless Wave: Good Times, Just Causes, Great Fights, and Other Appreciations*, Simon & Schuster, 2019

McCarthy, Dennis V.N., *Protecting the President – The Inside Story of a Secret Service Agent*, Dell Publishing Co., 1985

McClellan, Scott, *What Happened: Inside the Bush White House and Washington's Culture of Deception*, PublicAffairs, 2008

Melanson, Philip H., *The Secret Service – The Hidden History of an Enigmatic Agency*, Basic Books, 2005

Meloy, J. Reid, Sheridan, Lorraine and Hoffman, Jens, *Stalking, Threatening, and Attacking Public Figures – A Psychological and Behavioural Analysis*, Oxford University Press, 2008

Miller, Merle, *Lyndon – An Oral Biography*, Ballantine Books, 1980

Miller, Scott, *The President and the Assassin – McKinley, Terror, and Empire at the Dawn of the American Century*, Random House Trade Paperbacks, 2013

Milton, Joyce, *The First Partner – Hillary Rodham Clinton*, William Morrow, 1999

Moldea, Dan, *The Killing of Robert Kennedy*, Norton, 1995

——, *A Washington Tragedy: Bill & Hillary Clinton and the Suicide of Vincent Foster*, moldea.com, 2015

Nelson, Jack, *Scoop: The Evolution of a Southern Reporter*, University Press of Mississippi, 2012

Olson, Barbara, *Hell to Pay: The Unfolding Story of Hillary Rodham Clinton*, Audible Inc., 1999

Oppenheimer, Jerry, *The Other Mrs. Kennedy: Ethel Skakel Kennedy: An American Drama of Power, Privilege, and Politics*, St Martin's Press, 1994

Parmet, Herbert S., *George Bush – The Life of a Lone Star Yankee*, Prentice Hall, 1993

Parr, Jerry with Carolyn Parr, *In the Secret Service – The True Story of the Man Who Saved President Reagan's Life*, Tyndale, 2013

Patrick, Curtis, *Reagan – What Was He Really Like?*, Vol. 1, Morgan James Publishing, 2011

——, *Reagan – What Was He Really Like?*, Vol. 2, Morgan James Publishing, 2018

Pearlstein, Rick, *The Invisible Bridge*, Simon & Schuster, 2015

Petro, Joseph, *Standing Next to History – An Agent's Life Inside the Secret Service*, Thomas Dunne Books, 2005

Poumpouras, Evy, *Becoming Bulletproof: Life Lessons from a Secret Service Agent*, Icon Books, 2020

Powell, Jody, *The Other Side of the Story* William Morrow, 1986

Priess, David, *How to Get Rid of a President*, Public Affairs, 2018

Ray, Alex, *Hired Gun: A Political Odyssey*, University Press of America, 2008

Reagan, Ronald, *An American Life – The Autobiography*, Threshold Editions, 2011

Rothman, Hal, *LBJ's Texas White House*, Texas A & M University Press, 2001

Rush, George, *Confessions of an Ex-Secret Service Agent – The Marty Vencker Story*, Donald I. Fine, 1988

Sandbrook, Dominic, *Eugene McCarthy: The Rise and Fall of Postwar American Liberalism*, Foder's Travel Publications, 2005

Saunders, Frank, *Torn Lace Curtain*, with James Southwood, Holt, Rinehart and Winston, 1982

Scheer, Robert, *Playing President: My Close Encounters with Nixon, Carter, Bush I, Reagan, and Clinton—and How They Did Not Prepare Me for George W. Bush*, Acashic Books, 2006

Seigenthaler, John, *A Search for Justice*, Aurora, 1971

Shirley, Craig, *Reagan's Revolution*, Thomas Nelson Publishers, 2009

——, *Rendezvous with Destiny*, Intercollegiate Studies Institute, 2014

Shogan, Robert, *The Double-Edged Sword – How Character Makes and Ruins Presidents, From Washington To Clinton*, Westview Press, 2000

Skinner, Kieran K. (ed.), *Reagan In His Own Hand*, Free Press, 2001

Smith, Richard Norton, *On His Own Terms – A Life of Nelson Rockefeller*, Random House, 2014

Solberg, Carl, *Hubert Humphrey – A Political Biography*, Minnesota Historical Society Press, 2003

Spignesi, Stephen, *In the Crosshairs: Famous Assassinations and Attempts from Julius Caesar to John Lennon*, Barnes & Noble Books, 2004

Starr, Kenneth, *Contempt – A memoir of the Clinton Investigation*, Sentinel, 2018

Summers, Anthony, *The Arrogance of Power: The Secret World of Richard Nixon*, W&N, 2000

——, *Goddess – The Secret Lives of Marilyn Monroe*, Phoenix Paperback, 2012

Taraborrelli, J. Randy, *After Camelot*, Grand Central Publishing, 2012

——, *The Kennedy Heirs*, Griffin, 2020

Thomas, Evan, *Robert Kennedy – His Life*, Simon & Schuster, 2002

Timmerman, Kenneth R., *Shakedown – Exposing the Real Jesse Jackson*, Regnery Publishing, 2002

Tye, Larry, *Bobby Kennedy – The Making of A Liberal Icon*, Random House, 2016

Tyrell, Emmett, *The Clinton Crack-Up – The Boy President's Life After the White House*, Nelson Current, 2007

Uschan, Michael V., *Joe Biden*, Lucent Books, 2010
Wead, Doug, *Inside Trump's White House*, Biteback Publishing, 2019
White, Theodore H., *In Search of History*, Harper & Row, 1st edn 1978
——, *The Making of the President 1964*, Harper Perennial, 2010
Wilber, Del Quentin, *Rawhide Down*, Picador, 2012
Wills, Garry, *Under God – Religion and American Politics*, Simon & Schuster, 1991
Witcover, Jules, *85 Days – The Last Campaign of Robert Kennedy*, Ace Publishing Corporation, 1969
——, *Marathon*, Viking Press, 1977
Young, Andrew, *The Politician,* Thomas Dunne Books, 2010
Youngblood, Rufus W., *20 Years in the Secret Service – My Life with Five Presidents*, Simon & Schuster, 1973

Names Index

General Index